HUMAN-COMPUTER INTERACTION SERIES

VOLUME 7

From Brows to Trust

Evaluating Embodied Conversational Agents

Edited by

Zsófia Ruttkay

and

Catherine Pelachaud

KLUWER ACADEMIC PUBLISHERS
DORDRECHT / BOSTON / LONDON

A C.I.P. Catalogue record for this book is available from the Library of Congress

ISBN 978-90-481-6713-5 (PB)
ISBN 978-1-4020-2730-7 (e-book)

Published by Kluwer Academic Publishers,
P.O. Box 17, 3300 AA Dordrecht, The Netherlands.

Sold and distributed in North, Central and South America
by Kluwer Academic Publishers,
101 Philip Drive, Norwell, MA 02061, U.S.A.

In all other countries, sold and distributed
by Kluwer Academic Publishers,
P.O. Box 322, 3300 AH Dordrecht, The Netherlands.

Printed on acid-free paper

Contents

Part IV Evaluation of Applications

Contributing Authors

Sarkis Abrilian is a researcher at the Laboratoire d'Informatique pour la Mécanique et les Sciences de l'Ingénieur - Centre National de la Recherche Scientifique (LIMSI-CNRS) in France, working in the field of multimodal human-computer interfaces. He graduated in Computer Sciences and Cognitive Sciences. He has mainly worked on the design of multimodal input interfaces for interacting with 2D agents and on the definition of the Tycoon Markup Language in XML, for representing the multimodal behaviour of these agents. He can be contacted at: sarkis@limsi.fr.

Stéphanie Buisine is currently a PhD student in Cognitive Psychology at the Laboratoire d'Informatique pour la Mécanique et les Sciences de l'Ingénieur - Centre National de la Recherche Scientifique (LIMSI-CNRS) in France. She holds an academic master's degree in Experimental Psychology and a professional master's degree in Ergonomics. Her research interests focus on bi-directional multimodal interfaces, especially experimental evaluation of multimodal interfaces with and without ECAs, and model of user's multimodal behaviour when interacting with such systems. She can be contacted at: stephanie.buisine@limsi.fr.

Richard Catrambone is an Associate Professor in the School of Psychology at the Georgia Institute of Technology. He received his B.A. from Grinnell College (Iowa, USA) in 1982 and his PhD in Experimental Psychology from the University of Michigan (USA) in 1988. His research interests include problem solving, analogical reasoning, educational technology, and human-computer interaction with a focus on using cognitive principles for the design of teaching and training material that helps students learn basic tasks quickly and promotes transfer to novel problems. He has served on the editorial boards of the Journal of Experimental Psychology: General and the Journal of Experimental Psychology: Applied and has published in those journals and a variety of others. He can be contacted at: rc7@prism.gatech.edu.

Loredana Cerrato is a PhD student at the department of Speech Musing and Hearing (TMH/CTT) at the Royal Institute of Technology (KTH) in Stockholm, and is a participant in the Swedish Graduate School of Language Technology. She received her Master's degree you may want to use MA, like all others do in Foreign Languages and Linguistics from the University of Naples 'Federico II' (Italy) in 1992. Her current research is concerned with the analysis of feedback phenomena in human-human and human-machine communication. Particular attention is paid to the analysis of prosodic and gestural cues of feedback expressions across different modalities and across different languages. The main aim of the investigation is to formalize some aspects of human communication that can be implemented in the design of human-computer interfaces. She can be contacted at: loredana@speech.kth.se.

Noor Christoph is a PhD student at the Department of Social Science Informatics at University of Amsterdam. She has been involved in various European Union funded projects. The Lilienthal aimed at developing and evaluating an interactive learning environment for theoretical instruction of airline pilots. The KITS project focused on developing and evaluating a gaming simulation environment for the domain of knowledge management. In her PhD she addresses the role of metacognitive skills on learning to solve ill-defined problems. She can be contacted at: noor@swi.psy.uva.nl.

Courtney Darves is currently a PhD student in the Department of Psychology at the University of Oregon. Her research focuses broadly on adaptive human behaviour, both in the context of human-computer interaction and more generally in terms of neural plasticity. She can be contacted at: courtney@alumni.reed.edu.

Claire Dormann is currently a researcher at the Human Oriented Technology Lab, Carleton University, Canada. Her background is Psychology and Computer Graphics. Her PhD addressed human-computer interaction and rhetoric. She participated in the project GAIA (Generic Architecture for Information Availability) to support electronic brokerage and multimedia in the home. Lately, she became interested in ECAs and virtual environment. Her research interests include usability evaluation, affective applications, computer mediated persuasion, and emotions and humour in user interfaces. Some of her recent works relates to evaluation, emotional appeal, and cultural differences. She can be contacted at: cdormann@ccs.carleton.ca.

Patrick Doyle is a doctoral candidate in the Knowledge Systems Laboratory at Stanford University. His research focuses on embedding knowledge in virtual environments that ECAs can use to improve both their effectiveness and the quality of their believability. His interests also include the design of ECA architectures and the social and psychological issues in building ECA interfaces. He has designed and taught several courses on the creation of intelligent characters, with an emphasis on their use in computer games. He can be contacted at: pdoyle@cs.stanford.edu.

Susanne Ekeklint is a PhD student at the School of Mathematics and Systems Engineering at Växjö University in Sweden. She is also one of the participants in Graduate School of Language Technology (GSLT), which is collaboration between leading centres of research and teaching in language technology in Sweden. Her PhD thesis concerns information requests especially natural language questions, mainly with respect to open-domain question answering systems. She graduated from Göteborgs University with a Master in Computational linguistics 2000. She can be contacted at: sek@msi.vxu.se.

Martine Grice is Professor of Phonetics at Cologne University, Germany. She holds an MA and PhD in Linguistics, and a Habilitation in Phonetics and Phonology. Her main area of research is intonation theory, in particular the structure of tonal representations, and the relation between prosody and articulatory gestures. She has developed schemes for the database annotation of tonal and junctural phenomena, both for Standard German (GToBI) and for a number of varieties of Italian (IToBI). She is also currently investigating the interaction between linguistic and paralinguistic factors determining voice quality and intonation. She can be contacted at: mgrice@coli.uni-sb.de.

Kristina Höök is currently working as a Professor at the Department of Computer and Systems Sciences at Stockholm University. She also holds a part-time position at Swedish Institute of Computer Science (SICS). Her research has focused first on user-centred design of human-computer interaction from a situated action approach as reflected in her thesis, and then on social navigation, following the traces of others, as an alternative way to achieve adaptivity in the interface. Her work on affective interaction follows the same line of reasoning: a user-centred approach and a better basis in how human cognition really works will achieve better design of interaction than theory- or technology-driven approaches. She can be contacted at: kia@dsv.su.se.

Katherine Isbister is a visiting scholar in the Communication Department at Stanford University. She teaches a course in the Computer Science Department's Human Computer Interaction series on the design of characters for computer games. Isbister received her PhD and MA from Stanford, with a focus on using principles from psychology to design embodied agents. Her research interests include developing ECAs and socially augmented avatars to support inter-cultural contexts, and investigating the psychological foundations of successful game characters, towards broader applications of these principles in ECA and social interface design. She can be contacted at: ki@katherineinterface.com.

Mervyn Jack is Professor of Electronic Systems at the University of Edinburgh. A Fellow of the Royal Society of Edinburgh, he leads a multi-disciplinary team of twenty researchers investigating Usability engineering of eCommerce services. His main research interests are dialogue engineering and virtual reality systems design for advanced eCommerce and consumer applications. He is author of some 230 scientific papers and 5 textbooks. He can be contacted at: Mervyn.Jack@ed.ac.uk.

Emiel Krahmer is an Assistant Professor in the Communication and Cognition group at Tilburg University. He has an MA (1991) and a PhD (1995) in computational linguistics, both from Tilburg University. After completing his PhD he worked for six years at Center for User System Interaction (IPO) at the Eindhoven University of Technology. His research concentrates on multimodal information presentation, with an emphasis on spoken language generation and audio-visual prosody. He can be contacted at: e.j.krahmer@uvt.nl.

Brigitte Krenn is Senior Scientist at the Austrian Research Institute for Artificial Intelligence. She holds a Master's Degree in German Language and Literature, Psychology, Philosophy and Pedagogy, and a PhD in Computational Linguistics. Since 1990 she has worked in a variety of research projects in the field of computational linguistics. Her current research focuses on animated conversational character technology, including multimodal interaction and affective communication. She can be contacted at: brigitte@ai.univie.ac.at.

Jean-Claude Martin is Assistant Professor and head of the Conversational Agents Team created in 2003 within the Architecture and Models for Interaction Group (AMI) at LIMSI-CNRS, France. His research concerns multimodal communication including typologies of cooperation between modalities; creation, annotation, and analysis of corpora of multimodal human-human and human-computer interactions, design of bidirectional multimodal interfaces and their application to user interface of games. He has been involved in European research project about International Standards for Language Engineering (IST-ISLE), Natural Interactive Communication for Edutainment (NICE), Computer Mediated Communication (MagicLounge). He can be contacted at: martin@limsi.fr.

Helen McBreen currently works as a Research Engineer with Digital Fashion Limited, Osaka, Japan. She completed her postdoctoral research at The University of Edinburgh in 2002 under the supervision of Professor Mervyn Jack. Her thesis, entitled "Embodied Conversational Agents: Extending the Persona Metaphor to Virtual Research Environments" explored, through extended empirical evaluation, the usability of 3D conversational characters in a variety of eRetail applications. Her research on the subject has been published in notable proceedings, journals and books. She can be contacted at: helen_mcbreen@yahoo.co.uk

Hazel Morton is a Research Associate at the Centre for Communication Interface Research at the University of Edinburgh. She holds a Masters degree in English, a Masters degree in Applied Linguistics and is currently pursuing a PhD. Her work involves experimental design, testing and evaluation of applications with conversational agents, with particular interest in the perceived personality of agents and the evaluation of the effectiveness and user acceptability of animated conversational agents in eCommerce and eLearning applications. She can be contacted at: Hazel.Morton@ccir.ed.ac.uk.

Barbara Neumayr is responsible for product development within the sysis NetLife platform and for project management of research projects. As a co-founder of the Austrian company sysis, she has been working for sysis on a part time basis since 1994. Following her studies of business adminstration and economics, she had worked as an assistant professor in both teaching and research at the Vienna University of Economics and Business Administration for four years before joining sysis on a full time basis in 2000. She can be contacted at: barbara.neumayr@sysis.at.

Han Noot is a software engineer at the Center for Mathematics and Computer Science (CWI) in the Netherlands. He has an MA in theoretical physics (1973). His professional interests include computer graphics, lip-sync visual speech and computer animation systems. He can be contacted at: han@cwi.nl.

Sharon Oviatt is a Professor and Co-Director of the Center for Human-Computer Communication (CHCC) in the Dept. of Computer Science at Oregon Health and Science University (OHSU). Her research focuses on human-computer interaction, spoken language and multimodal interfaces, and mobile and highly interactive systems. Examples of recent work involve the development of novel design concepts for multimodal and mobile interfaces, robust interfaces for real-world field environments and diverse users, and adaptive conversational interfaces with animated software partners. She is an active member of the international HCI, speech and multimodal communities. She can be contacted at: oviatt@cse.ogi.edu.

Catherine Pelachaud is currently a professor at the IUT of Montreuil, University of Paris 8, directing the research team 'Technology and Communication'. She has been involved in research on Embodied Conversational Agent for a long time, looking at several aspects such as the link between facial expression and intonation, lip movements and coarticulation, facial and gesture communicative behaviours. She has been participant in several EU-projects as well as she was co-organisers of workshops on ECAs. Her current research interest includes conversational agent and human behaviour simulation, individual agents and representation language for agent. She can be contacted at: c.pelachaud@iut.univ-paris8.fr.

Zsófia Ruttkay is senior research at the Center for Mathematics and Computer Science (CWI) in Amsterdam, where she is head of the group 'Social User Interfaces'. She has been doing research on facial animation, hand gesturing and style for ECAs. She was involved in empirical evaluation of talking heads. With a background in AI, she applied constraint satisfaction to define facial expressions in a declarative way, and used logic programming for hand gesturing. She is also interested in beyond realism possibilities for virtual characters; she was co-author of the CharToon system to model and animate cartoon talking heads. She can be contacted at: zsofia.ruttkay@cwi.nl.

Christoph Schmotzer has been working for sysis in Austria as a content developer, project manager and usability researcher. He holds an MA degree in Psychology from the University of Vienna. His focus of research lies on empirical study design, test construction, psychological diagnosis and media psychology. Major areas of his current work at sysis are psychological user modeling, game design and interface ergonomics. He can be contacted at: christoph.schmotzer@sysis.at.

John Stasko is an Associate Professor in the College of Computing and the GVU Center at the Georgia Institute of Technology, where he is Director of the Information Interfaces research group. He received the BS degree in mathematics from Bucknell University in 1983 and the ScM and PhD degrees in computer science from Brown University in 1985 and 1989. His research interests are broadly in HCI, with a particular focus on information visualization, user interfaces, and software agents. He has been author or co-author of over 80 journal and conference papers. He can be contacted at: stasko@cc.gatech.edu.

Marc Swerts is now a senior researcher in the Communication and Cognition group at Tilburg University. He works on the project 'Functions of audiovisual prosody', sponsored by the Netherlands Organisation for Scientific Research (NWO). After having studied Germanic linguistics at Antwerp University, Marc Swerts got a Ph.D. (1994) in experimental phonetics from the Eindhoven University of Technology. Then he worked as a visiting researcher at various institutes in the USA, Japan, Sweden and Italy. He can be reached at: m.g.j.swerts@uvt.nl.

Qianying Wang is a PhD candidate of Stanford University, Communication Department. Her advisor is Professor Clifford Nass. She is interested in Human-Computer Interaction, human factors, cognitive and social psychology. From 1997 till 2001, Qianying worked as a staff research member for IBM Research and earned multiple IBM Research division awards. She is the author of nine filed patents worldwide. Qianying earned her B.S. and a M.S. cum laude in Electric Engineering from Shanghai JiaoTong University. She can be reached at: wangqy@stanford.edu.

Jun Xiao is a PhD student in the College of Computing at Georgia Institute of Technology. His research focuses on the evaluation of interface agents. In particular, he is gathering a set of experimental data through empirical studies to provide insights for understanding the conditions under which users could best benefit from interactions with interface agents. He received his B.S in Computer Science from Fudan University in Shanghai. She can be reached at: junxiao@cc.gatech.edu.

Preface

Embodied conversational agents (ECAs) are more or less autonomous and intelligent software entities with an embodiment used to communicate with the user. They have entered the research field some 10 years ago, and in recent years the first commercial applications have been launched. The ECA may act as an apprentice for the user in performing some task by a traditional piece of software (like the PaperClip providing help on using MSWord), take a specific role well-known from real-life scenarios (e.g. acting as a salesperson or a tutor), or represent individuals in virtual environments with or without parallels in real life, such as chat forums or multi-user games. One can come across a wide range of technical terms for ECAs: avatars are representatives of and directly controlled by users; in the case of talking heads the embodiment is a head with the capability of speech. Other terms like virtual characters or humanoids have been used too, emphasizing yet further characteristics of agents.

The diversity of terms is related to that of the decisions taken (some of them apparently self-evident) when designing an ECA. For instance, to convey some information in a most effective way, one designer may assume that the best solution is to create a talking head, while another may choose a torso with gesticulating hands, or even a full body with changing postures. Which design decision to prefer? The more modalities used, the better? Should the embodiment be anthropomorphic, and as realistic as possible? What are the features necessary to make such an impression? Should the agent be invading and omni-present? Should it be pro-active? Is it good or bad to give the impression of human intelligence by the behaviour, while the underlying processing is much more limited than that of real people?

Questions like these are essential for the research and development of ECAs. However, for most of them no simple answer is available. The reasons are manifold. First of all, as the research field is still very young, researchers have been focusing on some specific problems which are prerequisites for developing full-fledged multimodal ECAs: e.g. to model muscle contraction and wrinkle appearance, to get the hands move, or to let faces talk with acceptable quality. To develop the accurate use of single modalities, like synthetic speech sounding as real speech, or eyes gazing like a real human does requires years of research by specialists. Moreover, the evaluation of single modalities often cannot be done without taking into account the (unwanted) influence of other modalities.

The context becomes richer when one is interested in the added value of ECAs. There have been a few demonstrators developed in the research community to show the potentials of the technology in applications like tutoring or information services. The diversity of the techniques, tools and terms used, the context of using the ECA and the differences in the evaluation setting makes it difficult to assess the results. Secondly, though the commercial mass-application of ECAs is now emerging, there is hardly any feedback on the strong points or the deficiencies of these applications. Thirdly, human-human communication itself is extremely complex. The mechanisms of using modalities depend on factors like culture, personal features and the particular situation. One can turn to disciplines like psychology and sociology for a foundation of computational models of complex phenomena such as culture, emotion or personality. These disciplines provide some very precious qualitative and quantitative information that are indispensable to consider. But the approach undertaken by these disciplines (often working from examples to theory) as well as the intrinsic complexity of the phenomena (the enormous quantity of factors to consider and the various aspects to integrate) do make it difficult to create succinct computational models of all aspects of human-like communicational phenomena needed for a given application context. Finally, the empirical evaluation of ECAs has to be done in a methodologically sound way, which, in itself, has to be established for researching this new medium. This is particularly important as it has to be identified what aspects are relevant to be looked at, and also how to measure these, often subjective and not succinctly defined aspects.

In the present volume, we focus on methodologies for evaluating ECAs. The ECA technology has become mature enough for evaluation, and several authors, both advocates and opponents of the technology have pointed out the necessity of this (see e.g., the Chapter by Catrambone et al. for an overview). We believe that evaluation is essential for many reasons.

Morally, the research community should be aware of the potentials of the technology being developed. It is a thrilling position to be able to create synthetic humans and to exploit the power of this technology to influence real people. What social role could an ECA have, if it is able to engage and maintain a conversation with a user? Would ECA as a general new user interface turn users 'lazy and stupid'? For instance, a pro-active ECA may not only save some efforts by performing a tedious task (like gathering information from the web) on behalf of the user, but may perform evaluations, make suggestions or even take decisions instead of the user. To which degree should an ECA be allowed to fool users as being so believable that the users mistake him for a real person?

From a more pragmatic point of view, a common terminology and sound evaluation results with clearly stated scope would foster further development. Researches could rely on design guidelines on how an ECA should use certain modalities to exhibit certain qualities, as well as on what qualities of an ECA are essential for a certain application context. While the re-use and adaptation of models and low-level capabilities (for example fast inverse kinematics for hand positioning or TTS engines for speech) become common, the re-use of knowledge, models or algorithms to design ECAs to suit particular expectations is hampered by the lack of insight into the scope of applicability of individual recommendations.

For a broader scientific context, a realistic, detailed and by experimentally verified assessment of the pros of ECAs would help to gain recognition for the technology as a new form of human-computer interaction. By presenting the result and setting a research agenda grounded on evaluation, we should be able to avoid that ECA research will go through a life-curve similar to that of the machine translation of natural languages: after the first small but spectacular results the expectations were set unrealistically high, which led to the hibernation of a promising research field.

Last but not least, evaluation is essential to the real successful applications of ECAs, where the ECA has added effect in dimensions other than the attraction of novelty.

In this volume we have collected recent works on most of the above introduced different aspects of ECA evaluation. The concept and most of the contents of the book are the result of the workshop on "Embodied conversational agents — let's specify and evaluate them!", held at the 2002 AAMAS conference in Montreal.

The works in Part I address ECA design and evaluation from a methodological point of view. The Chapter by Isbister and Doyle gives an overview of the diverse opinions just about understanding the concept ECA, the necessity for turning the 'crafting' practice into a mature discipline, and outlines a research agenda for the necessarily interdisciplinary research. The Chapter by Ruttkay et al. discusses the problems inherent in designing and evaluating ECAs due to the lack of common understanding of terms, objectives and success criteria. They propose a common taxonomy for the design parameters and evaluation aspects and discuss ways to measure these aspects. The Chapter by Noor looks at ECA evaluation from the broader context of evaluating user interfaces. This chapter is a 'quick guide' on when and how to do empirical evaluation in a proper way, from identifying the goals via selecting the right subject groups to interpreting collected data. Finally, the Chapter by Cerrato and Ekeklint suggests to use prosodic and paralinguistic features as novel measures for user satisfaction based on the study of corpuses of real-life applications.

Part II consists of two papers which put the user in the focus. Höök claims that the user and her affective feedback have to be a main driving factor for ECA evaluation and design. She also points out the challenges and pitfalls of inducing and interpreting affective reactions by looking at three example applications from her own practice. She proposes a two-tiered approach for design and evaluation. Nass et al. argue that ECAs should appear as humans in their behaviour, and it is not the actual capability but the appearance which the user will assess. They give guidelines based on an extensive body of psychological studies on how to make an ECA be perceived as if it were paying attention to the user.

Part III consists of micro-level evaluation studies, where the target of evaluation is a single aspect of an ECA. How to choose the many parameters for the ECA embodiment in order to achieve some performance? For instance, what should the eyebrows be doing during speech? It turns out, as investigated in the Chapter by Krahmer and Swerts, that eyebrow movements have a different role in the perception of focus for speakers of Italian and Dutch, which has implication on ECA design with respect to the language spoken by the ECA. Thus when translating visual speech, it is not sufficient to get the visemes and lip-synch right only. Another, somewhat similar question is if and how hand gestures should be used. Buisine et al. looked at the effect of multimodal strategies used for combining verbal and nonverbal behavior for the design of ECAs. According to their small-scale experiment, there is a difference in preference depending on gender of the user. Catrambone et al. present here a piece of work meant to be the first step in a series of systematic evaluation studies to judge the utility of ECAs. First they set up a framework, where the features of the user and the task are influential factors in judging an ECA. In their current experiment they found that the perception of the ECA was influenced by the task, while the design of the ECAs had little effect.

Part IV reports on experience with ECAs in different applications. Darves and Oviatt found that children between 7 and 10 were stimulated very much to learn about marine biology by the possibility of conversing with an animated digital fish. They also pointed at the impact of the auditory embodiment on children's engagement: an extrovert speech had more effect than an introvert speech. Morton et al. investigated the effect of ECAs in three different eCommerce applications, from different points of views in each case, such as overall acceptance of an ECA, preference for ECAs with specific 'voice personae' including linguistic style, and the effect of text output redundant to speech on trust. Finally, Krenn et al. give an account on experience with commercial web applications in contrast to the previous 'laboratory experiments'. In the case of the web applications avatars were applied, meant to be representative of the users, and were used to gain — commercially interesting and other — information about the user. From their analysis of long-term usage data in three different countries, one can get an idea about what types of users like to interact via avatars, and in what ways.

The many-foldedness of ECA evaluation is reflected by the structure of the book. Several chapters could be assigned under more than one of the main themes. For instance, the importance of the user can be considered as an evaluation methodology principle (as argued by Höök, but also concluded by the experiments reported by Buisine), as well as an inspiration for design and guidelines on using modalities on a micro-level (as suggested by Nass et al.). Individual experiments and the systematic design of a series of experiments in a pre-set framework also address methodological aspects, like the framework used by Catrambone et al. or the analysis of commercial mass-applications reported by Krenn et al. Besides the consonances, the reader may discover dissonances between the chapters. The disciplinary and methodological rigor asked for by the works in the first part may not always be met in the works reporting on evaluation studies, or — as the authors themselves state — additional data with real life applications should have been collected in order to be able to perform a more detailed evaluation. With the collection of works dedicated to one or other aspect of evaluation, per se, we hope to give an impetus to future work. By getting more and more empirical results, gained by sound methods, presented with reference to common terminology and related to findings reported by others a detailed picture of the merits of ECA will emerge. The somewhat chaotic bulk of univocal or contradictory pieces of conclusions will be replaced by design guidelines with a clear scope of applicability. There is much to be done till then, so we ask everybody involved in ECA research and application to contribute.

January 2004

ZSÓFIA RUTTKAY
Amsterdam

CATHERINE PELACHAUD
Paris

I

EVALUATION METHODOLOGY

Chapter 1

THE BLIND MEN AND THE ELEPHANT REVISITED

Evaluating Interdisciplinary ECA Research

Katherine Isbister and Patrick Doyle

> *We shall not cease from exploration,*
> *And the end of all our exploring*
> *Will be to arrive where we started*
> *And know the place for the first time.*
>
> —T. S. Eliot

Abstract   The construction of embodied conversational agents is an ambitious, complex, and essentially interdisciplinary process. This is inevitable given the depth, sophistication, and many modalities of the products we seek to create. Other chapters in this book address methods for evaluating ECAs as artefacts or according to their usability. In this chapter, we offer a complementary perspective: grounding the evaluation of ECAs in the context of the different disciplines that have merged to create the research community constructing them.

Different research areas have different goals and criteria for success, and without understanding what these are and how they relate, we cannot intelligently recognise what contributions other groups are making, a necessary requirement for integrating work done on one aspect of ECAs with work on another. Our goal is to help our community ultimately to create the high-quality interdisciplinary products necessary for this discipline to mature.

Keywords: Conversational agents, design categories, evaluation criteria, interdisciplinary research.

Z. Ruttkay and C. Pelachaud (eds.), From Brows to Trust, 3–26.
© *2004 Kluwer Academic Publishers. Printed in the Netherlands.*

1.   Introduction

The goal of embodied conversational agent (ECA) research is to produce an intelligent agent that is at least capable of certain social behaviours and which can draw upon its visual representation to reinforce the belief that it is a social entity. Almost all researchers in this area have additional goals that revolve around giving their agents additional capabilities in presentation, behaviour, task knowledge, etc.

Efforts to create these agents are necessarily interdisciplinary. Creating a fully-realized ECA requires the application of research in areas ranging from agent architectures and issues in artificial intelligence, synthetic speech, natural language processing (Bates et al. (1992); Blumberg (1996); Cassell et al. (2000); Hayes-Roth et al. (1994); Loyall and Bates (1991); Reilly (1996); Johnson and Rickel (1997)), emotions (Elliott (1992); Elliott et al. (1999); Ortony et al. (1988); Picard (1997)), graphics (Badler (1997); Goldberg (1997)) and interface design (Laurel (1990); Rist et al. (1997)), to sociology and psychology (Fiske and Taylor (1991); Nass et al. (1995); Isbister and Nass (2000); Nass et al. (1994); Zimbardo and Leippe (1991)), and art, drama, and animation (Lasseter (1987); Thomas and Johnson (1981)).

The need to integrate this wide range of work causes three unavoidable problems. The first and most obvious problem is that no one can possess a comprehensive knowledge of all this research; there is simply too much of it. The effect is that very often simple solutions are re-invented over and over again for problems that, unbeknownst to us, have already been explored in detail elsewhere in the literature. Effort is expended in developing solutions that already exist.

ECA research has been praised by the artificial intelligence community on the grounds that we are attempting to address the "whole problem." Much of contemporary AI research has shifted away from working on general intelligence in favour of focusing on what Nilsson (1995) calls "performance programs" (such as expert systems) that are exceptional at narrowly-defined tasks while losing their relevance to the original goal. While our goal is not to create a general intelligence, ECA researchers nevertheless are working on complete agents. We expect an implementation to have an embodiment, an input-recognition system, a behaviour engine of some kind, some model of personality and possibly of emotion — in short, we expect our research artefacts to be 'complete,' if limited in one respect or another.

This approach is both a strength and a weakness, and leads to the second fundamental problem we face. The advantage of building complete agents is that most work (e.g., Andre (1997); Badler (1997); Hayes-Roth et al. (1997); Isbister et al. (2000); Stone and Lester (1996); Trappl and Petta (1996)) is grounded in the ultimate goal of producing an entire ECA. The disadvantage is that research groups generally do not have the resources to implement substantial solutions to all the problems involved in building an entire ECA. Instead, certain aspects of an ECA's design are avoided or given minimal treatment in favour of focusing on others. One system may have excellent facial animation; another a flexible emotional model; a third may be adept at handling social interactions. These ECAs must be placed into carefully-designed test environments in which these deficiencies do not weaken the agent's effectiveness. The result is that while there are many proposed complete ECAs, they are difficult to compare because they do not always offer comparably sophisticated solutions to each problem. This also means that it is generally not possible to test ECAs in broad and complex ways because it is generally not possible for any one group to build an ECA that possesses all the necessary mechanics.

These first two problems — the breadth of related work, and the desire to create ECAs that are complete, even if unavoidably limited in some ways — lead to the third problem, which is the lack of suitable evaluation criteria for ECAs. As with artificial intelligence research (Koller (1996)), a primary difficulty in ECA research is the vague and intuitive description of the basic problem we are trying to solve. There are no formal, widely-accepted definitions of core terms such as *believable*, *social*, or even *conversational* (see Chapter 2 by Ruttkay et al. for a discussion on the importance of rigorous definitions on the quality of research evaluations).

This situation is comparable to that in the parable of the blind men and the elephant. Each man reached out to touch the creature in order to identify it. One felt its trunk, and concluded that the elephant was like a snake. Another felt its tusk, and decided that elephants were like spears. A third ran his hand along its broad sides and declared that elephants were like walls. Each was partly correct, but none was completely accurate, and the view each man held of what an elephant was coloured his understanding of everyone else's interpretation. Similarly, in ECA research, each contributing research community working on the construction of these ECAs has its own view of what an ECA is and what qualities are significant in evaluating it. Only by making explicit what those disparate views are, and clearly delineating what each community is seeking to accomplish and what constitutes success to that community, can we have create meaningful, quantifiable criteria for evaluating what make 'good' ECAs.

As ECA research is a relatively new field, it is reasonable that strict evaluation criteria did not immediately appear. It has taken time to explore the space; define, however intuitively, our goals; and experiment with various theories and techniques. The field has been in what Kuhn (1996) calls the *pre-paradigm* phase, in which many different views of the basic concepts have been proposed and have been subject to multiple interpretations. There have been many *ad hoc* theories but there is no overarching formulation of the problem or its solutions that is widely accepted. ECA research is a discipline, and not yet a science, because we do not yet have formal theories to explain our discipline, and we do not yet have standard evaluation criteria for our contributions.

The purpose of this chapter is not to criticise the state of ECA research. On the contrary, these limitations are not the result of flawed research but the necessary compromises made in the exploration of a new research area, and one in which nearly every architectural or design decision is dependent upon a combination of factors springing from widely different bodies of knowledge. However, to continue to mature as a discipline, we will have to develop criteria for design and evaluation that are based upon those of these various disciplines. As an interdisciplinary research area, we need to communicate our results to the disciplines from which we draw inspiration; and to do that successfully, we must evaluate our work using criteria that they will recognise and respect.

As a first step toward this admittedly lofty goal, we offer a broad taxonomy of the research areas contributing to the creation of embodied conversational agents. There are two purposes in doing so. First, to make the distinctions between these divisions clear, so that researchers can clearly indicate where they are making novel contributions and where they are not. Second, the hope is that a basic taxonomy will be a starting point for developing evaluation criteria for each division. While ultimately we hope this will result in criteria that can be applied to entire ECAs, in the shorter term we believe this will assist us in evaluating existing ECAs, whose strengths and weaknesses can be assigned to these categories.

2.   The Taxonomy

To construct our taxonomy, we began by following the approach of Franklin and Graesser (1997), examining several foundational definitions for conversational agents, intelligent characters, believable agents, etc.

Loyall (1997) writes: "Believable agents are personality-rich autonomous agents with the powerful properties of characters from the arts."

A believable agent has personality, emotion, self-motivation, change, social relationships, consistency, and presents the illusion of life (appearance of goals, concurrent pursuit of goals, parallel action, reactive and responsive, situated, resource bounded, exists in a social context, broadly capable, well-integrated capabilities and behaviours).

According to Blumberg (1996), "...an autonomous animated creature is an animated object capable of goal-directed and time-varying behaviour." A creature must react, be seen as having an independent existence, have choices to make, reveal its intentionality, appear to care what happens to it, adapt, and display variability in its responses to users and to the environment.

Reilly (1996) says that believable agents are "autonomous, interactive agents that have the qualities that have made the non-interactive characters of traditional media believable." They may not be intelligent or realistic, but they will have strong personalities.

Hayes-Roth and Doyle (1998) claim that "animate characters" redefine traditional agent design problems. In addition to possessing empathy, personality, and a capacity for social relations, their behaviours must be variable rather than reliable, idiosyncratic instead of predictable, appropriate rather than correct (that is, they must be reasonable within the context, without necessarily being the most logical or rational choices of behaviour), effective instead of complete, interesting rather than efficient, and distinctively individual as opposed to optimal.

Stone and Lester (1996) describe animated pedagogical agents as possessing three key properties: timely domain coverage (that is, they present the topics they are meant to discuss or to teach at the appropriate times and at appropriate levels of detail), contextuality (appropriate explanations for the situation), and continuity (coherent behaviours, pedagogically and believably).

Perlin and Goldberg (1996) are concerned with building believable characters "that respond to users and to each other in real-time, with consistent personalities, properly changing moods and without mechanical repetition, while always maintaining an author's goals and intentions."

Trappl and Petta (1996) describe synthetic characters as needing different abilities in different contexts; "animators might be assisted in the delicate and ephemeral task of ensuring consistent and believable patterns of behaviour in yet other settings, achieving e.g. various degrees of agent autonomy that can play an essential role in providing effective assistance to users..."

In characterising believable agents, Bates (1992) requires "only that they not be clearly stupid or unreal." Such broad, shallow agents must "exhibit some signs of internal goals, reactivity, emotion, natural language ability, and knowledge of agents as well as of the micro-world."

For Foner (1993), the critical issues are autonomy, personalisability, discourse (ability to carry on two-way dialog), trustworthiness, domain (appropriate domain for the agent), graceful degradation, ability to cooperate, anthropomorphism, and choosing a setting in which users' expectations for the agent can be met.

Most of the researchers we cite here belong to computer science departments, or to computationally-based media arts programs. Yet their definitions combine qualities from traditional software agent design, such as autonomy, responsiveness, reactivity, situatedness, and goals, with qualities that come from media arts or social science — engaging personality, mood, emotion, and idiosyncrasy. Success at achieving such qualities is difficult to measure with traditional, quantifiable benchmarks for software performance.

Historically, ECA researchers have reached out to other disciplines to help them achieve these goals, drawing upon artists' and animators' techniques, those of media specialists from drama, film and other disciplines, and social sciences such as psychology and sociology. Yet, in the past, research teams did not also borrow evaluation criteria from these disciplines. Early evaluations of agent performance did not take full advantage of all that is known in the arts and the social sciences about isolating and testing whether something 'reads' as engaging and lifelike. For example, simple surveys asked users if they thought a character was 'believable' — an unreliable way to measure effects, as one cannot isolate exactly how or why the 'believability' is occurring, nor even what the term actually means to the respondent.

Just as ECA research has benefited from the use of structures, methods, and techniques from these various disciplines, we also believe that it will benefit from the application of their different approaches to evaluation. A mature discipline must have clear and meaningful ways of distinguishing the extent and significance of its results. It should also be possible to communicate those findings back to the other disciplines from which we have drawn inspiration in terms that researchers in those areas will recognize and accept.

As a starting point, we propose a set of four research concentrations within the ECA field, each with its own standards. These areas are agency and computational issues, believability, sociability, and task/application domains. We have chosen these areas through an examination of how ECA research has developed historically.

The development of embodied conversational agents began within the field of computer science; it was an outgrowth of the attempts to create artificial intelligence and artificial life. As the focus on ECAs moved from programs that could act intelligently to agents that could behave in lifelike ways, the discipline began to make use of art, animation, drama, theatre, and literature, which had been preoccupied with that problem for centuries. Once we began to build working ECAs, techniques from social science were needed in order to examine how they interacted with human beings and how humans responded to computer-based personalities. In the last decade, the field has begun to produce ECAs for use in real-world applications, which has led to a need for understanding issues such as stability, robustness, and completeness that are the concern of industrial design and production in particular task domains.

Consider believability. Believability researchers seek to create demonstrably lifelike and engaging character appearance and behaviour. Believability research draws upon the arts, psychology, and physiology. Evaluations of this work require the introduction of two new methods of evaluation:

Systematic empirical evaluations: Psychologists and physiologists conduct controlled experiments to test whether their hypotheses about causes and effects hold true. They make use of well-established existing measures where possible, so that other researchers can easily understand and replicate results. ECA believability research that draws upon these fields should leverage this technique, as well as the standard instruments used to measure effects (moving beyond the "is this believable, do you think?" paradigm of early efforts). An example: applying the facial coding system Ekman and Friesen (1976) developed for researching human emotions to the construction of ECA emotional expression, and then validating the legibility and plausibility of these expressions, using similar empirical tactics to those of the original researchers. The contribution of this kind of evaluation is evidence that such an approach to creating lifelike emotions could work in other ECAs.

Expert evaluation of the polished whole: Use of expert peer review and/or target audience surveys to evaluate the overall believability and effectiveness of an ECA. This approach is borrowed from the arts and media fields. Believability researchers should draw upon these methods for evaluating impressions of their ECAs. An example: designing an ECA modelled upon a famous animated character, to interact with visitors to a web site about that character. Using character experts from that company to evaluate the agent during design (is it true to the character's film personality, does it engage with high enough production values and realism), then using web site visitor surveys to find out how the agent was received once it is released. The contribution of this kind of evaluation is typically bounded by the single ECA instance. However, over time, these sorts of evaluations produce accumulated observations about tactics for effective design for particular audiences and contexts which can be tested and applied to similar ECA projects.

Sociability researchers are interested in implementing human-like social skills and interaction strategies in ECAs. Like believability researchers, sociability researchers draw upon both systematic empirical and expert evaluation techniques. However, sociability researchers draw upon work from different areas of the social sciences than believability researchers — social psychology, linguistics, sociology, and anthropology.

Finally, application domain researchers are those who seek to create complex, domain-specific scenarios or full-blown implementations. Tutoring, military training, health counselling, and customer service are some examples of these domains. In order to adequately plan and test ECAs on meaningful benchmarks for these domains, research teams include task-domain experts, who bring their evaluation standards along with them, leading to a third new method of evaluation of ECAs:

Outcome testing: Use of audience surveys and observation of behaviour to gauge the effectiveness of an ECA in achieving particular task domain outcomes. The contribution of this sort of evaluation is confirmation that the steps the research team took led to effective outcomes, allowing others who hope to tackle similar domains to leverage their knowledge and tactics.

To summarise, the evolution of the field has gradually moved us from teams of computer scientists to teams that include artists, psychologists and other social scientists, as well as domain experts. Each group brings established evaluation standards to the field that we can benefit from in our own literature.

Given the range of evaluation approaches and standards we outlined above, it becomes crucial to select appropriate evaluation criteria for any given project. For a large project, this could be a combination, with different project team members focusing on different types of contributions and outcomes. A wonderful example of a broad research project that encompasses many researchers and complementary agendas is the work done at the University of Southern California's Information Sciences Institute and Institute for Creative Technology on ECAs for training[1]. This work includes contributions to computational technique, work on

Table 1.1. Major categories of Embodied Conversational Agent research

Category	Criteria for Success	Evaluation Techniques
Believability	Agent conveys 'illusion of life' to the viewer/user.	Subjective: Does the user find the agent's appearance, voice, and words, and reactions and responses believable? Does an expert? Objective: Does the user react physiologically and behaviourally as if dealing with an equivalent 'real' person? Does the user engage in ways that demonstrate s/he treats the agent's behaviour as believable (reactions to behaviours, attribution of goals and emotions).
Sociability	User is able to interact socially in an intuitive and natural way with the agent.	Subjective: Qualitative measures from user of agent's friendliness, helpfulness, social qualities, communication abilities. Also, user's evaluation of overall experience — speed, ease, satisfaction. Objective: Measures of elicited social responses to the agent. Behavioural changes predicted by social tactics used (more influence of agent on user's answers, more reciprocal aid of agent, etc.).
Application domains	Agent performs domain-specific role in a manner that achieves the desired outcome and creates a satisfying experience for the participant.	Subjective: Measures of user satisfaction with task and interaction. Objective: Behavioural outcomes (performance on tasks, memory, etc).
Agency and computational issues	System/technique meets good design criteria and performance benchmarks. Also, believability and sociability goals above.	Subjective: Elegance of system, parsimony. Objective: Successful operation of the agent in 'real-world' domains according to criteria of speed, efficiency, optimality, reliability, error handling, etc. Subjective and objective measures of 'believability' and 'sociability' as specified in prior sections.

applying training tactics toward achieving measurable outcomes, and modelling human emotions to generate more lifelike character actions and reactions. The final product (e.g. the Mission Rehearsal Exercise) is held to media best practices standards and tested with real users. Thus this project uses all four evaluation strategies, to accomplish different ends.

The crucial thing, from our perspective, is that each contribution can be written up and subjected to different sorts of peer evaluation, and should be expected to advance the field in different ways.

Toward that end, we've constructed a taxonomy of research sub-agendas around primary contributions that lead to predominant evaluation strategies. Table 1.1 summarises these areas. In the following sections we provide more details to clarify what each area consists of, what its contributions are, and how work in that area should ideally be evaluated, with examples from existing research programs. Note: though agency and computational issues is historically first, we discuss it last, as it integrates the discussions of all the other areas.

2.1   Believability

Definition: Those who work on believability are tackling the problem of how to create the general, visceral 'illusion of life' for those who observe and engage with the embodied agent.

By this, most in our field do not mean literally recreating a moment-by-moment, highly realistic imitation of a real person or animal's behaviour. Instead, the approach is to selectively imitate and heighten qualities of humans and animals that will engage a person's belief that this is an animate creature. Even if the person does not fully believe the agent is real, s/he is able to enjoy and engage with the agent, and is not disrupted by feelings that the agent is somehow mechanical or machine-like.

Within the umbrella category of believability, there are many problems. Broadly speaking, they can be divided into two classes:

- Making the 'surface' of the agent believable — its appearance, voice, and movement.

- Making the 'intentionality' of the agent believable — that is, actions and reactions that create the impression of an independent entity with goals and feelings.

Researchers who focus on surface believability investigate topics such as refining facial or body expressivity, experimenting with different levels of abstraction and detail in clothing and props within the ECA's world, or creating realistic and emotionally engaging prosody in speech. Researchers in this area draw heavily upon work in traditional, noninteractive media such as literature and animation, as well as studies of human behavioural patters, locomotion, expressivity, etc.

An example of this kind of work is that of Norm Badler and his colleagues at the Center for Human Modelling and Simulation[2]. With their EMOTE system, this group has used the Laban Movement Analysis "human movement observation system" (Laban (1974)) as a basis for creating parameters applied to animated actions. Characters with this system in place perform everyday motions in a manner that is consistent with the observations of Laban, and which are 'read' properly by human observers (Badler et al. (2002)). Another example is the work done by Cahn on generating affect in synthesised speech (Cahn (1990)).

Believable intentionality researchers put their efforts into producing convincing behaviour in interactive characters — plausible goals and strategies for achieving them, demonstrable awareness of the environment and of other entities in it, etc. The Oz project at Carnegie Mellon University (Bates (1992)), and Bruce Blumberg's Synthetic Characters group at the MIT Media Lab[3] have focused their development efforts on producing ongoing convincing behaviour in interactive characters. Roz Picard's research on tracking and responding to emotion is another example of developing aspects of believable intentionality (Picard (1997)). Researchers in this area draw upon traditional media techniques as well as observations from the study of human and animal behaviour.

Criteria for success: Some form of response from end users that the character quality being produced is 'lifelike' or 'larger than life' in the appropriate way. Bates (1992) writes: "To our knowledge, whether an agent's behaviour produces a successful suspension of disbelief can be determined only empirically."

Evaluation strategies: Believability research combines both systematic empirical evaluation, and expert peer review and audience testing.

Researchers applying principles from the study of human or animal behaviour need to isolate and analyse the effectiveness of using these models on believability goals. Where possible, they should draw upon well-known measures. For example, if one is examining emotional expressions, the facial encoding system of Ekman and Friesen (Ekman and Friesen (1976)) provides a such a standard structure for description. It is best when researchers state the planned outcome ahead of time — measurable outcomes such as more positive ratings of the character or more reciprocal facial expressions. (See Table 1.1 for a list of subjective and objective measurement techniques in this area). Ideally, researchers should test versions of their ECA with and without the component, to get a true picture of the contribution of that component (though as Ruttkay et al. point out elsewhere in this book, this can be challenging).

It is also true that an ECA must be sufficiently holistically engaging and believable to support adequate testing of a sub-component system that is thought to increase believability. Collaboration with media partners (e.g., the current collaboration between Breazel, a social robotics researcher, and Winston, a Hollywood animatronics expert, to produce the Leonardo robot (SIGGRAPH (2003)) is one way to ease the burden of producing high-quality lifelike components that are not part of the target research. For example, if the research is about producing lifelike reactions by the ECA to users in real time based upon sensor input and computation, the media experts could ensure that the gestures and facial expressions of the agent are sufficiently lifelike to support this work.

Finally, there is room for research and case studies about fully realized believable ECAs and their impact on audiences, as well as critique by expert peers (e.g., practitioners from the entertainment industry who must evaluate and make decisions on commercial character projects). This is in contrast to evaluation by untrained examiners, which often include the researchers themselves. Uninformed intuitions about which behaviours seem lifelike may have served during our initial exploration of the field, but are not a suitable way of comparing present systems against the theories we are evolving.

2.2   Sociability

Definition: Sociability focuses on producing lifelike social interactions between ECAs and users. The goal is to produce both theories and techniques that will enable the creation of such interactions.

This speciality innovates and enhances the manner in which people interact socially with embodied conversational agents. This includes conversational skills, appropriate interpersonal reactions and adaptations, awareness of social context (e.g. physical or cultural), empathy, and the ability to work from individual goals toward mutual social agendas with the user. It also includes designing fluid and natural methods for interaction with agents, such as voice or gesture recognition. Researchers in this area draw upon the study of human interaction in the social sciences (social psychology, sociology, anthropology, linguistics), and also upon traditional media techniques for engaging sociability.

An example of this kind of work is the conversational skills built into Justine Cassell's REA project (Cassell et al. (2000)). Cassell and her group developed appropriate gestures, eye gaze, and use of small talk to facilitate believable conversation with an agent. They made use of sensing techniques to enhance the agent's ability to intervene at socially appropriate moments.

Other examples: the work of Isbister and Nakanishi (Isbister et al. (2000)) exploring the use of social agents to facilitate cross-cultural human-human conversations; Poggi and Pelachaud's use of performative facial expressions in agent-human conversation (Poggi et al. (2000)); and Nass and Reeves' ongoing program of research examining the application of human social psychological findings to interaction with media (Nass and Reeves (1996)).

Criteria for success: Some form of qualitative and quantifiable response from end users that the character interaction being produced is engaging, helpful, and/or intuitive in the manner that would be predicted by application of the relevant social tactics.

Evaluation strategies: Sociability research (like believability) combines both systematic empirical evaluation and expert peer review and audience testing.

Researchers seeking to apply principles borrowed from social psychology, linguistics, or other related fields, need to use subjective and objective measures to confirm that their implementations are having the desired effects on social encounters with users. These might include surveys or interviews of users, confirming the positive social perceptions predicted by application of the technique (friendliness, helpfulness, legibility of appropriate personality or role cues, ease of interaction through gesture, etc.). Objective measures include shifts in user behaviour toward the agent, which would be predicted given the underlying principles. For example, if one hypothesised that people prefer working with and are more influenced by those similar to themselves, one might test the extent to which a user changed his/her answers on a quiz based on the advice of an ECA that was either similar or dissimilar in personality. Ideally, researchers should test their sociability solutions against a parallel implementation without that particular innovation, to help isolate causality. Where possible, researchers should borrow established measures from related disciplines. For example, those studying personality can make use of the Myers-Briggs inventory (Murray (1990)) or the Wiggins interpersonal scale (Wiggins (1979)), rather than inventing a new scale of personality. The social sciences have a rich body of measures to draw upon for evaluative purposes.

As with believability, there is room for research and case studies about fully realized sociable ECAs and their impact on audiences, as well as critique by expert peers. In this case, the measures and/or critique would be focused on how intuitive and successful the social interaction with the ECA was, rather than on surface or intentional believability of the target ECA.

2.3 Task and Application Domains

Definition: Crafting ECAs that support real-world task domains, such as education, health care, or sales, with measurable target outcomes for users (e.g., learning, change in health behaviour, increased likelihood of buying a product).

This speciality, rather than beginning from generally applicable qualities of ECAs, begins from a particular application domain in which ECAs may provide value. The focus is on thoroughly researching such an application domain, designing and implementing an ECA to meet needs and fill a suitable role within that domain, and then testing the completed agent with real users, using benchmarks drawn from the domain.

Researchers working in this speciality must generate agents that are sufficiently believable and sociable to support the task context, but their focus is on developing these qualities around the particular task at hand, such as creating a believable and engaging mathematics tutor or health counsellor. Researchers draw upon disciplines related to the task space they've chosen; they may also make use of techniques and knowledge from psychology, sociology, and interaction design of other media.

Lester's work on tutoring agents (Lester et al. (1997)) is an excellent example — his group created animated agents who tutored students on various topics, and tested the effect of these agents upon learning and satisfaction with the experience. Bickmore's work in the health domain (Bickmore (2003)), on an exercise advisor agent, is another strong example of specific task domain agent research. Bickmore tested his agent's effectiveness in an empirical trial with end users. Work at the University of Southern California on training agents (mentioned in the taxonomy introduction) is yet another example of this kind of research.

Criteria for success: Production of a successful character that achieves the goals of this application area (e.g., increase learning, increase weekly exercise rate, selling more cars). Role usefulness as perceived by domain experts as well as end users.

Evaluation strategies: For applications research, outcomes testing is the most important type of evaluation. Uncovering standard outcome benchmarks (such as increased memory of materials for tutoring, or increased exercise for health counselling) during the literature review stage is important. Researchers should make use of existing benchmarks where possible. Ideally, researchers should test their ECAs against these benchmarks with a control group — people performing the same tasks without any ECA assistance. For applications research, it is also very important to test the ECA with the relevant target user population.

Having application area experts do peer review and critique of such ECAs is a way to glean further insight about why a particular agent implementation does or does not work well in the target domain.

2.4 Agency and Computational Issues

Definition: Researchers in this area are concerned with the creation of algorithms, systems, and architectures that control ECAs. This ranges from work on particular subsystems, such as vision, speech recognition, natural language understanding and generation, and kinematics for motion control, to complete architectures for creating autonomous agents that incorporate memory, planning, decision making, behaviour selection, and execution.

Much of the work done on these kinds of problems is broadly applicable to any intelligent agent systems, and not just to ECAs, because the core issues are common to both. In many cases it is possible to create an effective ECA that either simply simulates these kinds of capabilities (owing to the fact that believability rather than functionality is often the primary consideration for ECAs), but it is still ultimately desirable that ECAs possess these capabilities.

Work on agency specifically for ECAs tends to focus on systems that either make trade-offs that favour believability rather than traditional computational measures of success (such as optimality or correctness) or on the creation of control or reasoning systems that mimic living beings in ways that make it easier or more natural to produce believable behaviours. Architectures that use explicit models of emotion, for example (Doyle (2003); Hayes-Roth et al. (1994); Reilly (1996)), or architectures that are directly inspired by ethological models of animal behaviour (Blumberg (1996)) are examples of research on agency that is focused especially on ECAs.

Research in this area is inspired by traditional computer science, and especially artificial intelligence, graphics, and robotics, although it also frequently draws upon formal models of the behaviours of living beings from areas such as psychology, neurobiology, ethology, or sociology.

Criteria for success: The criteria for success of subsystems such as natural language understanding or vision are generally tied to the capabilities of humans to solve comparable problems; in many cases the goal is to build a system that can function at least as rapidly and correctly as a person can at the same task. For other systems, such as planning or learning, the goals may be to produce 'optimal' results, where optimality can be measured mathematically. Finding the shortest sequence of steps or learning the most general solution to a particular kind of problem are examples of this type.

Researchers developing entire architectures, even within purely artificial intelligence domains, frequently suffer difficulties in finding sufficiently formal evaluation criteria just as ECA researchers do, owing to the broad capabilities that these architectures are intended to exhibit. There have been recent proposals addressing this problem (e.g., Wallace and Laird (2003); Wooldridge and Jennings (1998)), but it is still an open issue. Parsimony, elegance of the architecture, extensibility, efficiency, accuracy, and optimality within the task domain are traditional measures of success.

Evaluation strategies: Many systems in this area are amenable to formal (mathematical) analysis and evaluation. How many faces were correctly recognized, the number of steps in the best plan found by the system, or the predictive accuracy of the learning routine are examples of the kinds of analysis that are generally applied.

For complete ECA architectures, evaluation has generally been broken down into two aspects: the intrinsic properties of the architecture, which can often be measured in according to the criteria mentioned above (elegance, extensibility, etc.), and the quality of the overall behaviour produced by the architecture, which is evaluated according to the criteria of the other areas of our taxonomy (believability, sociability, effectiveness at the task or application).

An example of the former category is Doyle's work on embedding annotations in virtual environments that enable characters to better understand how to behave believably (Doyle (2003)). Examples of the latter type are the work of Bates's Oz project or Blumberg's Synthetic Characters group (both described in Section 2.1) which are concerned with producing architectures whose characters are believable and lifelike to users, and which therefore require evaluation by users to determine their quality.

3.   Applying the Taxonomy

We propose that researchers in our community might use this taxonomy in several ways.

1. Use it to clarify and communicate primary skills.

Identify one's area of expertise and deep knowledge, and make this known to the community. Individual researchers can make clear their core discipline (e.g. computation, psychology, animation, linguistics) and the evaluation techniques that they are knowledgeable about and willing to carry out on the team's ECA to further the general research agenda.

2. Use it to assemble appropriate teams during project planning.

If a team makes clear where they hope to make a major contribution (surface believability or intentionality, sociability, task domain, agency/computation, or some combination of these) it will guide decisions about the needed competencies. It may be necessary to build from a core team to include others who have complementary competencies, or to plan to borrow components from others to cover areas that the team does not want to innovate upon, to ensure sufficient overall believability of the agent. It may also be necessary to find and involve experts in related disciplines in order to ensure quality evaluation.

3. Use it to set evaluation benchmarks.

Each interdisciplinary research group should set evaluation benchmarks and plans for each area in which they plan to make a contribution, relying on the evaluation expertise of each specialist. Ideally, researchers should begin to draw upon measures used by others to address similar questions in ECA development, so we can establish a body of standard measures within our field for common objectives. It is also very important that ECA researchers make use of standard evaluation instruments from the disciplines they draw upon, where possible. The social sciences and application domains often have well-tested measures of the concepts we seek to evaluate (personality, attractiveness, memory, recall, etc.), and a paper that did not use these standard measures within that subfield would need to carefully explain why. ECA research borrowing from these areas should be held to the same standards.

4. Use it to contextualize work for others in our community.

When reporting results, make it clear where the primary goals and contributions lie, and remind the audience of the appropriate standards of evaluation.

The research community can help to bolster this approach by setting different standards of evaluation for each type of contribution. We should expect rigorous, objectives-based testing of anything that claims to address a real application need. We should expect empirical evaluation by appropriate target audiences of any advance in believability techniques. We should expect peer-reviewable descriptions of any new architecture or computational technique, and if it claims to address a real interaction need as well, accompanying user evaluation of the success of the manifestation of that technique. We should allow for research papers that are case studies about design best practices.

It also behooves the research community to encourage the development of extensible, reusable components and tools for authoring ECAs. The creation of such artefacts would have a significant value for the community as a whole, partly because it would minimize the need to recreate the same essential components from one project to another, a process that is costly, time-consuming, and to a large extent devoid of useful contributions to the discipline, and partly because they would provide some degree of standardization across projects that would facilitate comparative evaluations.

5. Use it to contextualize work for others outside our community.

Making our field's sub-agendas more clear, and setting up stable pockets of applied technique and rigorous evaluation from related disciplines will help those who join our teams from other disciplines report their findings back to applied journals, using criteria for success and rigour that are acceptable to those disciplines. This will allow for more sustainable cross-disciplinary collaborations to improve ECAs.

In addition, enforcing the use of standard benchmarks from applied areas (e.g., commercial entertainment audience ratings, training and health outcomes expectations) will make it more likely that our research will be accepted and extended by those application areas, helping to ensure that our work is both relevant and useful to workers in those areas. Strengthening our connections to other communities for whom ECAs are a tool provides them with new means of exploring their problem areas, provides the ECA research community with critical feedback about where our systems are succeeding and where more work must be done, and gives us opportunities to expand our understanding of how and where ECAs can fruitfully be applied.

4. On Production Values

Though it is not part of our formal taxonomy, we wanted to include a brief comment on the value of good production values and techniques. By *production values* we mean the extent to which the ECA is made ready to be used in real-world settings, including the visual quality of its appearance, the quality of recorded sound or speech synthesis, the range and sophistication of its behaviors, and its smooth and convincing operation in general. Often in research projects the kind of polish we would expect to see in a real-world product is not achieved, because it is not important to the research effort. However, replicating the animation and voice acting quality of a Pixar film in one's project, for example, could produce quite different reactions to the ECA than if one used a very rudimentary set of animations and voice recordings made by an engineering student with no arts training or experience. Techniques used to assure high quality overall production values in character looks and behaviours, and smooth integration and performance of all components, are valuable inputs to ECA research and practice. As the technologies that we use shift, so do best practices for achieving the level of professionalism necessary to elicit the user responses we seek.

Such techniques are more frequently presented at conferences such as SIGGRAPH and GDC (the Game Developers' Conference) and published in trade venues. We would encourage ECA researchers to consider the reporting of such findings as valid contributions to our field.

Researchers describing results in this area might share tactics for creating consistent quality in final visuals, dialog, behaviour, and interaction mechanisms, as well as recommendations for the smooth integration of the whole. Contributions in this area could include sharing successful tactics for mapping and gathering the resources (people, hardware, software) needed to complete a project, creating schemes for file handling and asset processing, managing cycles of iteration and user testing, and quality testing before release. Providing information for other practitioners about potential pitfalls and best practices for using new technologies (e.g. input devices) would also be a valuable contribution in this area. Since many projects involve collaboration between multiple locations, best practices papers on achieving good results given this context would also be very useful.

As an example, Lally (2003) describes techniques used to create the engaging and believable animations in the video game *Ratchet and Clank*. The paper includes descriptions of production techniques such as testing the fit of the animation in the game world with prototypes, automation to speed animation production, technical interface between animation production tools and the game engine, and technical animation solutions for creating realistic movement and facial expression. Such papers are a valuable addition to the ECA literature.

5.   Further Classification

The taxonomy we have described here makes only broad distinctions between communities of practice (such as between those working on computational models of agency and those working on social interface questions). There is ample room for refinement.

The most obvious area for further subdivision is believability. Within that category there are many areas to draw upon for inspiration: traditional film studies, the copious animation literature, motion studies, drama and acting, literature and writing, perceptual psychology, etc.

Each brings its own particular strategies for evaluation. Further refining believability contribution areas and evaluation criteria as the field matures will help ensure rigour and allow us to communicate and build upon one another's findings.

Another kind of subdivision can be made along the philosophical approaches to agency and believability, which we have not touched on here. Most of the groups mentioned take the dramatic approach of determining what behaviours are recognisably lifelike and then producing agents that exhibit those behaviours in such a way as to maximise their believability. These agents are comparable to actors who consciously think about how to convey certain emotions or expressions to an audience, without necessarily experiencing the stimuli that provoke them. The alternative approach (exemplified in, e.g., Blumberg (1996)) is to create agents that simulate natural systems and whose lifelike behaviour arises from ethological considerations, e.g., the agent slowly becomes hungry over time and will therefore go in search of food, with its stomach growling. Given that the inspirations for these two lines of work are so dissimilar, we may find over time that evaluation criteria for these approaches should and do differ.

6.   Conclusions

Researchers studying embodied conversational agents draw upon work from many fields to define, create, and analyse their creations. The benefits of this diversity are balanced by the difficulty it creates in clearly indicating where individual contributions lie, and also in the problem of creating measurable evaluation criteria that can be applied to all ECAs. However, without addressing these difficulties, we will be unable to measure our progress as a discipline, and will miss opportunities to improve upon past work as we move toward the ultimate goal of creating fully-functional ECAs.

The taxonomy we provide is intended to be the basis for an explicit recognition that different research products contribute to different parts of the overall endeavour. We hope that it, or some variation upon it, will be used by researchers to classify their contributions, and that their work will be evaluated accordingly. It is also hoped that the preliminary explanations of the different kinds of evaluation criteria will be the starting point for the ECA community to develop formal metrics of a sort that we can use to transform research on embodied conversational agents from a discipline into a science.

Notes

1. http://www.isi.edu/research.html#Autonomous_Agents
2. http://www.cis.upenn.edu/~hms/home.html
3. http://www.media.mit.edu/characters/

References

Andre, E., editor (1997). *Notes of the IJCAI-97 Symposium on Animated Interface Agents: Making Them Intelligent*, Nagoya, Japan.

Badler, N. (1997). Real-time virtual humans. In *Pacific Graphics*, pages 4–14, Seoul, Korea.

Badler, N., Allbeck, J., Zhao, L., and Byun, M. (2002). Representing and parameterizing agent behaviors. In *Proceedings of Computer Animation*, pages 133–143, Geneva, Switzerland. IEEE Computer Society.

Bates, J. (1992). The nature of characters in interactive worlds and the Oz project. Technical Report CMU-CS-92-200, School of Computer Science, Carnegie Mellon University, Pittsburgh, PA.

Bates, J., Loyall, A. B., and Reilly, W. S. (1992). An architecture for action, emotion, and social behavior. Technical Report CMU-CS-92-142, School of Computer Science, Carnegie Mellon University.

Bickmore, T. (2003). *Relational Agents: Effecting Change Through Human-Computer Relationships*. PhD thesis, Media Laboratory, Massachusetts Institute of Technology, Cambridge, MA.

Blumberg, B. (1996). *Old Tricks, New Dogs: Ethology and Interactive Characters*. PhD thesis, Media Laboratory, Massachusetts Institute of Technology, Cambridge, MA.

Cahn, J. (1990). The generation of affect in synthesized speech. *Journal of the American Voice I/O Society*, 8:1–19.

Cassell, J., Bickmore, T., Vilhjalmsson, H., and Yan, H. (2000). More than just a pretty face: Affordances of embodiment. In *Proceedings of Intelligent User Interfaces 2000*, pages 52–59, New Orleans, LA.

Doyle, P. (2003). *Annotated Worlds for Animate Characters*. PhD thesis, Stanford University. Forthcoming.

Ekman, P. and Friesen, W. (1976). Measuring facial movement. *Journal of Environmental Psychology and Nonverbal Behavior*, 1(1):56–75.

Elliott, C. (1992). *The Affective Reasoner: A Process Model of Emotions in a Multi-Agent System*. PhD thesis, The Institute for the Learning Sciences, Northwestern University, Evanston, IL.

Elliott, C., Rickel, J., and Lester, J. (1999). Lifelike pedagogical agents and affective computing: An exploratory synthesis. *Lecture Notes in Computer Science* 1600:195–212.

Fiske, S. and Taylor, S. (1991). *Social Cognition*. McGraw-Hill, New York.

Foner, L. (1993). What's an agent, anyway? A sociological case study. Agents Memo 93-01, Media Laboratory, Massachusetts Instutite of Technology, Cambridge, MA.

Franklin, S. and Graesser, A. (1997). Is it an agent, or just a program: a taxonomy for autonomous agents. In Müller, J., Woolridge, M., and Jennings, N., editors, *Intelligent Agents III*. Springer-Verlag, Berlin.

Goldberg, A. (1997). IMPROV: A system for real-time animation of behavior-based interactive synthetic actors. *Lecture Notes in Computer Science* 1195:58–73.

Hayes-Roth, B., Brownston, L., Huard, R., van Gent, R., and Sincoff, E. (1994). Directed improvisation. Technical Report KSL-94-61, Knowledge Systems Laboratory, Stanford University.

Hayes-Roth, B. and Doyle, P. (1998). Animate characters. *Autonomous agents and multi-agent systems* 1:195–230.

Hayes-Roth, B., van Gent, R., and Huber, D. (1997). Acting in character. In Trappl, R. and Petta, P., editors, *Creating Personalities for Synthetic Actors*. Springer-Verlag, Berlin.

Isbister, K., Nakanishi, H., Ishida, T., and Nass, C. (2000). Helper agent: Designing an assistant for human-human interaction in a virtual meeting space. In *Proceedings of CHI 2000*, pages 57–64, The Hague, Netherlands.

Isbister, K. and Nass, C. (2000). Consistency of personality in interactive characters: Verbal cues, non-verbal cues, and user characteristics. *International Journal of Human-Computer Studies*, 53(2):251–267.

Johnson, W. L. and Rickel, J. (1997). Integrating pedagogical capabilities in a virtual environment agent. In *Proceedings of the First International Conference on Autonomous Agents*, pages 30–38, Marina del Rey, CA.

Koller, D. (1996). Structured representations and intractability. *ACM Computing Surveys* 28(4es):8.

Kuhn, T. S. (1996). *The Structure of Scientific Revolutions*. University of Chicago Press.

Laban, R. (1974). *Language of Movement: A Guidebook to Choreutics*. Play, Inc., Boston, MA.

Lally, J. (2003). Giving life to Ratchet and Clank: Enabling complex character animations by streamlining processes. Gamasutra. Available online at http://www.gamasutra.com/features/20030211/lally_01.shtml.

Lasseter, J. (1987). Principles of traditional animation applied to 3D animation. *Computer Graphics* 21(4):35–43.

Laurel, B. (1990). *The Art of Human-Computer Interface Design*. Addison-Wesley, Reading, MA.

Lester, J., Converse, S., Kahler, S., Barlow, T., Stone, B., and Bhogal, R. (1997). The persona effect: Affective impact of animated pedagogical agents. In *Proceedings of CHI '97*, pages 359–366, Atlanta, GA.

Loyall, A. B. (1997). *Believable Agents: Building Interactive Personalities*. PhD thesis, School of Computer Science, Carnegie Mellon University.

Loyall, B. and Bates, J. (1991). A reactive, adaptive architecture for agents. Technical Report CMU-CS-91-147, School of Computer Science, Carnegie Mellon University.

Murray, J. B. (1990). Review of research on the Myers-Briggs type indicator. *Perceptual and Motor Skills*, 70:1187–1202.

Nass, C., Moon, Y., Fogg, B. J., Reeves, B., and Dryer, C. (1995). Can computer personalities be human personalities? *International Journal of Human-Computer Studies*, 43:223–239.

Nass, C. and Reeves, B. (1996). *The Media Equation*. Cambridge University Press, Cambridge.

Nass, C., Steuer, J., and Tauber, E. (1994). Computers are social actors. In *Proceeedings of CHI '94*, pages 72–78, Boston, MA.

Nilsson, N. J. (1995). Eye on the prize. *AI Magazine* 16(2):9–17.

Ortony, A., Clore, G., and Collins, A. (1988). *The Cognitive Structure of Emotions*. Cambridge University Press, Cambridge.

Perlin, K. and Goldberg, A. (1996). Improv: A system for scripting interactive actors in virtual worlds. *Computer Graphics*, 30:205–216.

Picard, R. W. (1997). *Affective computing*. The MIT Press, Cambridge, MA.

Poggi, I., Pelachaud, C., and de Rosis, F. (2000). Eye communication in a conversational 3D synthetic agent. *AI Communications* 13(3):169–182.

Reilly, W. S. N. (1996). *Believable Social and Emotional Agents*. PhD thesis, School of Computer Science, Carnegie Mellon University.

Rist, T., Andre, E., and Müller, J. (1997). Adding animated presentation agents to the interface. In *Proceedings of the International Conference on Intelligent User Interfaces*, pages 21–28, Orlando, FL.

SIGGRAPH (2003). Android dreams: the present and future of autonomous robotics. In *Program and Buyer's Guide of SIGGRAPH 2003*, p. 7, San Diego, CA.

Stone, B. and Lester, J. (1996). Dynamically sequencing an animated pedagogical agent. In *Proceedings of the Thirteenth National Conference on Artificial Intelligence*, pages 424–431, Portland, OR.

Thomas, F. and Johnson, O. (1981). *The Illusion of Life: Disney Animation*. Hyperion Books, New York.

Trappl, R. and Petta, P., editors (1996). *Creating Personaities for Synthetic Actors.* Springer-Verlag, Berlin.

Wallace, S. A. and Laird, J. E. (2003). Comparing agents and humans using behavioral bounding. In *Proceedings of the 18th International Joint Conference on Artificial Intelligence*, pages 831–836, Acapulco, Mexico.

Wiggins, J. S. (1979). A psychological taxonomy of trait-descriptive terms: the interpersonal domain. *Journal of Personality and Social Psychology*, 37:395–412.

Wooldridge, M. and Jennings, N. (1998). Pitfalls of agent-oriented development. In *Proceedings of the 2nd International Conference on Autonomous Agents*, pages 385–391, Minneapolis, MN.

Zimbardo, P. and Leippe, M. (1991). *The Psychology of Attitude Change and Social Influence.* McGraw-Hill, New York.

Chapter 2

EMBODIED CONVERSATIONAL AGENTS ON A COMMON GROUND

A Framework for Design and Evaluation

Zsófia Ruttkay, Claire Dormann, and Han Noot

> *The one who seeks truth is a scientist. The one who wishes to realize the free flow of his subjective thought is a writer. But what can be done if one needs a way between these two possibilities?*
>
> —Robert Musil

Abstract   One would like to rely on design guidelines for embodied conversational agents (ECAs), grounded on evaluation studies. How to define the physical and mental characteristics of an ECA, optimal for an envisioned application? What will be the added value of using an ECA? Although there have been studies addressing such issues, we are still far from getting a complete picture. This is not only due to the still relatively little experience with applications of ECAs, but also to the diversity in terms and experimental settings used. The lack of a common, established framework makes it difficult to compare ECAs, interpret evaluation results and judge their scope and relevance. In this chapter we propose a common taxonomy of the relevant design and evaluation aspects of ECAs. We refer to recent works to elicit evaluation concepts and discuss measurement issues.

Keywords: Embodied conversational agents, design, evaluation framework, methodology.

Z. Ruttkay and C. Pelachaud (eds.), From Brows to Trust, 27–66.
© *2004 Kluwer Academic Publishers. Printed in the Netherlands.*

1.   Introduction

In this chapter we set out to provide a framework to evaluate and compare ECAs. We undertake this task with the following objectives in mind:

- We wish to provide a framework to categorise the extensive literature on ECA design and evaluation and hence to help us in interpreting and understanding the findings reported.

- We encourage the ECA community to start agreeing upon a common set of concepts used to report on ECA research. This will make comparison of results (much) more meaningful than it is now.

- Hopefully, the end-result of the use of a common framework by the ECA community will be the emergence of design rules for ECAs stating what properties an ECA should have in order to fulfil certain functions.

We are well aware of how challenging and ambitious such a task is. One might ask if it is a realistic and timely task at all. Yet we are convinced that a common evaluation framework will facilitate the judgement and proliferation of empirical results and theoretical guidelines, as well as help to identify fundamental research to be done on specific characteristics to such an extent that it is certainly worthwhile to start developing such a framework now. On the other hand, our framework put forward here will probably need some refinement and readjustment, as more academic results will be available on human-human communication and more empirical evidence will be collected on using ECAs in all kinds of application domains

When proposing a common framework, we do rely on the work done so far. Namely, we have done our best to locate all recent works addressing evaluation of ECAs. Dehn at al. (2000) give a critical summary of works done earlier. We have used the relevant studies from the ECA literature to elicit concepts, to point out controversial issues and draw attention to methodological problems. However, the references are meant to be illuminative, and not to give a complete list of all occurrences of certain evaluation issues.

An ECA can be considered as a novel user interface. We have examined if we could profit from established user interface evaluation methods in HCI. However, in the case of ECAs it requires extra effort and attention to separate the cumulative effect of the underlying application, of the mental and of the embodiment aspects of the ECA.

In the next section of this chapter, we discuss ECAs from a design perspective. First we give a general description of the software environment in which we envisage an ECA to operate and define the concept of an ECA by delineating it from the other software components it interacts with. Then review all the properties of ECAs which may be relevant for comparison of existing ECAs and specification of new ones with certain expected functions. In section 3 we turn to the methodological aspects of evaluation of an ECA, discussing critical issues as setting base-line for evaluation, the types of evaluation studies and design guidelines abstracted and the problematic of defining evaluation concepts. We outline the characteristics of tests subjects which may influence the evaluation, and methods available to collect and evaluate empirical data. Section 4 is devoted to the definition and discussion of concepts relevant to evaluate ECAs. In the concluding section we give a summary of the long-term potentials of our proposed framework, and make some concrete recommendations on ECA evaluation.

In the rest of this section we give the motivations for our endeavour.

1.1 Motivations and Problems

The evaluation of the capabilities of ECAs in the light of those of humans would require that the multitude of aspects of human-human communication have been described in a normative way and with the granularity matching the design parameters of ECAs. This is not the case. Unfortunately, there are not enough sources from the fields of socio-psychology, sociology, cultural anthropology and psycho-linguistics to rely upon for a complete description of, for instance, what a tutor should look like, how he should talk and gesture, given an application domain and a target group. Actually, the introduction of ECAs has motivated research in human-human communication, by posing new, succinctly formulated questions, some of which could be answered only by using ECAs as controllable mediums that exhibit the effects to be tested (see Chapter 7 by Krahmer et al. in this book). Moreover, it has to be justified if it is a correct objective to try to mimic human behaviour when creating ECAs. The technology does allow the creation of non-human, non-realistic creatures, but the problem of devising the 'right' communicational skills for such creatures and evaluating their merit is no less challenging.

One could rely on usability tests with the ECAs developed so far. Then the 'what to measure and how' problem arises. While one can come up quickly with aspects like 'ease of use' and 'believability' of the ECA as desired objectives, these concepts are not clearly defined. Moreover, they may have different connotations for experts from different fields as psychology, sociology, ergonomy, and computer science. These concepts are likely to have different interpretations depending on the application domain, such as e-commerce, banking or tutoring. One cannot be sure if the similar concepts reported in different studies were used with the same meaning. Moreover, the diversity in the settings for empirical data collection and in the evaluation methods used makes one uncertain if a reported conclusion is sound and general enough to be taken as a design guideline.

Finally, there has been relatively little done on ECA evaluation, and with a series of different objectives. Some researchers, interested in the potentials of applying ECAs in a specific domain, or endowing an ECA with mechanism to exhibit some specific characteristics, collected empirical data to test how people react to the ECA with the new feature. These reports are typically found as one of the last sections of a paper, and often account on experiments done with one or two dozens of computer science students as test subjects. Since a few years ago one can read more extensive works dedicated per se to evaluation of ECAs used in operating environments (Moundridou and Virvou (2002); Buisine et al. (2003); Bickmore and Cassell (2003); Lester et al. (1997); Cassell and Vilhjálmsson (1999); Höök et al. (2000); Isbister and Hayes-Roth (1998); McBreen et al. (2000); McBreen et al. (2001); Mori et al. (2003)) or to figure out how basic design parameters for an ECA influence the users impression (Barker (2003); Cassell and Bickmore (2000); Cowell and Stanney (2003); Isbister and Nass (2000); King and Ohya (1996); Koda and Maes (1999); Nass et al. (2000); Nass and Lee (2000); Sproull et al. (1996)). Only recently, some researchers of ECAs have addressed evaluations dimensions and methodologies as such (Sanders and Scholtz (2000); Isbister and Doyle (2002); Chapter 9 by Catrambone et at. in this book).

2.   ECAs from a Design Perspective

The user will react to an ECA based on both *what* it communicates, and *how*. To differentiate between the matters of producing syntactically correct output signals by using one or more modalities to present some message and the matters of deciding what to express, in the literature the *body* and *mind* distinction has been used. The mind aspect has been associated by Pelachaud et al. (2002) with *reasoning* and the AI techniques used to implement reasoning. In our discussion, we keep the *body aspects* but replace the mind with the *mental aspects* concept. We wish to have a broader category encompassing also phenomena like personality, which are static and do not necessarily involve the kind of intelligence and reasoning associated with the mind. Moreover, in our design-oriented discussion we are not concerned with the underlying *mechanisms* of triggering the communicational behaviour of the ECA, but only with the *effect* of it. Barker (2003) claims the 'illusion of life' can be achieved without any cognitive processing mechanism, by carefully designing the embodiment of the ECA.

We set our focus for ECA evaluation by concentrating on *design aspects*: what is the effect of certain characteristics of an ECA? The *embodiment design parameters* define the *look* of the body (static characteristics like gender, race, cartoon or realistic design) and the *capabilities of the communication modalities* (dynamic characteristics of facial and body gesturing). The *mental design parameters* are responsible for *conversational, personality* and *social role* characteristics. These parameters will have an effect on how things get presented for the user. In order to delineate the topics discussed in this chapter, we describe a conceptual architecture of the ECA and the assumed software environment in which it operates. Note that we only consider the ECA in its role as communicating to the user, about the communication channel from user to ECA analogous remarks can be made.

In Figure 2.1 we give an overview of the aspects of an ECA to be dealt with. The following steps are relevant in determining the behaviour of the ECA:

1. At the basis there is an *application* which produces information. This output may be in a textual form, close to one used in human-human communication (e.g., news items collected from the web), or data in a coded form (e.g., time-table items, numerical values of measurements, images, video etc.).

2. The agent translates the content provided by the application into a form which can be used for presentation for the user. This translation is done by using (one or more) *application interface* modules; resulting in a content the ECA can deal with further. One such form is text marked up with meaning tags, expressing different meta-information on the content.

3. The *agent*, with the use of its mental capabilities, decides about when and how the content is to be presented. Two types of task are essential:

   - coordinating the communication between the user and the application.
   - presenting the information provided by the application interface.

In its simplest form the agent just transmits information between the two (while maybe changing some formats); in a complex form the agent is truly autonomous and proactive. In that case it may for instance monitor the user's activity to determine when to get active.

4 The ECA performs the presentation, by using the possibilities of its *embodiment*. Besides the dynamical characteristics of the verbal and nonverbal presentation capabilities (e.g., facial expressions, speech, gestures), the static characteristics (the look) will also contribute to the impression it makes on the user.

2.1   The Embodiment

We use the term *embodiment* in a broad sense, for all low-level aspects which contribute to the *physical appearance* of the character, namely: body design and rendering, voice, head, face, hand gestures and body postures, the quality of the corresponding motions. Each of these aspects may have an effect on the perception of mental aspects of the ECA, or directly on the performance effect achieved by the ECA.

2.1.1   Look

Personification   Does the body of the ECA represent a human person, or some other living creature, or a non-living object? In case of a human-like ECA, is it made to be recognized as some individual real person, or to represent a category of persons (e.g., by profession, age), or to be an individual new person? In case of a non-human ECA, is it anthropomorphic?

The majority of ECAs are designed with a human look, with attributes suggesting a professional role like medical consultant, sales assistant, newsreader, or representing the user in virtual worlds or chat forums. There is cautiousness with applying and evaluating non-human living characters; we know of dogs (Isla and Blumberg (2002); Isbister et al. (2000); Koda et al. (1996)). The reason for this can be in the hidden assumption that "the more human-like the ECA is, the better". This assumption is not justified, in this generality. People attribute more intelligence and trust to human-like ECAs (King and Ohya (1996)), but a (well-designed) non-human character may be more appealing and entertaining. Moreover, in one case the dog appearance was chosen (Isbister et al. (2000)) to avoid that users assume and expect highly intelligent mental capabilities from the ECA. As of objects, we have Microsofts paper clip. (Unfortunately, we cannot refer to studies on its popular-

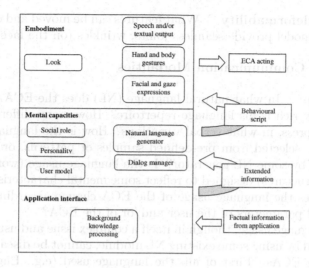

Figure 2.1. The conceptual framework for design aspects of an ECA.

ity, and wonder if the embodiment has been evaluated in any stage of its design). It is a challenge to find out which objects are appropriate candidates as ECA embodiment, both from technical points of view (they should have some face, some means of gesturing, some coding of human-like expressions) and of user reactions.

Physical details What parts of the body are present in the model: head, head plus neck, torso, full body.

Faces have been extensively used, due to the attractive power of the human face. A common application is a talking head, to enhance the intelligibility of speech (see Massaro (1998)). The application context may make it clear if hands (e.g., used for pointing) or the full body (e.g., to change location) are an absolute necessity. In general, it is not true that "the more of the body used the better" is a good design principle. There are some experiments confirming that users spend most of the time looking at the ECA's face (Witkowski et al. (2001)).

Realism Is the model (meant to be) realistic, or is it artistic, may be exaggerated cartoon-like? Is the level of realism the same, or is there a realistic face on a cartoon-like body?

Dimensions The model can be 2D, spruit (2D cut-out, which can change orientation) or 3D.

General deformability   What features can be moved and deformed?
Does the model provide seamless joints, wrinkles (on the face)?

2.1.2   Communication Modalities

Language   In what natural language (NL) does the ECA communicate? How rich is his language repertoire? How many different things
can he express, in what verbal variations? How is the language output
generated: selected from pre-defined samples or patterns, or generated
on the fly by some NL generator? Is the language usage (words, grammatical structures) designed to reflect some mental characteristics of the
ECA? Does the language usage of the ECA change according to some
dynamical parameters of the user and/or of the ECA?

The language usage, though in itself a complex issue and usually taken
for granted by using some existing NL module, cannot be discarded when
evaluating ECAs. First of all, the language used (e.g., English) may
imply some cultural connotations for the ECA. According to Isbister et
al. (2000), English as the language of communication may be a bias
for the Japanese users when interacting with a conversational mediator
ECA which was designed to bridge cultural and communicational gaps
between Japanese and American users. It is a subtle but important
point to remember, even if we tend to believe in such a statement as "the
language of the Internet is English". Further, according to Prendinger
and Ishizuka (2002) language is powerful in conveying personality and
social role aspects of the ECA.

Textual or verbal output   An ECA may be designed not to 'tell'
anything, just to be present and communicate without words. But in
most of the cases, an ECA is endowed with a separate text window
or body-related text bulbs for verbal output, or is able to speak. In
the latter case, are the utterances produced as pre-recorded audio, or
generated by some text to speech (TTS) engine? How understandable
is the (synthesized) speech? Does the speech sound natural? Is it in
accordance with the static embodiment (gender, age) and mental characteristics (personality, social role) of the ECA? What can be expressed
by meta-speech characteristics (intonation, speech rate, etc), for instance
punctuation, emphasis, emotions, certainty? Is the speech spontaneous
(with errors, gap filling sounds, non-speech elements like breath, laugh-
ter) or 'perfectly sterile'?

With the development of the quality and accessibility of synthesized
speech, talking is becoming a common modality of an ECA. All the
same, one can still find examples of text bulb usage or even textual

communication in a separate window, as examples of output redundant to speech. The pros (increased intelligibility) and cons (extra mental load) of using both speech and textual output, as well as the ideal design for the content, form and function (e.g., numerical data are shown only, in form of tables) are to be investigated.

As to the importance of tuning meta-speech characteristics of synthesized speech, experiments by Nass and Lee (2000) have shown that users do recognize personality characteristics in synthesized speech, and presenting personality in speech modality alone is sufficient to induce a different personality image of the ECA, and thus a different reaction by the user.

Facial display   The face can be used to express (exclusively, or in co-ordination with other modalities) several functions. In case of speech output, does the face provide lip-sync, and of what quality? Can it exhibit other phenomena of visual speech, namely providing facial expression for: emphasis, punctuation, regulation of discourse, conversational feedback, certain characteristics of objects the ECA refers to verbally? Can the face express emotions (which ones), cognitive states (which ones)? What does the face indicate in its idle state (what expression, blinking and head motion)? Do the eyes move and the pupils change size? Does the head move? Are other, maybe non-realistic features (like hair rising, eyes bulging) used for expressions? Does a given set of facial expressions get repeated in the same way, or is there some variety? Is superposition and concatenation of facial expressions supported, on what basis? Can the face change colour (redden, turn pale)? Are the facial expressions meant to be realistic, may be characteristic of a given real person, or of some group (by culture, by profession), or generic? Are the facial expressions designed as cartoon-like?

The effect of speech punctuation by facial expression has been investigated, recently in more depth and for different cultures too (see Chapter 7 by Krahmer et al. in this book). It has been shown that a subtle and static difference in the basic expression results in difference in the effectivity of task performance and in subjective impression of the task (Sproull (1996)). The facial display has been shown to be successful in expressing friendly-unfriendly personality aspects (Prendinger and Ishizuka 2003). Gaze has been shown to be relevant for dialogue regulations, and expressing personality (Krahmer et al. (2003)).

Hands   Are hands used in coordination with speech, to structure and punctuate speech (beat, gestures for enumeration, contrast, change of topic, dialogue turns)? Are hands used to point, if so, to what, and in what way (precision)? Are emblems used (which ones), metaphors to indicate characteristics (like form, motion and temporal aspects)? Are hands used (alone, or together with body and/or face) to indicate emotional and cognitive states (which ones)? Are hands used to demonstrate certain specific actions, to manipulate objects?

Body   Are body postures used in coordination with speech, to indicate change of topic, dialogue turns? Does the body move in accordance with hand gestures? Is the body used to express physical, emotional or cognitive states (which ones)? How about the idle state? Can the character change location, in what way (sliding, walking, running) and in what space? What other movements can the body perform? Are body movements typical of a real person, or a group (e.g., of the same profession)?

Modality coordination and motion generation   How are the different modalities used? What aspects of the ECA (such as personality, social role) are reflected in the modality usage and motion characteristics of the gestures? Are there stills used, or animations? What are the motion parameters of animations? The simplest case is when some (single or fixed set of) modalities with given animation are used to express some meaning. In a more sophisticated scenario the selection and fine-tuning of the gestures is done dynamically, according to the characteristics of the situation. How are the problems of blending and concatenating gestures and channel allocation conflicts solved?

2.2   The Mental Aspects

Humans use the body and the voice to express different aspects of a piece of factual content, according to a given situation. The knowledge and mechanisms of an ECA to enhance factual information with meta-aspects like emotions or certainty are referred to as (part of) the mental capabilities of the ECA.

2.2.1   Personality   Is the ECA designed to have a certain personality? What personality model is used? In what aspects of the embodiment (speech characteristics, gestures, postures, design of look) and other mental aspects (wording and structure of language used, dialogue management) is the personality manifested?

There exist established personality models in psychology. Probably the one most used in the field of ECA evaluation is the five factors model (see McCrae and John (1992)). The factors are agreeable, extroverted, neurotic, conscientious and open. There exists abundant evidence based on empirical evaluation that there are strong interactions between user personality, perceived ECA personality, and subjective evaluation dimensions discussed in 4.2. (see Dryer (1999); Nass and Lee (2000); Cassell and Bickmore (2000)). So ECA designers should take the ECA's personality in this technical sense serious, and perform the required evaluations.

2.2.2   Social Role   The social role of an ECA roughly corresponds to some professional category like teacher, salesperson, and clerk. However, these roles can be further refined, e.g., in the case of teacher to 'expert providing professional feedback' or 'educator providing motivational feedback'; or 'ally for the user' versus 'examiner of the user'. In the above sense, it is important to design the intended social role of the ECA, and reflect it in its embodiment and mental aspects.

Ideally, the manifestation of the social role in behavioural and presentation parameters should be evaluated (and, maybe also, designed) with reference to sociological and anthropological investigation. Isbister et al. (1998) give an example of such an evaluation when they analyse the behaviour of an agent playing the role of a bartender in a chat application. Prendinger and Ishizuka (2002) report on the perceived social role effect (power relationship to user) of ECAs.

The ECA technology allows cases without parallels in real life. For instance, in a real shop the user is communicating with a single salesperson who acts according to some mixture of his own interests of selling certain items and of the interest of the user. The two interests can be manifested in two ECAs, confronting positive and negative aspects of products, as shown by André and Rist (2000).

2.2.3   Emotions   What emotional states can the ECA get into? Are the possible emotional states exclusive categories, or mixtures? Is there some emotional model used, also for changes in emotions? Is it verified that the emotions the ECA is claimed to have are indeed perceived as such by users? When the ECA may be in a mixed emotional state it should be verified that the facial (and possibly other) manifestation of it, even if it is not recognised as a blend of certain emotions, is perceived as a believable expression, one which may occur on real faces. Cunningham et al. (2003) have pointed out, by using video recordings, that such non-interpretable but believable expressions do occur on faces of real people.

2.2.4   Adaptation to the User   Is it possible to tune the behaviour of the ECA according to (static or dynamic) characteristics of the user? Does the ECA maintain a model of the user, with aspects like expertise in the domain, age, gender, ethnicity, cultural and socio-economic background and personality? How is this acquired: by asking for the user profile, or by the ECA learning it? In what way does the user model influence the communication of the ECA (e.g., discourse strategy, being aware of safe or unsafe topics, what gestures should or should not be used in the users cultural context)?

Most of these aspects are far beyond the capacities of present-day ECAs, partly because of the lack of robust input possibilities (e.g., vision, voice analysis) in ECA applications to gain data about the user. The exploration of how single, static characteristics of the user influence her judgement of ECAs provides a basis for designing ECAs, to suit e.g., culturally different users the best. See the work of Isbister et al. (2000) discussed in section 2.4.3.

2.2.5   Discourse Capabilities   An ECA may be more or less reactive. The extremes are the presenter and the pro-active conversational agent. In the first case, not only the content to be presented by the ECA, but all other information on the presentation is canned. In the latter case, the content of the presentation as well as meta-information on how to present it are generated on the fly, based on dynamically changing parameters of the conversation. These parameters may reflect aspects like emotional state, history of the conversation, status of task fulfilment.

Control   How is the ECA controlled: by the application (in case of a presentation ECA), by the user (in case of most avatars in virtual forums), or by both (often the case for educational ECAs)? In the latter case, is there an explicit discourse model used; can the ECA display intention of turn-taking/turn-giving? How complex discourse patterns are allowed?

Is the ECA prepared to recover from erroneous input (content, timing), react to lack of input (after some time)? What modalities are used to indicate discourse states? Is feedback given to differentiate 'busy','idle', and 'waiting for input' states? Finally, how autonomous is the ECA, i.e. to what extent does it control itself? Does it take the initiative, for instance to signal a user that new information of interest has arrived?

According to Cassell and Thórisson (1999), non-verbal conversational signals of the ECA (e.g., averting gaze and lifting eyebrows when taking turn, performing beat gestures when providing content) are more valuable for the user than non-verbal emotional signals (e.g., smiling at the user). In their evaluation they used both objective measures of the users behaviour (e.g., number of hesitations) and subjective judgement by the user. Cassell and Vilhjálmsson (1999) have shown that in a chat environment avatars with autonomous non-verbal behaviour to express interest in conversing with others were considered more natural, more expressive and, interestingly, more easy to control, in contrast to avatars without any autonomous behaviour.

Input modalities of the user   Though monitoring the reactions of the interlocutor plays an important role in human-human communication, current ECA design has been concentrating on its presentational aspects, probably because of the technological bottleneck in perception. However, for reactive ECAs and for a symmetrical role in the interaction, it would be beneficial to endow ECAs with perception and sensing capabilities. So it should be a design concern to define how and what should be perceived of the user.

2.3   Implementation Aspects

In order to be able to re-use and adapt an ECA, the technical requirements must be clear. Stating the technical parameters also helps to judge the design of the ECA independent of the limitations of the implementation or technical resources available.

For the ECA *body*, it is informative to know the modelling principle (polygon mesh or smooth surfaces, are textures used) and complexity of the model of the ECA (size of mesh). By what means was the model produced? Are there different levels of detail variants available? As of *non-verbal capabilities*, the quality (frame per second) of the rendered animation is relevant. The animation may have been designed by professional animators, or based on captured motion. As of *speech* and *natural language generation*, the external modules used (TTS, dialogue manager, NL generator) are relevant.

For judging the *conversational behaviour* of the ECA, the following implementation-related questions are important: In what form and detail should the relevant information be given? Is it in some standard format, like XML compliant markup tags? How long does it take to specify a typical input; what is the level of the input instructions which control the ECA's behaviour? How long does it take for the ECA to process these instructions, that is, to produce the final behaviour? It may be relevant to distinguish time spent on separate tasks (e.g., discourse management, generation of textual output, generation of speech).

The *operational requirements* may limit the applicability of the ECA. What software and hardware are necessary for using the ECA? What are the upgrading possibilities, considering hardware and software components used? What are the assumed operational parameters (e.g., noise in the environment, size of screen, data transfer mode, real-time versus off-line generation of output)?

2.4   Range of Applicability

The application context determines, by and large, what characteristics and ECA should have. As of application context, we distinguish presentation ECAs, information ECAs, educational ECAs, sales ECAs, entertainment ECAs and ECAs as research tool used to learn about (multimodal) communication. An ECA may be suitable as an interface for several examples of an application type (e.g., a talking head may read news items, weather reports, mails), or may be designed as a 'one-case' ECA specific for an application. Adaptability to different user groups depends on whether the ECA was designed in a parameterized and modular way. For instance, by providing access to the natural language, the non-verbal repertoire, the look, an ECA could be tailored for users of different cultures.

From a technical point of view, conformation to standards and modular design are relevant. Does the ECA body and animation conform to some standard (MPEG4, VRML)? Could it be re-used, can some of its aspects (e.g., look, accessories, body geometry) be modified? Can it be replaced by another model? Is it technically easy to modify or extend the repertoire of the ECA for each modality? Can the ECA be up/downgraded in terms of modality usage, e.g., according to the computer system capacity?

3.   On Evaluation Methodology

Human-human communication and hence human-ECA communication is extremely complex, many parameters are involved, several of which are not clearly understood or, maybe, not even known. For instance, when finding a person nice, we (unconsciously) base our judgement on many aspects, such as look, way of speaking, gesturing, moving, usage of language. Hence evaluation work with different objectives is needed: to find out about the qualities of an ECA, compared to those common among humans, and to find out if an ECA has added value in a certain application context, and what is the best ECA for such a case. For the first case, the hidden assumption that ECAs should resemble humans, must be verified itself. In case of different applications, different aspects of the ECA may be relevant, and different users may have different expectations from and reactions to an ECA. In Chapter 9 by Catrambone et al. in this book, the importance of the nature of the application task is discussed in detail and illustrated by an experiment. When judging the merits of ECAs, the main issue is the identification of evaluation criteria, their interpretation and measurement. As these criteria involve responses (often subjective judgements) from the user, the criteria, and design rules abstracted from the evaluations, are more or less restricted in their scope of applicability. Finally, the collection and interpretation of empirical data should be done in a methodologically sound way.

In this section we address these issues briefly. First, we discuss the possible goals for ECA evaluation research, the types of design rules one may want to gain from the evaluations, and the relation of research on human-human communication to design and evaluation of ECAs. Then we address the problem of identification of evaluation criteria, in general. A sub-section is devoted to all the aspects of users which may influence their judgement of an ECA. Finally, we briefly sum up the sources and methods of collecting and evaluating data. For more in-depth discussion of doing evaluation research, see the Chapter 3 by Christoph in this volume.

3.1   Why to Evaluate?

A conscious setting of the goal is essential for the proper design of the evaluation and interpretation of the results. Basically, the target of evaluation is one of the following:

1 Find out the effect of single or multiple basic design parameters of the ECA on the perception and performance of the user (evaluation of the ECA itself). Specifically, the goal can be:

   (a) testing if a specific ECA fulfils some expectations;
   (b) finding out how to set certain parameters of the ECA to achieve some desired characteristics.

2 Find out about the merit of using ECAs for a given application (ECA as user interface evaluation). In this case too, one may be interested in:

   (a) testing if a specific ECA has added value;
   (b) investigating what ECA is the best for a given application.

Note that while the context differentiates the two cases, the sub-cases are similar in the sense that in case a) a concrete design has to be tested/verifified, while case b) requires exploration of the design field.

The first case corresponds to the micro-evaluation of ECAs, investigating the effect of certain modalities, the criteria to achieve a single characteristic (like intelligibility of speech, ability to indicate certain emotions). Testing if an ECA meets expectations (Case 1.a) is in particular relevant when ECAs are designed using artistic skills (at this date a common practice), and not explicit design guidelines. The required effect needs to be verified, as well as some additional, undesirable effects need to be excluded.

The second case corresponds to classical usability studies in human-computer interaction.

3.1.1   ECAs Like Humans?   We tend to take it for granted that a good ECA should communicate as humans do. But this, as a basic design principle, needs to be verified itself. Namely, are we sure that humans will be 'fooled' to perceive a piece of moving object on the screen as a human being, with emotions and personality? There has been quite some evaluation work suggesting that the answer is yes. Surprising deceptions, associated with slight difference in the (static) facial expression (Sproull et al. (1996)) and human-like embodiment (King et al. (1996)) were reported. The extensive work by Nass and his colleagues led them to coin the 'computers as social actors' (CASA) hypothesis (see Reeves and Nass (1996)). It was shown that humans do perceive subtle differences in virtual characters, as voice characteristics, look, use of eyebrows, and interpret them similarly as they do in human-human communication. Bailenson et al. (2001) showed that people treat their own virtual alter-egos specially, in terms of reducing the size of the personal space respected around them. With other virtual characters, the distance patterns known from human-human communication were observed. Another sign of treating ECAs as humans is, when the user communicates with the ECA in an erroneous and somewhat messy way which is common in daily conversation. For instance, Cassell and Thórisson (1999) suggest that overlap between the user and the ECA talking can be interpreted not only as a dialogue error, but as a positive sign of the user taking the ECA as a real person, expecting him to interpret overlap in speech a sign of turn-taking intention.

These findings verify that we are on a good trajectory when making efforts to endow synthetic characters with embodiment and communicational traits used in human-human communication.

Ideally, the manifestation of the ECAs social role (e.g., salesperson, tutor, medical advisor) in behavioural and presentation parameters should be analysed with reference to sociological and anthropological investigation. The ECAs dialogues and behaviours should be compared to the role model. Isbister et al. (1998) give an example of such an evaluation of an agent playing the role of a bartender in a chat application. Prendinger and Ishizuka (2002) report on the social role effect (power relationship to user) of ECAs.

Based on the above finding, ECAs can also be used as research instruments for psycholinguists, psychologists and sociologists, to learn about the norms present in human-human communication.

But, of course, the above arguments do not imply that "the closer to realism the better an ECA is", neither that anthropomorphic ECAs should be the only possibility. Virtual characters have the potential of using additional, non-realistic cues, as has been demonstrated by the success of traditional animation characters. Moreover, the emphasis on non-realism possibly adjusts the expectations and frame of judgement of the user to a level more appropriate to the mental capabilities of the ECA.

3.1.2   Separation of the Application and the ECA   The purpose of using an ECA is to provide better, or even a novel computer application. When interested in the added value of an ECA for an application, the base-line for verification, ideally, is the ECA-less version of the application. This, however, is much more problematic than with a traditional interface. The user has a single perception of a piece of software with an ECA embedded, and she might attribute aspects of the application (e.g., relevance of information provided, competence) to the agent's mental capabilities. For evaluation purposes it is important to separate what is the responsibility of the ECA and the underlying application, respectively. For instance, an ECA reacting with delays will be judged by users as unattractive and inefficient. But the cause of the delay can be very different:

1 It takes too long to generate the verbal and/or non-verbal signals to communicate the answer, promptly provided by the application.

2 It takes a long time for the application to produce the content of the answer (e.g., by searching a huge data resource), and the ECA is not prepared to inform the user that his answer is being produced by the application.

Clearly, in the first case the ECA is to blame. In the second case the essential cause of the delay is in the application. All the same, the ECA is still guilty, by missing a feature which could compensate for the inherent delay characteristic of the application. The deficiency may be on the mental level of the ECA: it might have a big expression repertoire, with the capability to indicate a processing state, but its view of the flow of communication is poor, not considering the processing state as one of interest for the user. But it can also happen that the ECA signals the processing state in a way which got misinterpreted or unnoticed by the user.

Moreover, the ECA technology allows entirely novel types of application which have not had an ECA-less counterpart, that is a system with traditional UI, because of the essence of the system is in the communicational capabilities of an ECA. It is impossible to imagine a version of the Erin the bartender system[1] with identical functionalities, but without an embodied bartender. In such cases it is interesting to compare the experience with the ECA with that of a real human in a similar role.

Another subtle point is that most of the current ECAs are designed for output. That is, the user is forced to communicate with the ECA by text input, requiring more time to perform and allowing for erroneous and irrelevant input. By introducing an ECA, on the output side the user interface is improved (at least that is the intention), on the input side it may become more cumbersome and error-prone.

3.1.3   Towards Design Guidelines   An ultimate goal of evaluating ECAs is to produce design guidelines. Design guidelines may be of three kinds, depending on the cast of role of the independent/dependent variables.

- *ECA embodiment – performance* guidelines map embodiment parameters onto evaluation parameters (e.g., an ECA as a bank-clerk with formal dress is liked more than in a casual dress).

- *ECA mental aspect – performance* guidelines tell about a mental aspect parameter to be preferred for a certain performance objective (e.g., an ECA with extrovert speech will be liked more by extrovert users, than by introvert ones, see experiment by Nass and Lee (2000)).

- *ECA embodiment – mental aspects* guidelines tell how to choose some embodiment parameters to reflect the desired mental characteristic (e.g., Cowell and Stanney (2003) provide guidelines on how to achieve impression of trust by setting facial and gesturing characteristics).

Some design guidelines may be independent of the task and application context. E.g., to test the intelligibility of speech, depending on fine-tuning of speech synthesis parameters, and the effect of intonation, may be of general use for every application context. However, even such rules may need to be fine-tuned, with respect to application context: the ideal children story telling speech is surely different of the speech expected from a financial news reader.

For the applicability of rules mapping mental aspects to performance, or embodiment parameters to mental aspects, the application context is likely to be decisive.

Besides the above guidelines which are meant to specify aspects of an ECA directly, in order to meet some performance criteria, there are design guidelines which act on a higher level and express more complex relationships than mapping design and performance variables. Examples for such rules are: "The ECA should be consistent, that is, all relevant body and mental aspects should correspond to identical personality, social role, gender etc.". "The ECA's personality should match the personality of the user."

In case of all types of design rules, one should not forget about stating their scope, with respect to application type and user group. The rule on consistency is of general scope, valid for all applications and user groups. Contrary, the rule above telling that an ECA should have a personality matching that of the user, is of limited scope, and is applicable only to users who, in their human-human interaction are attracted by identical personalities. Isbister and Nass (to appear) conducted several experiments on this issue, and discuss the importance of all details in interpreting the results. One of the causes of the seemingly contradictory conclusions spread about ECAs is that conclusions and design guidelines are quoted without the scope of experimentation and applicability.

3.1.4 Evaluation for Evolution In an ideal software development scenario, evaluations are planned at different stages, to verify that the developed ECA fulfils expectations, or as a preliminary study to find out how users react to an ECA in the given application domain (see the Chapter 3 by Christoph in this book for more on evaluation at different stages). As the application of ECAs is still in its infancy, most of the evaluations are done on a small scale, at the place where the research has been carried out, to verify the potentials of the ECA technology. In the evaluations, especially when unexpected negative effects are experienced, it remains open to speculation if the effect is due to the design, the deficiency of some ECA components (like the quality of synthesized speech), to the incomparable measurements in this and other evaluations or to some hidden flaws in the methodology.

The design and implementation of an ECA should be an iterative process, where the next version is improved based on evaluations of the previous version, or of alternative versions. Some authors use the design-and-test loop concept, mainly to gain preliminary ideas about embodiment or test if some basic modalities function as assumed (e.g., if an implemented smile is recognized as such). We are not aware of long-term evaluations, except in a few cases of repeated experiments, to eliminate the novelty effect. The question arises if the results from one-session experiments carry over to situations where ECAs are used over months or years on a daily basis. It would be useful to hear about experience with mass applications developed by commercial companies, like Cantoche[2], Charamel[3], Headpedal (Griffin et al. (2003)) or sysis (see the Chapter 12 by Krenn et al. in this book).

In the future, the availability of design guidelines, with a clear scope of applicability, would make some (but not all!) evaluation stages superfluous.

3.2   How to Define the Evaluation Variables?

In an evaluation context, dimensions for judgement are to be selected, with corresponding variables of discrete or continuous values and methods to obtain these values from empirical data. In case of evaluating ECAs, one encounters major problems at all of the three stages: identifying the evaluation aspects, defining them in terms of measurable variables, and providing methods to measure them.

The origin of the problems is in the complexity of human-human communication. For instance, we often state that we like or trust somebody, but it is hard to find commonly accepted definitions of these natural-language terms (see e.g., the web site [4]). As discussed in section 3.1.3 with respect to the scope of design rules, trust may be different if it is to be applied to a bank clerk, or a game player. And there may be cases, like entertainment, when trust is of no relevance at all. Moreover, many synonyms and similar concepts are in use. In the ECA evaluation literature too, one encounters different working definitions of the same concepts, or similar definitions but given for different evaluation concepts. Sometimes there is no explicit definition at all, the concept is defined implicitly by the way it is measured. Several measurement techniques, like the most often used questionnaire, are based on lists and alternatives of further, fuzzy concepts, often made up for each study by the researcher. So one is puzzled how, for example, 'fun' in one study relates to 'likeability' in another? Or which possible sense of believability is meant: believable as a living entity, or as a believable action?

Furthermore, some evaluation criteria will clearly depend on certain perceived qualities of the ECA. E.g., likeability may depend on the personality of the ECA, on the intelligibility of its speech, etc. Some evaluation criteria may not be completely independent of each other. For example, showing friendship may be an important aspect of inducing trust in the user and thus enhance the usability of an electronic commerce application. In our discussion we will refer to *high-level*, or *compound evaluation criteria* which involve others, as opposed to *low-level*, or *basic evaluation criteria*.

So when setting the evaluation aspects, the following two choices are to be made explicit:

1 Which (objective or subjective) evaluation criteria are of interest?

2 How are these interpreted, related to each other and to the qualities of the ECA?

Ideally, it is the task of experts in psychology, sociology and of the application domain to identify what aspects are relevant in certain application scenarios. Sessions with ECAs can serve as experimental settings to find out also about these aspects. What the main task for the ECA evaluator is, is to find out how to decompose a subjective aspect (e.g., likeability) into aspects which can be related to ECA design. Such aspects may be some objective performance aspects (e.g., understanding well what the ECA says), may concern mental aspects of the ECA (personality judgement) or some aspects of embodiment (e.g., gender or aesthetic appeal). These composite factors (not only their values!) may differ in different contexts. Hence one should be careful when defining a concept a priori in terms of others, without giving verification rooted in the application context.

This observation leads to the methodological deficiency in measuring these fuzzy concepts. Mostly, a set of questions are bunched together as measurements for one concept, without any verification of using just those and not other questions, and the way of gaining a single measurement value (e.g., by averaging) based on the answers to the questions. In particular, the relation between the definition of the concept and the way it is measured remains unclear. It remains problematic if the data obtained by the measurement are valid, in particular when a psychological construct is evaluated (see the Chapter 3 by Christoph in this book for the discussion of validity). One should make clear the relationship between collected data and evaluation variables. Two different approaches are used.

One possibility (and common practice), as discussed in the Chapter 3 by Christoph in this book in detail, is to define a complex evaluation variable in terms of its (directly measurable) phenomena in advance. For basic variables, the measurement method may be widely accepted; for instance arousal can be measured by blood pressure, or by observing facial expressions. For compound variables there may be measurement methods used in psychology, like for instance the desert survival problem to judge trust, or different methods to test intelligence. Note that in this case an alternative of measurement methods is offered, and it depends on the situation which one(s) to use.

For compound variables which do not yet have accepted measurement methods, in the previous sense, another, exploratory approach can be used. The compound variable is decomposed into simpler, independent components, which each get measured. For instance, for liking, arousal may be one component, subjective judgement of appeal another, helpfulness (in itself a complex variable) yet another. From these measurements, an aggregate value for the high-level variable is derived, e.g., by averaging (as is mostly done), or by some more subtle partial comparison of the measurement results for the components. Note that in this case all components need to be measured. It is possible that for a component well-proven alternative measurement methods are available, as explained earlier.

The identification of the components of a high-level evaluation variable is a non-trivial task in itself, as explained earlier. At the present state of the art of ECA technology and evaluation, an unbiased, mathematical approach, as used by, for instance, Nass et al. (2000) and Cowell et al. (2003), seems to be the most appropriate for us to learn also about the relevant evaluation aspects and their relationship.

It would be an interesting research topic to identify some categories of tasks or application contexts, and provide some objective definition and measurement methods for the relevant evaluation criteria, by using mathematical methods for decomposing the concepts into components, and established methods to measure those. This would produce a common ground for evaluating ECAs to be used in the same application context.

For the measurement of evaluation variables, expertise in related fields could be used. There are examples of adopting psychological tests and case-problems to judge perceived personality and trust (even in an application independent sense!). One could consult experts to forge a new measurement method. Moundridou and Virvou (2002) have asked 15 classroom tutors to come up with measurement for attention of students communicating with a tutoring ECA.

3.3 Testing by what Users?

When performing usability tests, the group of subjects should be selected carefully, as users with different characteristics may interact with and judge an ECA differently. Below we outline the aspects which may be relevant for ECA users, and refer to findings obtained so far.

3.3.1 Demographic Data The following demographic aspects of the user may be relevant for the ECA usage: gender, age, fluency in the language of communication, ethnicity, computer skills and familiarity with ECA technology.

Gender Most of the evaluation studies are aware of the potential importance of gender, as the gender distribution of the subjects is almost always reported. However, the results are still scattered and sometimes contradictory, so not sufficient to formulate design guidelines with respect to the gender of the users. Comparing different designs of full embodied agents for a retail application, McBreen et al. (2000) suggest that females may prefer to interact with agents of their own gender. Buisine at al. (2003) did not find such a correlation between the gender of the ECA and of the user, but reported on gender difference in preference for different non-verbal strategies of the ECA.

Age The age of the user has hardly been considered as an influential factor for ECA evaluation. Most often it is assumed that the experimental subject's age (usually student age) is the same as the target groups age. It would be interesting to investigate how age influences preferences for the looks and communicational modalities of an ECA. Describing an emotional expression model for chatterbots, Paradiso and L'Abbate (2001) stated that it was important to take into consideration the age of the user as the expressiveness of an agent should be stronger for younger users.

Ethnicity Ethnicity is meant to indicate the ethnicity of a person as visible from her looks. Studying the effect of the ECA ethnicity, Nass et al. (2000) found that when ethnicity of users and agents matched, the ECA was regarded as socially more attractive.

Language In the evaluation literature authors describe the level of language knowledge of the experimental subjects in a variety of terms, like "first language is English", "fluent English", or implied by being "3rd year student at American university X". The precise characterisation of the level of the communicational language skills may be relevant when mental aspects of the agent are to be judged, or if efficiency is measured by recall or task performance.

Computer skills   One may expect that users who know more about the mechanisms of computer applications and have a high proficiency in using computers perceive ECAs as less attractive, and also gain less (or even lose) in efficiency by using them. All the same, small-scale evaluations are often done by computer science students, who cannot be considered as good representatives of an intended user group. Proficiency in using computers should be established on the basis of a series of factual questions concerning using computer at work and in private life, as done e.g., by Cowell et al. (2003).

Familiarity with ECA technology   It is often mentioned that the 'novelty effect' biases a user's judgement. In practice, almost all test experiments are prone to this effect. On the other hand, the testing subjects should not know more about the ECA technology than the intended user group, as people from the ECA research field might be biased in their judgement and skilled in using ECAs.

3.3.2   Psychological Data   The mental characteristics of the user (other than language skills) are surely reflected in his preferences for ECAs. Research on what the relevant user characteristics are, and how they should be taken into account when designing an ECA, is still in its infancy.

Personality   The following personality characteristics of the user have been considered in the context of ECA evaluation: self-esteem, introversion/extroversion, and locus of control. Resnick and Lammers (2000) showed that users with low or high self-esteem reacted differently to error messages. Studying trust through relational conversational strategies, Cassell and Bickmore (2001) claimed that social dialogue had a positive effect on trust for users with a disposition to be extroverts. Nass et al. (2000) found that individuals had more fun with agents whose non-verbal cues matched their own personality. Rickenberg and Reeves (2000) showed that the locus of control of the user was relevant in the anxiety evoked by the ECA (see section 4.2.5 for discussion).

Affect intensity   Affect intensity is used in psychology to characterise the intensity of emotional response of the user to a given level of affect stimulus (Larsen (1987)). It appears that high affect intensity individuals, when exposed to emotional stimuli, produce more affect related cognitive responses as well as experience stronger emotional reactions. Thus users emotional reactions to an ECA as well as their preferences for certain types of ECAs could be related to their emotional profile or level of affect intensity.

Cognitive style   Cognitive style is the collection of stable aspects of how people organize their thoughts, deal with sensory input and communicate ideas. In HCI cognitive style has been used as a common entry of user profiles (Benbasat et al. (1981)). Modelling user cognitive style might be particularly relevant for pedagogical agents. User cognitive style might also influence their preferences for specific styles of multi-modal communication in other applications.

Perception and body capabilities   Among the users there may be ones who have deficiencies in using some communicational channels. Hearing and the capability to read faces have been used to pre-test users to exclude anomalies. Handedness of the user may have consequences on the judgement of gesturing of an ECA, especially in case of instructional tutoring applications.

3.3.3   Culture   A culture's impact on a person is to be noticed in his communication, norms and beliefs (de Rosis et al. (2001)) and behaviour (Hofstede (1997)). Thus culture should also be an aspect of the user profile, when designing an ECA to be used by a multicultural public, e.g., via the web. Isbister et al. (2000) examined the effect of the agent on crosscultural communication. They found that two cultural groups with very different interaction styles and norms; namely American and Japanese had different impressions on the same agent and they reacted in different ways.

While ethnicity can be decided at a glance, there is much discrepancy in how to elicit the user's culture (and what is meant by it). One comes across cultural descriptions like "CS student of Chinese origin" or "with Western/Eastern philosophical tradition" (King et al. (1996)). It requires further research to provide methodology to set useful categories of culture. Will a student, fluent in English and having spent 10 years in the USA, perceive and judge the non-verbal gestures of an ECA in a similar way as an American born student?

3.4   How to Collect and Evaluate Data?

Once it is clear what aspects of an ECA are to be evaluated and in what context, one has to design a setting for collecting relevant data, and a way of interpreting them. Chapter 3 by Christoph in this book is devoted entirely to evaluation methodology, in this section we give a brief summary of the most important issues.

3.4.1   Empirical Data Collection   According to Dehn and Van
Mulken (2000), an ECA may have influence at three levels:

- the user's behaviour during interaction,

- the user's subjective perception of the interaction, and

- longer term effects on the user.

The effects at the three levels do not always coincide, the subjective
perception of the user may differ from the conclusions based on observation or testing the final outcome. Höök et al. (2000) evaluated their
Agneta and Frida system, and noticed that the same user who was often
smiling while interacting with the system, did not like the characters,
according to the post-session questionnaire on subjective impressions.

Below we list the data collection methods most appropriate for evaluating ECAs.

Observation of user behaviour takes place at the work-place or in the
laboratory, in order to get basic impressions of ECA usage.

Experiment is used for a systematic evaluation of ECA designs or
elicitation of characteristics of human-human communication.

Benchmarks and comparative tests are standardized forms of experimental procedures, based on carefully constructed standard tasks. It is
still a challenge to define benchmark scenarios to test different aspects
of ECAs in an application independent way, as a function of certain
characteristics of the ECA. Choice Dilemma Situations and the Desert
Survival Problem have been used by Nass et al. (2000) to test the effect
of ECAs in an way independent of the domain of the application. Recall
rate can be used for testing the learning effect in arbitrary domains.

Questionnaire and interview are done with paper-and-pencil, and face
to face, respectively. It is known that the interview technique may bias
the subjects answers.

Usage data provides some quantitative characteristics of interaction
of the user, based on logged users input action or recorded non-verbal
behaviour like eye gaze or head movements (registered automatically
during the entire session with the system).

Biomedical data are gained by measuring directly some biomedical
characteristics of the user during the interaction. Blood pressure and
skin conductivity have been used by Mori et al. (2003) to get an objective
picture of affect arousal of the user during the entire interaction.

3.4.2   Interpreting the Data   The interpretation of collected
data may be a source of flaws for the experiment. Mistakes range from
misusing the data (e.g., misjudging them as indicators for some phe-

nomena) to the incorrect use of statistical methods. In a nutshell, the following major points must be taken care of:

- Most often, it is decided a priori that one measurement dimension, or the average of several different measurement dimensions is used as the value for an evaluation variable. Such an approach implicitly determines the evaluation aspect in terms of the measurement data. Verification of such an implied definition should be given, by referring to common practice or to some theoretical foundation. If these are not available, the motivation for the chosen measurements and mapping should be stated.

- When it is not yet well established what the evaluation dimensions should be, exploratory data analysis should be considered. Instead of an a priori interpretation framework, correlation between different data (e.g., answers to different questions) should be investigated by some sound method, like principle component analysis. By such an approach one can derive a few characteristic compound dimensions (consisting of sub-variables corresponding the specific aspects, each represented by a separate entry in the initial data collection) to judge the ECA.

- Simple comparison of numerical data or respective averages is sufficient only as descriptive evaluation.

- To draw conclusions, statistical tests are to be conducted, with carefully chosen and documented parameters.

- To perform specific statistical tests, data from a sufficient number of properly selected users are needed.

- Certain user characteristics might have a discriminative effect, which should be checked.

- If user observation data are labelled by evaluators, care should be taken that the labelling is correct (usually by using multiple evaluators and ensuring agreement between their judgments).

4.   Dimensions of Evaluation

In this section we identify aspects that, in our view, are most relevant for evaluation. We provide a definition for each evaluation criterion. Then we discuss the different usage and measurement of the concept in the literature.

In the first subsection, we deal with the aspects which are strictly related to the performance of an ECA as an interface. The performance-related aspects can be evaluated basically by objective measures of behaviour and results achieved. As 'good performance' is beneficial in all application domains and for all users, these objectives are universal, though the 'good performance' may have different meaning for different applications.

In the second subsection, we turn to the issue of the users experience with an ECA. The corresponding evaluation criteria are subjective and are more difficult to measure. Furthermore, it depends on the application domain and the user group, which of the possible qualities perceived are relevant for the ECA.

4.1   Usability

As a starting point for usability, we refer to the concept as described by Nielsen (1993) for general HCI. In this section on usability we discuss the *task performance* dimensions, namely *learnability, efficiency, memorizability* and *error*. Nielsens fifth category, satisfaction goes to the next section in a strongly modified form, as a dimension of user perception. In this way we separate the evaluation criteria related to objective performance and to subjective perception of the user.

In HCI, there are generally accepted heuristic guidelines to judge an interface. For instance, in order to judge the consistency of a user interface, the use of shortcuts, menus and other selection and navigation devices, layout and colours should be looked at and compared with common practice in other applications as well as multiple use in the given application. One can spot easily if, for instance, the usage of red colour or the shortcut key Ctrl-C are not consistent with common practice. So a 'quick and dirty' evaluation of a traditional user interface can be done by checking heuristic design rules.

In case of ECAs, we do not have yet such a complete and fixed set of heuristic design rules. The suggestion by Sanders and Scholtz (2000) provides rules to judge the natural language dialogue capabilities of an ECA. Many of the objectives stated in the heuristics for traditional user interface design are very likely desirable also when the interface is an ECA, though this has to be verified. The major problem is to be able to tell if a given ECA fulfils a requirement. Using the previous example, the question of consistency of an ECA is a far more complex issue than that of a traditional user interface. It involves the subtle correspondence of almost all design aspects. As discussed before, the identification of the evaluation criteria as well as the realization of the desired effects, in terms of the design parameters of the ECA, are open issues themselves, asking for multidisciplinary research.

This is the reason why in ECA evaluation the method of heuristic evaluation conducted by experts is hardly present, but empirical tests (also used in testing traditional software) are more often performed. In different, designed scenarios test subjects interact with the ECA. In order to measure the usability concepts as dependent parameters, data sets are collected and metrics are developed.

4.1.1   Learnability, Memorizability and Ease of Use

Learnability is the easiness/difficulty of figuring out how the ECA 'works', from the point of view of maintaining a discourse with it. *Memorizability* is to express how easy it is for users to remember those interaction strategies. *Ease of use* is a compound criterion, consisting of learnability and memorizability

The main motivation of having an ECA as an interface is its ease of use. Ideally, the user communicates with an ECA just as she does with a real person. In this ideal case, there is hardly anything to be learnt, as the user has been practising the type of natural communication in his daily life. As in practice ECAs are far from full-fledged humans in their communicational means, there are several concerns to judge learnability: Are users provided with sufficient instructions to understand how to interact with the ECA? Does the ECA tell, by way of introduction or when appropriate, what his limitations and powers are? Are the agent's limitations and capabilities (communication and mind) clear from his behaviour, or are wrong expectations generated? How natural it is (compared with human-human interaction) to communicate with the ECA?

Memorizability is quite important for novice users. Actually memorizability plays a role as a factor in learnability too. If some steps in the interaction process are hard to memorize, this, of course, hinders learning.

4.1.2   Efficiency

Efficiency is the relation between the success (accuracy and completeness) in achieving certain goals and the mental resources and time spent on it.

Efficiency can be defined as the degree to which the ECA enables the task to be completed in an effective and economical fashion. Depending on the kind of task, efficiency has different measures. When there is a clear-cut task which gets either performed or not (e.g., booking a flight), the number of goals/tasks achieved in a period of time, or the time needed to complete the task, can be measured. In order not to consider the extra time spent with the ECA 'for its sake', the *on-task time*, devoted to solving the task, should be considered. For other domains (e.g., learning), task fulfilment quality must be evaluated (e.g., by comprehension or recall). As of *mental resources*, low-level components like fatigue, stress and perceived mental load are measured. Stress and mental load relate the concept to perceived task difficulty (discussed in 4.2.6).

Apart from evaluating task performance efficiency in an ECA application one could evaluate the efficiency of the ECA's communicative functions by itself. For instance, the ECA's communicative skills are a general property which could be evaluated by experts separately from a specific application context. One could also design experiments to evaluate them, possibly using a context tuned to this evaluation purpose.

4.1.3   Errors   *Errors* indicate the relative amount and type of mistakes occurring while interacting with the ECA.

Common error categories can be identified, such as: misunderstanding (as of information content) of the ECA by the user or of the user by the ECA; problems in the dialogue management (whose turn it is, is the ECA idling or still active, deadlock situation). The relative number of occurrences of different types of error, as well as relative time spent on recovering from them, are good indicators how error-prone the ECA is. A related issue is whether the ECA provides active help for the user to recover from errors by, for instance, asking to repeat her input, or taking the initiative to recover from interaction errors.

4.2   Evaluation of User Perception of ECAs

In this section we discuss evaluation aspects of the ECA which essentially have to do with the perception of the user. Some of the aspects have a corresponding or related usability dimension (like satisfaction and usability), others like engagement and trust can be measured by observing the behaviour as well as by questioning the user.

4.2.1   Satisfaction   *User satisfaction* is the perception by the user that her interaction with the ECA serves ones intentions in a rewarding and agreeable way.

Though one of the most measured aspects, user satisfaction is a difficult concept. It is related to objective usability: if an ECA is inefficient and difficult to use, the user will be, basically, unhappy with using it. However, it has been suggested by several experiments (see discussion in 4.2.6), that the subjective impression may deviate from the objective performance: an ECA makes the user perceive the interaction and even the quality of the service more positive. This so-called 'persona effect' is another major motivation of applying ECAs.

A user's reactions to an ECA depend on several subjective factors, such as the importance of achieving some goal with the application, her (positive or negative) prejudice of the outcome of using the ECAs. A weakness of many of the experiments with test subjects is that the situation is not 'real', there are no consequences like passing or not an exam after sessions with a tutoring ECA, or gaining or losing money when following the advice of a broker ECA.

User satisfaction is a vague and in itself multi-dimensional concept, with possible components like *emotional liking* and *arousal*, assessment of *attractiveness*. It depends very much on the user's own characteristics, what is 'attractive' and 'pleasant' for her. In order to get insight into the factors of user satisfaction, one should carry on evaluation research where the possible dimensions of the concept and the user profile are taken into account, as discussed in Section 3.

For instance, Nass et al. (2000), investigating the consequences of ECA's personality, use fun as one of the concepts that indicates user satisfaction. Based on a factor analysis of responses to a questionnaire they define fun (triggered by using an ECA) as a high-level concept of the following components: enjoyable, exciting, funny and satisfying. Thus, instead of just evaluating for 'pleasant versus unpleasant', a more complete model of emotion is needed to cover all aspects of emotional assessment. Such a model is the pleasure, arousal dominance model described by Mehrabian and Russell (1977). Evaluating user experiences should include evaluating all relevant emotional as well as social aspects of the ECA.

4.2.2   Engagement   An *engaging (involving, appealing)* ECA motivates the user to spend time dealing with it while perceiving the activity as pleasurable in itself. Engagement is a high-level experience dimension. Its constituents depend on the application context. For instance, for an ECA as personal assistant these include likeability and trust, but if the ECA acts as tourist guide, these factors are less decisive, but the level of entertainment is. In our sense, engagement is even stronger than user satisfaction. One cannot be engaged by an ECA if one does not feel satisfaction while interacting with him. On the other hand, one can be satisfied with a non-engaging ECA, for instance when the ECA helps with a task one does not like doing, but has to do. In that case one will not be inclined, in spite of the satisfaction, to spend more time with the ECA. In the literature, this point of view is not always shared. Koda and Maes (1996) treat satisfaction on the same level as likeability and intelligence.

Both the relevance of the services of the ECA and its design aspects (look of the body, gesturing and speech, personality) have an effect on engagement. A correlation between user personality and ECA engagement is reported by Bickmore and Cassell (2000). Active users (who take the initiative in talking to the ECA) found the estate-agent REA more engaging when she got them involved in small talk, passive users when there was no small talk.

4.2.3   Helpfulness   An ECA is *helpful*, if in the users perception the ECA behaves in a cooperative way to assist her in achieving her goals and in resolving difficulties.

A way to paraphrase the definition is that the ECA should behave as a good assistant. Obviously, the perception of helpfulness is related to a large extent to usability aspects like how, when and what information the EAC presents. But less obviously, the ECA's visual design characteristics also play a role. For instance, Lester et al. (1997) conducted experiments with an educational ECA giving advice on two different levels (principle-based or task specific), with or without instructional animations. Subjects rated the ECA version with principle-based advice, demonstrated by animations as significantly the most helpful. McBreen et al. (2000a) evaluated retail agents, where the controlled variables were gender and visual characteristics. As for helpfulness they found that the fully realistic (video) head scored higher than the 3D talking heads. What was more interesting, that the *male* 3D talking heads (also with male voice) scored even lower than either of the stills. The last result is difficult to interpret for a reason which is paradigmatic for a general problem with this kind of evaluations. When manipulating gender in this example, more than one (high level) parameters are manipulated: visual characteristics and voice. This is unavoidable because the ECA has to be consistent!

4.2.4   Naturalness and Believability   An ECA is *natural (life-like)*, if it is in line with the expectations of the user about a living, acting creature with respect to its embodiment and communicative behaviours. When on top of that its task performance is perceived as meeting the expectations, it is *believable (credible)*.

The user judges the ECA based on its look and communicational behaviour. These should be consistent at each moment and at different points of time. They all should give the impression of a real living creature. For instance, a robot-like voice, or the lack of idle motion destroy the illusion of life, and thus, naturalness. Furthermore, consistency with the domain the ECA functions in is expected too: information should be provided in such a way that the user is willing to take the information seriously. Believability in this sense is not equal to taking the ECA as *real*. ECAs often have deliberately a non-realistic design, with non-realistic features. Not only the (yet significant) shortcomings of the technology do not allow to produce perfect clones of real humans, the realm of non-realism has additional advantages, like the enhanced expressivity of cartoons. But in case of non-realistic embodiment too, believability is an important evaluation criterion.

We found two examples of evaluations of believability, where the concept was used in accordance with our definition. In a teaching application Lester et al. (1997) ask test subjects: "Did you believe the advice you got from Herman the bug (the teaching agent)?" which we interpret as: "Did you take the advice by Herman as an advice given by a teacher?" In the literature on ECA evaluation, the distinction between believability, trust and credibility is sometimes quite unclear. For instance Nash and Lee (2000) talk about *voice credibility* (for a synthetic voice of a reviewer) as a high-level concept composed of the following three qualities: credibility, reliability and trustworthiness. Another evaluation concept was credibility of the ECA (in the role of a book reviewer), which was measured by a standardized trust scale.

4.2.5   Trust   *Trust (credibility)* is the belief that the ECA has benevolent intentions towards the user and has the competence to put those into effect.

Cassell and Bickmore (2000) further differentiate trust: "A useful distinction can be made between a cognitive state of trust and trusting behaviours. Trusting behaviours involve making oneself vulnerable to other people in any one of a number of ways." In their experiment the same authors provided evidence (Cassell and Bickmore (2001)), that the users subjective statement about her trust in the ECA does not necessarily coincide with a trusting behaviour towards the ECA. They also showed that small talk increased the trust in the agent, but among extrovert users only. Cowell et al. (2003) have reported on the correlation of perceived trust and task performance, as well as other perceived qualities of the ECA.

Rickenberg and Reeves (2000) tested the reaction of subjects (distinguished on the internal/external locus of control dimension) who had to perform tasks on web sites in the presence of an ECA which behaved as if monitoring the user. Monitoring produced anxiety especially for subjects with external locus of control, yet in the monitoring condition subjects trusted the website more than the same website without an ECA.

In McBreen et al. (2001) users report not having trust in an e-banking application, featuring an ECA because "they have not enough confidence in the technology yet". Given the accepted status of e-banking, this result points at the danger of adding an immature ECA on top of a proven application.

4.2.6   Perceived Task Difficulty   *Perceived task difficulty* is the subjective judgement of the difficulty of the task.

This is one of the parameters referred to in the discussion about the persona effect, initially coined by Lester et al. (1997). Namely, that the presence of an ECA makes the user perceive the task as easier, without a measurable difference in task performance. Such effect has been reported with tutoring systems in different domains, like the operation of a pulley system by Van Mulken et al (1998), linear equations by Moundridou and Virvou (2002) or biology by Lester et al. (1997). Recently, Baylor (2003) conducted an experiment which suggests the superiority of the 'split-persona effect': having two separate pedagogical agents with different roles improved learning performance and perceived value of the agents. On the other hand, the experiments by Van Mulken et al. (1998) suggest that the assistance of an ECA has no effect on short-term learning; moreover there was no persona-effect at all in case of the less technical application which dealt with photos of human faces.

4.2.7   Likeability   An ECA is perceived as *likeable* (sympathetic) if the user feels positive about (some of) its traits and behaviours.

Likeability is a compound concept too. In a loose sense, it is the judgement of the ECA, also its personality. As this judgement is user-dependent, one should not equal likeability to a kind, friendly personality of the ECA. (Think of how one can dislike a 'keep smiling character too.) Moreover, additional design (like look) and perceived aspects (helpfulness, trustworthiness) of the ECA also play a role. A difference with respect to engagement is that the ECAs competence as a task performer and the relevance of the performed task do not enter here. In this case too we encounter terminology problems in the literature. Buisine et al. (2003) and Koda and Maes (1996) evaluate likeability by directly including the term in a questionnaire. Rickenberg and Reeves (2000) on the other hand used a compound concept (derived by factor analysis of a sixteen-item questionnaire), containing items like enjoyment, fun and boredom.

4.2.8   Entertainment   An *entertaining* ECA is amusing in a non-task related way, thereby making performing the task more agreeable for the user.

Both the relevance of the services of the ECA and its design aspects (look of the body, gesturing and speech, personality) have an effect on engagement. Van Mulken et al. (1998) report on a technical explanation (of a pulley system) and a non-technical recall task (remembering data on new employees) presented with and without an ECA. In the technical case the explanation with the ECA was judged significantly more entertaining. No difference was found for the non-technical task. Although the authors are not sure how to interpret this difference, to the ECA designer it shows the importance of the application context.

5.   Conclusions

We proposed a framework for comparing and evaluating ECAs. We introduced the general and most important issues one has to take care of when starting research on evaluating ECAs. We discussed the design parameters of ECAs in detail. Then we took a critical look at the relevant literature to elicit common terminology of evaluation aspects. While we did our best to provide a complete list and acceptable working definitions for fuzzy concepts which have been used widely and controversially, we do not claim that our list is closed. Just the opposite, we will be happy if our work will induce some debate and will lead to improvements and extensions on evaluation aspects. In our discussions we emphasized the proliferation in methodology. The next step is to settle some methods (till the detail of questions to be asked) and provide benchmarks as the standard way to evaluate certain aspects of ECAs.

Our secondary goal was to draw attention to the necessity of a common framework. In our view, a common reference framework will facilitate many tasks in the ECA community:

- To compare ECAs, from a design and technical point of view;

- to facilitate the re-use and adaptation of existing ECAs;

- to help researchers doing evaluation to converge to some design guidelines;

- to point out 'white spots' in human-human communication, and in ECA evaluation.

We claim that by taking a systematic and critical look at design categories, evaluation criteria and evaluation methods, the research efforts can be spent better. Not only on a short term, by avoiding pitfalls of making unsound conclusions or developing superfluous features. But also on a long term, by having a clearer view within the research community, and presenting a, maybe, more subtle but sound and not less challenging image of our field for the outside world about what has been achieved and what we are after.

But with the near future in mind we want to conclude with the following concrete recommendations to researchers in this field:

- Keep in mind that all the design parameters mentioned in section 2 (and possibly further ones) may influence the impact of your ECA in often yet unknown ways.

- When trying to find design guidelines, vary only one of the parameters at a time, i.e. comparing a 2D cartoon to a 3D cartoon and a 3D cartoon to a 3D realistic ECA is more instructive than comparing a 2D cartoon and a 3D realistic one. The latter kind of evaluation makes sense in practical cases only, where two alternatives to choose from are available, but it does not lead to general design guidelines.

- When evaluating an ECA with an application, take care to separate the effect of the two (see 3.2) if you want to draw conclusions on the effect of the ECA. When possible at all, use the application without an ECA as baseline.

- Ask yourself what the intended user group is. Take demographic data and user characteristics into consideration (see 3.4).

- Whenever possible, use evaluation dimensions and measurement methods also used by others. When not possible, discuss why and define them.

- Lets try to reach agreement on evaluation (especially user perception) dimensions, their definition and measurement method in order to leave behind us the incompatibility problems discussed in section 3.3

Notes

1. www.extempo.com
2. www.cantoche.com
3. www.charamel.com
4. http://dict.die.net/trust/ for several alternatives

References

André, E. and Rist, T. (2000). Presenting Through Performing: On the Use of Multiple Lifelike Characters in Knowledge-Based Presentation Systems. In *Proc. of the Second International Conference on Intelligent User Interfaces*, pp. 1–8.New Orleans, Louisiana.

Bailenson, J. N., Beall, A. C., Blascovich, J., Raimundo, M. and Weisbuch, M., (2001). Intelligent Agents Who Wear Your Face: Users Reactions to the Virtual Self. In De Antonio, A., Aylett, R., Ballin, D., editors, In *Proc. of the Third International Workshop Intelligent Virtual Agents, IVA 2001*, pp. 86–99, Madrid, Spain, Lecture Notes in Computer Science 2190, Springer.

Barker, T. (2003). The Illusion of Life Revisited. In *Proc. of the AAMAS03 Workshop on Embodied Conversational Characters as Individuals*, Melbourne, Australia.

Baylor, A. L. (2003). The Split-Persona Effect with Pedagogical Agents. In *Proc. of the AAMAS03 Workshop on Embodied Conversational Characters as Individuals*, Melbourne, Australia.

Benbasat, I., Dexter, A. and Masulis, P. (1981). An Experimental Study of the Human/Computer Interface. *Communication of the ACM*, 24(11): 752–762.

Bickmore, T. and, Cassell, J. (2001). A Relational Agent: A Model and Implementation of Building User Trust. In *Proceedings of the CHI'01*. pp. 396–403.Seattle, Washington.

Buisine, S., Abrilian, S., Rendu, C., and Martin, J.C. (2003). Evaluation of Individual Multimodal Behavior of 2D Embodied Agents in Presentation Tasks, In *Proc. of the AAMAS03 Workshop on Embodied Conversational Characters as Individuals*, Melbourne, Australia.

Cassell, J. and Bickmore, T. (2000). External Manifestations of Trustworthiness in the Interface. *Communications of the ACM*, 43(12): 50–56.

Cassell, J. Thórisson, K. R.(1999). The Power of a Nod and a Glance: Envelope vs. Emotional Feedback in Animated Conversational Agents. *Applied Artificial Intelligence*, 13: 519–538.

Cassell, J. and Vilhjálmsson, H. (1999). Fully Embodied Conversational Avatars: Making Communicative Behaviors Autonomous. *Autonomous Agents and Multi-Agent Systems*, 2(1): 45–64.

Cowell, A.J. and Stanney, K.M. (2003). On Manipulating Nonverbal Interaction Style to Increase Anthropomorphic Computer Character Credibility. In *Proc. of the AAMAS03 Workshop on Embodied Conversational Characters as Individuals*, Melbourne, Australia.

Dehn, D. and Van Mulken, S. (2000). The impact of animated interface agents: a review of empirical research. *Int. Journal of Human-Computer Studies.* 52: 1–22.

De Rosis, F., Pelachaud, C. and Poggi, I. (to appear). Transcultural believability in embodied agents: A matter of consistent adaptation. In Payr, S. and Trappl, R., editors, *Agent Culture: Designing Human-Agent Interaction in a Multicultural World.* Laurence Erlbaum Associates, New York.

Dryer, D. (1999). Getting personal with computers. *Applied Artificial Intelligence.* 13: 273–295.

Griffin, P., Hodgson, P., and Prevost, S. (2003). Character User Interfaces for Commercial Applications. In *Proc. of the AAMAS03 Workshop on Embodied Conversational Characters as Individuals*, Melbourne, Australia.

Hofstede, G. (1997). *Cultures and Organisations: Software of the Mind.* McGraw-Hill, New York.

Höök, K., Persson, P., and Sjölinder, M. (2000). Evaluating Users Experience of a Character Enhanced Information Space, *Journal of AI Communications*, 13(3): 195 – 212.

Isbister, K. and Doyle, P. (2002). Design and Evaluation of Embodied Conversational Agents: A Proposed Taxonomy. In *Proc. of the AAMAS02 Workshop on Embodied Conversational Agents: Lets Specify and Compare Them!* , Bologna, Italy.

Isbister, K. and Hayes-Roth, B. (1998). *Social Implications of Using Synthetic Characters: An Examination of a Role-Specific Intelligent Agent.* KSL-98-01 Stanford, Knowledge Systems Laboratory.

Isbister, K., Nakanishi, H., Ishida, T., and Nass, C. (2000). Helper Agent: Designing an Assistant for Human-Human Interaction in a Virtual Meeting Space. In *Proceedings of the CHI 2000*, pp. 57–64. The Hague, The Netherlands.

Isbister, K. and Nass, C. (2000). Consistency of Personality in Interactive Characters: Verbal Cues, Non-Verbal Cues, and User Characteristics. *International Journal of Human-Computer Studies*, 53: 251–267.

Isla, D. and Blumberg, B. (2002). Object Persistence for Synthetic Creatures. In *Proc. of AAMAS02*, pp. 1356–1363.

King, J. and Ohya, J. (1996). The Representation of Agents: Anthropomorphism, Agency, and Intelligence. In *Proc. CHI96*, pp. 289–290.

Koda, T. and Maes, P. (1996). Agents With Faces: The Effects of Personification of Agents. In *Proc. of HCI'96*, pp. 98–103. London, UK.

Larsen, R.J. and Diener, E. (1987). Affect Intensity as an Individual Difference Characteristic: A review. *Journal of Research in Personality*, 21: 1–39.

Lester, J., Converse, S., Kahler, S., Barlow, S., Stone, B., and Bhogal, R. (1997). The Persona Effect: Affective Impact of Animated Pedagogical Agents. In *Proc. of CHI97*, pp. 359–366, ACM Press, New York.

Massaro, D. (1998). *Perceiving Talking Faces*. The MIT Press, Cambridge, MA, USA

McBreen, H.M., Shade, P., Jack, M.A., and Wyard, P.J. (2000). Experimental Assessment of the Effectiveness of Synthetic Personae for Multi-Modal E-Retail Applications. In *Proc. of Fourth International Conference on Autonomous Agents*, pp.39–45.

McBreen, H. M., Anderson, J., and Jack, M. (2001). Evaluating 3D Embodied Conversational Agents in Contrasting VRML Retail Applications. In *Proc. of AAMAS01 Workshop on Representing, Annotating, and Evaluating Non-Verbal and Verbal Communicative Acts to Achieve Contextual Embodied Agents*, Montreal, Canada.

McCraae, R. R., and John, O.P. (1992). An Introduction to the Five-Factor Model and its Applications. *Journal of Personality*, 60: 175–215.

Mori, J., Prendinger, H., and Ishizuka, M. (2003). Evaluation of an Embodied Conversational Agent with Affective Behavior. In *Proc. of the AAMAS03 Workshop on Embodied Conversational Characters as Individuals*, Melbourne, Australia.

Moundridou, M. and Virvou, M. (2002). Evaluating the Persona Effect of an Interface Agent in an Intelligent Tutoring System. *Journal of Computer Assisted Learning*, 18(3): 253–261.

Nass, C., Isbister, K., and Lee, E. J. (2000). Truth is Beauty: Researching Embodied Conversational Agents. In Cassell, J., Sullivan, J., Prevost, J., Churchill, E., editors, *Embodied Converastional Agents*, pp. 374–401, MIT Press, MA, USA.

Nass, C. and Lee, K. M. (2000). Does Computer-Generated Speech Manifest Personality? An Experimental Test of Similarity-Attraction. In *Proc. of CHI 2000*, pp. 329-336. The Hague, The Netherlands.

Nielsen, J. (1993). *Usability Engineering*. Morgan Kaufmann, San Francisco.

Paradiso, A. and L'Abbate, M.A. (2001). A Model for the Generation and Combination of Emotional Expressions. In *Proc. of the AAMAS01 Workshop on Representing, Annotating and Evaluating Non-Verbal and Verbal Communicative Acts to Achieve Contextual Embodied Agents*. Montreal, Canada.

Pelachaud, C., Carofiglio, V., De Carolis, B., de Rosis, F., and Poggi, I. (2002). Embodied Contextual Agent in Information Delivering Application. In *Proc. of First International Joint Conference on Autonomous Agents and Multi-Agent Systems*, Bologna, Italy.

Pelachaud, C. and Poggi, I. (2002). Subtleties of Facial Expressions in Embodied Agents. *Journal of Visualization and Computer Animation*, 13: 301–312.

Prendinger, H., and Ishizuka, M. (2002). Social Role Awareness in Animated Agents. In *Proc. of AAMAS02*, pp. 270–277.

Prendinger, H. and Ishizuka, M. (2003). Designing and Evaluating Animated Agents as Social Actors. *IEICE Transactions on Information and Systems*. E86-D(8):1378–1385.

Reeves, B. and Nass, C. (1996). *The Media Equation — How People Treat Computers, Television and New Media Like Real People and Places.* Cambridge University Press, Cambridge.

Resnick, P.V. and Lammers, H.B. (1985). The Influence of Self-esteem on Cognitive Responses to Machine-Like Versus Human-Like Computer Feedback. *The Journal of Social Psychology*, 125: 761–769.

Rickenberg, R. and Reeves, B. (2000). The Effects of Animated Characters on Anxiety, Task Performance, and Evaluations of User Interfaces. In *Proc. of CHI 2000*, pp. 49–56. The Hague, The Netherlands.

Russell, J.A. and Mehrabian, A. (1977). Evidence for a Three-Factor Theory of Emotions. *Journal of Research in Personality*, 11: 273–294.

Sanders, G. and Scholtz, J. (2000). Measurement and Evaluation of Embodied Conversational Agents. In Cassell, J., Sullivan, J., Prevost, J., Churchill, E., editors, *Embodied Converastional Agents*, MIT Press, pp. 347–373.

Sproull, L., Subramani, M., Kiesler, S., Walker, J.H., and Waters, K. (1996). When the Interface is a Face. *Human-Computer Interaction*, 11: 97–124.

Van Mulken, S., André, E., Müller, J. (1998). The Persona Effect: How substantial is it?. In *Proc. of HCI1998*, pp. 53–66. Sheffield, UK.

Witkowski, M., Arafa, Y., and De Bruijn, O. (2001). Evaluating User Reaction to Character Agent Mediated Displays Using Eye-Tracking Technology. In *Proc. of the Workshop on Information Agents in E-commerce; Agents and Cognition*, AISB Convention, York, UK.

Xiao, J., Stasko, J., and Catrambone, R. (2002). Embodied Conversational Agents as a UI Paradigm: A Framework for Evaluation. In *Proc. of the AAMAS02 Workshop on Embodied Conversational Agents: Lets Specify and Compare Them!*, Bologna, Italy.

Chapter 3

EMPIRICAL EVALUATION METHODOLOGY FOR EMBODIED CONVERSATIONAL AGENTS

On Conducting Evaluation Studies

Noor Christoph

> *If we knew what it was we were doing, it would not be called research, would it?*
>
> —Albert Einstein

Abstract   The objective of this chapter is to identify the common knowledge and practice in research methodology and to apply it to the field of software evaluation, especially of embodied conversational agents. Relevant issues discussed are: how to formulate a good research question, what research strategy to use, which data collection methods are most appropriate and how to select the right participants. Reliability and validity of the data sets are dealt with and finally the chapter concludes with a list of guidelines that one should keep in mind when setting up and conducting empirical evaluation studies on embodied conversational agents.

Keywords: Embodied conversational agents, evaluation, methodology.

Z. Ruttkay and C. Pelachaud (eds.), From Brows to Trust, 67–99.
© *2004 Kluwer Academic Publishers. Printed in the Netherlands.*

1.   Introduction

In this chapter an attempt is made to bring the best of two worlds together. On the one hand, there is a growing body of knowledge about the development and implementation of software applications such as embodied conversational agents. On the other hand, much is known about the methodology of conducting empirical research. Many good handbooks have been written that deal with choosing research strategies, formulating research questions, selecting data collection methods, and checking the reliability and validity of data (see further in this chapter). Conducting evaluation studies on embodied conversational agents (ECAs) or avatars needs the input of both worlds. The objective of this chapter is to identify the common knowledge and practice in research methodology and to apply it to the field of evaluating ECAs. In order to achieve this, several illustrative examples (not necessarily the best ones) are drawn from the existing research literature on ECAs.

The chapter is structured in the following way. First, various types of evaluation research are discussed. The scope of the research depends on the developmental stage the ECA is in and this influences how the research should be designed. Secondly, a method is described that helps to formulate a well-designed set-up of the research in which the phenomena to measure are clearly defined. The strategies to choose from for conducting evaluation research on ECAs is described next and in the subsequent section the actual data collection methods such as questionnaires, observation and the like are discussed. In section six some important issues concerning the sample are brought up. Additionally, the reliability and validity of data is elaborated upon. In section seven, some words are said about methods for data analysis and finally in section eight, a number of guidelines are introduced that capture the scope of this chapter.

2.   Types of Evaluation Research

In order to start this chapter properly, the first question to address is: what is evaluation research all about. One of the definitions of evaluation research is the collection of information about how a *specific* software application works for a *specific* group of users in a *specific* predefined context. What is evident in this definition is the contextualized situation. All of these aspects should be specified in the research design in order to conduct a study that is sufficiently plotted out and clear. Reeves and Hedberg (2003:27) discuss additional background concerning the definition and different paradigms of evaluation research, which ranges from a measurement perspective to a more constructivistic perspective that implies much richer descriptions of phenomena.

One intuitively assumes that the most appropriate moment to evaluate a piece of software is when the application is in the final stage of development, when one wants to find out what users think of it. However, during each stage of software development, one should perform one form or another of evaluation research. The main advantage is that it saves time and resources to find out what potential users think of the application (or only just conceptual ideas) well before it has reached the final design. Making adjustments to the final version of an application is a lot more costly than changing, adding or refining user requirements.

2.1 Star Life Cycle

The *Star life cycle* (Hix and Harston (1993)) describes the most commonly distinguished stages of software development. Evaluation research can be performed in each of these stages. Alternative ways of software development are the waterfall model or the spiral model Boehm (1988).

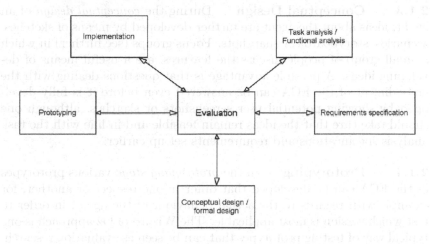

Figure 3.1. Star life cycle Hix and Harston (1993).

In each of the phases of software development of the Star life cycle (see Figure 3.1), one should perform evaluation research with a specific focus.

2.1.1 Task or Functional Analysis
Developing a software application usually starts with performing *task analysis or functional analysis*. In this stage information is collected about features of the task

to be performed and what functionality it should cover. One possibility is to observe potential users of the ECA in a natural setting in order to collect data about the specific constraints and goals for a task at hand. Collecting this information about the task and functionality is a form of evaluation research that can be done by using relatively free format methods such as interviews and observations. One of the pros of performing task analysis is that in an early stage one acquires hands-on experience and feeling with the setting, participants and task to develop the ECA for.

2.1.2   Requirements Specification   Following task analysis, the *requirements specification* phase is completed during which the actual requirements for the embodied agent are specified. One way of collecting this information is to involve potential users and ask them about the desired requirements, for example, by conducting interviews. The aim is to construct a list of requirements that sufficiently describe the functionality of the ECA.

2.1.3   Conceptual Design   During the *conceptual design* of an agent, ideas about the agent are further developed by means of sketches, scenarios, storyboards or snapshots. Focus groups (see further) in which a small group of people discuss the features, are a useful means of developing ideas. A possible advantage is that questions dealing with the embodiment of the ECA can be answered even before it is fully developed by showing potential user screenshots or sketches, although one should take care that the ideas remain feasible and in line with the task analysis specifications and requirements set up earlier.

2.1.4   Prototyping   In the *prototyping stage* various prototypes of the ECA can be developed that differ in one respect or another, for example with regards to the actual behaviour of the agent, in order to test which version is most applicable. The Wizard of Oz approach is one typical way of testing prototypes that can be seen as evaluation research. The Wizard of Oz approach entails simulating the fully functional software behind the ECA. The user is unaware of this. The developers of SenToy (Andersson et al. (2002)) used this approach in order to develop the design of this agent.

2.1.5   Implementation   In the *final stages* of software development, when the embodied agent is ready and implemented in a specific environment, one can perform evaluation studies that have more profound research questions that concern, for instance, learning effects, or that investigate the acceptability of the final design in the work place or in an information system in a shopping environment. This is the first time the agent is fully developed and implemented in the intended situation and it is now possible to collect information on future updates or potential functionality extensions or refinements.

2.2   Formative and Summative Evaluation

Another distinction that can be made in types of evaluation research is the one between *formative* and *summative* evaluation. Formative evaluation takes place when the application is being developed and data is continuously being collected. The main objective is to shape ideas in order to come to an appropriate tool. Summative evaluation takes place when the software is implemented in the intended context or is in its final development. The main objective for summative evaluation is to give an impression of how the software is being used in the field, and to collect information for possible updates. This type of research focuses more on processes that take place when users work with the system. According to the Star life cycle depicted above, summative evaluation mainly takes place after the implementation phase, in all the other phases the research is more or less formative in nature.

The actual design of the evaluation study will depend greatly upon the developmental phase of the application. For example, a more exploratory study with mainly qualitative methods can be applied when the conceptual design of an ECA is at stake.

When determining the degree of femininity of an embodied agent, one could draw several sketches and make several screenshots and present these to potential users working on a particular task. Open interview questions and free format observation could yield the desired results in order to determine what the ECA should look like for specific types of tasks. A more experimental study is called for when measuring the effectiveness of different versions of an ECA in helping hearing-impaired people to lip-read in order to investigate which version works best. This type of research will most probably be conducted when the agent is in the implementation phase of software development.

Apart from all the possible research questions and themes one could formulate for evaluating an ECA, some attention is drawn here to the theme 'usability'. Usability as defined by Nielsen (1993), is concerned with five major aspects of software usage: learnability, efficiency, memorability, errors and satisfaction. Usability can be defined as the extent to which a participant is able to use the functionality of the software. In each of the developmental phases depicted above one could investigate the usability of the (potential) application and focus on one or more of these aspects. However, scientific questions in each of these developmental phases may also arise, such as questions dealing with the validity of a behavioural model of an ECA.

3.   Research Model, Research Question and Construct

Preece et al. (1994) discuss several research themes one can adopt once the ECA is fully implemented:

- *Understanding the world.* For example, Buisine et al. (2002) pose the following questions to be investigated in their study: does the use of a conversational agent enhance the ergonomics of the interface; the effectiveness of the interaction and the satisfaction of the user?

- *Comparing designs.* For example, Xiao et al. (2002) manipulate the appearance (lifelike versus iconic) and the nature of the user's task (carrying out procedures versus providing opinion) in order to see what effects it has on the user-perception of the agent in terms of helpfulness.

- *Engineering towards a target.* For example, Morishima and Nakamura (2002) report developing a multi-modal ECA that is able to translate from English to Japanese and vice versa and also translates the user's speech motion while synchronizing it to the translated speech.

- *Checking conformance to a standard.* Firm standards in the field of ECAs are still lacking though it seems that MPEG4, VRML or H-anim compatibility are commonly accepted.

Each of these four lines of research implies a very different type of research, ranging from theoretical to practical, and therefore a different research question and type of design. In order to conceptually elaborate upon the research design, one should create a research model that describes the objective and set-up of the study. Based on the research model one should develop a well-formulated research question. Finally, one should define the construct that is mentioned in the research question. This will be elaborated upon in the next sections.

3.1   Research Model

In a *research model*, one gives a *schematic* and *visual representation* of the main steps to be taken in empirical research. It gives an overview of the study in a nutshell ranging from the *objectives* of the study to the *theories* taken into account (Verschuren and Doorewaard, (1999)).

3.1.1 Research Objective

The study of Moundridou and Virvou (2002) is chosen as an example. They investigate the effects of implementing an agent in a learning environment. Their abstract says: "This paper describes the evaluation of the persona effect of a speech-driven anthropomorphic agent that has been embodied in the interface of an Intelligent Tutoring System (ITS). [...]The participants in the experiment were divided into two groups: half of them worked with a version of the ITS which embodied the agent and the rest worked with and agent-less version. [...]the hypothesis that the presence of the agent improves short-term learning effects was rejected based on our data."

The first step is to formulate the *objective* of the research. The purpose of the research can be either to create or add to an existing base of theory or to contribute to the solution of a practical problem. Moundridou and Virvou (2002) describe that the aim of their experiment was to examine how the presence of the agent would affect the students in terms of learning, motivation and learning experience. This can be reformulated briefly as is shown in *part A* in figure 3.2.

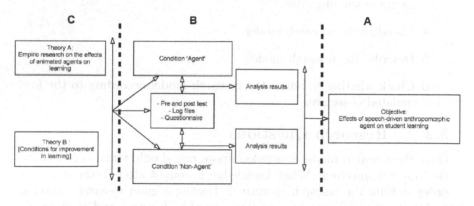

Figure 3.2. Research model made for the study by Moundridou and Virvou (2002).

3.1.2 Nature of the Research

Subsequently one should address how to achieve this aim by declaring the *nature of the research* and how to study this. Types of research are, for example, theory testing research or diagnostic research. When conducting theory-testing research, one will test hypotheses. When performing diagnostic research, one should determine possible causes of malfunctioning. Clearly the study by Moundridou and Virvou (2002) is concerned with hypotheses testing. Two conditions are contrasted, a condition in which the agent is included in the learning environment versus a condition in which the agent is absent (see *part B* of figure 3.2).

3.1.3 Sources of Information Then one should identify the different ingredients or *sources of information* to rely on for performing the study. Here, the authors have reviewed empirical studies on the effects of animated agents on learning. Another source of information is possibly literature on conditions under which learning takes place. This last step is depicted in *part C* of figure 3.2.

Verschuren and Doorewaard (1999) suggest to work backwards when creating the research model, that is, the research objective is formulated first.

1 Formulate the objective of the research briefly and crisply in a few words.

2 Determine the nature of the research perspective.

3 Choose relevant literature and experts based upon the main elements of the objective.

4 Visualize the research model.

5 Describe the research model.

6 Check whether to adapt the research model according to the formulated objective.

3.2 Research Questions

Once the research model is decided upon, one should start to formulate the *research question*. What knowledge is sought after in the study in order to fulfil the research objective? Having a good research question makes it more efficient to contribute to the objective and it gives direction as it makes clear what should happen in the study and what material to collect. In Chapter 2 by Ruttkay et al. valid objectives for investigating effects of ECAs are mentioned. Swanborn (1997) states that the research question should indicate, among other things, the domain, the variables and the population, and if relevant, the time and place. The research question should also make clear what type of problem one wants to solve, for example, a descriptive, an explanatory or a design problem. Referring back to the study conducted by Moundridou and Virvou (2002) one could formulate the following research question:

Does the the agent WEAR, implemented in an intelligent tutoring system for algebra related domains, result in a more positive attitude of students towards the learning environment; more attention for the learning environment; higher learning performance, when compared to the same learning environment without the agent?

3.3   Psychological Construct

When having identified the research objective, the research question and having a general idea of how to conduct the study, it is important to describe and define the phenomenon one aims at measuring. Sometimes, the formulation of the phenomenon of interest is described in an abstract manner. For instance, one aims at investigating the experienced altruism, believability or trustworthiness of an ECA. In order to study the phenomenon correctly, one needs a useful definition in order to increase the perceptibility of this phenomenon. This phenomenon can be a *construct*. A construct is an underlying psychological attribute that cannot be measured directly. It is a hypothetical variable, a mental state or a concept. Examples of constructs are: trust, liking, happiness, intelligence, learnability or altruism. Because a construct is non-tangible, one needs to operationalise or define it into variables that can be measured and perceived (see Figure 3.3). Chapter 2 by Ruttkay et al. also discusses ways to develop evaluation variables. To operationalise means to define the construct by specifying behaviours or phenomena that can be measured directly by means of variables. A variable is any class of events on which observations are made and potentially differing values are assigned to (Neale and Liebert, 1986). Variables can differ according to their level of aggregation and measurement. One can operationalise a construct by reviewing literature on definitions and finding standard measurement methods that are used. Another way of operationalising is to define the construct, choose variables and develop the measurement methods yourself.

In order to assert whether the operationalisations one has made, are valid, or 'true' one needs to check the construct validity (cf. Neale and Liebert, 1986). Construct validity deals with the extent to which a particular instrument measures the construct and the procedure involves examining the relation between various test scores and observations (see also validity). This is especially important when measurements are not generally accepted methods. Then it is wise to use more than one measurement method that supposedly measures the construct in order to compare results.

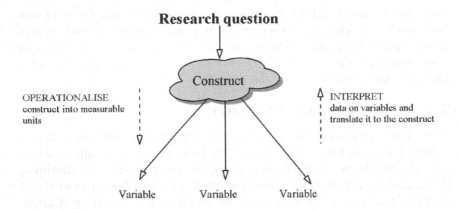

Figure 3.3. Measuring a construct.

Coolican (1994) describes constructs like this: "We build up a concept (or 'construct') of [for example] extraversion or anxiety or attitude from learning what are signs or manifestations of it. Biting lips and trembling voices may show anxiety, for instance. The important question is, does our internal (mental) 'construct' of extroversion relate to any real identifiable phenomenon which affects people's behaviour in a regular or predictable manner? We do not observe something called 'extroversion' as such - we observe what we assume is evidence of it in a person - unafraid of complaining in shops, first to dance at parties and so on. So how are we to establish that the 'psychological construct' of extraversion is a scientifically valid one?" (Coolican (1994:41))

Some of the evaluated parameters measured in various studies on ECAs can be considered psychological constructs. Ruttkay et al. (2002) mention 'trust' which can be considered a psychological construct. Variables mentioned in this overview that are not a construct are eye gaze or turn taking. These phenomena often can be measured *directly* without operationalising although it is wise to define them as well.

4.   Research Strategy

The *research strategy* of a study concerns identifying the way one conducts research. Several basic research strategies can be identified when answering the following questions (Verschuren and Doorewaard (1999)): are you aiming for breadth or depth of information? Do you need qualitative or quantitative data? And do you prefer empirical or desk research? A survey will deliver information in the breadth, whereas a case study delivers information in the depth. Information collected from focus groups or interviews is qualitative in nature, whereas the information collected by means of reaction time tasks is mostly quantative in nature. And every now and then it is likely that a review study will be published which is regarded as desk research in contrast to empirical research. Desk research uses existing literature or data sets and reviews it in a new perspective. A special form of desk research is the meta study in which a large number of articles and papers is reviewed and concluded upon. For example, Dehn and Van Mulken (2000) published a meta study on the impact of animated interface agents. One of their conclusions is that the results of the studies under review are hard to relate to each other as some of the studies appeared to have contrasting results and the methodologies adopted differ to a large extent.

Three research strategies will be looked at more closely as they seem to be most appropriate for the evaluation of ECAs. These strategies are: *survey, experiment* and *case study*. Referring back to the stages of development of an ECA one could say that the survey and experiment are most suitable for evaluating the ECA that is in the final stages of development. The case study is more appropriate for evaluating the conceptual design of an ECA or earlier stages of development.

4.1 Survey

The goal of a *survey* is to collect information from a sample of participants in order to obtain a good picture of the total population referred to in the research question. So one wants to collect information in the *breadth* and one will *randomly* sample a *large number* of participants. This will normally guarantee that the results can be *generalized* towards the population. As the number of participants is rather large, the data collection method is *labor extensive*, that is one uses for instance a questionnaire with mainly closed questions. There are three major techniques in survey research (Neale and Liebert (1986)): the distributed questionnaire, the phone survey and the interview. The distributed questionnaire is by far the most used data collection method in the survey strategy. In this case participants are invited (either by mail or in person or nowadays through the Internet) to complete a series of items concerning a topic. The major disadvantage of this approach is that self-selection can easily bias the results as the non-response group can become rather large. One possibility is that only those participants that are favourable towards a specific type of ECA fill in the questionnaire; the others do not respond. A survey has the following characteristics:

- Large number of participants (more than 50) participate.

- Participants are randomly selected.

- Data collection methods are used that require not much labour, such as a questionnaire.

- Quantitative data analysis is most appropriate for the collected data.

4.2   Experiment

An *experiment* aims at identifying a causal relationship. For instance, inclusion of a particular ECA (the intervention) in an interface changes the attitude and behaviour of participants compared to an environment without the agent. The conditions for conducting a true experiment are:

- Having an experimental and a control condition.

- Random assignment of participants to conditions.

- The experimenter decides which condition is the experimental one (not the participants).

- All other circumstances equal except for intervention.

Ideally, one should also have pre-intervention tests to measure the baseline and afterwards another equivalent test if one wants to know the effect size of the intervention. When one wants to justify a causal relationship, one should take special care in setting up the study. Confounding factors might bias the results of an experiment. They can originate from the participants being studied (e.g., self-selection: maybe only those participants that are positive towards the ECA want to participate; Hawthorne effect: improvement of a process because of being observed; time-on-task: the amount of time spent working with the ECA could have an effect; social desired behaviour: answering the questions in a socially desired way) or the experimenter testing the participants (self-fulfilling prophecy: the experimenter (unconsciously) strives to fulfil his own hypotheses; interpretation bias: consequently wrongly interpreting certain data sets). One example of an experiment is given in the study conducted by Krahmer et al. (2003). This study investigates whether facial expressiveness can contribute to the perception of extraversion, see Table 3.1. Their hypothesis is that the presence of eyebrow movements (the intervention) will be associated with extraversion, while the absence of such movements (control group) indicates introversion. In fact, this study covers eight conditions, as the introversion and extraversion conditions of gaze and speech are included as well. The 'control' group or baseline concerns the condition in which all personality cues are introvert. Most often, a control group is the group that receives

Table 3.1.   Fulfilment of the conditions for an experiment by Krahmer et al. (2003).

Condition	Fulfilment in Krahmer et al. (2003)
Having an experimental and control condition	Eight experimental conditions
Random assignment to conditions	24 participants randomly assigned
Experimenter decides experimental condition	Not reported upon
All the other circumstances equal	Each talking head utters a similar phrase of poem. The eight different animations are administered in one go. Two (random) orders of the animations are created. Participants work individually and self-paced watching and listening to the animations as often as desired.

no 'experimental treatment' or intervention. However, the issue for an experiment is that one needs a baseline to measure against. In this case the conditions are contrasted with condition eight in which all personality cues are introvert. The control or baseline group follows from the hypotheses formulated concerning the research question.

4.3   Case Study

A *case study* is appropriate for collecting information in the depth about a specific phenomenon. The data collected will be mostly qualitative in nature. The characteristics of a case study are:

- Small number of participants (eight or less).

- Labour intensive data collection methods such as observation, interviews.

- Qualitative data analysis.

- Deliberate selection of participants.

The main advantage of a case study is that detailed information about a specific phenomenon becomes available and one is able to further investigate peculiarities that arise during the study as one goes along. It is the most flexible research strategy. The downside of this flexibility is that it is hard, if not impossible to generalise the results to the population and that data collection is labour intensive. For example, scoring video material is a cumbersome task. Examples of a case study can be found in Chapter 5.

Table 3.2. Overview of match between research strategies and data collection methods.

Data collection method	Survey	Experiment	Case study
Questionnaire	Yes	Yes	
Interview	Yes		Yes
Observation		Yes	Yes
Log files		Yes	
Biological measures		Yes	

5.   Data Collection Methods

The research strategy chosen restricts to a large extent the actual *data collection method* to employ. A questionnaire is mainly used in experiments and surveys, whereas observation is typically suitable for collecting data in a case study. Table 3.2 gives an impression of which data collection methods are mainly used in each research strategy. This should not be understood as restrictive, it all depends on the actual research question.

Triangulation yields the most informative data. Triangulation is concerned with using a combination of data collection methods for example using a questionnaire, an observation protocol and an interview technique in one study. This way, the validity of the data can be examined and improved.

The data collection methods are either *qualitative* or *quantitative* in nature. Qualitative data collection methods predominantly deliver data that is qualitative in nature, that is not numeric. Qualitative data is descriptive data on a nominal level of measurement (nominal data can be divided into different categories, for example male, female (participant) or positive and negative remarks). It can be written down as in transcripts or consist of visual material like photographs. For example, typical qualitative methods are: the open interview or the free format observation. An open interview generates a transcript of the opinion of a user about a specific feature of an ECA. Free format observation generates remarks about peculiarities in user behaviour while interacting with an ECA. These peculiarities can be divided into several distinct categories. Quantitative data collection methods predominantly deliver data that is numeric in nature. Quantitative data consist of numbers and is measured on ordinal (data have a natural sequence), interval (data can be rank ordered with equal intervals) or ratio level (data have an absolute zero value). However, a qualitative data collection method can generate quantitative results as well, for example, the various opinions of users on an interview with open questions can be transformed to numerical data, usually by counting the answers and creating frequency distributions. According to the level of measurement you can perform descriptive or inferential statistics on your data.

5.1 Qualitative Methods

5.1.1 Interview and Focus Groups

The *interview* is a data collection method that mainly delivers qualitative data, as it concerns opinions and attitudes of people. A *focus group* is a special type of interview; in this case it is an interview conducted with a group of people. A moderator leads the discussion. Normally, the focus group is semi-structured; some open questions are formulated beforehand, but during the interview the moderator is free to embark on specific topics not specified beforehand. When it concerns an application that is in the conceptual design phase, usually parts of the system (either on PC or on paper) are shown to the participants. It is important that participants can express their opinion about the application. Therefore it does not seem wise to have the developer moderate the discussion; this person is probably too much involved in the process of developing the agent. An assistant can make notes of all the remarks of participants and a video camera can be used in order to collect information.

5.1.2 Informal or Descriptive Observation

Informal observation produces qualitative data in the form of notes, pictures or sketches. For example, one can observe a person that is learning Italian from a language teacher and make notes of anything that seems interesting in terms of the research question. Later on these notes can be used to generate the requirements for the ECA that replaces the teacher. This is contrasted with systematic observation, which will be covered later in this section. Informal or descriptive observation is often performed in the early stages of research, for example, when conducting a pilot study, because it leads to more defined research questions and the development of appropriate methods to address those questions. Wilkinson nicely addresses the value of informal observation: "Observing a situation with relatively open eyes, ears and mind can provide valuable insights and yield information indispensable for subsequent decisions about the best location in which to make the observations and for developing the categories to be used in systematic observation. It is essential to make notes of casual observation, as first impressions are usually the most vivid and most useful when written down immediately." (Wilkinson (1995:216)).

A special form of informal observation is participant observation. As the name implies, participant observation means that the observer is part of the events being studied. The advantage of this approach is that enables access to possibly more private events, which participants would not allow an outsider to observe. The main criticisms of this technique are that it is impossible for the participant observer to be objective, and ethical problems play a role as normally the participants are not aware of the fact that they are observed (Wilkinson (1995)). It could also be problematic to collect data, as the observer has to find a way to do this without the participants noticing. More information about participant observation can be found in the work of Spradley (1980).

5.2   Quantitative Methods

5.2.1   Questionnaires   Useful advice of how to design *question-naires* is given by Mangione (1995). Broadly one can distinguish two types of questions: open ended and closed ones. Open-ended questions have no specific answering categories, participants can write down the answer in their own words. This generates qualitative data. The difficulty with analysing open-ended questions is that it takes time and a lot of interpretation and this interpretation can make the analyses less objective. Another issue is that participants often do not feel like writing down large amounts of text, therefore often producing less data than desired. Closed questions exist in many types and forms of which two formats will be shortly described here.

The *semantic differential* question format concerns describing the *quality* of an object. The question involves a series of opposite adjectives and the participant is to choose a number between the two extremes, that best describes his or her feelings. For example, Krahmer et al. (2003) report to measure the perceived personality in terms of introversion and extraversion by using 7-point semantic differential questions with five pairs of adjectives, see Table 3.3. The participant should judge the ECA on each of the five scales and choose which option best reflects the participants feeling towards the personality of the ECA.

Rating scales are very commonly used in questionnaires. A rating scale includes a list of alternatives that ranges from 'not much' of a particular quality to 'a great deal' of that particular quality. A special type of rating scale format questions is the Likert scale. The Likert scale measures the extent to which a person agrees or disagrees with the question. The most common (interval) scale is 1 to 5. Often the scale will be 1=strongly disagree, 2=disagree, 3=not sure, 4=agree, and 5=strongly

Table 3.3.   Example of the semantic differential question format adapted from Krahmer et al. (2003).

Introvert pole								Extravert pole
Shy	1	2	3	4	5	6	7	Enthusiastic
Inward	1	2	3	4	5	6	7	Outgoing
Bashful	1	2	3	4	5	6	7	Perky
Unrevealing	1	2	3	4	5	6	7	Open
Non-vivacious	1	2	3	4	5	6	7	Vivacious

agree. Mangione considers several factors to take into account when constructing rating scales:

- *Psychological distance* of answering options. The scale points should be formulated in such a way that the participants consider the distance between the answering options to be equal. Only then, the data generated by these questions can be said to be measured on the interval level instead of on the ordinal level, which implies one can use more powerful statistics.

- *Number of response alternatives.* Depending on the research question one can vary the number of response items. Normally it is between three and seven. There is a trade-off between the granularity of the answers and the time it takes the participants to answer all questions. Additionally one wants to give the participant ample 'room' for his or her opinion or judgement.

- *Odd versus even numbers* of choice. Taking an odd number of answering options results in a 'natural' middle point. This middle point could be the 'Average', 'Neutral' or 'Unsure' option. It is a trade-off between forcing participants to answer versus receiving less informative data.

Mangione also describes some guidelines for creating questions: write brief and clear brief questions (define key terms, don't use expert jargon and avoid double negatives), stay in touch with reality (do not assume too much and do not ask hypothetical questions), write unidimensional questions, use mutually exclusive response categories and create exhaustive categories and do not write loaded questions. And finally, pilot test the questionnaire. Distribute it to two or three participants that are member of the research population.

5.2.2   Systematic Observation   *Systematic observation* is defined as: creating a reduced image of reality that quantifies certain aspects of that reality according to specific rules (Van de Sande (1999)). In a nutshell this definition can be explained as follows. As reality is quite complex, observation or perception of this reality involves making a selection and therefore a reduction of this complex reality in order to study it. It is done according to specific rules so another investigator can replicate the results. The result of the observation is a conclusion with a quantitative character; for example, certain behaviour occurs more or less often.

Two main principles play a role in systematic observation: *selectivity* and *subjectivity* of the perception. Selectivity of perception is concerned with the fact that as reality is complex one cannot observe everything and therefore a selection has to be made. This is done by creating a so-called category system. A category system or ethogram is a schematic overview of different behavioural elements that are observed. When the construct extraversion is the subject of study, it can be operationalised and split in the following behavioural elements for example: pitch of speech (e.g. rated on a scale from 1 to 5), mobility of facial elements (e.g. rated on a scale from 1 to 5), and direction of the gaze (e.g. on screen, on experimenter, elsewhere). The behavioural elements are measured in terms of frequency, latency, intensity and or direction of the behaviour. Subjectivity of perception deals with the fact that the human being (namely the observer) is the measurement instrument. As each of us has a different reference framework and background this can bias the observation. For example, what one observer considers a smile could be considered a neutral expression by another observer. Additionally, random and systematic errors and errors of perception and of interpretation can blur the observation. Therefore subjectivity of perception should be minimized by performing a pilot study and discussing the behavioural elements and the scoring of them in order to use them in a systematic and objective way. Furthermore, one should always have more than one observer so the reliability of the data can be checked.

Two informative works on performing systematic observation are a course on how to perform observational research (Van de Sande (1999), Christoph and Van de Sande (1999)) and the software application fOCUS (Oates et al. (2000)) for the domain of observational research.

5.2.3   Log Files   *Log files* can be considered as an automatic data collection method. The system that is investigated can have some sort of data capturing module that automatically logs user behaviour. One can think of capturing the commands the user applies, or the navigation of the user through the system or the error logs that are generated. The advantages of using log files is that it requires not much labour to collect data and it is unobtrusive for the user as he or she will probably not notice it. This will touch upon ethical concerns, though. However, on the other hand the disadvantages are that one receives an overwhelming amount of data that should be analysed. When the data is on a low level (e.g. keystrokes) interpretation issues can play a role as well. For example, when one sees from the log files that a user takes quite some time at a specific point in the application, this user could have lost its way in the application, he or she is thinking through the next steps or perhaps this person is distracted? This has consequences for the interpretation and thus the validity of the data.

5.2.4   Heuristic Evaluation   A special form of a data collection method for evaluating an ECA is *heuristic evaluation* (Nielsen (1993)). Heuristic evaluation is concerned with testing the usability of a piece of software. During heuristic evaluation, a software expert reviews the ECA on a set of heuristics. Generally accepted usability heuristics are: learnability; efficiency; memorability; errors and satisfaction. Other frameworks or sets of guidelines exist as well in order to judge the usability of an application. Kabel et al. (1997) developed a framework based on the work of Norman (1986) with which user remarks can be easily elicited and categorised in meaningful categories so developers can more easily solve these problems. Therefore it is a data collection method that on the one hand helps the participant in articulating the problems he or she has with the application and on the other hand helps the developer in categorising and solving the problems.

5.2.5   Biological Measures   Another rather special data collection method in the field of evaluating ECAs is the use of biological or biomechanical measures such as heart rate or skin conductance. Mainly, these measurement are taken from participants with the purpose to have more *objective* data instead of solely using self-report questionnaires or observational techniques that can be prone to subjectivity of measurement. The underlying thought often is that participants could not actually report what they truly experience while working with the ECA and therefore is could be worthwhile to have more objective measures aside. In some ways this could be true, however, one should take special care with biomechanical measures especially to overtly formulate the supposed relationship between the construct one aims at measuring and the hypothised effect on the biomechanical measures including any alternative explanations. For instance, investigating the amount of stress induced by working with the ECA could generate results from a questionnaire that indicates that participants did not experience stress, whereas the biomechanical measures depict the opposite picture. But, the mere fact that participants were subjected to these biomechanical measures could have induced stress.

5.3   More Data Collection Methods

Concluding, the data collection methods discussed above are some of the methods to use in order to collect data. However, various other techniques can be considered for evaluating an embodied conversational agent as well such as the *cognitive walkthrough*, a *cart-sorting task*, or a *usability review* depending on the research question to be addressed. A nice overview of additional methods is presented at the website of Information and Design[1]. Another source of information for several convenient evaluation tools can be found at the Georgia Institute of Technology[2].

6.   Samples, Reliability and Validity

Having tackled the choice for an appropriate research design and data collection methods, one should consider the number of participants to select. On the one hand one can take constraints such as time, resources or practical issues into account to take this decision. On the other hand, one should fulfil the conditions of scientific research. Additionally, data should be reliable, that is repeatable, and valid.

6.1   Samples

Neale and Liebert (1986)insight in issues of sampling. A *sample* is a subset of a population and one should decide:

- *Which* participants should be included, and

- *how many* participants should be included in the study.

According to Neale and Liebert these questions can be answered in terms of *representativeness* and *variability*. The first question one should ask is whether it is vital for the study to aim for a representative sample of the population for the phenomena that one wants to study. When the issue of representativeness of the sample is at stake it is important to have samples that are not biased. "A sample is said to be biased when it is not representative of the population to which the investigator wishes to generalize." (Neale and Liebert, (1986:32)) How can one create a non-biased sample? By conducting random sampling, that is, every member of the population has equal chance to be selected in the sample and the selection of one participant does not change the chances of the others, the condition of representativeness of the sample can be fulfilled. Techniques for random sampling differ, one example is using random number tables.

Sometimes, think about using case studies, the issue of representativeness of participants is not a condition that one wants to fulfil. Verschuren and Doorewaard (1999) mention three strategies in this respect:

1 Choosing participants that differ minimally from each other.

2 Choosing participants that maximally differ on the main aspects of importance but that are maximally alike or equal in all other aspects.

3 Choosing participants one by one.

Each of these strategies has its benefits and pitfalls. When conducting an exploratory study it might be of use to choose participants who are quite similar to each other in order to generate hypotheses about the phenomena of study without being distracted by all kinds of variations. By choosing participants that differ maximally only with respect to the phenomena of study one can develop a broad view on the whole picture. Thirdly, one can start with choosing one participant and based upon the results of the first case study, one selects another participant and so on.

The concept of variability is of importance for determining the sample size. When studying a particular phenomenon the number of participants to include in the study depends on the variability of this phenomenon (or target variable). If the phenomenon has a large variation, then one needs to include more participants than when the phenomenon does not vary as much. A general rule is that the larger the sample, the more precise the estimate of the phenomenon of study of the population will be.

Reasoning from another perspective, one can consider the statistics one wants to apply to the data and take this as a starting point for deciding the sample size. Firstly, each (non)-parametric test comes with its own conditions. Parametric tests require that variables are measured on interval or ratio level and (most of the time) the samples should be distributed normally. Nonparametric tests are used when these conditions cannot be fulfilled. Nonparametric tests are based on the rank orders of the data and in general these types of tests are less powerful than parametric tests. Less powerful in this sense signifies that the chance not to reject a hypothesis that should have been rejected, is larger.

For example, it is acceptable to use the parametric Students t-test for comparing means when one can comply with the condition of normality (that is, the variable is normally distributed in the population) *or* the sample size is larger than 30 participants in each condition. So the choice one should make in advance about which statistics to use does have an impact on the number of participants to select.

One can actually calculate the sample size by using the power of a specific statistical test. The power is concerned with the probability of rejecting a false null hypothesis which is computed by using a specific significance level (alpha) and a particular effect size. The formula for calculating the sample size depends on the actual test one wants to use (cf. Triola (2002)). An overview of available software for calculating the sample size can be found on the Internet[3] and a user-friendly software program that can do this is GPower[4] Erdfelder et al. (1996). For example, when performing a Student's t-test (two-tailed) for comparing two means taking into consideration an alpha of 0.05, a power of 0.95 and an effect size (estimated effect) of 0.5 the total number of participants should be 210 (105 in each group).

6.2   Reliability

The first and foremost condition for data is that they are *reliable*. Reliable data are data that are *true*, meaning *repeatable* or *reproducible*. In essence, a data collection method, such as a questionnaire or an observation carried out by a human observer, should generate reliable data, that is, when conducting the study again and using the same data collection method under the exact same condition, one should find similar results. There are various ways of testing the reliability of data, depending on the data collection method used. The following procedures are briefly discussed here (Neale and Liebert (1986)): test-retest reliability, interitem reliability, interrater reliability and item sampling.

6.2.1   Test-retest Reliability   One possible way of testing whether a data collection method such as a questionnaire delivers reliable data is to collect the data twice, under the same circumstance. The questionnaire is distributed to the participants and some time later the questionnaire is distributed again under the same conditions and to the same participants. The questionnaire is said to be reliable when both data sets are highly correlated. The scores are then stable. Neale and Liebert (1986) however do say that the absolute test scores of the first and second session need not be the same. Test scores should be *relatively* identical. Figure 3.4 demonstrates this.

In case I the participants obtain the same scores during the retest. In this case the scores are reliable as they are interchangeable between the test sessions. In the second case the participants obtain higher scores during the retest session, however, the relative distance to each other

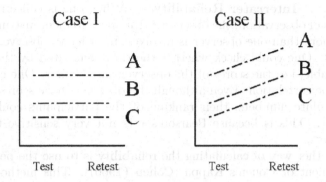

Figure 3.4. Hypothetical data for two possible sets of test-retest scores for three groups of participants adapted from Neale and Liebert (1986).

stays the same. So, although the participants have possibly learned something (and therefore have obtained higher scores during the retest session) the relative distance to each other has stayed the same and therefore the scores are still interchangeable between sessions. In both cases the reliability is perfect.

One can check the test-retest reliability by calculating the correlation, which should be as high as possible. Pearson's correlation coefficient or Spearman's rho (see Guilford and Fruchter (1978) or Howel (1982) for an overview) can be used to do this depending on the measurement scale of the data (respectively interval or higher level or ordinal level).

6.2.2   Interitem Reliability   The *interitem reliability* is concerned with creating in some way 'two halves' of the test and calculating a correlation. This way of testing the reliability of for example a questionnaire does not require two or more distributions of the test. One can use the split-half procedure. For example, one way of doing this is to split up a questionnaire in odd and even items and to calculate the correlation between them. When one finds a high correlation, one could say the test scores are reliable or internally consistent. One can calculate the interitem reliability by means of the split-half procedure or Cronbach's Alpha (Cronbach (1951)). The split-half test actually calculates the correlation between two halves of the test. Cronbach's alpha is a coefficient that describes how well a group of items focuses on a single idea or construct, this is called inter item consistency. Alpha assumes that there is only one construct being measured. Usually an alpha of 0.65 or higher is considered sufficient.

6.2.3   Interrater Reliability   When one is collecting data by means of observation, the observer is the measurement instrument. Usually more than one observer is involved in order to observe the participants. One could check whether the data generated by the observers is reliable, i.e. the scores of the observers are similar. One could calculate the correlation. Even although the observers have scores differently in absolute numbers, their ranking of the participants could be quite similar. This is because Pearson's r is not very sensitive to absolute numbers.

Another way of calculating the reliability is to use the percentage of agreement or Cohen's Kappa (Cohen (1960)). This method does not use the relative ranking but focusses on the exact scores and checks whether they are identical over observers. Cohen's kappa in fact uses the percentage agreement and corrects it for chance.

6.2.4   Item Sampling   Last but not least, *item sampling* is based on the fact that the reliability of a test increases when the number of items (such as questions in a questionnaire) increases. One should aim on the one hand for the full set of *potential* items in the test and on the other hand deal with time constraints of the test. Or putting it differently, in a questionnaire measuring a specific phenomenon one should aim for including all the potential questions concerning the phenomenon and take into account time and resources one has in order to administer the test.

6.3   Validity

Validity concerns the extent to which one measures those features that one intends to measure. Data can be reliable but not valid. For example, the study by Cowell and Stanney (2003) aims at finding out how the embodiment can alter the user's perception of an agent, specifically the trustworthiness of the agent. The authors use four questionnaires in their study of which two of them measure the construct 'Trustworthiness': the Agent Trust Survey (ATS), the Inter Personal Trust Survey (IPTS).

The question concerning the validity of the data collected in this study is whether these two questionnaires actually measure the construct 'Trustworthiness'. The first questionnaire is based upon the Rempel and Holmes trust scale (Rempel and Holmes (1986)), the second questionnaire is adapted from the behavioural model of inter personal trust (De Furia (1996)). One can aim at achieving valid results by using existing, generally accepted and validated instruments in order to measure the construct or one can take these as a starting point. If one decides to home-develop measurement instruments, a pilot study that includes not only the newly developed instrument, but also a standard measure, should give sufficient explanation about the validity of the results.

There are many ways of looking at the concept of validity and one can distinguish different types of validity, for example *internal* and *external validity*. Internal validity deals with the extent to which a study shows a cause-effect relationship between the independent and dependent variables. External validity is concerned with the question of whether the responses of the participants can be generalized to the target population or beyond that to any population of interest. A practical way of approaching this important concept is advocated by Van de Sande (1999) and Christoph and Van de Sande (1999) that is based on Campbell and Fiske (1959). One can consider data valid when:

1 The results of the measurements of the construct correspond with other measurements of the construct conducted with different measurement methods (convergent validity).

2 The results differ from measurements on another but related construct (divergent or discriminant validity.

6.3.1   **Convergent Validity**   *Convergent validity* is concerned with having a correspondence between the results of different measurement methods that all aim at measuring the same construct. This requires that the construct is well defined. For example, physiological measures such as skin conductance, heart rate, eye movements or muscle tension can be used in order to measure the construct 'nervousness'. The question then is whether an increased heart rate or more skin conductance actually denotes that a participant is more nervous than before (when heart rate and skin conductance were much lower). In order to assert this, one should at least have another source of data collected with a different measurement method (e.g. a questionnaire or interview in this case) that can be compared to the original measurement. By calculating the correlation one can draw a conclusion about the extent to which the data of the measurement methods correspond. When the correlation is high, one can say that the methods measure the same construct, in this case 'nervousness'. In this case the correlation between the data of the eye movements, questionnaire I and the interview should correlate highly in order to say that they all measure the construct 'nervousness' (see Figure 3.5).

6.3.2   **Divergent Validity**   Other constructs that are closely related to the one that is focus of the study can be measured accidentally (see Figure 3.5). In order to be sure that one did not accidentally

Construct

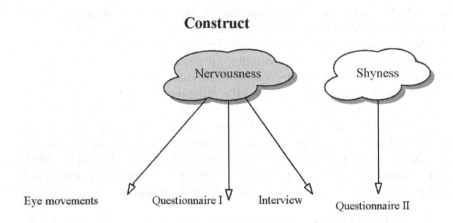

Figure 3.5.   Convergent and divergent validity illustrated.

measure another, closely related construct, one should create a data
collection method that aims at measuring this related construct. The
correlation between data from this method and the methods measuring
the initial construct (which is the *divergent validity*) should be low. In
this case, correlation between questionnaire II on the one hand and the
eye movements, questionnaire I and the interview on the other hand
should show a low correlation.

7.   Data Analysis

After having performed reliability and validity checks on the data collection, one can start analysing the data in order to come to conclusions. There are handbooks with the essentials of statistic procedures
(cf. Triola (2002); Johnson (1988), Neter, et al. (1990)) so here, merely
a short introduction is given.

Performing analyses on data can be done in two major ways. Firstly,
one can apply *descriptive statistics* on the data set. The purpose of
descriptive statistics is to present (quantitative) data in an orderly and
insightful manner. Descriptive statistics include summarizing data with
frequency tables, measures of the centre, variation and position and
presenting graphs. A frequency table depicts classes or categories of
values along with frequencies of the number of values that fall into each
class. Reasons for making frequency tables is this way one can effectively
show the distribution of the data over various categories. Measures of
the centre include the mean, mode and median. As Triola (2002) states,
there is no single best answer to the question which measure is best

for the centre. The different measures have different advantages and disadvantages. Depending on the skewness of the data set these measures vary. The mean is relatively stable. The standard deviation is a measure for the variation in the data set. It is one of the most important concepts in statistics. The higher the standard deviation, the more variation in the data and vice versa. Measures of the position include z-scores (converting values to standardised scales) and percentiles (quartile and deciles). These measures enable the comparison of different data sets or to compare values within one data set. Finally, various graphs can be used to depict data, such as, histograms, stem-and-leaf plots, pareto charts, pie charts and scatter diagrams. When it concerns qualitative data, then one could categorise, summarize and interpret the data. More information on analysing qualitative data can be found in Silverman (2000) or Berg (2001).

Secondly, one can apply *inferential statistics* on the data set. The purpose of applying these statistics to data is to make inferences and generalisations from the collected data to a bigger setting (the population). An overview of the main methods is given in Table 3.4. In order to give an example of using these statistics inferred from the Agneta and Frida study (see Chapter 5 by Höök), one could imagine a comparison of 20 participants surfing web pages *with* and 20 without Agneta and Frida. One measures the amount of time spent with the system (interval / ratio level). This results in a student's t-test if one fulfils the conditions for this test (random samples, samples are normally distributed *or* both contain at least 30 cases). If these conditions cannot be met, then one could use the Mann-Whitney test for ordinal data which is less powerful but requires less strict conditions. Should one have more than two independent samples (e.g. a third independent sample with system X), then analysis of variance is a useful technique.

Depending on the level of measurement of the data one can either apply parametric or non-parametric tests. The work of Mosteller and Rourke (1973) gives a good account of how to deal with non-parametric tests. Some words about the (non-)importance of *significant* results: the significance of a result (for example a correlation between two measures or the difference between a pre and a post test) describes the fact that a result does not appear by coincidence. Indeed, something seems to be happening, for example an ECA *does* have effect on the attitude of people. However, it is the effect size that is really important. A significant effect that is small, is often not of great practical interest. For instance, a significant correlation of r $= 0,20$ between two variables actually means that only 4% of the variance is explained by the variables.

	Nominal data	Ordinal data	Interval / ratio data
Comparing distributions			
Two independent samples	Chi square test	Mann-Whitney test	Student's t-test
Two dependent samples	Chi square test	Wilcoxon test	Paired t-test
More independent samples	Chi square test	Kruskal-Wallis test	Analysis of variance
Comparing theoretical distributions	Chi square test for one sample, binomial test	Kolmogorov-Smirnov test for one tample	
Associations between variables			
Associations between two variables	Chi square test and nominal measures of association	Spearman's rank order correlation, ordinal measures of association	Correlation and regression
Associations between more variables	Chi square test over sub groups		Partial correlation and multiple regressions

Table 3.4. Overview of (non-)parametric test procedures adapted from de Vocht (2002).

So even although the effect does not appear by coincidence, it is so small that one can wonder if it is of any importance.

In order to perform statistical procedures one could either use a spreadsheet program for simple calculations and for example STATDISK (2003) or the Statistical Package for the Social Sciences (SPSS (2002)) for more complex procedures. A useful guide for working with SPSS is written by Norusis (2002).

8.   Concluding: Guidelines for Evaluating ECAs

In this chapter an effort is made to make a crisp and sound but also practical account of how to evaluate ECAs and how to set up a proper study. To conclude this chapter several guidelines are added that one can keep in mind as a final help.

1 Create a research model that clearly describes the objectives of the study, the research question(s) and that gives insight in the main steps of how to answer the research question.

2 Identify and define the constructs and phenomena that are to be studied. By defining the constructs they are made concrete and measurable and it will help you in developing measurement methods.

3 Choose the right research strategy and accompanying data collection methods. Try to think, beforehand, of reasons why certain hypothetic results could be accounted for by (flaws in?) your research design.

4 Think about which participants should participate in your study and how to select them. Describe the population you want to select them from, and the selection procedure.

5 Check what statistics to use and what are the ideal numbers of participants in order to meet the criteria for (non) parametric tests to be conducted?

6 Perform counterchecks or, use triangulation. Measuring a phenomenon with three different data collection methods will help you gain insight in whether you are really measuring what you want (validity).

7 Pre-test your data collection methods. Do the participants understand your questionnaires and the concepts and terms that you use in them?

8 Create a 'code book' in which you make notes throughout the study about all the things you do and all the decisions you have to make. Also peculiarities that you notice during the study can be written down, they might help you later in explaining the results. Begin compiling data as you test.

9 Prepare the data input and analysis: know how you are going to present the data in your data files and which preliminary procedures such as reversing answers, to perform (keep an original!). Know how you are going to analyse the data in a statistics program.

10 Answer your research question. What is the (ultimate) conclusion and what are possible reasons for finding this result. And, (how) can you generalise? Also, if the results are unexpected, give several

hypotheses (either methodological or content-related) about what possibly could have influenced your research. Finally, what can future research clarify?

Acknowledgments

The author wishes to thank all the SWI students from the University of Amsterdam that during the years 2000 – 2003 followed the course 'Evaluation of interactive software applications' [EISS] for all the questions that they asked. The author also wishes to thank Wouter Jansweijer and Vanessa Evers for reviewing this chapter and Zsófi Ruttkay and Han Noot for the interesting discussions on the topic.

Notes

1. http://www.infodesign.com.au/ usabilityresources/default.asp
2. http://mime1.marc.gatech.edu/ MM_Tools/evaluation.html
3. http://www.insp.mx/dinf/stat_list.html
4. http://www.psycho.uni-duesseldorf.de/aap/projects/gpower/

References

Andersson, G., Höök, K., Mourão, D., Paiva, A., and Costa, M. (2002). Using a Wizard of Oz study to inform the design of SenToy. *Personal and ubiquitous computing*, 6(5-6): 378–389.

Berg, B.L. (2001). *Qualitative Research Methods for the Social Sciences*. Allyn and Bacon, Boston.

Boehm, B. (1988). *The spiral model of software development and enhancement. IEEE Computer*, 21(5): 61–72.

Buisine, S., Abrilian, S., Rendu, C., and Martin, J. (2002). Towards experimental specification and evaluation of lifelike multimodal behaviour. In *Proceedings of AAMAS 2002 workshop: Embodied conversational agents - let's specify and evaluate them!*, Bologna, Italy.

Campbell, D.T. and Fiske, D.W. (1959). Convergent and discriminant validation by the multi trait-multi method matrix. *Psychological Bulletin*, 56: 81–105.

Christoph, L.H. and Van de Sande, J.P. (1999). *Werkboek gedragsobservatie: systematisch observeren en The Observer [Workbook observing behaviour: systematic observation and The Observer]*. Wolters-Noordhoff, Groningen, The Netherlands.

Cohen, J.A. (1960). Coefficient of agreement for nominal scales. *Educational and Psychological measurement*, 20: 37–46.

Cronbach, L.J. (1951). Coefficient alpha and the internal structure of tests. *Psychometrika.*, 16: 297–334.

Coolican, H. (1994). *Research Methods and Statistics in Psychology.* Hodder and Stoughton, London.

Cowell, A.J. and Stanney, K.M. (2003). On manipulating nonverbal interaction style to increase anthropomorphic computer character credibility. In *Proceedings of AAMAS 2003 workshop: Embodied conversational characters as individuals*, Melbourne, Australia.

De Furia, G.L. (1996). *A behavioral model of interpersonal trust.* Unpublished Ph.D. thesis. St. John's University, Springfield, L.A., USA.

Dehn, D.M. and Van Mulken, S. (2000). The impact of animated interface agents: A review of empirical research. *Int. J. human-computer studies*, 52(1): 1–22.

Erdfelder, E., Faul, F., and Buchner, A. (1996). GPOWER: A general power analysis program. *Behavior Research Methods, Instruments, and Computers*, 28: 1–11.

Guilford, J.P. and Fruchter, B. (1978). Fundamental statistics in psychology and education. McGraw-Hill, New York.

Hix, D. and Harston, H.R. (1993). *Developing user interfaces: ensuring usability through product and process.* Wiley, New York, USA.

Holm, R., Priglinger, M., Stauder, E., Volkert, J., and Wagner, R. (2002). Automatic data acquisition and visulatization for usability evaluation of virtual reality systems. In *Proceedings of Eurographics Short Presentations*, Saarbrücken, Germany.

Höök, K. (2002). Evaluation of affective interfaces. In *Proceedings of AAMAS 2002 workshop: Embodied conversational agents - let's specify and evaluate them!*, Bologna, Italy.

Howel, D.C. (1982). Statistical methods for psychology. Duxbury Press, Boston, Mass.

Johnson, R. (1988). *Elementary statistics.* PWS-kent publishing company, Boston.

Kabel, S., De Hoog, R., and Sandberg, J. (1997). *User interface evaluation and improvements: A framework and empirical results.* Internal report SWI-UVA.

Krahmer, E., van Buuren, S., Ruttkay, Zs., and Wesselink, W. (2003). Audio-visual personality cues for embodied agents; an experimental evaluation. In *Proceedings of AAMAS 2003 workshop: Embodied conversational characters as individuals*, Melbourne, Australia.

Mangione, T.W. (1995). *Mail surveys: Improving the quality.* SAGE publications, Thousand Oakes, CA.

Morishima, S. and Nakamura, S. (2002). Multi-modal translation and evaluation of lip-synchronization using noise added voice. In *Proceedings of AAMAS 2002 workshop: Embodied conversational agents - let's specify and evaluate them!*, Bologna, Italy.

Mosteller, F. and Rourke, R.E.K. (1973). *Sturdy statistics: Nonparametrics and order statistics.* Addison-Wesley, Massachusetts.

Moundridou, M. and Virvou, M. (2002). Evaluating the persona effect on an interface agent in an intelligent tutoring system. *Journal of computer assisted learning,* 18(3): 253–261.

Neter, J., Wasserman, W., and Kutner, M.H. (1990). *Applied linear statistical models: regression, analysis of variance and experimental design.* Irwin, Boston.

Neale, J.M. and Liebert, R.M (1986). *Science and behavior. An introduction to methods of research.* Prentice Hall International editions, New York.

Norman, D.A. (1986). Cognitive engineering. In, Norman, D.A. and Draper, S., editors. *User Centered Systems Design: new perspectives on human-computer interaction,* pp. 31–61, Erlbaum Associates, Hillsdale, NJ.

Nielsen, J. (1993). Usability engineering. Morgan Kaufmann, San Francisco.

Norusis, M.J. (2002). *SPSS 11.0, guide to data analysis.* Prentice Hall, New Jersey.

Oates, J., Gove, J., Goudge, A., Hill, R., Littleton, K., Christoph, L.H., Edwards, N., Gardner, R., Grayson, A., and Manners, P. (2000). *fO-CUS: a CD-ROM based application for developing observation skills.* Winner of the European Academic Software Awards (EASA), November 2000, Rotterdam, The Netherlands.

Preece, J., Rogers, R., Sharp, H., Benyon, D., Holland, S., and Carey, T. (1994). *Human-computer interaction.* Addison-Wesley, England.

Reeves, T.C. and Hedberg, J.G. (2003). *Interactive learning systems evaluation,* Educational Technology Publications, Englewood Cliffs, NJ.

Rempel, J.K. and Holmes, J.G. (1986). How do I trust thee. *Psychology Today,* 20: 28–34.

Ruttkay, Zs., Dormann, C., and Noot, H. (2002). Evaluating ECAs — what and how?. In *Proceedings of AAMAS 2002 workshop: Embodied conversational agents - let's specify and evaluate them!,* Bologna, Italy.

Sande, J.P., van de (1999). *Gedragsobservatie: een inleiding tot systematisch observeren [Observing behaviour: an introduction to systematic observation].* Wolters-Noordhoff, Groningen, The Netherlands.

Silverman, D. (2000). *Doing qualitative research: a practical handbook.* SAGE publications, London.

Spradley, J.P. (1980). *Participant observation.* Holt Rinehart and Winston, New York.

SPSS Inc. (2002). SPSS version 11.0 for Windows. SPSS Inc., Chicago IL.

STATDISK (2003). STATDISK version 9.5 for Windows. Addison-Wesley, Boston.

Swanborn, P.G. (1997). *Basisboek social onderzoek [Handbook of social research].* Boom, Meppel, Amsterdam, The Netherlands.

Triola, M.F. (2002). *Essentials of statistics.* Addison-Wesley, Boston.

Verschuren, P. and Doorewaard, H. (1999). *Designing a research project.* Lemma, Utrecht, The Netherlands.

Vocht, de, A. (2002). *Basishandbook SPSS 11 voor Windows (Handbook SPSS 11 for Windows).* Bijleveld press, Utrecht, The Netherlands.

Wilkinson, J. (1995). Direct observation. In. G.M. Breakwell, S. Hammond, and C. Fife-Schaw (Eds). *Research methods in psychology.* London, Sage publications.

Xiao, J., Stasko, J. and Catrambone, R. (2002). Embodied conversational agents as a UI paradigm: a framework for evaluation. In *Proceedings of AAMAS 2002 workshop: Embodied conversational agents — let's specify and evaluate them!*, Bologna, Italy.

Chapter 4

EVALUATING USERS' REACTIONS TO HUMAN-LIKE INTERFACES

Prosodic and Paralinguistic Features as New Measures of User Satisfaction

Loredana Cerrato and Susanne Ekeklint

The appearance of things change according to the emotions, and thus we see magic and beauty in them, while the magic and beauty are really in ourselves.
—Kahil Gibran

Abstract   An increasing number of dialogue systems are deployed to provide public services in our everyday lives. They are becoming more service-minded and several of them provide different channels for interaction. The rationale is to make automatic services available in new environments and more attractive to use. From a developer perspective, this affects the complexity of the requirements elicitation activity, as new combinations and variations in end-user interaction need to be considered. The aim of our investigation is to propose new parameters and metrics to evaluate multimodal dialogue systems endowed with embodied conversational agents (ECAs). These new metrics focus on the users, rather than on the system. Our assumption is that the intentional use of prosodic variation and the production of communicative non-verbal behaviour by users can give an indication of their attitude towards the system and might also help to evaluate the users' overall experience of the interaction. To test our hypothesis we carried out analyses on different Swedish corpora of interactions between users and multimodal dialogue systems. We analysed the prosodic variation in the way the users ended their interactions with the system and we observed the production of non-verbal communicative expressions by users. Our study supports the idea that the observation of users' prosodic variation and production of communicative non-verbal behaviour during the interaction with dialogue systems could be used as an indication of whether or not the users are satisfied with the system performance.

Keywords: Conversational agents, evaluation, multimodal interface, non-verbal behaviour, communicative gestures, prosodic cues.

Z. Ruttkay and C. Pelachaud (eds.), From Brows to Trust, 101–124.
© *2004 Kluwer Academic Publishers. Printed in the Netherlands.*

1.   Evaluation of Dialogue Systems

The fact that evaluation plays a crucial role for speech and natural language applications is no surprise: several methods have in fact been proposed and used to perform different evaluation tests, both on component level and on system level (see McTear (2002)). However most of the methods have been developed to evaluate individual components. One example of this, is a standard way to evaluate speech recognition and language understanding modules: Given a certain input compare the actual output to the desired output. Many systems generates some kind of confidence scoring of recognized utterances (see Glass (1999); Lippman (1997)). Another example of a module that might be evaluated separately is the dialogue manager. As suggested by Danieli and Gerbino (1995), the total score for the dialogue systems robustness can be measured in terms of the dialogue manager's ability to perform both implicit and explicit recovery when the speech recognition or the language understanding unit fails.

Overall performance evaluation is carried out mainly to measure system performance in specific areas. This evaluation is significant only if a pre-defined baseline performance is available. The different baselines that have been proposed so far to evaluate dialogue systems are however mainly based on the performance of separate modules.

1.1   Evaluation of User's Satisfaction

User satisfaction is also an important measure to evaluate on a system. One of the more recent tools for evaluation of qualitative issues in spoken dialogue systems is PARADISE (presented in Walker and Littman (2000)). This method uses various parameters to calculate an estimation of user satisfaction. The PARADISE paradigm breaks down the term user satisfaction into costs and success - the goal is to maximize the success and minimize the costs. PARADISE takes into account several parameters when calculating user satisfaction, for example, counting number of rejects, cancels, time-outs and mean recognition score. Other things taken into account are number of turns, requests for help, barge-ins, elapsed time, etc. Rejects, for example, are the number of times that the recognizer cannot produce a result with enough confidence.

User satisfaction is a subjective metric, which depends on individual differences among users. Asking users to answer specific questions about how the interaction with the system went is not always the most appropriate way to evaluate user satisfaction. The judgments of the users can be influenced by many factors and moreover there are particular questions, which are difficult to formulate, such as whether the interface has influenced the users' feelings and expectations during the interaction. Furthermore there are the issues of costs, time and users' integrity. Even if the individual point of view of the users is very important for the aim of evaluation, it is often difficult to collect individual judgments and combine them with other component level based metrics in order to formulate generalizations in the final evaluation.

1.2 Evaluation Criteria for Multimodal Dialogue Systems

Being a relatively new field, the development of conversational multimodal dialogue systems lacks both specific evaluation tools and established sets of evaluation criteria (see Gibbon et al. (2000)). Usually for the evaluation of multimodal systems, evaluation methodologies used for the various sub-fields are applied, for instance speech recognition, speech synthesis, gesture recognition, evaluation of talking heads (see Massaro et al. (1998); Beskow (2003)).

The more modalities that are used in a system the more complex the evaluation of the individual components will be, since each component needs to collaborate with a larger number of components. The objectivity when looking at separate modules may also be influenced by other modules since one module's weakness may very well be saved by another module (see Carlson and Granström (1996)). For example if the speech recognizer is not good enough, a well working dialogue manager may fix some of the problems of the speech recognizer. The evaluation of multimodal dialogue systems endowed with embodied conversational agents (ECAs) seems to neglect the assessment of the benefits that agents can have on aspects such as entertainment, mental load and system efficiency (see Sanders and Scholtz (2000)) and in particular on the overall user satisfaction. Of course multimodal interactions with systems endowed with ECAs are hard to evaluate for many reasons, mainly because they are difficult to record under normalised and easily reproducible conditions, and because they are highly dependent on user behaviour.

Our idea is to focus more on the users' points of view, without necessarily needing to submit the users a questionnaire after the interaction has been accomplished. We suppose that some new parameters for the evaluation of user satisfaction can be found in the prosodic and non-verbal side of speech communication. With a futuristic view in mind, we hypothesise the possibility of using some prosodic cues and non-verbal communicative behaviour as 'on-line' help for the system itself to evaluate how the interaction is going. Our method does not aim at providing an overall evaluation for dialogue systems, but it proposes to exploit prosodic information and non-verbal communicative behaviour as a complement to other traditional subjective and modular evaluation methods. The reasons for the degree of user's satisfaction will not be given by the measurements we are looking for, but we believe that these measurements could be useful to point out when something does not go as well as expected during the interaction.

2.   Prosodic Cues and Non-verbal Behaviour as new Evaluation Measures

Prosodic cues and non-verbal communicative behaviour are both features that make human communication natural. Researchers from different fields are therefore trying to capture this naturalness in order to reproduce it in ECAs. To do so they first look at how human beings communicate with each other, trying to infer prosodic models and non-verbal communicative models to reproduce into ECAs (see Thórisson (1997); Poggi and Pelachaud (1999); Cerrato and Skhiri (2003)).

Studying human behaviour in communicative interactions is essential both to improve the naturalness and the expressiveness of ECAs and to develop more natural interaction-based systems. However defining what is meant by 'natural' in the field of human-machine interaction is quite a hard task. The interpretation of the concept of naturalness is very subjective and, to our knowledge, there are no empirical studies that have tried to investigate what the users consider being 'a natural ECA' and 'a natural interaction with an ECA'. What we mean by natural interaction refers to whether or not the users feel at ease while interacting with an ECA. This condition of 'feeling at ease' can depend on many factors and it is not necessarily correlated to the quantitative measures used for evaluation (success of the task, number of turns, word error rate etc.); it might also be influenced by the visual realism of the ECA, by the emotional condition of the user, by the particular interest or how familiar the user is with machine interaction, by the topic of the interaction and so on.

Our assumption is that when users feel at ease interacting with a multimodal dialogue system, they tend to behave more naturally, which results in the production of prosodic variation and communicative gestures.

There are several prosodic and communicative non-verbal behaviours, which can be taken into account when analysing human-machine interactions. However, to remain realistic, we have limited our analysis to prosodic variations, which are rather easy to detect automatically (variations in F0 contours) and communicative gestures, such as head nods and facial displays produced to signal feedback and turn taking. These features are all likely to be modelled and improved on ECAs in the near future. Prosodic variation and communicative non-verbal behaviour, such as facial expression and body postures, are also the main physical means by which emotional states are typically expressed.

2.1 Prosodic and Visual Cues of Emotions

Prosody in a traditional way consists of a series of suprasegmental variations of the speech signal correlated with stress, prominence, timing, and phrasing. Prosody not only gives information on the syntactic structure of the uttered speech, but also plays a significant role in signalling emotions. Studies on how to reproduce the acoustic correlates of simulated emotions in speech synthesis have shown for instance that variation in pitch and tempo can be used to reproduce sadness and surprise. Whereas the reproduction of happiness and anger can use acoustic properties, such as spectral balance and vocal tract characteristics (see Montero et al. (2002); Mitchell (2000)). Prosody and emotions also have visual correlates. For instance, F0 rises are often accompanied by eye brow rises (see Cave et al. (1996); Graf et al. (2002)), stressed syllables are often punctuated by a head movement and the visual correlates of vowel-articulations can be affected in different ways by the emotion expressed (see Nordstrand et al. (2003)).

2.2 Prosodic and Visual Cues of Emotions and Evaluation

Prosodic and visual correlates of emotional speech can therefore also be used as cues to the emotional state of users of dialogue systems. The physiological correlates of emotions have been studied by Ekman whose results show that there are some basic emotions (happiness, sadness, fear, disgust, surprise and anger) each of which seems to have its own set of unique facial muscle pattern movement. The basic emotions are expected to have universal common patterns even if variability can occur across speakers (see Ekman (1993)). For this reason it seems possible to model these common patterns in the development of ECAs (see Pelachaud et al. (1996); Massaro (2000); Fabri et al. (2000)). The prosodic and visual correlates of emotions can be very interesting cues to be taken into account also in the evaluation of user interactions with ECAs. The emotional state of the users might play a relevant role in the course of interaction with ECAs. For this reason it would be useful to provide ECAs with the ability not only to express emotions, but also to perceive and reason about communicative situations in terms of the emotions they raise. The capability to make a cognitive assessment of a communicative situation on the basis of physical expressions of emotion could give the system the ability to decide how to react to a given emotional state of the user in terms of which emotions to express and which dialogue strategy to use (see Picard (1997)).

3.   The Investigation

The aim of our investigation is to propose new parameters and metrics related to the users of multimodal dialogue systems endowed with ECAs. We believe that these parameters can be found in the prosodic cues and in the non-verbal communicative behaviour of the users during the interaction.

To test our hypothesis we carried out analyses on different multimodal corpora of interactions between users and multimodal dialogue systems. We analysed the way in which users ended their interactions with the system by carrying out an acoustic analysis of some prosodic cues of the final utterances and where possible observing the production of non-verbal communicative expressions by users. We also examined the physical manifestation of the emotional state of the users caused by the course of interaction. By observing behaviour, gestures, and body postures we tried to understand whether the users were engaged or unengaged in the interaction, whether they were bored or amused and whether they got irritated or frustrated during the interaction. However an in-depth analysis of the visual correlates of the users' emotional state is beyond the scope of our investigation. More detailed investigations aiming at analysing and reproducing objective visual correlates of emotional states in talking heads and aiming at providing technological baselines and methodologies for comparative evaluations of visual correlates of emotional speech in talking heads are being carried out in the framework of the European project PF-Star[1].

3.1   Material

To carry out our analysis we selected three corpora from available material previously collected for other research purposes by means of two experimental Swedish multimodal conversational dialogue systems: *August* and *Adapt*. Table 4.1 reports the number of users in each corpus.

3.1.1   The August System   The August system was developed for research purposes at CTT/KTH in 1998 (see Gustafson et al. (1999)). It was endowed with an ECA having a distinctive personality resembling

Table 4.1. Number of users in each corpus.

Corpus	Number of users
August corpus	274
Adapt corpus I	32
Adapt corpus II	6

the Swedish author August Strindberg. Figure 4.1 gives a snapshot of the August system interface. The system was placed at the Stockholm Cultural Centre, as part of the Cultural Capital of Europe 1998 program. The set-up environment was quite harsh in terms of acoustic conditions, in particular due to background noises produced by people visiting the centre and other technical equipment that were placed there. Users received no instructions about how to interact with the system however they were invited by the agent to try the system.This way they were induced by the agent to socialize with the system, rather than just seek for straightforward information. The users where recorded with a directional microphone that was placed in a metal grid box.

The system was able to give information about three different domains: KTH (the Royal Institute of Technology), the city of Stockholm and the life and work of the August Strindberg. The material collected consists of more than 10.000 utterances produced by 2685 users, all visitors at the Stockholm Cultural Centre. The material is quite heterogeneous,since it contains recordings from users of different ages, languages and background (see Bell and Gustafson (1999b)). Moreover a single user does not always carry out the interactions with the system individually: sometimes groups of users tries to interact with the system overlapping or alternating each other in the turns. Many of the recorded dialogues are quite short (less then 5 turns). From the material collected with the August system we selected a sub-corpus of 274 interactions among those that presented more than 5 turns in which the users did not overlap with each other. We will refer to this material as the *August corpus*.

3.1.2 The Adapt System The Adapt system is an experimental Swedish conversational multi-modal dialogue system developed at CTT/KTH in collaboration with Telia Research (Gustafson et al. (2000)). The system is endowed with an ECA that is able to produce speech and gestures as output (see Beskow (2003); Beskow et al. (in press)). The ECA's name is Urban and he provides information about

Figure 4.1. Snapshot of the August system interface as reported by Beskow (2003).

apartments for sale in Stockholm. Figure 4.2 presents a snapshot of the Adapt system interface. The dialogues collected with the Adapt system can be described as information browsing since the users were instructed to ask for information about apartments for sale in Stockholm. Two major data collections were conducted with the Adapt system.

The first collection of data with a prototype of the Adapt system was performed in 1999 by means of the Wizard of Oz technique. The aim of this first collection was to obtain data for an evaluation of the system under development. This data includes a total of 50 dialogues produced by 33 users. From this collection we selected 32 dialogues. We will refer to this material as the *Adapt corpus I.*

In 2002 a second collection of interaction between 24 users and the Adapt system was carried out (see Edlund and Nordstrand (2002)). This time the users were also video-recorded, both when listening to the instructions given by the test leader and when interacting whit the system. One of the main aims of this further collection was to obtain materials for an evaluation of 3 different set-ups of the system using the PAR-

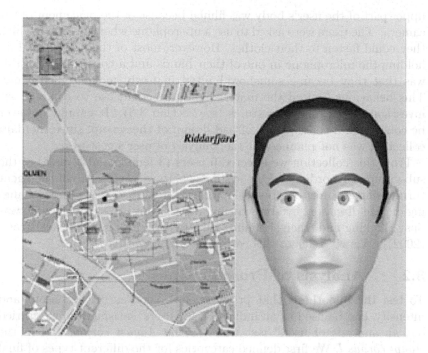

Figure 4.2. Snapshot of the Adapt system interface as reported by Beskow (2003).

ADISE paradigm, the evaluation is presented by Hjalmarsson (2002)). The users were divided in 3 sub-groups; each sub-group interacted with a different set-up of the Adapt system for half an hour. The three different set-ups were characterized respectively by:

- presence of the agent turn-taking gestures;

- absence of the agent turn-taking gestures;

- absence of the agent turn-taking gestures and presence of an hour-glass icon to signal when the system was busy.

The users were instructed to look for information related to apartments for sale in Stockholm that they would have an interest in. After half an hour the test leader interrupted them. For this reason we could not use this material to analyse how users ended their interaction, but thanks to the video-recordings of the interactions we could analyse the non-verbal behaviours of the users. The users were sitting in front of the computer screen and behind the screen a video-camera was attached. Only the upper part of the user's body was filmed because of the placement of the camera. The users were asked to use a microphone when speaking, which they could fasten to their clothes. However, most of the users ended up holding the microphone in one of their hands and a consequence of this was that they became somehow limited in freely moving their hand. This behaviour limited the material that we could use to conduct our investigations on bodily gestures (see section 3.3). It cannot however be considered a consequence of bad design of the set-up, since the data collection was not planned for the analysis of user's gestures.

From this collection we selected 6 users (3 female and 3 male) of the sub-group of recordings of the system set-up with presence of the agent turn-taking gestures. In this set-up the agent used some gestures (changing of gaze direction, eye-brow rising, head tilting) to show when he was busy thinking and when signalling turn-taking (Edlund and Nordstrand (2002)). We will refer to this corpus as *Adapt corpus II*.

3.2   Analysis of Prosodic Cues

To test the hypothesis that prosodic cues, such as pitch contour and intensity, can be used as an indication for users' satisfaction, we carried out an analysis of users' last turns in the *August corpus* and in the *Adapt corpus I*. We first defined categories for the different types of final utterances and then we carried out an acoustic analysis of pitch contour and intensity of some of the words included in the final utterances.

3.2.1   August Corpus   For the August corpus we started by categorising the final utterances using the typology proposed by Bell and Gustafson (1999a). They suggest a grouping of the utterances in the August database into two main categories: socializing and information seeking. To these two main categories they added subcategories which are reported in Table 4.2.

Table 4.2.   Utterance typology proposed by Bell and Gustafson (1999a).

Socializing	Information seeking
Social	Domain
Insult	Meta
Tests	Facts

Bell and Gustafson divided the socializing type of utterances into social, insult and test. They explain that the social category includes greetings and remarks of a social kind while the insult category consists of negative comments and swearwords. The test category on the other hand consists of utterances produced with the intention of testing the system.

The distribution of the last users' turns in our August corpus is reported in Figure 4.3. The majority of final utterances have been categorised as social. Also in the whole August database a great number of utterances were categorised as social and Bell and Gustafson explained this result by the existence of the animated agent, an explanation that we support.

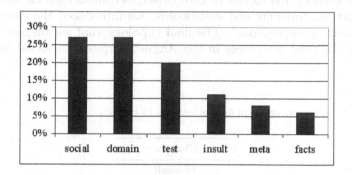

Figure 4.3. Distribution of the last utterance in the August corpus, according to Bell and Gustafsson's typology given in Table 4.2.

The number of final utterances that fall under the categorisation of socializing (social, test, insult) is quite high, as reported in Figure 4.3. The sub-categorisation of socializing utterances proposed by Bell and Gustafson however does not completely serve our purpose of analysing the final utterances, since it was intended to describe all the utterances in the database. For a categorisation of final utterances we thought it could be appropriate to take into account the notion of conventional closures, as presented by Schegloff and Sacks (1977). A conventional closure is expected to appear at the end of a spoken interaction between humans. A goodbye, a thank you or some other kind of courtesy expressions such as "it has been nice talking to you", can be considered conventional closures.

Results in support of the idea that people apply politeness norms when interacting with text-based computers have been previously shown by Nass and Moon (1996). As a consequence it can be assumed that humans interacting with dialogue systems (and in particular with dialogue systems featuring embodied conversational agents) also would end their interactions with conventional closures. This has been supposed for instance in the Dialogue Act Tagging Scheme for Evaluation of

Spoken Dialogue Systems -DATE- (see Walker and Passonneau (2001)). DATE uses ten categories to label speech acts. Among these, the opening/closing speech act category is intended for the categorisation of utterances that open and close the dialogues.

Analysing the August database we noticed that the dialogues did not always end with a conventional closure. In fact 35% of final utterances consisted of negative comments or even swearwords, which cannot be considered, in our opinion, as conventional closures. To group all those final utterances that cannot be categorised as conventional closures, such as negative comments and swearwords, we introduced the category of 'non-courtesy expressions'. The final typology that we suggest to categorise the final utterances in the August corpus is reported in Table 4.3.

Table 4.3.   Categorisations of final utterances in closures.

Closures
Farewell
Thanks
Courtesy expression
Non courtesy expression

Figure 4.4 reports the distribution of the socializing final utterances in the August corpus according to the sub-categories in Table 4.3.

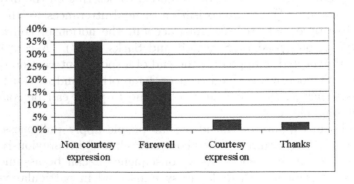

Figure 4.4.   Distribution of the subcategories of the socializing final utterance in the August corpus.

Many dialogues (39%) in the August corpus do not end with an utterance that we can consider a closure. We cannot judge if the turns categorised as non-closures depend on the user's choice of concluding the interaction without a closure or whether they are due to the alternation of users in the interactions or to some flaws in the recordings.

This categorisation of final utterances was carried out on the basis of lexical analysis. By this we simply mean that we categorised final utterances by looking at the words without taking eventual suprasegmental information given by the prosodic cues into account. For example when an utterance included the word "goodbye" we categorised this as a "farewell".

It is well known that by means of prosody, a different meaning can be given to an expression depending on the attitudinal intentions and the emotional state of the speaker. For instance a "goodbye" uttered with an ironic tone may imply that the user wishes to express his/her dissatisfaction with the interaction. We therefore performed an acoustic analysis of the final utterances to find the acoustical correlates that can be used for a deeper semantic interpretation. We used the software package *Wavesurfer* to analyse pitch contour intensity and duration of some of the words included in the final utterances (see Sjölander and Beskow (2000)).

We selected words from the farewell ("hej", "hej då") and thanks ("tack") groups. We noticed the following trends:

- a farewell or a thanks with a rising pitch contour is typical when the user has had a successful interaction with the system;

- a farewell or a thanks with a falling pitch contour is typical when the user has not had a successful interaction with the system, due to problem of reciprocal understanding or because the user was asking questions outside the domains;

- a thank you or a farewell with a higher intensity and longer duration (respect to the rest of the words in the utterance) were produced by some users who had not had a successful interaction with the system. These users, in our opinion sounded 'ironic'.

The results reported here seem to suggest that the human-like appearance of the agent induces users to have a more social behaviour towards the system. This is an important observation to support the idea that special evaluation methods are needed for multimodal conversational dialogue system. Even if it is difficult to propose a general typology for the categorization of final utterances, the results of our analysis show that there is a tendency among the users to end their interaction with the system with a conventional closure. A rising pitch contour can be noted as typical when the interaction when the system has proceeded without immense problems of mutual understanding.

3.2.2   Adapt Corpus I   When using the Bell and Gustafson typology to categorise the final utterances in the Adapt corpus we found that the utterances could be assigned to two categories only: social (63%) and domain (9%).

As in the August corpus, the majority of final utterances are categorized as socializing, but in the Adapt corpus there are no final turns consisting of insults. This is probably due to the fact that the majority of the interactions with the Adapt system went on in a positive way, that is, with just a few reciprocal misunderstandings, while in the August corpus many interactions went on in a problematic way because of problems with reciprocal understanding. Another explanation may be that the user of the August system were interacting with the system in a less controlled way compared to the user of the Adapt system, for this reason they probably felt the freedom of insulting the system at the end of a problematic interaction.

44% of the users of the Adapt system positively completed their task (i.e. finding the apartment they were interested in).

28% of the users could not find the apartment they were looking for (because there were no similar apartments in the system database), but they still managed to have an interaction without problems with the system. The fact that the users of the Adapt system never insulted the system at the end of the interaction can be seen as an indication of the fact that the interactions with the system went on without great problems of understanding.

For the remaining 28% of the users the final turns consist of an empty sound file. This can be both due to the personal choice of the users of not concluding the interaction using a conventional closing utterance or it might as well be due to some problems with the recordings.

The results of the sub-categorisation of the socialising final utterances in the Adapt corpus is reported in Figure 4.5. When we tried to use the closure typology proposed in Table 4.3 to sub-categorize the socializing final utterances in the Adapt corpus I, we realized that some final utterances could be assigned to more than one category, for instance an utterance like: "thank you and good bye" can be assigned both to the 'farewell' category and to the 'thanks' category. For these cases we need to add a 'joined category' such as 'thanks + farewell'.

An acoustic analysis of the expression 'adjö' in the farewell category, produced by 7 different users, was carried out to test our hypothesis that

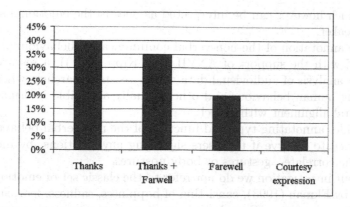

Figure 4.5. Distribution of the subcategories of social final utterances in the Adapt corpus I.

the users' intentional variation of pitch can be interpreted as a cue to how satisfied they were with the way the interaction with system went on. The results show that the 3 users that successfully completed their task pronounced 'adjö' with a rising pitch contour while those 4 users who did not get the information they required produced 'adjö' with a falling pitch contour. Falling pitch contour seems to be a typical characteristic of the farewell and thanks uttered by users whose interaction with the system did not proceed smoothly.

3.3 Analysis of Non-verbal Communicative Behaviour

To test the hypothesis that the production of non-verbal communicative behaviour can be used as an indication for users' satisfaction, we carried out an analysis of non-verbal communicative behaviour of the users of the Adapt system, *Adapt corpus II*.

By non-verbal communicative behaviour we refer to those gestures that users produced during the interaction with the system with a specific communicative intention, such as, giving or eliciting feedback, signaling turn-taking. The gestures we focused our attention on are:

- head movements (nods, jerks, waggles, side-way turns);

- facial expressions (eyebrow movements, gaze, smile).

Of course the users also produce other gestures such as shoulder shrugs, hand and trunk movements, not always with a communicative intention, but which however can be interpreted as cues to the emotional state of the speaker.

The annotation of the non-verbal communicative behaviour was performed with the support of ANVIL (see Kipp (2001)), a research tool for the analysis of audiovisual data which assists researchers when transcribing human behaviour and other visually accessible information in temporal alignment with speech.

Besides annotating type and function of the non-verbal behaviour we also tried to observe if the users signalling any emotions, by means of acoustic correlates, gestures or body postures.

In our investigation we do not refer to the classic set of emotions proposed by Ekman (1993), consisting of happiness, sadness, fear, surprise, disgust and anger. We only use emotions (or emotional expressions) that we consider likely to arise during the course of interacting with the system that we looked at (Adapt corpus II).

We believe that each user has a neutral emotion by 'default' when starting the interaction with the system. The course of the interaction with the system may trigger other emotions. As a consequence the user might show some facial expressions that communicate boredom, tiredness, amusement, irritation, frustration.

It might be argued that the number of communicative gestures that a speaker produces is highly dependent on the personal keenness to gesture production. The only way to verify this is to have some kind of baseline measurement of the user's gesture production in human-human communication. Unfortunately we did not have recordings of the users in everyday human-human communication, but we had the video-recordings of the users listening to the test leader's instructions before the actual interaction with the system started.

During the reading of the instructions, which lasted between 4 and 5 minutes, all the users showed an 'active listening attitude', which means that they gave verbal and non-verbal feedback to the person that gave them instructions. Their communicative gestures consisted of head nods, jerks and smiles with the function of giving feedback. Table 4.4 reports the total number of communicative gestures produced during the instruction phase, mapped against the number of gestures produced during the interaction with the system. The numbers in the Table 4.4 show that all users produce more gestures while listening to the test leader reading than when interacting with the system. It also needs to be added, that while the interaction with the test leader lasted between 4 and 5 minutes, the interaction with the system lasted between 25 and 30 minutes. The number of communicative gestures produced by the subjects during the interaction with the test leader therefore does not seem to be correlated with the number of communicative gestures produced during the interaction with the system.

Table 4.4. Number of communicative gestures in Human-Human and Human-Machine interactions for each Subject.

	$S11$ male	$S12$ female	$S13$ female	$S16$ male	$S08$ male	$S22$ female
Feedback & turntaking gestures in H-H	14	17	20	16	20	11
Feedback & turntaking gestures in H-M	6	0	4	0	2	3

Except for user $S11$ the number of communicative gestures during the interaction with the system is very low, and in two cases null. In order to better interpret our results we correlated them to a measure of user satisfaction, based on a data collection performed by Hjalmarsson (2002) on the same material.

Hjalmarsson carried out an evaluation of the Adapt system using the PARADISE paradigm (see Walker and Littman (2000)). The data for the users satisfaction measure were collected by means of a user survey based on the questions proposed in the PARADISE paradigm (see appendix in Hjalmarsson (2002)). The questions concern the evaluation of TTS Performance, ASR Performance, Task Ease, User Expertise, System Response, Expected Behaviour and Future Use. Two extra questions were added, with the attention to capture the multimodal features of the Adapt System:

- Did you benefit from the graphical interface in getting the information you wanted?

- How did you like the graphical interface?

Furthermore four specific questions were added in the questionnaire to obtain users' ratings of the different set-ups of the dialogue system ADAPT. Since we only used material from one set-up of the system (the one with the agent's turn-taking gestures), we did not find it necessary for our purposes to take all four questions into account, therefore we only kept the following one:

- Did you think that the interaction with the system worked smoothly?

The answer to this question, in our opinion, can be seen as a general indication of the user's point of view on how the interaction with the system went on. In total we had 10 questions. All question responses ranged from the value "no, almost never" to "yes, almost always". Each response was mapped to an integer (from 1 to 5) so that the final measure of user satisfaction would be given by a number ranging between 10 and 50: the higher the number, the more satisfied the user.

While in PARADISE a questionnaire was completed after each task, in the Adapt survey the users filled in just one questionnaire at the end of their interaction. For this reason Hjalmarsson (2002) states that the user satisfaction in her survey can be considered as an overall evaluation of the dialogue and cannot be associated with a specific task.

Table 4.5 shows for each user the number of communicative gestures mapped against the measure of user satisfaction and in particular against the answer given to the last question: *Did you think that the interaction with the system worked smoothly?* None of the users seem to have liked the interaction very much and in particular *S*08 did not seem to have liked it at all. He is in fact the one who has the lowest score on the last question and one of the lowest user satisfaction scores. Under the course of the interaction with the system this user appears quite irritated when the system does not reply to his requests. The user satisfaction score shows cross-gender differences: female users gave higher scores than male users.

Table 4.5. Number of communicative gestures for each user, mapped against the measure of user satisfaction, the answer given to the last question and the emotional state of the user.

	*S*08 male	*S*16 male	*S*11 male	*S*12 female	*S*22 female	*S*13 female
User satisfaction score	20	23	26	27	30	31
Last question score	1	2	2	3	3	3
Feedback & turn-taking gestures in H-M	2	0	6	0	3	4
Dominant signalled emotional state	irritated	bored un-engaged	engaged	tense frus-trated	Engaged at the beginning, tired towards the end	Engaged at the beginning, neutral afterwards

With the exception of user $S11$ who produces 6 turn-taking gestures, consisting of eye-brow raising and a little head nod at the end of the uttered request to Urban, the communicative gestures produced during the interactions by the other users are very few, if any. If we ought to interpret this result according to our hypothesis we should conclude that given the low number of communicative gesture produced, none of the users had a natural interaction with the system. In fact the score of user satisfaction is not high for any of the users. However there seems to be no straightforward correlation between the number of communicative gestures produced during the interaction and the measure of subjective user satisfaction.

Table 4.5 also reports the emotion signalled by each user. We tried to interpret users' emotions so that we were given an indication of whether or not they were feeling at ease while interacting with the system.Important cues to emotions can be given by the posture that the user holds during the interaction. This assumption is supported by some results obtained in the field of psychology and AI (see Laban (1976); Damasio (1994); Höök (2002)) according to which emotions reside both in the mind and in the body of human beings.This means that emotion felt as a state can be displayed by means of facial expressions, gestures and body postures. This assumption can lead to the supposition that particular body postures and gestures might encourage or constrain the expression of emotions.

This assumption seems to be supported by the behaviour of the six users of the Adapt corpus II. During the interaction with the system five of them sat mostly with their arms crossed in a tense and still position, or were constrained by holding the microphone in one hand and holding the other hand under their chin. This posture is likely to have limited them in their production of gestures during the interaction with the system. For instance user $S12$, who does not produce any communicative gestures during the interaction, appears very tense. She keeps still during most of the interaction, she hyper-articulates speech and gives the impression of being quite frustrated when Urban does not understand her requests.

Users $S22$ and $S13$, who both have rather high user satisfaction scores, appear very engaged during the first half of the interaction with the system, and it is in this first half that they produce their communicative gestures. User $S22$ in the second half of the interaction shows evident signs of tiredness, such as positioning one of her hands under her chin or sinking down on the desk hanging on her elbows. User $S16$ does not appear very engaged in the interaction, he yawns several times, and fidgets in the chair. He gets very bored during the interaction and this is signalled both through his voice, which undergoes some variations in pitch (lowering), and through his facial expression and mainly his body postures: corners of the mouth downward, gaze directed in space, 'hanging' body posture with his head bent on one side, or supported by a hand positioned under his chin or holding one side of his face.

4.   Conclusions and Further Investigation

Our investigation aimed at proposing new parameters and metrics related to the users, in order to evaluate some aspects of multimodal dialogue systems, which could be used as a complement to traditional evaluation methods. Our assumption is that the intentional use of prosodic cues and the production of communicative non-verbal behaviour by users can give an indication of their attitudes towards the system and might also help to evaluate the users overall experience of the interaction.

To test our hypothesis we carried out analyses of interactions between users and two Swedish experimental multi-modal dialogue systems, endowed with ECA (August and Adapt). The results we obtained, even though quite limited in their amount, seems to support our idea of using prosodic cues and non-verbal communicative behaviour produced by users interacting with ECAs as new parameters for evaluating some aspects of user satisfaction. Moreover the observation of users' behaviour shows that there seems to be hints of correlation between the physical signals of emotion and the user satisfaction score.

However a more thorough investigation is needed to better support our hypotheses. In particular we would need to collect data specifically for our investigation purposes. It has to be pointed out that the materials we used for our analyses were previously collected for other research purposes and were collected at different stages of the development of the ECAs included in the systems; August and Urban have in fact been further developed (the improvements are reported by Beskow (2003)).

Since the user satisfaction can depend very much on the visual realism of the ECAs and on how well ECAs reproduce human verbal and non-verbal behaviour, we believe that in order to make humans' communication with ECAs more similar to the way they would communicate with other humans, it is necessary to keep improving the visual realism of the ECAs and their human-like features and at the same time continue to improve specific evaluation methods for multimodal applications with ECAs.

Even though the analysis of the prosodic and paralinguistic parameters we propose do not cover all the aspects of user satisfaction, we believe it has several appealing elements:

- The results of the analysis can be used as an indication of whether or not the system is working as well as the user expected it to.

- The analysis of acoustical cues can be implemented at low-cost, since it is possible to extract the cues automatically.

- In a futuristic vision even the detection of some non-verbal communicative gesture could be conducted automatically, by means of gesture recognition.

- The detection of acoustical cues coupled to negative emotions (disappointment, irritation, boredom) can be used as a trigger to start certain modules, for example help modules.

- Finally prosodic cues can be used as a parameter to decide when to save data from dialogues for further investigation.

Acknowledgments

This study was carried out at CTT, Centre for Speech Technology, a competence centre at KTH, supported by Vinnova (the Swedish Agency for Innovation Systems), KTH and participant Swedish partners. All the materials analysed in our study were previously collected at CTT, for this reason we would like to thank all the people who took part in the August and Adapt projects. In particular we thank Jens Edlund and Magnus Nordstrand for their help and technical support. This work was also sponsored by GSLT, the Swedish Graduate School of Language technology and Växjö University.

Last, but not least we would like to express our sincere gratitude to our supervisors, David House and Joakim Nivre, for their valuable advice and patient proofreading of early and final versions of this work.

Notes

1. European project PF-Star webpage June 2003: http://pfstar.itc.it/

References

Bell, L. and Gustafson, J. (1999a). Utterance types in the August System. In *Proceedings of the Third Swedish Symposium on Multimodal Communication*, pp.81–84. Stockholm.

Bell, L. and Gustafson, J. (1999b). Interacting with an animated agent: an analysis of a Swedish database of spontaneous computer directed speech. In *Proceedings of Eurospeech'99*, Budapest, pp. 1143–1146.

Beskow, J. (2003). *Talking Heads Models and Applications for Multimodal Speech Synthesis*. Doctoral dissertation, KTH, Stockholm.

Beskow, J., Edlund, J., and Nordstrand, M. (in press). A model for generalised multi-modal dialogue system output applied to an animated talking head. In Minker, W., Bühler, D., and Dybkjaer, L., editors, *Spoken Multimodal Human-Computer Dialogue in Mobile Environments*, Dordrecht, Kluwer Academic Press.

Carlson, R. and Granström, B. (1996). The Waxholm spoken dialogue system, Palkova, Z., editor, *Phonetica Pragensia IX. Charisteria viro doctissimo Premysl Janota oblata*. Acta Universitatis Carolinae Philologica, 1: 39–52.

Cave, C., Guaitella, I., Bertrand, R., Santi, S., Harlay, F., and Espesser R. (1996). About the relationship between eyebrow movements and f0 variations. In *Proceedings of the ICSLP'96*, pp. 2175–2179. Philadelphia.

Cerrato, L. and Skhiri, M. (2003). Analysis and measurement of head movements in human dialogues. In *Proceedings of AVSP, ITRW on Audio Visual Speech Processing'03*, pp. 251–256, St Jorioz, France.

Damasio, A. (1994). *AR: Descartes' Error: Emotion, Reason, and the Human Brain*, New York, Grosset-Putnam.

Danieli, M. and Gerbino, E. (1995). Metrics for evaluating dialog strategies in a spoken language system. In *Working Notes AAAI Spring Symposium Series*, pp. 34–39, Stanford University.

Edlund, J. and Nordstrand, M. (2002). Turn-taking Gestures and Hour-Glasses in a Multi-modal Dialogue System. In *Proceedings of ISCA Workshop Multi-Modal Dialogue in Mobile Environments*, Kloster Irsee, Germany. pp. 181–184.

Ekman, P. (1993). Facial expression and emotion. *American Psychologist*, 48(4): 384–392.

Fabri, M., Moore, D.J., and Hobbs, D.J. (2000). Expressive Agents: Non-verbal Communication in Collaborative Virtual Environments. In *Proceedings of Workshop on Embodied Conversational Agents — Let's Specify and Evaluate them!*. AAMAS02, Bologna, Italy.

Gibbon, D., Mertins, I., Moore, R.K., editors, (2000). *Handbook of multimodal and spoken dialogue systems*. Kluwer Academic Press.

Glass, J.R. (1999). Challenges for spoken dialog systems. In *Proceedings of the 1999 IEEE ASRU Workshop*, pp. 430–435, Keystone.

Graf, H.P. et al. (2002). Visual Prosody; Facial Movements Accompanying speech. In *Proceedings of the 5th IEEE International Conference on Automatic Face and Gesture Recognition*, Washington. pp. 396–401.

Gustafson, J., Lindberg, N., and Lundeberg, M. (1999). The August spoken dialogue system. In *Proceedings of Eurospeech'99*, pp. 1151–1154, Budapest.

Gustafson, J., Bell, L., Beskow, J., Boye, J., Carlson, R., Edlund, J., Granström, B., House, D., and Wirén M(2000). AdApt - a Multimodal conversational dialogue system in an apartment domain. In *Proceedings of ICSLP'00*, 2, pp. 134–137, Bejiing.

Hjalmarsson, A. (2002). *Evaluating Adapt, a multimodal conversational dialogue system, using PARADISE.* MaS thesis. Department of Speech Music and Hearing KTH, Stockholm.

Höök, K. (2002). Evaluation of Affective Interaction. In *Proceedings of Workshop on Embodied Conversational Agents — Let's Specify and Evaluate them!*. AAMAS02, Bologna, Italy.

Kipp, M. (2001). Anvil — A Generic Annotation Tool for Multimodal Dialogue. In *Proceedings of Eurospeech'01)*, pp. 1367–1370, Aalborg.

Laban, R. (1976). *The Language of Movement a Guidebook to Choreutic.* Boston, Plays Inc.

Lippmann, R. (1997). Speech recognition by machines and humans. *Speech Communication*, 22: 1–15, Elsevier Science. ?

Massaro, D.W., Cohen, M., Beskow, J., and Cole, R. (1998). Developing and Evaluating Conversational Agents. In *Workshop on Embodied Conversation Characters'98*, pp. 287–318. Lake Tohoe.

Massaro, D.W. (2000). Multimodal emotion perception analogous to speech processes. In *Proceedings of the ISCA Workshop on Speech and Emotion*, pp. 114–121, Newcastle Northern Ireland.

McTear, M.F. (2002). Spoken Dialog Technology: Enabling the Conversational User Interface. *ACM Computing Surveys*, 34(1): 90–169.

Mitchell, J., Menezes, C., Williams, J., Pardo, B., Erickson, D., and Fujimura, O. (2000). Changes in syllables and boundary strengths due to irritations. In *Proceedings of the ISCA Workshop on Speech and Emotion'00*, pp. 98–103, Newcastle Northern Ireland.

Montero, J. M., Gutierrez Ariola, J., de Cordoba Herralde, R., Enriquez Carrasco, E. V., and Pardo Muoz, J.M. (2002). The role of pitch and tempo in Spanish Emotional Speech. In Keller, E., Bailly, G., Monaghan, A., Terken, J., and Huckvale, M. editors, *Improvements in speech synthesis Cost 258*, pp. 246–251, John Wiley & Sons, Chichester.

Nass, C. and Moon, Y. (1996). Social responses to communication technologies: A summary of four studies. Unpublished manuscript.

Nordstrand, M., Svanfeldt, G., Granstrm, B., and House, D. (2003). Measurements of Articulatory Variation and Communicative signals in Expressive Speech. In *Proceedings of AVSP, ITRW on Audio Visual Speech Processing'03*, pp. 233–238, St Jorioz, France.

Pelachaud, C., Badler, N., and Steedman, M. (1996). Generating Facial Expressions for Speech. *Cognitive Science*, 20(1): 1–46.

Picard, R. (1997). *Affective Computing*, Cambridge Massachusetts, MIT Press.

Poggi, I. and Pelachaud, C. (1999). Emotional Meaning and Expression in Animated Faces. In *Proceedings IWAI'99*, pp. 182–195, Siena, Italy.

Sanders, G.A. and Scholtz, J. (2000). Measurements and Evaluation of Embodied conversational agents. In Cassell, J., Sullivan, J., Prevost, S., and Churchill, E., editors, *Embodied conversational agents*, pp. 346–373, Cambridge Massachusetts, MIT press.

Schegloff, E.A. and Sacks, H. (1977). Opening Up Closings. *Semiotica* 8: 298–327.

Sjölander, K. and Beskow, J. (2000). WaveSurfer - an Open Source Speech Tool. In *Proceedings of ICSLP'00*, Bejing, pp. 464–467.

Thórisson, K.R. (1997). Gandalf an embodied humanoid capable of real time multimodal dialogue with people. In *Proceedings of the First ACM International Conference of Autonomous Agents*, pp. 536–537, California.

Walker M.A., Kamm C.A. and Littman, D.J. (2000) Towards Developing General Models of Usability with PARADISE. *Natural Language Engineering: Special Issue on Best Practice in Spoken Dialogue Systems, 2000*, 6.

Walker, M.A and Passonneau, R. (2001). DATE: A Dialogue Act Tagging Scheme for Evaluation of Spoken Dialogue Systems. In *Proceedings of Human Language Technology Conference'01*, pp. 66–73, San Diego. Available from: http://hlt2001.org/papers/hlt2001-15.pdf

II

THE USER IN FOCUS

Chapter 5

USER-CENTRED DESIGN AND EVALUATION OF AFFECTIVE INTERFACES

A Two-tiered Model

Kristina Höök

> *What a piece of work is a man! How noble in reason!*
> *How infinite in faculty! In form and moving, how ex-*
> *press and admirable!*
>
> —Shakespeare, Hamlet

Abstract   One obvious challenge for affective interfaces is to find ways of checking whether the expressed emotions are understood by users, and whether the system can interpret user emotions correctly. Even more challenging is whether the overall usage scenarios are achieving their purpose of being e.g. engaging, fun, believable, or creating a relationship with the user, and how much of this can be attributed to the emotion modeling and expression. We propose a two-tiered design and evaluation model. We exemplify this model through studies of three different affective interfaces: the *Agneta & Frida* system, the *Influencing Machine*, and *SenToy & FantasyA*.

Keywords: Affective interaction, synthetic characters, user evaluation, user-centred design.

Z. Ruttkay and C. Pelachaud (eds.), From Brows to Trust, 127–160.
© *2004 Kluwer Academic Publishers. Printed in the Netherlands.*

1.   Introduction

Affective computing, or the development of computational systems which
can be aware of and respond to human emotions, has become the focus
of a great deal of attention in the Artificial Intelligence (AI) community.

Recent developments, such as the results from Tristão & Isolda (Martinho and Paiva (1999)), and Influencing Machine (Sengers et al. (2002),
Höök et al. (2003)) suggest that a too narrow understanding of emotions will fail to address the important issues in interaction. The AI-
approaches to affective computing often focus on what one might call an
'informatics of affect', in which emotions are treated as units of information. Emotions are analyzed, classified, discretized, and formulated
as units whose purpose is to inform cognition or be communicated. The
often-used integrative cognitive theory of emotion of Ortony, Collins and
Clore (1988), for example, defines emotions in terms of a set of discrete,
basic types and focuses on the cognition or reasoning which may give
rise to them. Once a set of emotional units is defined, input devices
can be designed which can turn physiological responses into information. For example, Fernandez, Scheirer, and Picard's (1999) Expression
Glasses measure the movement of facial muscles and classify the resulting expression into a small, discrete set of emotions. Ark, Dryer and
Lu's (1999) Emotion Mouse extends a normal computer mouse to deduce users' emotional states from physiological information such as pulse
and galvanic skin response.

Frequently in this tradition, emotions are subsumed to rationality or
effectiveness. Damásio's (1994) influential arguments for the importance
of emotion in scientific research, for example, gain currency from the
idea that emotion is necessary for true rational behavior. Similarly,
Picard's (1997) ground-breaking work on Affective Computing argues
that computers must be able to process emotion in order to function
maximally effectively with human beings.

While defining, classifying, creating logical structure for, and understanding the relationship of rationality to emotions can be useful ex-
ercises, we believe this mindset is in danger of missing a fundamental
point: affect is not just a formal, computational construct, but also a
human, rich, complex, and ill-defined *experience*. Rationalizing it may
be necessary to make it computable, but an affective computation that
truly inspires and incorporates human emotion must include a broader
cultural perspective, in which the elusive and non-rational character of
emotion does not need to be explained away (Sengers et al. (2002)).
From this perspective, computation may be used, not to acquire and

reason about user's emotional states, but rather to create intuitive experiences of affect by the user during interaction.

A substantial design challenge in constructing a technical system that creates intuitive experiences and supports open interpretation, then, is the need to bridge the rational objectivity of the software and the hardware with the interpretational complexity of users' subjective experiences. Doing this well requires insights into how to develop the design. The line of argument presented here is that design and evaluation methods placing the user and usage at core, can be one key component in achieving the design goals of affective applications. Our starting point is a set of user studies the author has performed previously that we shall revisit and to some extent reanalyze. The methods that we have found to be most useful in capturing the idea of user experience are open-ended, subjective, interpretative studies performed through a two-tiered method. The first step in this method is to get the interface expression and interpretation right (usability). The second, more interesting step is to try and evaluate whether the affective aspects of the system do indeed contribute to the overall goal of the system, and users' experiences.

The work presented in this chapter should therefore be seen as an attempt to show that user studies interwoven into the design process can be crucial in the design process, but only if we can move away from simplistic measurements that 'prove' the efficiency of our affective interactive systems, and instead aim at deeper, interpretative understandings of what is really going on between user and system.

Let us start by outlining our philosophy underlying our method and the specifics of the method. We shall then go through previous work and in particular turn to a set of user studies performed according to our ideas[1]: a study of the Agneta & Frida system (Höök et al. (2000)), two studies of the Influencing Machine (Sengers et al. (2002), Höök et al. (2003)), and two studies of SenToy and FantasyA (Andersson et al. (2002), Paiva et al. (2003), Höök et al. (2003)). While all three systems are aimed at invoking affective responses from the user, they also examplify three quite different forms of Embodied Conversational Agents (ECAs), which is the focus of this book.

2. Underlying Philosophy and Method

As indicated above, the prevailing approach in the design of affective interaction is to construct an individual cognitive model of affect from first principles, implement it in a system that attempts to recognize users' emotional states through measuring biosignals, and through this try to achieve an as life-like or human-like interaction as possible, seamlessly adapting to the user's emotional state and influencing it through the use of characters in the interface or other affective expressions.

There has been quite some research on how to recognize users' emotional states through singular, one-off, readings of biosensor data, facial expressions, body posture, interaction with devices, such as mouse or keypad, or props, such as plush toys. However, repeatedly there seems to be the same conclusion: while some basic emotions (fear, stress, and arousal) may be recognized, the methods fail to get the whole picture and often contradictory results arise between users' self-reports of what they think and feel and their physical expressions (e.g Höök et al. (2000)). They also fail to understand any more complex and interesting emotional states that users might be in – such as shame, guilt, positive arousal, or flow.

It is probably impossible to detect fine-grained aspects of human emotion. People are interesting intelligent beings, and their emotion processing does not constitute some simple stimulus/response model. Human emotion relates to so many complex interactions that no modeling will ever be able to "detect" them. We have a personality, a mood, attitudes and value systems that are individual as well as cognitively related, we have bodily states that we influence and bodily states that we cannot influence (hormone levels, diseases...); we are influenced by the current context, and so on. An emotion state is usually not a single state – it is a mixture of several emotions along several scales such as arousal level, energy involved, long-lasting moods, more cognitively-induced versus more bodily-induced emotions, or valence (positive/negative) of the emotion. You might be in a melancholic mood that lies like a blanket on top of any emotion you have, or you might be in a context that does not allow for jumping around and thereby experiencing and reinforcing the strength of the inner emotion. It is hard to envision any modeling system that would be able to deal with and mimic such a complex and changing situation. As one of the studies discussed below showed, facial expressions of users only reveal one tiny aspects of how and why users react in certain ways to affective systems. Personality, value systems, ethics, and other individual differences also come into play as determinants to why we react in certain ways to these systems.

But the problem we would like to discuss here is not the problem of understanding how complex the human mind is, or how difficult it will be to try and correctly recognize users' emotional states from simple measurements of facial expressions or other biosignals, since we would like to stay clear of discussing counterarguments such as that this could be described as a problem due to lack of knowledge of how to model human emotions in machines, lack of sensors to recognise emotion states, or lack of correct theory of the human emotional processing system and consequently lack of good, computational models of emotions that can be inserted into these affective systems. Instead, we would like to argue that what is more crucial in creating affective interactive systems, is to understand how to influence the users' emotional states and be able to maintain and build user emotional involvement to create a coherent cognitive and emotional experience. With such a goal, bad modeling of human emotions lacking respect for the complexity of our inner life can be devastating. On the other hand, rightly used, affective interaction based on some emotional models can make us learn more, make better decisions, understand each other better in social applications and shared workspaces, and sometimes simply enjoy the application more.

Creating such systems is, obviously, a hard and very difficult goal to achieve. We know for sure that movies, novels, television shows, arts and music are indeed able to get people affectively involved. But we want to make end-users affectively touched by interacting with systems that model emotions, reason using emotions and express emotions. How can we aid the design process and make it more likely that we succeed? Our argument here is that one tool in the repertoire, among many others, could be a user-centered development methods. A user-centered approach throughout the development of affective interactive systems will aid designers to at least stay on track, focused on the end-user experience, even if it does not provide the whole answer to how to design these systems.

2.1   Our Philosophy

Our approach in the design of affective interaction has therefore had another starting point than that taken in Affective Computing. Our user-centred perspective does, in turn, influence how we think user evaluation studies should be done. We base our work on the following three assertions:

> **Assertion 1:** *People's affective reactions are parts of ongoing interactions embedded in a broader social context.*

People's affective interaction consists of much more than what can be understood from simplistic local measurements of their bodily reactions. Significant emotions (beyond elemental experiences such as of surprise, disorientation, or disgust) are to a large extent social phenomena that take place in specific cultural settings, taking on particular expressions colored by the culture and the group of people at a particular place. The meaning and expression of emotions like guilt or shame are given both by their local social context as well as by their cultural context.

Assertion 2: *Affective interaction has a broader scope*

Affective outputs should not be seen as an end product but rather be made part of the interactive coupling. Through affective input through affective toys, tangible input media, or affectiveware, and acquisition of an understanding of the affective output these generate, users will become more or less part of the system and will be more or less affectively involved. We believe that it is crucial to tap into those affective input and output modalities that speak more directly to our affective states, such as soundscapes, colors, imagery, and tactile media.

Assertion 3: *People's affective reactions are adapted to the current context*

Through experience, by watching others, by studying the specific culture at places, people will learn to portray affect through different behaviors under different circumstances. Thus, someone might scream out loud in happiness at a soccer game but only smirk in a research project meeting, all because of context and interaction with others and the setting. This becomes particularly relevant when we invent novel ways for users to interact affectively. While we can be inspired by theories of human emotion, the particular interactions we invent have to be designed and developed in ways that are particular to a specific activity and its purpose. We must be aware that people will pick up and learn how to interact in ways that are given by the specific interaction devices, the context and purpose of use, and the expressive behavior of the system. This interaction cycle has to be developed in a user-participatory design cycle in order to identify the particular difficulties and opportunities for design.

2.2   Our Method

There are very few user studies of the short-term and even fewer of the long-term effects of affective interaction. On the other hand, designers of artifacts, artists, musicians, writers, people in advertising, and more recently web- and game designers have played around with evoking emotions for ages. What differs here is the *interaction* between the artifact aimed at raising emotions or expressing emotions and the viewers'/listeners'/readers'/users' reactions and (affective) actions at the interface. Users will be involved in the loop in a more active manner – expressing their own emotions rather than only be influenced.

A lot of the work on affective interfaces is focused on implementing affective interaction through interactive characters, but affective interaction may also be realized in various other ways. In many affective interaction scenarios (besides interactive characters), the goal is to entertain. The HCI community has only recently started to debate how to take those characteristics into account when performing usability studies or providing input to design. These aspects are sometimes referred to as *hedonic usability factors* (Hassenzahl et al. (2000)) or pleasure-based human factors. Affective interfaces may also, of course, be used as part of learning systems, e-commerce applications, or general desk-top applications.

Open Interpretation   Since the field of affective interaction is fairly new, there is no general agreement on what to evaluate through a user study. Researchers in the field have been focused on issues like natural expressions, perfect models of the user's emotions, design of sensors and readings of sensor-data, and not really concerned with whether this aim for naturalness or the emotion models as such, do in fact contribute to the overall success of the system. While Bates, who first coined the expression *believability* of characters[2], was aiming for a design that could suspend disbelief (1994), other researchers have been using the concept believability in the more simplistic sense of 'naturalness' of face, body and voice of characters. The idea of 'suspension of disbelief' as coined by Disney, has been misinterpreted as meaning as 'human-like as possible'. As put by Persson et al. (2002) when discussing how to create Socially-Intelligent Agents (SIA):

> In order to develop believable SIAs we do not have to know how beliefs-desires and intentions *actually* relate to each other in the real minds of real people. If we want to create the impression of an artificial social agent driven by beliefs and desires, it is enough to draw on investigations on how people in different cultures develop and use theories of mind to understand the behaviors of others. SIAs need to model the *folk-theory reasoning*, not the real thing. To a shallow AI approach, a model of mind based on folk-psychology is as valid as one based on cognitive theory.

The approach suggested by Persson et al. is to look upon human-computer interaction (the 'shallow AI approach') as a constructivist perspective on users where they themselves make sense and create meaning out of their interactions with the world. Thus, instead of viewing end-users as passive viewers of what the 'perfect' system is constructing based on models of their emotional states, end-users are viewed as active co-constructers of meaning. Our approach is to agree with this perspective and add some practical methods for understanding how users react to the kinds of systems we want to build in order to further the understanding of the design process.

Informal Methods   Studies in other fields, such as natural language interfaces, adaptive interfaces and intelligent user interfaces show that there are principles and peculiarities particular to the design of human machine interaction (Dahlbäck et al. (1993), Höök, (2000)). A computer system is a designed artifact – not a 'natural' thing. While the field of HCI certainly recognizes that there are design considerations that should be built from knowledge of human abilities and limitations (see e.g., Norman (1990)), they also recognize that computers are part of human culture, and thus subject to change. Over and over, artifacts are designed that users then take into use in ways that are quite different from what the designer expected (Suchman (1987)). A design process that fails to involve end-users in the design loop, will fail to recognize the particular quirks and problems of how to design these artifacts.

Within HCI, formal user studies (quantitative-scientific) are the gold standard for evaluating computational systems. But the aim in the affective interaction systems might not be best captured using formal user studies as these rarely are able to capture end-user experience (in a broader sense). We believe that informality and open-ended interpretation of users experience is key here as done in the more ethnographically inspired parts of HCI. This approach is similar to how artwork is evaluated through art critics and informal encounters between the artist and the audience. This will not render results that are independent of time and culture – but the point is that no user evaluation studies are independent of time and culture anyway[3], something that we come back to below.

Informality can, e.g., be observed in the HCI literature on evaluation of art-influenced speculative design. For example, the Presence project was evaluated informally by describing the designers' experience in installing the system and observing user interaction (Gaver et al. (2001)).

Anecdotal evidence, informal chats between users and system-builders, tiny study sizes, forms structured to influence user interpretation, no discussion or analysis of results: this may sound like a to-do list for bad evaluation. But since the goal is to aid the process of improving the design until the end-user experience and the system interaction harmonize, we prefer a rich, narrative, and singular understanding before a simpler but rigorous and generalizable understanding (Höök et al. (2003)). This interest in singularity and narrative complexity allies well with the recent ethnographic turn in HCI; yet many ethnographers may feel uncomfortable in promulgating a personal vision to users to the same extent as we have done in some of the studies discussed below.

No Averaging – No Normal User   In looking for this rich, narrative, constructive understanding of what is going on between user and system, we are not looking for the average user reaction. We are interested in the richness and complexity of unique, individual users, cultural contexts, and resulting variety of interpretations and experiences of the system. Since affective interactive systems in many cases will make end-users engage in complex acts of interpretation, it would not be appropriate to summarize the results of a study into a few statements that are said to hold for everyone. Also, the statistical averaging and laboratory simplifications necessary for reliable scientific statements may wash out all the details that interest us.

Thus, we are not looking for representative user groups, or generalisable scientific results that last for ever – we are looking for input to the design process.

Two-tiered Method In our experience from the user studies and design work with the three systems presented here, we noted that it was necessary to divide the user studies into two different levels. The first obvious challenge for affective interfaces is to find ways of checking whether the expressed emotions are understood by users, and whether the system can interpret user emotions correctly. It might be that a design of an affective interactive character is perfectly valid and well-suited to the overall goal of the system, but the facial emotional expressions of the character are hard to interpret. Thus the overall design fails anyway. Or the other way around, the emotional expressions might be easily understood by the user, but the design does still not achieve its overall goal of entertaining or aiding the user.

Thus once the interpretation loop is bootstrapped and working, the second, even more challenging goal for evaluation of affective interfaces, is whether the overall usage scenarios are achieving their purpose of being e.g., engaging, fun, believable, or creating a relationship with the user, and how much of this can be attributed to the emotion modeling and expression. These two levels of evaluation will not necessarily be dividable into two different user studies or two different phases in the design process – instead they should be viewed as two levels of interpretation of what is going on when the system fails to achieve it goals.

What we are looking for, are ways of disentangling the *bad design* choices from the interesting interpretative experiences end-users have with affective systems that in many cases cannot be controlled (as they are attempting to adapt the users' emotional states and thereby changes over time) or understood in a narrow sense (as they are oftentimes portraying interesting narrative or character-based dramas).

Timing and Control As we shall discuss below, in the process of doing the studies, we found that there were some problems specific to affective interfaces that are not discussed much in the general HCI literature. These design problems concern the *timing of events* and the *level of control* handed to the end-user.

When an emotion is displayed to the user it has to come at the right point in time, and last for an appropriate length (Hendrix et al. (2000)). If an affective response from the user is the aim, then the interaction has to be carefully paced so that the user can follow it without being bored or puzzled.

As affective systems based on modelling of users' emotions are oftentimes pro-active, end-users are given less control over the interaction compared to direct-manipulation systems. The level of control and predictability needs to be balanced (Höök (1997)).

Anthropomorphism   Other researcher in the field also discuss the issue of *anthropomorphism*, which can be seen as a positive or negative effect of affective interaction – in particular when realized through characters in the interface. Synthetic characters tend to raise expectations of anthropomorphism of the system (Reeves & Nass (1996)). Such anthropomorphic effects seem to have many dimensions. On the one hand the user may expect the system to be intelligent and cognitively potent. Brennan and Ohaeri (1994) showed that users talked more to the anthropomorphic interface. King and Ohya (1995) showed that users attributed more intelligence to anthropomorphic interfaces. Koda and Maes (1996) showed that realistic faces are liked and rated as more intelligent than abstract faces.

Opponents of synthetic characters argue that raised anthropomorphic expectations may lead to frustration in the user when the system cannot meet the expectations (Shneiderman (1997)). For instance, the presence of a talking face might influence the user to expect the system to possess natural language and dialogue competence, which no system of today can live up to. The general conclusion is that the more 'natural' the interface, the higher expectations on intelligence in the system. The problem arises when there is a mismatch between the users expectations and the systems' ability and this causes the user to fall out of their 'suspension of disbelief'.

Using Existing HCI Methods   It should be noted that our contribution here is not an entirely new method for interactive design of affective interaction systems. We are simply picking up the methods existing within the field of HCI and attempt to see how they can be applied to this area. Thus, in the first study of the SenToy device, we used the well-known 'Wizard of Oz'-method. In the Agneta and Frida study, we used questionnaires and open-ended interviews. The Influencing Machine studies were typical laboratory-based video-recorded encounters with demo versions of the system.

Summary of Proposed Method In summary, the method we propose is to:

- bring in end-users several times during the design work;

- apply methods that allow for a rich interpretation of users' experiences of interacting with the system;

- separate the understanding of emotional input/output from the overall experience and success of the design;

- not average over some non-existent 'normal' user, but to bring in a richer understanding of the users' background into the interpretation of what is going on between user and system;

- put some extra attention to issues of timing, control of interaction and effects of anthropomorphism (positive and negative) when observing user behavior, as well as any gaps that cause end-users to fall out of their 'suspension of disbelief'.

3.   Studies of Three Affective Interfaces

The studies of the three different affective interaction systems, each illustrate a step in designing and to some extent evaluating the overall effects of affective interaction:

- The study of Agneta & Frida shows the importance of interpretation of the subjective experiences of affective systems and the risk of taking too simplistic measurements. It also shows the need to further study control and timing, and to be more open to how users' background and personality matters.

- The two studies of the Influencing Machine show the importance of first making sure that the affective output from the system is understood by users, before checking if the overall interaction idea is succeeding, thus showing the value of the two-tiered evaluation cycle. It also points to problems with control and timing, and the need for interpretative methods of analysing user study results.

- The studies of SenToy also illustrate how a study in an early stage of the design cycle can help bootstrap the design of affective input (performed through gestures with a toy) and how the second

Figure 5.1. Agneta and Frida reacting to the site of a film production company.

level of evaluation can address the overall purpose of the affective interaction system. It also shows the need to differentiate between 'natural behaviors' and how users really will interact with designed artifacts.

Since we did the Agneta & Frida study before the other three studies, we shall start by describing it and the inspiration we gained on study methods. In many ways, the flaws of this study are the basis and inspiration to how we set up the studies that followed.

4.   Agneta & Frida

Our first study was of the Agneta & Frida system (Höök et al. (2000)). The two animated female characters – mother and daughter – sit on the users' desktop, watching the user's browser more or less like watching television, see Figure 5.1. They make humorous and sometimes nasty comments of the web pages, the user actions, and sometimes just randomly talk to one-another.

Initial testing helped us find the right timing for the jokes – a crucial aspect of humor is to deliver it at the right moment. The early version was too slow in delivering the jokes and in particular the punch line.

Users would move on to other web pages before the joke was finished, and sometimes this meant that the joke became unintelligible.

In the following study of Agneta & Frida, we measured how many times users smiled or laughed, the amount of time they spent with the system, their mood before and after using the system, and their responses to questionnaire questions after their session with Agneta & Frida. 20 subjects tested the system with Agneta & Frida, and for comparison we also had 20 subjects who surfed the same set of web pages but without the company of Agneta & Frida.

4.1   Non-correlation of Measurements

Interestingly, none of the measurements correlated. Subject 16, for instance, smiled as often as 7.5 times per 10 minutes, spent 36 minutes (9 minutes above average) with the system, which would indicate that he had a good time. However, his post-usage view on Agneta & Frida's commentaries was only 3 on the 7-grade scale (where 7 was the highest grade). On the other hand, subject 1, who smiled the least, only 1.2 smiles per 10 minute, and only spent 16.5 minutes with the system, really liked Agneta & Frida – giving them grade 6 on the 7-grade scale. This might be because the measurements were bad and fuzzy, or because people are generally known to behave in a socially desirable way, i.e. according to what they believe the experimenter desires. But another way of explaining the non-correlation is to assume that the variables simply measure different things. We believe that although all of them try to capture the overall experience of the system, they may, in fact, measure different aspects of this experience.

For example, facial expressions of the subjects (how often they smiled or frowned) may provide indications of the immediate, un-reflected appreciation of the system. Facial expression will perhaps show the instantaneous reactions to the jokes, but not the retrospect overall appreciation of the whole experience of surfing together with Agneta & Frida. The post-usage replies, on the other hand, might reflect subject's 'afterthoughts' about the system, which may be influenced by moral and ethical preferences – the more official views of what humor and entertainment should or should not be according to a person's value system. This was in part confirmed by results such as the correlation we found between how much subjects were disturbed by Agneta & Frida and their web and computer experience. Users who had a lot of web experience were also more disturbed by Agneta & Frida (r=.54, p <.05), the same for computer experience (r=.60, p <.05). Computer experienced users may have a task-oriented and quite strict model of how to interact with computer interfaces and web browsing. Since Agneta & Frida blatantly break with this 'tradition', experienced users are more disturbed than users who do not have such strong expectations or 'preconceptions'. Especially subjects who are used to having complete control over the computer – from the insides of the operating system and out – may find it hard to accept characters in the interface and processes that run outside their control. In fact, before, after, or even during the session, some subjects said that they in general disliked interface characters for many of these reasons.

The mood measurement – which lands somewhere in-between the instantaneous reactions during use and the post-usage replies – will again measure something else than immediate reaction or the post-usage reflective evaluation. Since it showed that the Agneta & Frida subjects were in a better mood after the study compared to the subjects who surfed without Agneta & Frida, it provides us with some evidence that the system positively influences users' experience of the system on an emotional level. But being in a better mood does not necessarily mean that we appreciate every aspect of it. Our views on humor are reflections of our personality and who we want to be in the eyes of others. Sometimes Agneta & Frida make strongly ironic and sarcastic remarks about the computer and web culture, as for example:

> **Frida:** They say that computers save so much time. But sometimes I wonder... At work I often feel like I'm spending 90% of the time getting the damned thing to work, and about 10% of the time actually accomplishing things with it....
>
> **Agneta:** I don't really know... I'm not that experienced...
>
> **Frida:** Maybe we should buy a home computer...? Just for the fun of it...
>
> **Agneta:** Naa, I'd prefer a television set instead... there are more stories on TV....

Some jokes are concerned with the male dominance of the IT-world:

> **Frida:** Stupid! Nothing works! Who would ever publish a page like this?
>
> **Agneta:** A man?

Users might approve or disapprove of this type of humor or the views of Agneta & Frida. In order to determine and predict such processes, we would need a thorough investigation of subjects' attitudes towards humor, irony, and fictional characters in general, and attitudes towards these phenomena in interfaces in particular.

What aspect of experience is most important – and thus determining the appropriate method of measurement – is of course dependent on the design goals. If we aim to entertain for a onetime usage situation, then maybe it is more important that subjects smile a lot; if we want subjects to return to the system, then their post-usage evaluation should be emphasized. The fact that many users were disturbed by Agneta & Frida – but still enjoyed their company – indicated that we failed to create a feeling of flow or relaxed relationship to the space. If that had been our design goal, then other design solutions need to be sought.

Our results point at the difficulty of gathering facial expressions and using those as a means to measure subjects' affective reactions towards computer systems. Users' physical reactions of interactions with systems are not necessarily good predictors of users' inner mental states. In order to pinpoint finer distinctions in the emotional reactions, we have to consider the users interpretation, understanding, attitudes, and expectations of computer culture. The experience of jokes and irony, for instance, will be determined by personal expectations, but also by social and cultural context. As argued above, our views on humor are reflections of our personality and who we want to be in the eyes of others.

4.2   Narrative Experience

The most important design goal for the Agneta & Frida system was an idea that end-users would tie together the web surfing experience into a coherent whole: a story that would entail both the web page content and the jokes of Agneta & Frida nicely intertwined and thereby helpful to the end-user as a means of remembering the information space in a narrative form rather than as a spatially organized information space.

Apart from the measurements above, we did two kinds of analysis of the open-ended interviews performed after they had used Agneta & Frida. We asked the subjects to describe what had happened while using the system. Inspired by Maglio and Matlock (1999) and Lakoff and Johnson (1999), we performed a *metaphor analysis* of the interviews. From Maglio and Matlock's study we knew that web browsing is often perceived as a spatial activity: the user is viewed as an agent moving through the space of sites and web pages. Maglio and Matlock found this by examining the metaphors used when subjects described their surfing through web pages: 'I browse/surf the web'; 'I go to pages'; 'I enter/leave pages'; 'pages contain information'; 'the web is an information space in which I look for things'.

We decided to follow the method used by Maglio and Matlock, focusing on narrative versus spatial verbs and adverbs in the interviews that followed after out subjects had explored the system. The metaphor analysis revealed that the group of subjects who had encountered Agneta & Frida tended to talk about their experience in terms of narrative verbs and adverbs (68% narrative), while the group of subjects who only surfed the web pages without Agneta & Frida, used more spatial verbs and adverbs (only 45% narrative). The difference between the conditions was statistically significant (Mann-Whitney: p>0.95).[3] This seemed to indicate that users actually merged the narrative and the spatial structure into one experience. A qualitative analysis of the interviews, however, sketched a somewhat more complex picture. Subjects in our study did not gracefully merge Agneta & Frida and the web content into one narrative whole. Sometimes they enjoyed the contents of the web pages, sometimes they were amused by the comments by Agneta and Frida, and at some points web browsing and interaction was integrated into the story of the two characters, but mostly subjects divided these experiences into two separated experiences of what was going on.

Finally, we measured *disturbance* and *recall*. If the user was able to integrate the narrative of Agneta & Frida with the web content, we hypothesized, that subjects would be less disturbed by the two characters, than a case in which the Agneta & Frida story ran 'in parallel' to the web content. In the latter case, the comments and activities of the characters would be experienced as intrusive. As for recall, we assumed that the emotional reactions caused by the remarks from Agneta & Frida – e.g., laughs, frustration, moral judgment and agreeableness – would enhance the recall of the information remarked upon. We assumed that Agneta and Frida would encourage the user to construct a narrative context and associative links between information in the site, which would improve memory. Thus, we expected the Agneta and Frida subjects to perform better on a post-usage recall test, than would subjects without Agneta & Frida.

There was no difference between the two groups in terms of how much they remembered of the web pages. Out of the 38 randomly selected test pages, the Agneta & Frida group remembered 88% of the pages they had seen, while the group who surfed without Agneta & Frida remembered 89%. Subjects were able to accurately recall the comments Agneta & Frida had made at particular pages. It seems like Agneta & Frida failed to create the context needed to better tie the different sites in the space together into one coherent narrative experience.

4.3   Implications for Design Method

While these results basically only tells us that the design was bad in terms of achieving this particular goal (even if Agneta & Frida were indeed successful in many other ways), the results also tell us something really important about the need for open interviews and deep interpre-

Figure 5.2. Setup of the Influencing Machine.

tation of what is really going on between subject and system. Simplistic measurements of time spent, bodily reactions, or questionnaires will only provide a limited understanding of what users really feel and think about complex, interactive systems such as Agneta & Frida. In fact, if we would have decided to only tell the story of those measurements, then Agneta & Frida would have looked like a very successful system.

Second, we also learnt how crucial the background and subjective perspectives of end-users were in how they reacted to Agneta & Frida. For any evaluation of a desk-top program, end-users values, humor or personality would not be considered crucial to how they react to the system. In this case, those aspects became key.

The level of control given to the users was also crucial to some of the subjects. The computer-experienced users did not like the lack of control that they experienced when Agneta & Frida interrupted their interaction and acted independently.

5.   The Influencing Machine

We took many of the experiences from the Agneta & Frida study with us when we studied the Influencing Machine designed by Phoebe Sengers and colleagues (Sengers et al. (2002), Höök et al. (2003)).

The Influencing Machine explores the tension between machines and affective beings in affective computing; how people will relate to a machine whose emotions they can influence, but whose behavior they cannot control. In some ways it can be seen as a provocative piece of interactive art exploring some of the Artificial Intelligence (AI) dreams with a more critical, cultural perspective.

The Influencing Machine is supposed to work as follows. Two people enter a small room. Child-like scribbling appears across a wall: jagged lines, circles, spirals, and other shapes build up, overlap, fade away (see Figures 5.2 and 5.4). Scattered throughout the room are postcards with art prints or color fields; on a table stands a wooden mailbox (see

Figure 5.3. The constructed Mailbox.

Figure 5.4. Examples of generated scribblings.

Figure 5.3). One person picks up a card and tentatively puts it in the box. Unusual and musical sounds begin to play. Drawings change speed, color, pressure, form. The people begin sorting through cards, dropping them in the box and seeing how the graphics and sound change. They play, experiment, and discuss: "How is this reacting to us?" "How do you think this works?"

Technically, the system works by using the input postcards marked with machine-readable bar codes to influence an internal emotional model. These internal emotions trigger sounds and the selection of drawing behaviors and their dynamic parameters: speed, color, size, pressure, etc. When the machine receives input, system drawings tend to become gradually more complex; when it has not received input for several minutes, it restarts. While this technical description is precise and clean, the emotional interpretation of the graphical output and postcards by users is complex, incompletely specifiable, open-ended, and strongly culturally influenced.

5.1   Study Method

The *co-discovery method* (Dumas and Redish (1993)), where users are brought in two by two, was used with some slight modifications. We brought in users in different group sizes. Also, we were not interested only in the talk-aloud effect, but also in group dynamics around the art piece. Facial expressions and discussions among the subjects are much more interesting to study with a group of users as opposed to single users in front of a screen. Second, we asked more questions about the subjects' background and attitudes than in the Agneta & Frida study. Thirdly, we kept the interviews after their session much more open-ended to allow for them to express various views and ideas, rather than a simple "Yes, I like it" or "No I don't" in a questionnaire.

Agneta & Frida and the Influencing Machine are quite different systems. The Influencing Machine grew out of the affective computing field, but takes on a different stance. Affective computation generally focuses on the informatics of affect: structuring, formalizing, and representing emotion as informational units. Through the Influencing Machine Sengers and colleagues proposed instead an enigmatics of affect, a critical technical practice that respects the rich and undefinable complexities of human affective experience. The Influencing Machine bridges the subjective experience of the user and the necessary objective rationality of the underlying code. It functions as a cultural probe, reflecting and challenging users to reflect on the cultural meaning of affective computation. In doing so, it might not aim to please, as Agneta & Frida did, but instead to spur reflections and discussions.

But what exactly were we going to check once we brought the Influencing Machine and users into the lab?

The purpose of the Influencing Machine is to create a cultural provocation, challenging our views of what a machine can be, in particular whether it was capable of being emotional – but how would we check what the machine in fact was able to provoke? What if users did not get the idea at all, or if they only got frustrated and dismissed it entirely? A provocation entails an experience that is not necessarily easy or pleasant for users, so we may have the goal of developing painful or difficult situations. This is something standard usability strategies will try to avoid.

We had to disentangle frustration that came from *bad design* choices from frustration that came from actually encountering a machine that cannot be controlled – only influenced. The design of the Influencing Machine is balancing on a thin line between being predictable and controllable and thereby boring and not achieving its purpose, and being unpredictable and uncontrollable and thereby alienating its users, making them feel stupid and out of control entirely.

5.2   The First Influencing Machine Study

Our first study of the machine was done at a very early stage in the development cycle. The Influencing Machine did not have any sound system at this point. The evaluation was explorative in nature, as our main goal was to feedback into the design process.

Users were brought in small groups (six groups with in total 12 subjects) into a room with the Influencing Machine. Users were told that the installation had something to do with emotions, and were then allowed to play with the system as long as they liked. On average, they spent about 20 minutes in the room.

Generally speaking, users were first curious, then became frustrated. Often this frustration stemmed from not being able to control the machine. They had a great deal of trouble figuring out the relationship between postcards and drawings. For some users this became a barrier that stopped their interest in the machine. Some users found the Influencing Machine drawings too simple and drawn too slow. The mailbox itself was liked. Unfortunately, the bar code reader in the mailbox made a beep whenever a postcard was inserted. This led subjects to think of the mailbox as a machine rather than a form of communication with a semi-living being.

A complication was the frustration that users often developed with lack of control. Many users got irritated and frustrated when they could not figure it out. Certainly this is an affective reaction, but not one intended, unless leading to the kinds of discussions sought by the designer/artist. These thoughts and observations led to a number of system design changes performed by Sengers and colleagues.

Users were confused about the emotional meaning of the imagery. The addition of the sound system helps to clarify the agent's interpretation of input cards and its emotional state. Moreover, an internal emotional display was developed showing the level of each of the internal emotions. Although the designers of the Influencing Machine were reluctant to show these internals, by offering the user an opportunity to understand how the agent is designed to feel, users can and do engage in critical reflection on whether they believe that the drawings actually express the stated internal emotion state. This display can be set in a state were it will fade away over time, supporting users through their initial exploration without constraining further interaction.

Users were also confused about the nature of influencing versus controlling the system. With the above improvements to emotional expression, including direct sound feedback instead of mechanical Mailbox beeping for changes in emotion, users would hopefully have a better understanding of how they affect the system. At the same time, this concept is subtle and runs counter to users' everyday experiences with computers; it may simply be in its nature that it is hard for users to understand.

Finally, users were sometimes bored by the drawings themselves. Speeding up the drawings, reducing the persistence of behaviors so that new forms appear more quickly, and adding some more complex drawings will probably raise user interest. Also, transitions between drawings need to be handled more gracefully. In the old version, the system draws for a while and then clears the screen and starts over. The graphics was re-implemented to remove these rough breaks by layering over one another and gradually fading away.

In general, the first study achieved the first level of feedback to the design envisioned by our two-tiered design method discussed above. It made clear what aspects of the affective input means and the affective output from the system were understandable/failing to the users preventing them from going from a 'basic' level of understanding the input – output relation, to actually starting to reflect on the overall purpose of the machine.

5.3   The Second Influencing Machine Study

The second study was performed in a similar fashion to the first study, but on an improved and altered Influencing Machine. In this new version, the timing was faster, the scribblings more complex and interesting, and an explanatory 'emotion bar' was added to the top of the scribblings showing the emotional state of the machine.

The results from this second study showed that the design changes did indeed achieve the desired result; users were more positive, less confused, and more of them did understand the point and were willing to discuss the intended provocation than in the first study. The replies to the interview questions and the interactions the groups did with the machine indicated that the group who had the emotional display on did more easily grasp that the machine expressed emotions and could be influenced.

Subjects were more inclined to form theories of what was going on inside the Influencing Machine and we got more positive comments about the drawings and the overall experience. The subjects from the second study also used the Influencing machine twice longer in average than the subjects from the first study. But there were still those subjects who experienced frustration and who were less inclined to 'get the point'.

5.3.1   Video Analysis   The analysis of users' experiences of the Influencing Machine was done through carefully transcribing everything that the subjects did with the machine as well as their dialogue with one-another and not to avoid interpretation of what was going on and how subjects' personality interfered with their interaction. We will discuss the case of group 6.

#6 Two Teachers and a Husband   The three subjects were 61 (female), 65 (male) and 42 (female) years old. The two women were teachers, and one of them, was married to the man.

The two women did not look very carefully at the cards that they put in the machine. Nor did they analyze what was happening on the screen. The machine restarted after 3 minutes. Both women kept on entering cards very quickly. The man was quiet, kept to the background, and only gave away something of his theories after about 8 minutes. In general, one woman, his wife, was quite dominating and the man had a hard time convincing her that his theories could be proven. The two women realized that the machine kept on drawing even when they did not put any cards inside the machine, and used this as an argument that the man's theories could be dismissed.

The man did not give up, but discussed the emotional display and said that one has to put a card inside the machine in order to make the values in the emotional display fluctuate. He got some positive feedback on his theory from the machine, and albeit reluctantly, he got the two women to take part in some more theory forming. Unfortunately, the machine did not react to the postcard that the dominant woman inserted, at least not visibly. The man got more visible reactions to his postcards, which in turn made him think that the machine only reacted on him. He suspiciously turned around, staring at the video camera, wondering whether this was in fact where the 'control' was placed.

During this, the dominant woman made an interesting comment: she pointed at the computer under the table with the table cloth, and asked the man whether this computer was in fact connected to the machine. She meant that if it was, then the Influencing Machine was just a computer – not a machine in its own right. It seemed that to her a computer cannot be what she perceives that the Influencing Machine is (according to the man's theories). If it is a computer, it must be predictable, not influenced by them.

They stopped putting in cards for a while which caused the drawings to change color until they were white and the machine restarted. They put a few cards inside the machine and then they waited for it to restart again, just to see if the drawing would change color to white again before the machine restarted. Again, the man argued that the cards they put in the machine seemed to be influencing it, but the other two argued that the card is not important and that the machine just went around in a cycle: "placed on 'repeat'".

They waited for the machine to restart a third time, to check if the machine would start drawing even if they did not insert any cards, and they found that it did. They discussed whether the machine would restart if they stopped inserting cards or if it restarts after a certain time interval. They speculated about whether the emotions were connected with certain colors in the drawings. Finally, the dominant woman concluded that it was entirely random, while the man kept on insisting that there were certain relationships to his actions.

This summarised transcript shows how theories were formed and discussed, and how the Influencing Machine was even capable of spurring the kind of discussion of what a computer can/cannot be that the designer/artist sought.

In total, seven of the nine groups invented different theories that they tested during their session with the machine. They tried to make the machine respond in a particular way by putting a certain card or a specific category of cards inside the machine; for example, they tried to use only dark-colored cards in order to see the response from the machine. The groups that tested several different theories during the session seamed to have more fun during the session than the other groups, but after a while most of them got frustrated when the response from the machine was not what they expected.

5.3.2 Timing and Control In the Influencing Machine, the *timing* of emotion change and development, drawings, and system's reactions to inserted postcards is key. The interaction cycle must be slow enough for users to recognize the emotions, but fast enough to attract and keep the users' interest. The intent is not for the user to control the machine, but also not to make users too frustrated when they cannot control it at all. The second study showed that the design of the machine was closer to a reasonable balance point.

5.4 Implications for Design Method

The two studies of the Influencing Machine showed the need for in-depth interpretation and analysis of users' behavior. The study is an explicit attempt *not* to avoid the messiness of having several users together in the lab, interpreting their behaviors based on some subjective understanding of their personality and attitudes. Through such a study, we could give the designer of the Influencing Machine a *grounded feeling* for what works.

The study also showed the usefulness of first making certain that the affective input – output behavior could be understood, before studying the overall design against its purpose.

Problems that reappeared in this study had to do with perceived level of control – a natural consequence of provoking users preconceptions of machines as stupid, rational, and predictable – and timing of the affective behaviours. These two factors are not unrelated. After speeding up the response from the machine, users felt that that they could understand and control the machine to a larger extent than in the first study.

Laboratory evaluations helped us uncover problems in interaction design related to questions like: "Is this interaction cycle right? How is the timing? Do users understand the affective expressions?" In the case of the Influencing Machine this meant reaching the balance point between control and complete randomness (in the eyes of the users), finding good timing so that users are captivated (and not bored), finding the right level of interesting drawings, and getting better sound.

Finally, let us point out that evaluation of this kind can give answer to the question "Is it good interaction?", but not to the one "Is it good art?" If our question is "Is it good *interactive* art?," we may need to more fully integrate the perspectives of art and HCI. We suggest this may be done by a 'system critic,' who analogous to a literary, movie, or art critic is specialized in understanding the social, cultural, and intellectual context of the system and who simultaneously can evaluate the system using variations on standard HCI techniques.

6.   SenToy and FantasyA

Finally, the last system we have designed and studied was an affective input device – the SenToy – and a game named FantasyA (Andersson et al. (2002), Paiva et al. (2003), Höök et al. (2003)). SenToy is a doll with sensors that allows users to (partly) control their avatars in an adventure game. SenToy allows players[4] to influence the emotions of a synthetic character placed in FantasyA, a 3D virtual game. By expressing gestures associated with anger, fear, surprise, sadness and joy through SenToy, players influence the emotions of the character they control in the game. Players' characters will be drawn into duels where the expressed emotion determines which spell is cast at their opponents, the players' character will trade (using emotion expressions) with other characters to win magic stones, and so on.

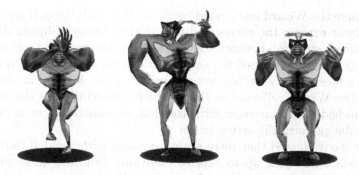

Figure 5.5. Fear and two versions of Gloat as expressed by one of the avatars (stills of animated behaviour).

The aim of SenToy is to 'pull the player into the game' through the use of a physical, touchable affective interface. With sensors in its limbs, sensitive to movement and acceleration, SenToy is designed to capture certain manipulations patterns from players, which in turn are associated with particular emotional expression.

The affective output in the system is shown through how the avatar that the player controls behaves, see Figure 5.5. This in turn also determines what the character will do next. Emotions as expressed through SenToy, controlling the avatars emotional state and subsequent actions is therefore the only way that the player can play the game.

6.1   Wizard of Oz

When designing SenToy it was hypothesized that players would manipulate the toy to express emotions by using a particular set of gestures. Those gestures were drawn from literature on how we express emotions through bodily movements and from emotion theories (Darwin (1872/1998), Davies (2001)). To evaluate this idea we performed a Wizard of Oz study (Andersson et al. 2002). Wizard of Oz studies have previously been used for natural language interface (Dahlbäck et al. (1993)) and intelligent agent design (Maulsby et al. (1993)) and we showed that it can effectively be used also in the domain of affective input design.

In a Wizard of Oz study, users are made to believe that they are interacting with a system, while in reality they are interacting with a human Wizard, sitting behind the screen pretending to be the system. This study was performed with dolls that did not have any sensors at all, but where the Wizard interpreted users' actions with the doll and made the avatar express the corresponding emotion. Since subjects divided their visual attention between the doll and the screen with their avatar, subjects sometimes missed the actual performance of an emotion of the avatar's face or body as they were focusing on the doll and moving the doll. The Wizard adjusted to this problem, delaying until the subject had finished their movement with the doll, or sometimes, even making the avatar perform the action twice.

The study showed that there are movements with the doll that most users will easily pick up to express emotions, but that these are not necessarily linked to any 'natural behavior'. First, users will not behave in the same way when expressing emotions through a doll rather than through their own bodily behaviors. There are numerous reasons for this, among them the cultural notions for how dolls and cartoon characters behave when expressing emotions. Secondly, we needed to put users in a loop where they are given feedback from the system through how the avatar reacts. Users will learn how to create the right behavior through watching the face of the avatar when they perform actions on the SenToy. Thus there is room for 'unnatural' learnt behaviors. In addition, imitation between avatar animation and end-users' movements with the doll, will probably take place (and did in fact happen during the last study).

The WoZ study also revealed some other aspects of the design of the doll and its interaction through the sensor technology, such as the preferred distance between user and screen, movements of limbs that

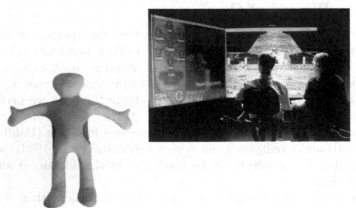

Figure 5.6. SenToy to the left and boys playing the FantasyA game through SenToy to the right.

will most likely occur, desired softness and size of the doll, and which facial expression it should have (neutral).

Based on the results from this study, the doll in Figure 5.6 was designed and implemented. The movements for each emotion are described in Table 5.1.

Table 5.1. Mapping of emotions to recognized expressions.

Emotion	Expression
Happy	Jumping/Dancing up and down
Sad	Lean the body forward at least 45 degrees
Gloat	Point right arm forward and jump up and down
Anger	Shake doll forwards and backwards or side to side
Fear	Hand(s) in front of eyes
Surprise	Jump back rapidly, and tilt backwards at end

6.2 Second Study of SenToy Used in FantasyA

In the second study of SenToy, we were able to use a functioning prototype of the toy based on the movements collected from the WoZ study and an early version of the adventure game named FantasyA. Users (players) were brought in as pairs and were encouraged to play together. In general, the conclusions were that SenToy was a great success, but that some of the emotions did not necessarily make sense in the context of the game. The game itself was also quite complex and only a few of the players did understand what was going on.

Subjects found it fairly easy to express most emotions, with the exception of the emotion Surprise. Surprise was also only rarely used during the game. The most used emotions were Gloat and Happy, on second place came Sad and Angry, on third place Fear, and finally, Surprise.

During the game most emotional expressions were very physical and encouraged players to act out the emotion. The exception from this rule was Sad where subjects sat very still, bending the doll over waiting to see the result on the screen. This is not necessarily a bad design choice since sadness is characterized by an inwards posture among people, thus encouraged by the design of the movement.

Some users, especially the kids, were really keen on having the doll and would pull it from the other player or interfere and try to help the other player in expressing some particular emotion. In the interviews, two kids commented that they would have liked to have a doll each and be able to play against each other.

In the comments field of the questionnaire, one player wrote:

> A few days after having played, I still like the doll very much. I really appreciated his direct contact to give commands, even if in that case, the commands were not that obvious and their result a bit fuzzy. (adult player)

One of the kids remarked that he would probably like to use the SenToy for a whole month before getting bored. Considering that he was 12 years old, this is a very good result.

After the game about 80% seemed to like the doll. The kids were in general more enthusiastic about the doll than the adults. In the interviews about the SenToy some players felt that they became one with SenToy, but others felt that a button-based interface would have made them feel more directly in control of it. In general, the impression given was that they could identify with the doll most of the time and act through it, but that the avatar was reacting in strange ways sometimes, thus they did not feel that they through the doll became the avatar.

Players also seemed to have an intellectual rather than emotional relationship to the emotions of their own avatar and to the emotions expressed through SenToy. They would "instrumentalize" the emotion to be one of the commands in the game, such as "cast blast" or "cast shield". They would be playing the strategic, intellectual game rather than being influencing on a basic instinctive emotional level. This was due to several different design decisions – some of which might be easily changed if the aim is to make the player more emotionally affected by the game.

On another level, players do get more and more involved with the game – especially when they win a few duels – but to the experimental leaders this seemed to be more in terms of "duel emotions" than the six emotions that can be expressed through the doll.

The FantasyA game is currently being redesigned by Paiva and colleagues to better cater for an emotional involvement between user, SenToy and their personification in the game as their avatar. The narrative structure connecting the game turns with the emotional states of their avatar will be the key to further developing the game, together with these study results.

6.3 Implications for Design Method

The design and user studies of SenToy and FantasyA show how user studies can be very relevant to do even before a system has been implemented or fully designed. The Wizard of Oz study saved a lot of energy in the project through pointing out the flaws in the theory of how people would move the doll to express different emotions. The design of SenToy, similar to the design of the mailbox in the Influencing Machine, also show how these affective interactive systems are indeed designed artifacts with their own interaction problems that cannot be solved simply through creating an even better theory of human emotions and emotion expression. Arriving at a good affective game or an interesting affective interactive art piece, is a process where the user studies can help to debug the particular interaction functions.

While not used as much in the studies of SenToy and FantasyA, subjective evaluation and interpretation of what where experiencing when using the system were crucial. It is through such an interpretative analysis that we could see that users did not identify directly with the emotions they were expressing in the game, such as sadness or surprise, but that they instead were reacting with a different set of emotions much more related to their game play experience. We believe that a careful analysis and redesign of the relationship between emotion and the next game turn could create a system where the two are more in harmony and players will start to experience the emotions they are expressing through the SenToy.

The two studies of SenToy and FantasyA again show the importance of first getting the affective input – output relationship right before attempting to evaluate, in this case, the success in terms of how well the affective game captures users' interest and achieves affective involvement. Since the design of this system is not yet finished, yet another study would probably be a good last step in the design cycle.

7. Discussion

The studies of the three different systems show the importance of bootstrapping affective interaction and making sure that the affective expressions or affective input opportunities are understood before the overall system can be evaluated. The studies also reveal some important issues to be dealt with once this bootstrapping has been done and the system is evaluated against its overall purpose. In particular, we find that the field of affective computing often make simplistic statements where it is claimed that e g users will more easily bond with an affective system, become more efficient if not stressed or disturbed at the right moment. The Agneta & Frida study and the Influencing Machine study show how complex the reactions are to these interfaces and how much depends on the users' background, age, attitudes and interest – to some extent this is different from normal usability issues.

Some general conclusions about design difficulties of affective interfaces can be drawn. First of all, all the studies confirm that issues of
timing are crucial. Agneta & Frida's jokes have to arrive at the right
moment, the Influencing Machine has to be influenced at the right level
and draw its drawings fast enough in order for the interaction to work,
and finally, the avatar reactions to SenToy has to be delayed or pro-
longed enough for the user to both handle the doll and watch the avatar
on the screen in order to understand what happens next in the game.

For SenToy, many lessons were learnt before the costly process of
creating a doll with sensors was started. All studies, but in particular
the SenToy study, definitely show that it will be a mistake to only aim
for "naturalness" in the affective expressions. From the theory of human
expression, a set of movements were extracted, but in the two studies,
these movements were not the ones that best fitted with the particular
game situation and how users did really behave with the doll. Most
interactive agents and affective interfaces are interesting in that they
are different from how we behave in human-human relationships, but
still similar enough for us to recognize them and have fun with them.
This concurs nicely with theories such as those presented by Suchman
(1987, 1997) or by Dourish (2002). Dourish argues that rather than
embedding fixed notions of meaning within technologies, we should allow
users to create and communicate meaning through their interaction with
the system and with each other through the system, since this is how
artefacts are given their meaning in human culture.

We need to do more of these open-ended explorative studies, early
on in the design process, before we can start doing the studies that
really matter: namely those that show that affect in interaction does
indeed contribute something different from other kinds of design. In this
process, we need to more openly discuss which measurements will indeed
be related to the overall goals of the entire system. The non-correlation
between measurements in Agneta & Frida shows how difficult it is to
separate an understanding of what kind of experience we want to evoke
from users' attitudes and values. It also shows that we need to be clear of
what kind of experience it is that we want to give the user: a short-term
fun thing, a post-usage positive attitude, a provocation that continues
even after using the system as for the Influencing Machine, or what?

While we have not presented a complete framework for how to bootstrap design and evaluate affective applications, we believe that our studies could be the inspiration to taking some more steps in this direction.
In particular, we hope to encourage taking users into the loop when designing the interaction cycle with respect to timing, narrative context,

understanding of affective input and output, and being more open to the effects of users' attitudes and cultural values.

Acknowledgments

Thanks to Gerd Andersson, Adrian Bullock, Pia Mårtensson, Per Persson, Ana Paiva and Phoebe Sengers who worked with me on the studies discussed here. Thanks to Petra Fagerberg and Anna Ståhl for reading and commenting this text. Thanks also to the anonymous subjects who participated in the studies. Most of the work was done within the EC-funded SAFIRA (Supporting Affective Interactions for Real-time Applications) project while the author was employed at SICS.

Notes

1. It should be pointed out that though the author was involved in all the user studies described in here, the designs and studies of the systems were performed by teams of researchers.

2. Believability refers to how well those characters are able to appear as living, coherent characters that users are willing to interact with.

3. An evaluation of a web-interface from 1994 done by users 2004 would tell us that it looks boring, old and unusable, has all its buttons in the wrong places, does not use frames properly, while an evaluation of the same interface done back in 1994 would probably show completely different results. Computer interfaces are cultural artefacts.

4. We use the term player rather than user throughout the description of this system to emphasise that the target domain is a game.

References

Ark, W., Dryer, D., and Lu, D. (1999). The emotion mouse. In *Proceedings of HCI International 1999*. Munich, Germany.

Andersson, G., Höök, K., Mourão, D., Paiva, A., and Costa, M. (2002). Using a Wizard of Oz study to inform the design of SenToy. Exhibit at *Designing Interactive Systems, DIS'02*, ACM Press, London.

Bates, J. (1994). The Role of Emotion in Believable Agents. *Communications of the ACM, Special Issue on Agents*, 37(7): 122–125.

Brennan, S.E. and Ohaeri, J.O. (1994). Effects of Message Style on Users' Attributions toward Agents. In *Conference companion on Human factors in computing systems, CHI'94*, pp. 281–282, Boston, Massachusetts, United States.

Dahlbäck, N., Jönsson, A., and Ahrenberg, L. (1993). Wizard of Oz studies—Why and how. In *Proceedings of the 1st international conference on Intelligent user interfaces*, pp. 193–200, ACM Press, Orlando, Florida, United States.

Damásio, A. (1995). *Descartes' Error*, Avon Books, New York.

Davies, E. (2001). *Beyond Dance: Laban's Legacy of Movement Analysis*, Seven Locks Press, Santa Ana, CA, USA.

Darwin, C. (1872/1998). 3rd ed. by Paul Ekman, *The expression of emotions in man and animals*. Oxford University Press, Oxford.

Dumas, JS. and Redish, J. (1993). *A Practical Guide to Usability Testing*, Ablex, Norwood, NJ.

Fernandez, R., Scheirer, J., and Picard, R. (1999) *Expression glasses: a wearable device for facial expression recognition*, MIT Media Lab Tech. Rep. 484, Cambridge, MA.

Gaver, W., Hooker, B., and Dunne, A. (2001). *The Presence Project.*, Royal College of Art, London.

Hendrix, J., Ruttkay, Zs., ten Hagen, P., Noot, H., Lelievre, A., and de Ruiter, B. (2000). A facial repertoire for avatars, *Proceedings of the Workshop Interacting Agents*, pp. 27–46, Enschede, The Netherlands.

Hassenzahl, M., Platz, A., Burmester, M., and Lehner, K. (2000). Hedonic and Ergonomic Quality Aspects Determine a Software's Appeal. In *Proceedings of the SIGCHI conference on Human factors in computing systems*, pp. 201–208, The Hague, The Netherlands.

Höök K. (1997). Evaluating the Utility and Usability of an Adaptive Hypermedia System. In *Proceedings of the International Conference on Intelligent User Interfaces*, pp. 179–186, Orlando, Florida.

Höök, K. (2000). Steps to take before IUIs become real. *Journal of Interacting with Computers*, 12(4):409–426, February.

Höök, K, Bullock, A., Paiva, A., Vala, M., Chaves, R., and Prada, R. (2003). FantasyA and SenToy. In *Proceedings of the conference on Human factors in computing systems*, pp. 804–805, Ft. Lauderdale, Florida, USA, ACM Press.

Höök, K., Persson, P., and Sjölinder, M. (2000). Evaluating Users' Experience of a Character-Enhanced Information Space. *Journal of AI Communications* 13(3): 195–212.

Höök, K., Sengers, P., and Andersson, G. (2003). Sense and Sensibility: Evaluation and Interactive Art. In *Proceedings of the conference on Human factors in computing systems*, pp. 241–248, ACM Press, Ft. Lauderdale, Florida, USA.

King, W.J. and Ohya, J.(1995). The representation of agents: A study of phenomena in virtual environments. In *Proc. of the 4th IEEE International Workshop on Robot and Human Communication ROMAN'95*, pp. 289–290, Tokyo, Japan.

Koda, T. and Maes, P. (1996). Agents with Faces: The Effects of Personification of Agents. In *Proceedings of Human-Computer Interaction*, pp. 239–245, London, UK.

Lakoff, G. and Johnson, M. (1999). *Philosophy in the Flesh: The Embodied Mind and Its Challenge to Western Thought*, Basic Books, New York.

Maglio, P. and Matlock, T. (1999). The Conceptual Structure of Information Space. In Munro, A. , Höök, K., and Benyon D., editors, *Social Navigation of Information Space*, Springer-Verlag, London.

Martinho, C. and Paiva, A. (1999). Pathematic Agents. In *Proceedings of the third annual conference on Autonomous Agents*, pp. 1–8, Seattle, Washington.

Maulsby, D., Greenberg, S., and Mander, R. (1993). Prototyping an intelligent agent through Wizard of Oz. In *Proceedings of the conference on Human factors in computing systems*, pp. 277–284, Amsterdam, The Netherlands.

Norman, D. (1990). *Design of everyday things, The Design of Everyday Things*. Doubleday, New York.

Ortony, A., Clore, A., and Collins, G. (1988). *The Cognitive Structure of Emotions*, Cambridge University Press, Cambridge.

Paiva, A., Andersson, G., Höök,K., Mourao, D., Costa, M., and Martinho, C. (2003). SenToy in FantasyA: Designing an Affective Sympathetic Interface to a Computer Game. In *Journal of Personal and Ubiquitous Computing*, 6(5-6): 378–389, Springer-Verlag, London Ltd.

Persson, P., Laaksolahti, J., and Lönnqvist, P. (2002). Understanding Social Intelligence. in Dautenhahn, K., Bond, A., Canamero, L. C., and Edmonds, B., editors, *Socially Intelligent Agents - creating relationships with computers and robots*, pp. 21–28, Kluwer, Dordrecht.

Picard, R.W. (1997). *Affective Computing*. MIT Press, Cambridge, MA.

Reeves, B. and Nass, C. (1996). *The Media Equation: How People Treat Computers, Television, and New media Like Real People and Places*, Cambridge University, Cambridge.

Sengers, P., Liesendahl, R., Magar, W., Seibert, C., Müller, B., Joachims, T., Geng, W., Mårtensson, P., and Höök, K. (2002). The Enigmatics of Affect. In *Proceedings of Designing Interactive Systems, DIS'02*, pp. 87–98, ACM Press, London.

Shneiderman, B. (1997). Direct Manipulation for Comprehensible, Predictable and Controllable User Interfaces. In Moore, J., Edmonds, E., and Puerta, A., editors, *Proceedings of 1997 International Conference on Intelligent User Interfaces*, pp. 33 – 39, ACM Press, Orlando, Florida.

Suchman, L.A. (1987). *Plans and Situated Actions: The problem of human-machine interaction.* Cambridge University Press, New York.
Suchman, L.A. (1997). From Interactions to Integrations. In Howard S., Hammond, J., and Lindegaard, G., editors, *Proceedings of Human-Computer Interaction INTERACT'97.* p. 3, Sidney, Australia.

Chapter 6

'USER AS ASSESSOR' APPROACH TO EMBODIED CONVERSATIONAL AGENTS

The Case of Apparent Attention in ECAs

Clifford Nass, Erica Robles, and Qianying Wang

The proper study of mankind is Man.

—Alexander Pope

Abstract   Traditionally, an optimal embodied conversational agent (ECA) has the same capabilities and appearance as an actual person. This chapter proposes a 'user as assessor' approach to evaluating ECAs that focuses on how ECAs manifest human capabilities independent of actual capabilities that an ECA may possess. Literatures on humans as producers of behavior and humans as interpreters of behavior are leveraged to draw implications for how ECAs should behave to seem most realistic to their human assessors. To illustrate the approach, we answer the question, "what will convince a user that an ECA is paying attention to him or her, whether the ECA truly is paying attention or not?" 'Apparent attention' is conceptualized in terms of two basic dimensions – selectivity and breadth – and their indicators and impacts. Using the proposed approach, the chapter provides guidelines for how agents, conversational agents, and ECAs can effectively exhibit attention.

Keywords: User as assessor approach, apparent attention, selectivity, breadth, evaluation methodology, design principle.

Z. Ruttkay and C. Pelachaud (eds.), From Brows to Trust, 161–188.
© *2004 Kluwer Academic Publishers. Printed in the Netherlands.*

1.   Introduction

The history of virtually every new medium follows a similar pattern. When the medium is first introduced, the technology generates the excitement; the content is simply a means of illustrating the medium's capabilities. For example, when hi-fis, record players that had much greater and clearer frequency range, were first introduced, all of the interest concerned the range of sounds. Thus, 'Songs of the Humpback Whale,' which was simply a recording of sounds that the whales made while communicating, was one of the hottest selling records of the era, even though environmental interest was very low. When the first musicals were introduced to Broadway, attendees were fascinated that actors could burst into song and dance; it was not until 'Oklahoma' that the songs became an integral part of character development and plot. Similarly, when 'special effects' were first added to movies, film critics' discussions focused on how remarkable the effects were and how difficult they were to create, instead of the current concern with appositeness of the effects for the particular story and genre ('The Matrix' notwithstanding). Finally, the early video games, such as 'Pong' and 'Space Invaders,' were engaging because the idea of controlling and interacting with images on a screen was startling;. It was not until 'Pacman' that characters and plot became part of the videogame industry. In sum, media are initially evaluated with reference to how the technologies are *built*; it is only later that media are assessed with respect to their *impact on users*.

It is not surprising, then, that embodied conversational agents (ECAs) have the same history. ECAs are synthetic, pictorial characters that can converse with the user (or with other ECAs) by one or more of the natural modalities of human-human communication (see Cassell (2000)). Traditionally, the definition of a 'better' ECA has been one that possessed more actual human capabilities and a more human appearance. Processing information like a human was *a priori* better than thinking like a machine; speaking and seeing was superior to being mute or blind; realistic articulations and fluent language were a greater success than mechanical-sounding speech and poorly-parsed sentences, and fully-elaborated, mobile human bodies were clearly more desirable than looking like a paper clip or being unable to move. 'Improvements' were those objectively measurable aspects of ECA cognition, behavior, and appearance that were closer to the ontological characteristics of human. The sole question was: "On what dimensions (see Nass and Mason (1990)) is the particular ECA *truly* human?"

As the design and development of ECAs has matured, the literature has begun to turn from technological attributes to the recognition that a successful ECA must also comport with user's *perceptions* of the agent's characteristics. Thus, assessments of ECAs now include subjective evaluations by the user as integral to the creation and assessment of a successful ECA. Under this view, agents are successful to the extent that they encourage the user to apply a mental model of the ECA as human, regardless of how accurate that model is (see Reeves and Nass (1996)). For example, Ruttkay, Dormann and Noot(see Chapter 2 by Ruttkay et al.) include *user perception* along with design, usability, practical usage and application as the bases for comparing and evaluating ECAs. Isbister and Doyle in Chapter 1 argue that *believability* and *social interface* are as important as agency and computational issues when evaluating ECAs. Persson et al. (2000) suggest that following a *folk theory* approach to ECA design, where users are integral parts of constructing meaning in an interaction, can provide just as much value as the traditional computational approach. Finally, Catrambone, Stasko, and Xiao in Chapter 9 suggest that the interaction between characteristics of the ECA and *characteristics of the user* are as important as the objective criteria of features of the agent and the task the user is performing.

Evaluations of agents, then, have as much to do with how people think about agents as the agents' actual competencies and behaviors (see Norman (1997); Reeves and Nass (1996)). For example, a conversational agent that generates its own sentences may 'think' more like a human than an agent that merely produces scripted utterances, but from the user's point of view, the greater fluency of the latter may cause it to be identified as *more* human. Conversely, if an agent has a human ability (e.g., vision) but the agent doesn't manifest that ability – either by explicit reference or by performing an action that necessitates the ability – the technological triumph has no impact on the user.

This user-oriented notion of success may seem unfair to the engineers who must struggle to solve extremely hard problems in symbol processing, human vision algorithms, natural language production and understanding, natural movements, facial expression, emotional modeling, etc. While the technologist must struggle to invent and build technologies that compete with 200 000 years of human evolution, the complaint goes, a designer can simply 'trick' users by building ECAs that 'hint' or 'imply' that the ECAs have human skills. If this view is correct, it is the technologists who should be hailed as the heroes.

As technologies become diffused and commonplace, however, designers or creators of ECAs become the focus of attention: compared and contrasted, lauded and criticized. Whether this is 'fair' in the case of other media is moot, but designers of ECAs have a strong argument for claiming that their job is actually much harder than that of the engineer. The argument is grounded in the relative understanding of what it is to be human and what it is to *seem* human.

The scientific study of the ontology of humans dates back at least as far as Aristotle. There are entire fields of study and enormous literatures for virtually every aspect of how humans do what they do, including think (psychology), use language (linguistics), see (vision studies), hear (audiology), move (kinesiology), etc. These literatures give the builders of technologies precise targets (e.g., what frequencies humans can discriminate, exactly how weight is shifted between the legs), metrics for how close a particular implementation has come to reality (e.g., standard sentences to evaluate parsing, exact acoustic properties of speech, detailed information on human color and face discrimination), and tremendous insights into how to build to the human 'spec.'. While there are certainly arguments as to whether the best way to implement a human ability is to replicate underlying processes or to leverage the unique strengths of computers and agents (e.g., Minsky (1986)), the literature at least provides numerous, well-articulated points of departure.

Designers, conversely, can find virtually no literature on how to *indicate* the existence of a particular human ability in agents, especially where such an ability has not been explicitly implemented. This omission is very reasonable, because human abilities tend to be very highly correlated with manifestations and perceptions of those abilities. People who cannot see generally cannot hide their lack of vision and those who can see navigate complex spaces effectively; those who do not have the requisite musculature cannot seem to walk while those who have appropriate muscle strength walk within the first year of life; and people in a foreign country can rarely hide their ignorance of a language, while native children speak very well by the age of three. Because ontology has historically been of much more concern than perception, the literature simply describes actual abilities and treats manifestations much more lightly (gesture and para-linguistic cues are two key exceptions). Even when an ability is not manifest, a person assumes that other people have the same basic abilities that they themselves have. Thus, when a person encounters another person, they automatically assume that the person has judgment, emotions, imagination, etc. (although this may not be the case for users encountering ECAs).

Where can designers turn for help when trying to create more human ECAs? How can they overcome the particularly difficult problem of making the ECA *seem* human-like, especially when it lacks human abilities? One's first instinct is to simply copy behaviors that are associ-

ated with humans, such as blinking and head-turning, small movements
when the ECA is idling, changing the comments over time, altering
facial expression, etc. Unfortunately, this approach is doomed to fail-
ure because without the behaviors being clearly and tightly linked to
the user or the context, there is a disturbing mismatch that makes the
ECA seem even less veridical and less human than if it didn't exhibit
these manifestations at all. For example, a cheerful voice that delivers
bad news (see Nass and Gong (2000)), a natural language system that
give identical answers to repeated questions (violating Griceian maxims;
Grice (1975); Reeves and Nass (1996)), and ECAs whose posture do not
match their personality (see Isbister and Nass (2000)) all lead to a sense
of the ECA as non-human, deceptive, or surreal.

How, then, can one adduce those behaviors that make ECAs lifelike without clear and explicit guidance from the literature or simple
observation? Two approaches prove fruitful. The first is to understand
the underlying processes that determine how humans think and feel in
a particular domain. That is, rather than simply mimic the surface
behavioral features of humans, we focus on the fundamental structural
elements of human information processing and communication (Cassell
and Stone (1999)) and adduce the likely physical and verbal behaviors
associated with particular internal states. From an understanding of the
link between the brain and the body, we can derive how a human would
respond, and hence how an ECA *should* respond.

The most effective ECA behaviors to create and assess using this
technique are *automatic responses associated with internal states*. There
are two reasons for this. First, these actions tend to be independent
of the situation, because they are tightly coupled to internal states of
the person. Second, these responses tend to be cross-cultural because
they are primitively grounded; thus, they are robust against differences
in users.

The second approach, conversely, *begins* with the user as an assessor of behavior. People have mental models of the meaning of various
human behaviors, models that are not always accurate. For example,
while humans tend to be very confident that they can accurately identify deception, most people are very poor at determining who is lying
and who is telling the truth (see Clark (1996)). Similarly, humans are
not perfectly attuned to the cues emitted by a person, attributing too
much to certain manifestations (e.g., eye gaze) and too little to other
manifestations (e.g., body posture). By starting with humans' *perceptions* of other people's behaviors rather than what those behaviors *truly*
represent, designers and evaluators of ECAs can gain insight into the
more nuanced aspects of ECA behavior. The two approaches can be

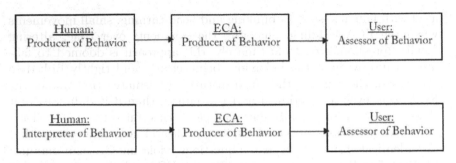

Figure 6.1. Two approaches for adducing how to make ECAs lifelike.

compared and contrasted as in Figure 6.1. These two approaches are not mutually exclusive. Whenever the manifestation of an internal state is consistent with people's beliefs about the meaning of the manifestation, the two approaches provide identical insights. In what follows, we will simply leverage whichever approach is more useful for addressing the particular design issue.

2.   Attention as an Example of the 'User as Assessor' Approach

To illustrate the 'user as assessor' approach to ECAs, we will focus on the concept of *attention*. Attention is at the very core of human communication (see Grosz and Sidner (1986)): Why should a person transmit information unless the other party is going to receive it and process it? Thus, to be a human-like interaction partner, it is critical that an ECA demonstrate that it is attending to the user.

2.1   How Do Humans Attend?

Before turning to the manifestations of attention in humans, it seems useful to present an overview of how humans actually pay attention. The processes of human attention have been a particularly active and vigorous area of research. As early as 1890, William James wrote: 'Every one knows what attention is. It is the taking possession by the mind, in clear and vivid form, of one out of what seem several simultaneously possible objects or trains of thought. Focalization and concentration of consciousness are of its essence. It implies withdrawal from some things in order to deal effectively with others' (see James (1980)). Following James, many other researchers proposed various theories to explain the mechanisms of attention. Each of these theories addresses James' notion that attention requires a 'withdrawal from some things', that is, selective effort. Among these theories, capacity theory is particularly informative and useful.

Capacity theory suggests that humans have a finite attentional resource pool. This limited ability to attend forces people to focus on certain stimuli instead of fully attending to every aspect of every stimulus in the environment (see Kahneman (1973); Wickens (1984)). However, people do have substantial control over how they choose to allocate their attention and divide their resources among various elements about which they may want to gather information. For example, a person can choose either to focus exclusively on a single element, or to divide her attention among multiple elements with less attentional resources devoted to each. Similarly, a person can decide how much information to obtain about a particular element. Selective focusing on a certain element and the amount of effort devoted to that element reflects the goals of the person who is paying attention.

Any attended element can be monitored by one or more sensory inputs. For example, imagine that John, a college senior, is approached by Mary, an attractive freshman, who has lost her way. John avidly watches her facial expressions, he listens intently to the melody of her voice, and he can detect the slight smell of her perfume. During this interaction, his best friend, Scott, passes by and calls out loudly. Unnoticed, Scott taps John on the shoulder, but John still doesn't seem to know that Scott is there. John has focused so exclusively on Mary that his limited attentional resources are fully consumed, leaving no room to monitor other elements in the environment, such as voices or physical contact.

Recent research suggest that humans use the same limited pool of attentional resources for different sensory channels, including vision, hearing, touch, and smell (see Latorella (1999); Spence et al. (2001)). That is why Scott's idea of using a non-engaged modality, touch, was nonetheless unsuccessful. Indeed, attention to multiple modalities is particularly resource-consuming. Supramodal control consumes attentional resource to integrate the different sensory inputs (see Biernet and Vescio (1993); Mirsky (1989)). Therefore, multiple sensory channels assigned to one element costs more attentional resource than using a single channel. This increased focus on one element decreases the possibility that other elements are attended to.

2.2   Conceptualizing Apparent Attention

Following the notion that the 'user as assessor' is at the heart of designing a successful ECA, we ask: *What will convince a user that an ECA is paying attention to him or her, whether the ECA truly is paying attention or not?* That is, we are interested in the user as a consumer and *evaluator* of the attentional behavior of the ECA; we are not interested in the much more common questions of what leads users to pay attention *to* ECAs nor in how to build ECAs that *actually* attend to the user.

Whether the role of the ECA be pedagogical, collaborative, assistive, or social, an ECA must manifest attention in order to fulfill its communicative function and to confirm their 'humanness' (see Isbister and Nass (2000); Traum and Rickel (2002)). Two steps are required to make a user feel that he/she is being attended to (whether the ECA is in fact attending to the person or not). First, the ECA must appear to be selecting the person for attention from a choice of other people or objects in the environment, a process we term *apparent selectivity*. Second, the ECA must appear to gather a variety of information about the person that it has (seemingly) selected, a process we term *apparent breadth*. We discuss each of the dimensions in turn.

2.2.1   Apparent Selectivity   The first dimension that influences the degree of perceived attention is apparent selectivity. Selectivity is the withdrawal of focus from some items in order to focus effectively on others. The selected item or items are preferentially identified, and they draw cognitive resources, mental effort, and concentration towards them. Conversely, the unselected items are filtered out or placed at the margin of the attentional space. This discriminating property of selectivity generates a strong perception of attention. The following example demonstrates how generalized agent selectivity can be understood.

Imagine that you live in a house equipped with an intelligent agent, standing by and awaiting your commands. One summer night, you come home with a group of friends, and everyone comments that your living room is a little stuffy. Knowing that you have an intelligent agent managing your home, one of your friends calls out: 'Open the window!' Nothing happens. A few others try to address your agent, but there is still no response. Finally, you say: 'Open the windows,' and the living room windows all slide open in response. Your friends joke about how loyal your house agent is.

In the above scenario, the agent seems to focus on one user, ignoring any input from others, illustrating the essence of selectivity. Of course, it is possible that the agent was simply programmed to respond to the tenth voice that asks to open the window; in this case, selectivity was perceived but not actual.

Although we highlight the *apparent* aspect of selectivity, apparent selection is certainly correlated with its real counterpart. For example, if a camera controlled by an ECA visibly and noisily zooms in on a user, the ECA is clearly selecting as well as apparently selecting. However, a differentiation between apparent selectivity and actual selectivity is critical because, at least for agents, they are frequently not correlated. For example, an ECA's camera that is zoomed in but hidden from the user would have selectivity but not apparent selectivity. Conversely, an ECA's camera that seems zoomed in but has a very wide-angle lens exhibits apparent selectivity but not selectivity.

Apparent selectivity is usefully viewed as a continuum rather than a dichotomy (apparently selective or not apparently selective). Zero apparent specificity would suggest that the user believes that the user and every other object in the environment is approached equally, i.e., there is maximum entropy in the selections. Conversely, maximum apparent selectivity would suggest that the user believes that absolutely nothing else in the environment is perceived by the ECA other than the user. There are clearly many points between these two extremes.

2.2.2 Apparent Breadth   Apparent breadth, the second dimension of apparent attention, is the degree to which the available inputs concerning an object are obtained. Once the agent has selected (or seemingly selected) the object to attend to, breadth describes how richly the selected object is examined. Agents can potentially collect content, state, trait, and behavioral input from a variety of sensory modalities-vision, hearing, haptics, etc.-and input devices-keyboard, mouse, sensors, etc.

Like apparent selectivity, apparent breadth is correlated, though not perfectly, with real breadth. For example, an ECA that used cameras, microphones, body sensors, and a keyboard and mouse to monitor a person would have both breadth and apparent breadth. An ECA that used hidden cameras, hidden microphones, surreptitiously read a person's email, and used skin conductance sensors imbedded inside a mouse would have breadth but not apparent breadth. Conversely, an ECA that controlled sensors that claimed to determine a wide range of attributes of a person but that could only detect skin conductance (providing only arousal information) would have apparent breadth but not real breadth.

Apparent breadth can also be defined as a continuum. Zero apparent breadth is the belief that although the user has been selected, the ECA has not inputted any information about the user. Conversely, maximum apparent breadth is represented by the belief that the ECA is gathering every possible piece of information about the user. Obviously, there are ECAs that could exhibit other levels of apparent breadth.

3.   Creating Apparently Attentive ECAs

Although it is traditional to consider ECAs as a bundle of characteristics, the best way to draw on and apply the extant literatures and understandings concerning how people manifest attention and how people recognize attention (the two approaches outlined above) is to remember that ECAs are *agents* that happen to *converse* and have access to *bodies*. Specifically, we first discuss how attention can be manifested by *any* agent, including ECAs, irregardless of whether or not the agent uses language or has an embodiment. We then go on to consider apparent attention in *conversational agents*, including ECAs, whether they have a body or not. Finally, we discuss how to leverage the 'unique affordances of the body' (see Cassell (2000)).

3.1   Apparent Selectivity in ECAs

3.1.1   Apparent Selectivity in Agents   Although the literature does not generally identify 'selectivity' as a characteristic of agent behavior, selectivity, at least apparent selectivity, is intrinsic to any agent implementation. Processing limitations prevent agents from responding to *every* stimulus in the environment, so agents are generally built to 'select' only certain types and values of inputs. Furthermore, no programmer could hope to characterize an environment along the extraordinary number of dimensions and degrees that can be discriminated by a person.

An agent can seem to be highly selective even when its actual capabilities exceed its perceived capabilities. For example, when a child covers the eyes of the Barney Actimates doll, the doll says, 'I can't see you.' Even though the doll only has light sensors, the reference to 'you' may lead the child to deduce that Barney is selectively paying attention to her and selectively ignoring all other stimuli.

Filtering agents are excellent examples of selective agents, in that they seem to only see information that fulfills their current goal (see Lieberman (1995)). For example, NewT, a news-filtering agent created by Sheth and Maes (1993) adapts over time to user's news preferences. As the agent develops ever-more sophisticated algorithms, either through learning more about the user's preferences or through updates, the user feels a heightened sense of attention from the agent. Users can also be made to feel selected when they receive different treatment than other users. Intelligent Room (see Coen (1998); Oh et al. (2002)), for example, uses a multi-person tracker and a pointing detection system to identify the user who is currently requesting data. By detecting the user's location and the objects that are close to the user, the room can provide information that the user requests on the display closest to the user. This level of selectivity creates a dramatic sense of perceived attention.

3.1.2   Apparent Selectivity in Conversational Agents   Attention in conversation is a dynamic process that serves to summarize information from previous utterances, including salient objects, properties, and relations, to capture the changing focus of a discourse (see Grosz and Sidner (1986); Grosz et al. (1995)). Because of the constraint on attention, only a limited number of entities in the discourse will be considered in processing (Walker (1996)), that is, selection is a crucial mechanism in discourse (see Grosz and Sidner (1986); Mann and Thompson (1987)). Schemes for creating actual conversational attention have been implemented by some conversational systems (see Haller et al. (1997); Poesio (1992); Reed (2002); Rickel et al. (2002); Shankar et al. (2000)).

Conversational agents consistently use selectivity because full natural language understanding is much too difficult a problem given current technology. Attentional states are maintained by selectively recording salient conversational objects, discourse goals, and discourse segments (see Murray (1991)). For example, famed computer therapist Eliza (see Weizenbaum (1966)) shows attention by selecting certain discourse segments for repetition. Eliza has almost no intelligence; she relies heavily on simple tricks like picking out keywords from the user's input, and generating canned response based on them. Nevertheless, Eliza's ability to manifest some level of attention to the user has resulted in it being mistaken for a human; People feel that she is genuinely attending to them and that attention indicates caring.

Similar to Eliza, the collaborative agent system COLLAGEN (Rich and Sidner (1998); Rickel et al. (2002)), a collaborative discourse system that is the substrate of numerous conversational agents, works by maintaining a focus stack which consists of the goals of discourse. The position of each goal on the focus stack allows the agent to select, or prioritize, the appropriate behaviors.

Responsiveness is a strong indication of how selective a conversational agent is (Eysenck (1997)). Latency in response indicates either low selectivity of the user, high selectivity of something else in the environment, or simply insufficient capacity to selectively attend to the user. An ECA might intentionally slow down its speech rate when another agent or person enters the environment, for example, simply to suggest that the agent is interested in the new person and is not simply focusing on the user.

3.1.3   Apparent Selectivity in ECAs   Three dominant behavioral categories can be used to manifest selectivity in agents with embodiments, i.e., ECAs: gaze, deictic gesture, and proxemics. We discuss each in turn.

Gaze   Gaze, or orientation of the eyes, is a strong indicator of selectivity. Because the eye does not have 180 degree, let alone 360 degree, visual capability, the overt position of the eye determines which regions of space can be observed and which regions cannot (see Chopra-Khullar and Badler (1999)). Therefore, gaze indicates where the current visual focus of attention is and what objects in the space are being ignored.

Positioning of the eyes, even when an ECA cannot actually see, can be a powerful method for manifesting apparent selectivity and apparent human-like behavior (see Argyle and Cook (1976); Vertegaal et al. (2002)). The direction of a listener's gaze is highly correlated to the location of the speaker in whom the listener is interested. Similarly, speakers are more likely to direct gaze towards their intended audience (see Vertegaal et al. (2001)). This design principle should be effective even when the agent is 'listening' to textual input or is 'speaking' via a word balloon. Because users show greater willingness to speak when gaze is directed towards them (see Vertegaal and Ding (2003)), gaze is a particularly useful technique when one is attempting to lead the user to disclose information (see Moon (1998)). Gaze can also suggest selectivity by providing visual feedback of comprehension and conversational turn-taking, as understanding and knowledge of who is speaking and who is listening requires and suggests attention (see Cassell et al. (2001); Kendon (1980); Vertegaal and Ding (2003)).

The importance of gaze accounts for its widespread use as a behavioral feature in ECAs to indicate selectivity and attention. The real estate agent, Rea, implemented by Cassell et al. (2001), directs gaze toward the user. Steve, a pedagogical agent, indicates attention by shifting gaze towards the current speaker (Rickel and Johnson (1999)). FRED, an attentive agent, looks towards the user when being addressed (Vertegaal et al. (2001)). If FRED is not addressed, he averts gaze from the user, signaling that he does not wish to initiate conversation. BodyChat, a semi-autonomous avatar system, indicates that users no longer want to give attention to their conversational partner by diverting avatar gaze (Vilhjálmsson and Cassell (1998)). Finally, AVA, an ECA explicitly intended to emulate the visual attending behaviors of humans, practices visual search and selection. AVA can scan its environment and then orient gaze towards the selected focus of attention (Chopra-Khullar and Badler (1999)).

There are several open issues in using gaze with ECAs. For example, amount of gaze and increased perceived selectivity may not be perfectly correlated. It may be that gaze that first surveys the field of vision and then settles on the user can create a greater feeling of selectivity as compared to constant gaze, consistent with the finding that an agent that adapts to become similar to a user is more liked than one that is continuously similar to the user (Moon and Nass (1996)). Another issue is whether extremely high levels of gaze are consistent with the limited attentional resource pool of people, thereby undermining the sense of believability. Finally, Bailenson et al. (2001)'s provocative idea of having each participant in a multi-avatar virtual reality system perceive the agent's gaze as focused primarily or exclusively on themselves merits much further research.

Deictic Gesture The second behavioral category, deictic gesture (pointing to an object(s) or event(s)) is a frequent method of demonstrating selectivity in human-human communication (see McNeil (1992)). Deictic gestures are co-verbal and associated with conversation. They are used to direct attention towards the point of reference in the course of a conversation (see Kettebekov et al. (2002)). Humans develop the ability at an early age to use deictic gestures as a means of directing another's attention toward distal objects, or events (see Krause (1997); Schmidt (1999)). By two years old, children can point to direct attention towards an interesting sight (Moore and D'Entremont (2001)) and learn to follow another's referential gestures (see Krause (1997); Leung and Rheingold (1981)).

The importance of utilizing deictic gestures to maintain conversational attention is well recognized by the ECA community (see Cassell (2000); Rickel and Johnson (1999); Lester et al. (1997); Traum and Rickel (2002)). Deictics towards a user creates a high level of perceived selectivity from the agent. For example, when a pedagogical ECA receives a correct answer from one of a group of student, the ECA could point at the answering student and say, 'Great answer!', increasing the seeming level of attention compared to the remark alone. An ECA can also distinguish the user from her surroundings and place her in the center of the attentional space, as when the agent points at the user and says, 'I love *you.*'

Deictic gesture can evoke high levels of perceived selectivity not just by pointing to the user but by pointing to objects that are part of the discourse focus. For example, Steve uses deictic gesture together with gaze and speech to refer to one out of the many objects in the virtual world (Rickel and Johnson (1999)). Similarly, Cosmo, another pedagogical agent (see Lester et al. (1997)) lives in a graphically rich virtual world simulating the routing system of the Internet. It uses deictic gestures in conjunction with recorded human speech to physically designate the referent within the environment.

As a clear denotation of selectivity, deictic gestures represent an effective way to confine the attentional space by disambiguating the referenced object. We suggest that as multi-user systems and complex virtual representations of spaces become common, deictic gestures will play an increasingly important role in inducing user's perceived attention.

Proxemics   Proxemics, or the use of gross body movements like motion, posture, and orientation, is an important manifestation of selectivity (see Grayson and Coventry (1998)). The act of orienting the body towards or away from an object is one of the most forceful ways to restrict the visual field and thus to select a focus for attention.

Research suggests that humans do utilize proximity cues in mediated environments (see Bailenson, et al. (2001); Jeffrey and Mark (1999); Grayson and Coventry (1998)). Though proxemics is meaningful in mediated communication, few agents utilize these manifestations to indicate selectivity. At a simple level, the paperclip character (Clippy) in Microsoft Office 2000 will lean its 'body' forward and tap on the screen to suggest that it notices that the user is not paying sufficient attention (see Chapter 9 by Catrambone et al.). More elaborated example of agents that leverage proxemics are Steve (see Rickel and Johnson (1999) and Cosmo (see Lester et al. (1997)). Both pedagogical agents inhabit rich environments, replete with numerous objects that may be referred to. The agents can physically approach their focus of attention, singling it out from the set of available objects. Steve can also orient his body towards the user to express attention.

There are many open questions concerning proxemics and agents. For example, it is unclear whether the different proximal zones in human-human communication-intimate, conversational, and far-are relevant to attention in agents, and if so, whether the same distance rules apply (see Sherman (1973)). It is also not clear whether the same proxemics rules apply to agents and avatars (see Bailenson et al. (2001)): Will the knowledge that there is a person 'behind' the picture influence people's perceptions and behaviors? There is also little known about the relationship between absolute and relative position of the ECA and perceived selectivity. Will a character that seemingly moves toward a person seem to be more selective than one that is forward from the very beginning?

The advent of virtual reality systems will allow researchers to use unobtrusive quantitative measures of responses to proximal cues in order to evaluate the user of ECAs (Bailenson et al. (in press)). Furthermore, as multi-user environments are more common, the relationship between agent body orientation and distance to the numerous users will become more complicated; guidelines for selectivity in this context are critical.

Finally, a truly understudied area in selectivity is the question of *low* attention. In general, researchers have struggled to make ECAS seem engaged in the activities of the user. However, there are numerous circumstances in which seemingly limited attention would be desirable. For example, perhaps pedagogical agents should visibly de-select a student when she is showing frustration or doing consistently poorly, either selecting other students or focusing on the blackboard. Similarly, when an ECA asks about personal questions, such as a nurse ECA requesting medical information, it might be useful to have the ECA appear to look away by focusing on one or more objects in the environment that are distant from the user.

These three behavioral categories of selectivity manifestations-proxemics, gaze, and deictic gesture-are likely not the sole behavioral indicators of selectivity and hence attention. However, they are the most powerful and most susceptible to assessment by researchers and manipulation by designers.

3.2 Apparent Breadth in ECAs

3.2.1 Apparent Breadth in Agents
According to Maglio and Campbell (2003), a fundamental characteristic of any attentive interface is that it 'gathers evidence about user behavior from multiple sources, possibly even across multiple modalities'; that is, attentive interfaces are high on breadth. For example, Maxims, an agent, continuously 'looks over the shoulder' of the user as the user deals with the electronic mail (see Metral (1993)). Keeping track of user actions and message content, Maxims provides assistance with email organization. Maxims' breadth of inputs, including which emails are filed or discarded, their content, etc., leads users to feel supported and attended to.

While Maxim achieves breadth through a single agent, the Simple User Interest Tracker, or SUITOR, is a collection of agents, each of which is responsible for monitoring one input channel from the user (see Maglio et al. (2000)). SUITOR is an attentive information system that provides suggestions to the user in a peripheral desktop pane. The input channels that are monitored by SUITOR include user's web browsing, eye gaze, screen content, and user history, all merging together to provide insights into user activities. Knowledge of user activities 'allow attentive agents to inform or notify the user of potentially helpful information at opportune moments' (Maglio and Campbell (2003)).

An important open question is the extent to which users are more influenced by heavy information gathering via one modality or the gathering of proportionately less information from multiple modalities.

3.2.2   Apparent Breadth in Conversational Agents

Breadth is critical for conversational agents because the agent must consider the context of any utterance or action in order to accurately attend to the discourse (see Reed (2002)). Collagen, for example, tracks, maintains, and prioritizes both user conversational content as well as user action. Tracking multiple input types allows Collagen to maintain the attentional state component of discourse structure proposed by Grosz and Sidner (1986), thereby creating a feeling of responsiveness.

The increased acceptance of available discourse elements is another indicator of the degree of involvement in conversation. Manifestly attentive conversational agents make reference to concepts and ideas scattered throughout the conversation, rather than just exhibiting a stimulus-response-like approach to conversation (as in ELIZA). Even ECAs that do not have large amounts of memory can remember one idea early in the conversation and strategically reference it at later points in the discourse, suggesting more breadth than the agent actually has.

Another powerful conversational technique to manifest breadth is alignment, the tendency to use the same linguistic form as the user (see Branigan et al. (2000); Brennan and Clark (1996)). For example, the conversational agent can look for user's use of unusual or regional words for common objects, such as 'hound' instead of 'dog' or 'pop' instead of 'soda,' and mirror those utterances. Similarly, the user might opt for the gerund form ('the man giving the woman the book') rather than the active form (e.g., ('the man gave the woman the book') when describing a situation; the conversational agent could adopt the same construct. Research suggests that even if the user is not consciously aware of the similarities in language patterns, they will nonetheless be influenced because it increases their sense of apparent attention (Branigan et al. (2000)).

Breadth can also be established by moving beyond words to the paralinguistic aspects of speech. ECAs that measure such cues as volume, fundamental frequency, frequency range, words per minute, cadence, etc. have a number of opportunities for manifesting attention. Paralinguistic cues allow conversational agents to contextualize utterances and actions and more consistently demonstrate attention (see Shankar et al. (2000)). Paralinguistic cues can also be very powerful indicators of personality (see Nass and Lee (2001)) and emotion (see Brave and Nass (2002)). ECAs can demonstrate recognition of the former through adopting language that is consistent with the user's personality (see Nass and Moon (2000)) and appreciation of the latter by facial expression and tone of voice (Brave and Nass (2002)). Even if processing of paralinguistic cues for meaning is impossible, simply mirroring the vocal characteristics of the user should be sufficient to demonstrate breadth, as suggested by Nass and Gong (2000)[1].

The conversational agent can also use paralinguistic cues to manifest its own attentional states. For example, speech cadence is an important indicator of how attentive the speaker is during discourse, because pauses and changes in speed or fluency suggest that cognitive capacity is being devoted to something other than the speaking task. Consistent pauses, especially in responses to the behavior of the other person, suggest high attention to the listener. Pauses that do not seem linked to the complexity of the content, on the other hand, suggest that the conversational agent is either broadening its inputs or changing its selectivity.

Conversation also provides a natural opportunity to indicate that the agent has obtained information from the user that goes beyond the conversation itself to focus on fundamental characteristic of the user. To the extent that an ECA seems to detect these traits, it will be following Dale Carnegie's (author of *How to Win Friends and Influence People*, one of the best-selling books of all time) first principle for how to get people to like you: Treat everyone as an individual (Carnegie (1990)).

Gender   Men and women behave differently in conversation (see Lakoff (1975); Tannen (1990)). Indeed, it has been argued that knowing the gender of a speaker is important for understanding content in most conversations (see Reeves and Nass (1996)). One general finding is that men are more instrumental and less expressive than women (see Rosenkrantz et al. (1968)). Thus, using more emotive language and references to the dyad for female users and more goal-oriented references for male users will tend to make everyone feel more attended to. Women and men also tend to be interested in different topics (see Nass et al. (1997)). An agent that does not provide direct indicators of its gender can at least focus on topics that are gender-appropriate for the user.

Ethnicity   Ethnicity is a readily observable physical feature of humans (see Biernet and Vescio (1993)). In human-human interaction, individuals assess others' ethnicity at the beginning of the conversation to quickly determine whether they are part of the same group or from a different group (see Tajfel (1982)). Similarity leads to more favorable responses in virtually all domains. Users will also assign an ethnicity to an agent and be influenced by that assignment (see Nass et al. (2000)). Although the most obvious markers of ethnicity come from the morphological features of a body, mere conversational agents can manifest ethnicity. For example, accents can suggest the ethnicity of the agent and can lead to social identification (see Nass and Gong (2000)). Acknowledgment of users' ethnicity can also be demonstrated by adapting conversational content to reference the particular culture.

Personality   Personality represents those characteristics of the person that account for consistent patterns of feelings, thinking and behaviors (see Nass and Moon (2000)). Personality is an excellent predictor of conversational patterns. For example, extroverts use long sentences, highly expressive language, and initiate conversations, while introverts do the opposite. Adopting both verbal and non-verbal behaviors to manifest personality (e.g., extroverts speak louder and more rapidly than introverts; see Nass and Lee (2001)) that matches the user will not only lead the user to more favorable assessments but will also suggest that the agent is gathering significant information from the user (see André et al. (2000); Nass and Lee (2001); Nass and Moon (2000); Rizzo et al. (1997)).

Conversational agents can manifest acquisition of other user features such as age, background or domain specific knowledge, computer experience, previous experience with the agent, etc., to demonstrate a striking degree of attentiveness. On the other hand, it is unknown at what point high levels of apparent breadth will actually put off a user, making the user feel that he or she is being 'stalked' or overly monitored.

3.2.3   Apparent Selectivity in ECAs   In general, bodies are more effective for manifesting selectivity than breadth. While every part of an embodiment can be used to demonstrate that a user or object has been selected, the only part of the body that clearly indicates breadth is the head and face.

Eye gaze, for example, has already been noted as a key strategy for illustrating selectivity. However, ECAs can also use eye gaze as a means to signal the search for information and feedback during conversation, i.e., breadth. For example, when the ECA wants the user to provide more information, it can switch from ambient gaze mode to looking steadily at the user.

Enlarged pupils indicate that the observer is taking in a large amount of information (see Hoeks and Levelt (1994)). Thus, apparent breadth can be readily indicated even if the ECA is 'blind.' Conversely, very small pupils would suggest that there was no depth to the information being gathered.

Head movements, such as nodding and shaking, indicate whether or not the speakers' content is accepted by the listener (see Bishop et al. (1998); Giges (1975)). ECAs have utilized nodding to reassure the user that they are paying attention to and understanding conversational content (see Cassell et al. (2001); Rickel and Johnson (1999)). Head movements provide ECAs with a channel to communicate that they are gathering conversational input even if the ECA is attending to another task at the same time. For example, an ECA may be working with and gazing at another object in the environment. To avoid suggesting that the agent is ignoring the user's input, the agent can nod as the user types or vocalizes. It is important to note that unlike pupil dilation, particular head movements are not cultural universals. In some parts of the world, a head shaking from side to side indicates disagreement, while in other parts (e.g., parts of India), the head movement indicates agreement.

Facial expressions can also be used to indicate information gathering. When facial animations are more expressive and facial movements are less random, the user will deduce that the ECA is gathering more information and thus exhibiting greater breadth/attention (see Coker and Burgoon (1987)). As long as the facial expressions are not incongruous, more range reflects more breadth.

4.   Conclusion

ECAs are remarkable technologies. Independently developing, let along integrating, artificial intelligence, natural language processing and understanding, high-quality graphics, models of motion, facial expressions, speech processing, etc., is a tremendous feat. Advances have been consistent, clearly definable, and striking in the ingenuity that has been brought to bear. ECAs are truly one of the triumphs of computing technology.

Although ECAs are technological marvels, they are quintessentially oriented toward humans. From a machine's point of view, it would be much more effective to strip out the conversational and pictorial elements of ECAs and just 'get to the facts.' Conversation and embodiment are affordances for people, not for technologies. Thus, it is wholly appropriate that the criteria for excellence in creating ECAs are grounded in how ECAs are perceived by people rather than by abstracted metrics and technological benchmarks.

This chapter argues for the 'user as assessor' approach to evaluating ECAs. Under this view, the critical question is how ECAs manifest their human-like abilities, whether or not those manifestations are consistent with the ECA's capabilities or not: "What the user sees is what the ECA is." That is, when one identifies an attribute that makes an ECA more human-like, it is imperative to determine how to make it *seem* more human-like. To perform well under this standard, we urge designers and evaluators to adopt an approach that starts with the literature on humans as producer of behavior and/or humans as interpreters of behavior and then draws implications for how ECAs should behave to seem most realistic to their human assessors.

To illustrate this approach, we focused on the concept of apparent attention. We identified and conceptualized two key dimensions of apparent attention: apparent selectivity and apparent breadth. For each of these concepts, we illustrated how designers and evaluators of agents, conversational agents, and ECAs could derive key insights from the 'user as assessor' paradigm by adducing a number of design guidelines and principles.

Although this chapter culled the literature for insights into apparent attention, there are many other agent capabilities that would be susceptible to an analysis that distinguish ontology from perception. Designers can utilize this distinction to improve seeming affect or intelligence of ECAs (see Chapter 5 by Höök; Brave (2003)). For example, in humans, the correlation between actual intelligence and perceived intelligence is very small. Such elements as attractiveness, glasses, smooth movements, rapid speech, etc., are very strong indicators of *being perceived as intelligent* but only weakly correlated with actual intelligence (see Reeves and Nass (1996); Borkenau and Liebler (1993)). Designers of ECA should leverage these indicators to make their ECAs seem as intelligent as they actually are (if not smarter!).

Leveraging indicators of various human abilities in the design of ECAs may create heightened expectations of a systems' capabilities (see Schneiderman (1997); Friedman (1997)). Opponents of such mismatches argue that when users come to understand that a system is capable of less than it indicates, they may feel misled or tricked. Furthermore, one can argue that deception is a priori a bad idea that, at least in the long run, harms ECAs, the user, and society more generally (Friedman (1997); Kant (1781/1929)). Unfortunately, space limitations have forced us to focus solely on those implementations in which 'faked' attention likely leads to better user experiences. As consolation, it should be noted that deception among human interactants provides numerous examples of acceptable appearance/reality mismatches. Flight attendants and Wal-Mart 'greeters', for example, manifest attention and concern towards each customer (Hochschild (1985)). When customers discover that this attention is directed equally towards everyone, they do not feel disappointed or deceived (cf. Beniger (1987)). Further investigation is required to determine precisely when an ECA must truly possess a trait, and when appearances will suffice.

While builders of ECAs might want to receive credit for objective technological performance, the bottom line, to paraphrase Alexander Pope, is that "the proper study (and studier) of embodied conversational agents are humans."

Notes

1. Mirroring in social contexts can express a diversity of intentions. It is important to view attention as only one concept that is implicated by mirroring (Chartrand and Bargh (1999); Bavelas et al. (1988)).

References

André, E., Klesen, M., Gebhard, P., Allen, S. and Rist, T. (1999). Integrating models of personality and emotions into lifelike characters, In *Proceedings of the International Workshop on Affect in Interactions: Towards a New Generation of Interfaces*, pp. 136–149, Siena, Italy.

Argyle, M. and Cook, M. (1976). *Gaze and mutual gaze*, Cambridge University Press, New York.

Bailenson, J. N., Blascovich, J. B., Beall, A. C. and Loomis, J. M. (2001). Equilibrium theory revisited: Mutual gaze and personal space in virtual environments. *Presence: Teleoperators and Virtual Environments*, 10(6): 583–C598.

Bailenson, J. N., Blascovich, J., Beall, A.C. and Loomis, J.M. (in press) *Interpersonal distance in immersive virtual environments*, Personality and Social Psychology Bulletin.

Bavelas, J.B., Black A., Chovil, N., Lemery, C.R., and Mullett, J. (1988). Form and function in motor mimicry: Topographic evidence that the primary function is communicative, *Human Communication Research*, 14: 275–299.

Beaumont, J. G. (1983). *Introduction to neuropsychology*, Blackwell, Oxford.

Beniger, J. R. (1987). Personalization of mass media and the growth of pseudo-community, *Communication Research*, 14(3): 325–371.

Biernet, M. and Vescio, T. K. (1993). Categorization and stereotyping: Effects of group context on memory and social judgment. *Journal of Experimental Social Psyhcology*, 29: 166–202.

Bishop, D. V. M., Chan, J., Hartley, J. and Weir, F. (1998). When a nod is as good as a word: Form-function relationships between questions and their responses. *Applied Psycholinguistics*, 19(3):415–432.

Borkenau, P., and Liebler, A. (1993). Convergence of Stranger Ratings of Personality and Intelligence With Self-Ratings, Partner Ratings, and Measured Intelligence, *Journal of Personality and Social Psychology* 65:546–653.

Branigan, H. P., Pickering, M. J. and Cleland, A. A. (2000) Syntactic coordination in dialogue, *Cognition*, 75: B13–B25.

Brave, S. (2003). *Agents that care: Investigating the effects of orientation of emotion exhibited by an embodied computer agent*, Unpublished doctoral dissertation, Stanford University.

Brave, S. and Nass, C. (2002). Emotion in human-computer interaction. In Jacko, J. and Sears, A. editors, *Handbook of human-computer interaction*, pp. 251–271, Lawrence Erlbaum Associates, New York.

Brennan, S. E. and Clark, H. H. (1996). Conceptual pacts and lexical choice in conversation. *Journal of Experimental Psychology: Learning, Memory, and Cognition*, 22: 1482–1493.

Carnegie, D. (1990). *How to win friends and influence people*, Pocket Books, New York.

Cassell, J. (2000). More than just another pretty face: Embodied conversational interface agents. *Communications of the ACM*, 43(4):70–78.

Cassell, J., Nakano, Y. I., Bickmore, T., Sidner, C. L., and Rich, C. (2001). Non-verbal cues for discourse structure. In *Proc. of the 41st Annual Meeting of the Association of Computational Linguistics*, pp. 106–115. Toulouse, France.

Cassell, J. and Stone, M. (1999). Living hand to mouth: Theories of speech and gesture in interactive systems. In *Proceedings of AAAI Fall Symposium: Psychological Models of Communication in Collaborative Systems*, pp. 34–42, Cape Cod, MA.

Chartrand, T.L. and Bargh, J. A. (1999). The chameleon effect: The perception behavior link and social interaction, *Journal of Personality and Social Psychology*, 76:893–910.

Chopra-Khullar S. and Badler N. I. (1999). Where to look? Automating visual attending behaviors of virtual human characters. In *Proceedings of ACM Autonomous Agents Conference*, pp. 16–23, Seattle, WA.

Clark, H. H. (1996). *Using Language*, Cambridge University Press, New York.

Coen, M. (1998). Design principles for intelligent environments. In *Proc. of the National Conference on Artificial Intelligence*, pp. 547–554, Madison, Wisconsin.

Coker, D. A. and Burgoon, J. K. (1987). The nature of conversational involvement and nonverbal encoding patterns. *Human Communication Research*, 13(4):463–494.

Eysenck, M. W. (1997). *Principles of cognitive psychology*, Psychology Press, New York.

Friedman, B. (1997). *Human values and the design of computer technology*. CSLI Press, Stanford, CA.

Giges, B. (1975). Using your head: Notes on nodding. *Transactional Analysis Journal*, 5(3):264–266.

Grayson, D. and Coventry, L. (1998). The effects of visual proxemic information in video mediated communication. *SIGCHI Bulletin*, 30(3):30–39.

Grice, H. P. (1975). Logic and conversation. In Cole, P. and Morgan, J. L., editors, *Syntax and semantics*, Volume 3: Speech acts. Academic Press, New York.

Grosz, B. J and Sidner, C. L. (1986). Attention, intentions, and the structure of discourse. *Computational Linguistics*, 12(3):175–204.

Grosz, B. J., Joshi, A. and Weinstein, S. (1995). Centering: A framework for modelling the local coherence of discourse. *Computational Linguistics*, 2(21):203–225.

Haller, S. M., McRoy, S. W. and Ali, S. S. (1997). Towards a model for mixed initiative in dialogic discourse. In *Working Notes of the AAAI Spring Symposium on Computational Models of Mixed Initiative Interaction*, pp. 78–80. Stanford University, California.

Hoeks, B. and Levelt, W. J. M. (1994). Pupillary dilation as a measure of attention: A quantitative system analysis. *Behavior Research Methods, Instruments and Computers*, 25: 16–26.

Hochschild, A. R. (1985). *The managed heart*, University of California Press, Berkeley, CA.

Höök, K., Persson, P., and Sjölinder, M. (2000). Evaluating Users Experience of a Character Enhanced Information Space, *Journal of AI Communications*, 13(3):195–212.

Isbister, K. and Nass, C. (2000). Consistency of personality in interactive characters: Verbal cues, non-verbal cues, and user characteristics. *International Journal of Human-Computer Studies*, 53(1):251–267.

James, W. (1890). *The principles of psychology*, New York: Holt.

Jeffrey, P. and Mark, G. (1999). Navigating the Virtual Landscape: Coordinating the Shared Use of Space. In Munro, A., Höök, K., and Beynon, D., editors, *Social Navigation of Information Space*, pp. 112–131, Springer, London.

Kahneman, D. (1973). *Attention and effort*, Prentice-Hall, Englewood Cliffs, NJ.

Kant, I. (1781[1929]). *The critique of pure reason*, Macmillan, London.

Kendon, A. (1967). Some functions of gaze direction in social interaction. *Acta Psychologica*, 32:1–25.

Kettebekov, S., Yeasin, M. and Sharma, R. (2002). Prosody based co-analysis for continuous recognition of coverbal gestures, In *Proc. of the International Conference on Multimodal Interfaces (ICMI'02)*, pp. 161–166, Pittsburgh, USA.

Krause, M. A. (1997). Comparative perspectives on pointing and joint attention in children and apes. *International Journal of Comparative Psychology*, 10(3):137–157.

Lakoff, R. (1975). *Language and woman's place*, Harper and Row, New York.

Lashkari, Y., Metral, M. and Maes, P. (1994). Collaborative Interface Agents. In *Proc. of the Twelfth National Conference on Artificial Intelligence*, pp. 444–449, Menlo Park, CA.

Latorella, K. A. (1999). Investigating interruptions: Implications for flightdeck performance. *NASA/TM-1999-209707*, National Aviation and Space Administration, Washington.

Lester, J. C., Voerman, J. L., Towns S. G. and Callaway, C. B. (1997). Cosmo: A life-like animated pedagogical agent with deictic believability. In *Working notes of the IJCAI '97 workshop on animated interface agents: Making them intelligent*, pp. 61–69, Nagoya, Japan.

Leung, E. H. and Rheingold, H. L. (1981). Development of pointing as a social gesture. *Developmental Psychology*, 17(2): 215-220.

Lieberman, H. (1995). Letizia: An agent that assists in web browsing. In *Proceedings of the Fourteenth International Joint Conference on Artificial Intelligence*, pp. 457–480, Montreal, Canada.

Maglio, P., Barrett, R., Campbell, C. S. and Selker T. (2000). SUITOR: An attentive information system. In *Proceedings of the International Conference on Intelligent User Interfaces*, pp. 169–176, New Orleans, Louisiana, USA.

Maglio, P. P. and Campbell, C. S. (2003). Attentive agents. *Communications of the ACM*, 46(3):47–51.

Mann, W. C. and Thompson, S. A. (1987). Rhetorical structure theory: A theory of text organization, *Technical Report RS-87-190*, International Computer Science Institute, Marina Del Rey, CA.

McNeill, D. (1992). *Hand and mind*, Chicago, IL: University of Chicago Press.

Metral, M. (1993). *Design of a generic learning interface agent. Bachelor of Science thesis*, Massachusetts Institute of Technology, Cambridge, MA.

Minsky, M. (1986). *The society of mind*, Simon and Schuster, New York.

Mirsky, A. F. (1989). The neuropsychology of attention: Elements of a complex behavior. In Perenman, E., editor, *Integrating theory and practice in clinical neuropsychology*, pp. 75–91, Erlbaum, Hillsdale, NJ.

Moon, Y. and Nass, C. (1996). How "real" are computer personalities? Psychological responses to personality types in human-computer interaction. *Communication Research*, 23(6): 651–674.

Moon, Y. (1998). Impression management in computer-based interviews: The effects of input modality, output modality, and distance. *Public Opinion Quarterly*, 62:610–622.

Moore, C. and D'Entremont, B. (2001). Developmental changes in pointing as a function of attentional focus. *Journal of Cognition and Development*, 2(2):109–129.

Murray, J. (1991). Anatomy of a new medium: Literary and pedogogic uses of advanced linguistic computer structures. *Computers and the Humanities*, 25(1):1–14.

Nass, C. and Gong, L. (2000). Social aspects of speech interfaces from an evolutionary perspective: Experimental research and design implications. *Communications of the ACM*, 43(9):36–43.

Nass, C. and Lee, K. (2001). Does computer-synthesized speech manifest personality? Experimental tests of recognition, similarity-attraction, and consistency-attraction. *Journal of Experimental Psychology: Applied*, 7(3):171–181.

Nass, C. and Mason, L. (1990). On the study of technology and task: A variable-based approach. In Fulk, J. and C. Steinfeld, C., editors, *Organizations and communication technology*, pp. 46–67, Sage, Newbury Park.

Nass, C. and Moon, Y. (2000). Machines and mindlessness: Social responses to computers. *Journal of Social Issues*, 56(1): 81–103.

Nass, C., Isbister, K. and Lee, E. (2000). Truth is beauty: Researching embodied conversation agents. In Cassell, J., Sullivan, J., Prevost, S., and Churchill, E., editors, *Embodied conversational agents*, pp. 374–402, MIT Press, Cambridge, MA.

Nass, C., Moon, Y. and Green, N. (1997). Are computers gender-neutral? Gender stereotypic responses to computers. *Journal of Applied Social Psychology*, 27(10):864–876.

Norman., D. A. (1997). How might people interact with agents. pp. 49–55. In Bradshaw, J. M., editor, *Software agents*, AAAI Press/The MIT Press, Cambridge, MA.

Oh, A., Fox, H., Kleek, M. V., Adler, A., Gajos, K., Morency, L. and Darrell, T. (2002). Evaluating look-to-talk: A gaze-aware interface in a collaborative environment. In *Proc. of the Conference on Human Factors in Computing Systems (CHI)*, pp. 650–651. Minneapolis, MN.

Persson, P., Laaksolahti, J., and Lönnqvist, P. (2000). Anthropomorphism: A multi-layered phenomenon. *AAAI Fall Symposium 2000, Technical Report FS-00-04*, pp. 131–135, North Falmouth, Massachusetts.

Poesio, M. (1992). Conversational events and discourse state change: A preliminary report. In *Proceedings of the 3rd International Conference on Principles of Knowledge Representation and Reasoning (KR'92)*, pp. 369–380, Cambridge, MA.

Reed, C. A. (2002). Saliency and the attentional state in natural language generation. In *Proceedings of the 15th European Conference on Artificial Intelligence*, pp. 440–444, Lyon, France.

Reeves, B. and Nass, C. (1996). *The media equation: How people treat computers, television, and new media like real people and places*, Cambridge University Press/CSLI, New York.

Rich, C. and Sidner, C. (1998). COLLAGEN: A collaboration manager for software interface agents. *User Modeling and User Adapted Interaction*, 8:315–350.

Rickel, J., Lesh, N. B., Rich, C., Sidner, C. L. and Gertner, A. (2002). Collaborative discourse theory as a foundation for tutorial dialogue. In *Proc. of the Conference on Intelligent Tutoring Systems*, pp. 542–551, Biarritz, France and San Sebastian, Spain.

Rickel, J. and Johnson, W. L. (1999). Animated agents for procedural training in virtual reality: Perception, cognition, and motor control. *Applied Artificial Intelligence*, 13(4-5): 343–382.

Rizzo P., Veloso M. V., Miceli M. and Cesta A. (1997). Personality-driven social behaviors in believable agents. In *Proc. of the AAAI 1997 Fall Symposium on "Socially Intelligent Agents"*, AAAI Press Technical Report FS-97-02,pp. 109–114.

Rosenkrantz, P. S., Vogel, S. R., Bee, H., Broverman, I. K. and Broverman, D. M. (1968). Sex role stereotypes and self concepts in college
students. *Journal of Consulting and Clinical Psychology*, 32:287–295.

Schmidt, C. L. (1999). Adult understanding of spontaneous attention-
directing events: What does gesture contribute? *Ecological Psychology*,
11(2):139–174.

Schneiderman, B. (1997). *Designing the user interface: Strategies for
effective human-computer interaction*, Addison Wesley, New York.

Shankar, T. R., van Kleek, M., Vicente, A. and Smith, B. K. (2000).
Fugue: A computer mediated conversational system that supports
turn negotiation. In *Proc. of the Thirty-Third Hawaii International
Conference on System Sciences Persistent Conversation mini-track*,
pp. 3035–3036, Maui, Hawaii.

Sherman, E. (1973). Listening comprehension as a function of proxemic
distance and eye-contact. *Graduate Research in Education and Related
Disciplines*, 7(1):5–34.

Sheth, B. and Maes, P. (1993). Evolving agents for personalized information filtering. In *Proc. of the Ninth IEEE Conference on Artificial
Intelligence and its Applications*, pp. 1–7. Orlando, FL.

Spence, C., Kettenmann, B., Kobal, G., McGlone, F.P. (2001). Shared
attentional resources for processing visual and chemosensory information. *Quarterly Journal of Experimental Psychology*, 54A(3):775–783.

Tajfel, H. (Ed.) (1982). *Social identity and intergroup behavior*, Cambridge: Cambridge University Press.

Tannen, D. (1990). *You just don't understand: Men and women in conversation*, Ballantine, New York.

Traum, D. R. and Rickel, J. (2002). Embodied agents for multi-party dialogue in immersive virtual worlds. In *Proc. of the First International
Joint Conference on Autonomous Agents and Multi-Agent System*,
pp. 766–773, Bologna, Italy.

Vertegaal, R. and Ding, Y. (2003). Explaining effects of eye gaze on
mediated group conversations: Amount or synchronization? In *Proceedings of Computer Supported Cooperative Work*, pp. 41–48, New
Orleans, Louisiana.

Vertegaal, R., Slagter, R., Van der Veer, G. C. and Nijholt, A. (2001).
Eye gaze patterns in conversations: There is more to conversational
agents than meets the eyes. In *Proceedings of ACM CHI 2001 Conference on Human Factors in Computing Systems*, pp. 301–308, Seattle,
Washington.

Vertegaal, R., Veer, G. and Vons, H. (2002). Effects of gaze on multiparty
mediated communication. In *Proceedings of Graphics Interface*, pp.
95–102, Montreal, Canada.

Vilhjalmsson, H. and Cassell, J. (1998). BodyChat: Autonomous communicative behaviors in avatars, In *Proceedings of ACM International Conference on Autonomous Agents*, pp. 269–276, Minneapolis.

Walker, M. A. (1996). Limited attention and discourse structure. *Computational Linguistics*, 22(2):255–264.

Weizenbaum, J. (1966). Eliza — a computer program for the study of natural language communication between man and machine. *Communications of the ACM*, 9:23 –28.

Wickens, C. D. (1984). Processing resources in attention. In Parasuraman, R. and Davies, D. R., editors, *Varieties of attention*, Academic Press, New York.

III

EVALUATION OF ECAS

Chapter 7

MORE ABOUT BROWS

A Cross-Linguistic Study via Analysis-by-Synthesis

Emiel Krahmer and Marc Swerts

> *The computer can't tell you the emotional story. It can
> give you the exact mathematical design, but what's miss-
> ing is the eyebrows.*
> —Zappa, The real Frank Zappa book

Abstract   In a seminal paper, Ekman (1979) remarks that brows can play an
accentuation role (e.g., to signal focus). However, the literature about eyebrows
is inconclusive about their exact role and as a consequence there is no agreement
among developers of embodied conversational agents about their precise timing and
placement. In addition, it is unclear whether eyebrow movements perform the same
role in different languages. In this chapter, an analysis-by-synthesis technique is used
to find out what the role of eyebrow movements is for the perception of focus and to
see whether this role is the same across different languages. Three experiments are
performed, both for Dutch and Italian, investigating where subjects prefer eyebrow
movements, whether brows influence the perceived prominence of words and whether
they are used in a functional way when subjects interpret utterances. The results
for Dutch and Italian are indeed different, but it is argued that these differences
can be reduced to prosodic differences between the two languages. The advantages
and potential limitations of studies via analysis-by-synthesis are discussed, and an
approach to compensate for the limitations is offered.

Keywords: Audio-visual prosody, eyebrow movements, pitch accents, focus, prominence, perception, analysis-by-synthesis, analysis-by-observation, cross-
linguistic comparisons.

Z. Ruttkay and C. Pelachaud (eds.), From Brows to Trust, 191–216.
© *2004 Kluwer Academic Publishers. Printed in the Netherlands.*

1.   Introduction

How can the *naturalness* of an embodied conversational agent[1] be improved? Arguably, one way is to use *variation*. An agent speaking in a monotonous way and with a static facial expression (only moving its mouth) will look unnatural and people presumably will find it unpleasant to interact with such an agent.

Variation in speech (both in humans and machines) has been the subject of many studies in the past. Some of the variation may be random, such as the smaller instabilities in pitch (jitter and shimmer) that are due to the limited capabilities of a human's vocal apparatus, and that may make synthetic speech more natural when properly implemented. In addition, research has shown that much of the variation in speech is also *functional* in that it can signal communicatively relevant information. Speakers may use pitch accents and prosodic boundaries, for instance, not to counter the monotonicity of their speech, but to give clues to the hearer about how the current utterance should be interpreted (see for instance Ladd (1996) or Cruttenden (1997)). There is some psycholinguistic evidence that processing of utterances is indeed enhanced by the 'correct' placement of pitch accents and boundaries (see e.g., Cutler (1984); Terken and Nooteboom (1987); and Sanderman and Collier (1997)).

But only variation in speech is not sufficient to create a natural embodied agent. Facial variation is required as well (besides visual correlates of producing the different speech sounds, i.e., movements in the mouth area). For this purpose, many current embodied agents employ some form of *Perlin noise* (Perlin (1995)), i.e., small random head movements. Even though Perlin noise certainly makes animations more natural and life-like, the resulting variation is small and not functional in the linguistic sense of the word.[2] Arguably, what is needed is some form of *audio-visual prosody*, where speech cues and facial cues can be used, alone and in tandem, to enhance both the naturalness and the expressiveness of embodied agents.

Arguably, not all facial cues have speech correlates and not all speech cues have facial correlates, but for certain functional aspects of communication there is reason to assume a connection between the two (see e.g., Pelachaud et al. (1996)). This implies that knowledge is required about the potential co-occurrence of auditory and visual cues. Concerning this, Pelachaud et al. (1996:32) stated that "there is a lack of empirical information on when an accent or other intonational components are accompanied by a facial action". Unfortunately, this situation has not changed much in recent years, despite a growing number of empirical studies involving embodied conversational agents. One possible way to further this discussion is as follows. As a starting point, one can look for relevant claims made in the literature, in particular in the many descriptive (non-empirical) studies of non-verbal communication. These claims can subsequently be implemented in an embodied conversational agent. Many researchers and developers of embodied conversational agents indeed follow this strategy, but one can go even further and use the agent implementation to empirically verify, as it were, the original claims. This method could be called *analysis-by-synthesis* and is, in different disguises, applied in Granström et al. (1999, 2002); Nass et al. (2000); and Krahmer et al. (2002a, 2002b), to name but a few.

In this chapter, the analysis-by-synthesis method is used to gain insight in one aspect of audio-visual prosody, namely the signalling of important bits of information in an utterance (the *focus*), via pitch accents and eyebrow movements. It will be argued that analysis-by-synthesis is a powerful evaluation tool, but one that should be used with some caution.

2.   About Brows

In a seminal paper, Ekman (1979) describes the role of eyebrow movements as emotional and conversational signals. Sometimes the distinction between these two kinds of signals is difficult to make (for instance because both often occur during conversation). Still clear differences between the two exist: conversational signals typically do not occur when a person believes (s)he is unobserved, while emotional signals do. Moreover, emotional but not conversational signals are believed to be universal.

While the use of eyebrows as emotional signals has been addressed in many studies (already in Darwin (1872)), the conversational use is still relatively understudied and most of the work that has been done in this area is based on intuitions and impressionistic observations. This is surprising, since eyebrow movements are according to Ekman (1979:183) "probably among the most frequent facial actions employed as conversational signals". Various authors have suggested that eyebrow movements can be used to emphasize important pieces of information (see e.g., Birdwhistell (1970); Eibl-Eibesfeldt (1972); Condon (1976); Ekman (1979)). Ekman observes that eyebrows can play this accentuation role in two different ways: they can function as a *baton* (in the terminology of Efron (1941)), which may be used to accentuate a particular word as it is spoken, or they can function as an *underliner* (in Ekman's own terminology), where the emphasis stretches out over more than one word.

It is well-known that speakers may use *auditory* speech signals to emphasize words as well. For instance, speakers of Germanic languages (such as Dutch, English and German) can use pitch accents to indicate the information status of words: accents tend to distinguish information that is *in focus* (since it is *new* or *contrastive*) from information which is given from the prior discourse context (see e.g., Chafe (1974); Terken (1984); Hirschberg (1993)).

That both eyebrow movements and pitch accents can be used to signal focus, suggests that there is close correspondence between the two. This correspondence has indeed been noted by Morgan (1953) and Bolinger (1985:202ff). The latter formulated his *Metaphor of Up and Down* which implies, among other things, that when the pitch rises or falls, eyebrows tend to follow the same pattern. As an illustration of this metaphor, it is instructive to try and utter a two-word phrase, say "blue square," with a pitch accent (and no corresponding eyebrow movement) on the word "blue" and an eyebrow movement (but no pitch accent) on the word "square". Most people find this a difficult exercise. Yet, speakers have no problems whatsoever to produce the utterance with pitch accent and eyebrow movement on the same word.

One of the few empirical studies devoted to the connection between pitch accents and eyebrow movements is Cavé et al. (1996), who conducted a small production experiment (i.e., they recorded speakers). They found a significant correlation between the two (in particular, and surprisingly, for the *left* eyebrow). This implies that eyebrow movements often co-occur with pitch accents. It is important to realize that the opposite is not the case. Ekman (1979:184): "There are many occasions when people mark emphasis in their speech without either a baton or an underliner." People do *more* with their pitch than with their eyebrows, as the reader can easily verify by looking at an arbitrary speaker.

If not all emphasized words are accompanied by an eyebrow movement, which words are? This is still an open question. Ekman (1979:184) is "not optimistic about being able to predict when a baton or underliner will be used and when emphasis will be carried just by voice, although perhaps there might be some weak relationship with overall involvement in what is said."

It thus appears that the literature on non-verbal behavior is inconclusive about the role of eyebrow movements for communication. As a result, it is no surprise that among developers of embodied conversational agents there is no consensus about the timing and placement of eyebrow movements. Pelachaud et al. (1996) assume that the conversational use of eyebrow movements is affect dependent (e.g., it is assumed that a disgusted person uses more eyebrow movements than, say, a sad one). In response to the question *I know that Harry prefers* POTATO *chips, but what does* JULIA *prefer?*, a disgusted agent would respond with:

$$(\overline{\text{JULIA}} \text{ prefers})_{\text{theme}} \ (\overline{\text{POPCORN}})_{\text{rheme}}$$

(Here and elsewhere, small caps indicate a pitch accent, and over-lined words are accompanied by an eyebrow movement.) Cassell et al. (2001: 482) use eyebrow movements (or *flashes* as they call them[3]) more sparingly. The eyebrows are raised only when an *object* is introduced in the rheme. So, in response to the question above, the *beat* algorithm of Cassell and co-workers would not produce an eyebrow movement on Julia. It is worth noting that neither Pelachaud et al. (1996) nor Cassell et al. (2001) report on empirical evaluation. As a result we get no insight in the effectiveness of the animations; it is unknown, for instance, whether eyebrow movements influence the way human listeners process the information.

The general picture that emerges is that both pitch accents and eyebrow movements may be used to signal focus. Eyebrow movements tend to accompany pitch accents, but the opposite is not the case; often words may be emphasized in speech, but not accompanied by an eyebrow movement. On the basis of such observations, Cavé and co-workers suggest that eyebrow movements and pitch do not link up automatically (e.g., due to muscular synergy), but rather coincide for *communicative* reasons. Naturally, one wonders what these communicative reasons might be. In general, it is uncertain what the function of eyebrow movements for the perception of focus is. Do they help in emphasizing a particular word as it is spoken? Do they influence the way human listeners process information in a functional way?

There is still another complication. Various researchers have stressed the functional link between eyebrow movements and pitch accents. However, pitch accents have different functions in different languages; they play an important role in Germanic languages as signallers of information status, but this is not a linguistic universal. In Romance languages (such as Italian and Spanish), for instance, less use is made of pitch accents (and prosody in general) to mark information status (certainly within syntactic constituents, Ladd (1996:177ff)). Instead, word order variation may be used for this purpose. This raises the question what the function of eyebrow movements is for Romance languages. It is not obvious that eyebrow movements perform the same function for focus perception in Romance languages as they do in Germanic ones. In sum, the general picture raises (at least) two questions:

Question one What *is* the role of eyebrow movements for the perception of focus?

Question two Is this role the same across languages?

Below these questions are addressed via an analysis-by-synthesis method, applying it to both Dutch (a Germanic language) and Italian (a Romance one). In section 3 the stimuli used in the three experiments are described. The first experiment (section 4) is about *subjective preferences*, asking both Dutch and Italian subjects where they prefer to see eyebrow movements in relation to pitch accents. In the second experiment (section 5) it is investigated what the contribution of eyebrow movements is for the *perceived prominence* of words in Dutch and Italian. The third experiment (section 6) is a *functional study*, investigating to what extent Dutch and Italian subjects use pitch accents and eyebrow movements to interpret incoming utterances. We end with a general discussion, in which we attempt to answer the two general questions introduced above. In addition, we discuss the pros and cons of the analysis-by-synthesis method, and offer a general remedy to alleviate some of the cons of this method.

3.   Materials

In all three experiments the stimuli consisted of animations of a male Talking Head uttering the Dutch phrase "blauw vierkant" (*blue square*) or the Italian phrase "triangolo nero" (*black triangle*).

3.1   Speech

The Dutch and Italian speech materials were collected in a (semi-) spontaneous way in two earlier production experiments (for more details see Krahmer and Swerts (2001) or Swerts et al. (2002)). This was done using a simple dialogue game, played by four Dutch pairs and four Italian pairs of speakers, thus giving eight speakers per language. All Dutch subjects were students and colleagues working in the south of the Netherlands and speaking standard Dutch. The Italian speakers were all living in Italy and were native speakers of the Tuscan variety of Italian.

The dialogue game is essentially an alignment task of figures played by two subjects, call them A and B, who are separated from each other by a screen. In each game, both players have an identical set of eight cards at their disposal, each card displaying a geometrical figure in a particular color (such as a blue square or a black triangle). Four of these cards are put on a stack in front of the subjects, the remaining four are in a row before them. The four cards in the *stack* of A are the same as

Table 7.1. Example contexts for collection of target utterances in Dutch ("blauwe vierkant", *blue square*) and Italian ("triangolo nero", *black triangle*).

Context	Dutch	Italian
CC	A: rode driehoek	A: rettangolo rosa
	B: blauwe vierkant	B: triangolo nero
GC	A: blauwe driehoek	A: triangolo rosa
	B: blauwe vierkant	B: triangolo nero
CG	A: rode vierkant	A: rettangolo nero
	B: blauwe vierkant	B: triangolo nero

those in the *row* of B, and *vice versa*. The task for both subjects is to create an identical ordered list of geometrical figures. The game consists of a series of turns in which one participant describes the figure on top of his or her stack and instructs the other participant to select this card. Once a card has been described, both players discard it by placing it in the ordered list. After each turn the subjects change roles, so that the instruction-giver in one turn is the instruction-follower in the next turn. The game is over when both players are out of cards. There are no winners or losers. Each pair of subjects plays eight games. There is always a two minute break between games. Speakers found it an easy game to play.

The data thus obtained allow for an unambiguous operationalization of the relevant contexts. A property is defined to be *given* (**G**) if it was mentioned in the previous turn, and it is *contrastive* (**C**) if the figure described in the previous turn had a different value for the relevant attribute. Here we ignore initial dialogue contributions, so all properties are either given of contrastive. We say that a phrase is *in focus* if it is contrastive.

By systematically varying the order of the cards in the stack, we collected target utterances ("blauw vierkant" for Dutch and "triangolo nero" for Italian) in three different contexts: all contrast (**CC**), contrast in the final word (**GC**) and contrast in the pre-final word (**CG**). Note that in the two-letter abbreviations of the contexts the first letter represents the information status of the first word and the second letter that of the second word in the utterance. Table 7.1 summarizes the three contexts of interest and illustrates them with Dutch and Italian examples.

A distributional analysis was performed for all target utterances by three independent labellers for Dutch and three independent ones for Italian. All labellers were intonation experts and did not know the dis-

Figure 7.1. Two stills from the Talking Head uttering "blauw vierkant" (blue square) with a raised eyebrow on the first word (left) and no eyebrow action on the second word (right).

course context of the utterances while labelling them. For the utterances used in the three experiments below, the results are unequivocal. In Dutch, words receive a pitch accent when they are in focus (here: contrastive). In Italian, every word is always accented, irrespective of the discourse context. All Italian speakers produce the same intonation contour in all contexts: a double accent (the pitch contour may be likened to a "flat hat"), with the second accent downstepped with respect to the first (the hat is dented). Thus, the first accent is stronger and more prominent than the second, which is reflected, among other things, in that it has a larger pitch excursion size (i.e., a larger difference between the minimum and maximum F_0, Swerts et al. (2002:643)).

In sum, the distribution of pitch accents is context-dependent in the Dutch data and clearly reflects the information status of words; a focussed (contrastive) word carries a pitch accent, an unfocussed (given) word does not. The distribution in the Italian data is different in that it is always the same irrespective of the context; it provides no clues about the focus of the utterance.

3.2   Animations

The animations used in the experiments were made with the *CharToon* environment (e.g., Ruttkay and Noot (2000)), and take a 2D head of a male character as their basis, see Figure 7.1. CharToon animations are based on constraints over control points (Ruttkay (2001)). As speech materials we used the utterances of "blauw vierkant" and "triangolo nero" that our male speakers produced in the relevant contexts. Visual speech is generated on the basis of a set of 48 visemes. Phonemes from the input speech are mapped to corresponding visemes with a sampling rate of 100ms, while intermediate stages are computed using linear interpolation. Rapid eyebrow movements coincide with the stressed syllable of either the first or the second word in the relevant utterances. Notice that these are eyebrow counterparts of focus on the first word and focus on the second word respectively. We mark the presence of an eyebrow movement by placing a line over the relevant character; thus, for instance, a $\overline{C}$G animation uses speech that was collected in a CG context (the first word is contrastive, the second given) and the first word is associated with an eyebrow movement.

The eyebrow movements always had the same pattern: first, a 100ms dynamic raising part, then a static raised part of 100ms, and finally a dynamic lowering part of 100ms. The overall length of the movement is comparable with the average duration of rapid eyebrow movements of human speakers ($\pm$375ms, Cavé et al. (1996)). We opted for slightly shorter movements due to the overall short duration of the spoken utterances. The 300ms long movement also aligned nicely with the onset and offset of syllables in the Dutch and Italian words used in our stimuli. The brow movement always corresponds with Action Unit AU 1+2 (Ekman and Friesen (1978)).

4. Experiment 1: Subjective Preference

4.1 Method

In the first experiment, subjects were presented with minimal pairs of stimuli. The members of these pairs were always identical in terms of their sound properties, including the pitch accent distribution. They only differed in that one member had an eyebrow movement on the first word while the other had an eyebrow movement on the second word. Subjects were asked in which of the two sound and image were best synchronized.

Subjects were 25 native speakers of Dutch for the Dutch experiment and 25 native speakers of Italian for the Italian experiment.[4] They watched and listened to the Talking Head uttering the different pairs of two-word phrases "blauw vierkant" (Dutch) and "triangolo nero" (Italian). Two male voices were used for each language. All pairs of stimuli, in both AB and BA order, were presented randomly. Subjects could watch and listen to each pair twice, and were encouraged to select, by forced choice, the most natural animation from the pair after the first presentation, and then verify their initial choice during the second showing. Before the actual experiment subjects entered a brief training session (consisting of three pairs of stimuli) to make them acquainted with the experimental setting and the kind of stimuli. No feedback was given on the 'correctness' of their answers and there was no further

Table 7.2. Preference judgements (Dutch) for eyebrow movement on first or second word as a function of context ($N = 300$; 12 stimuli $\times$ 25 subjects).

	Eyebrow preferred on	
Context	First word	Second word
CC	.60	.40
GC	.38	.62
CG	.75	.25

communication with the experimenter. The experiment itself consisted of 12 stimuli per language: 3 different contexts (CC, GC, CG) $\times$ 2 voices $\times$ 2 orders (AB and BA). Subjects were not informed about the kinds of cues they could pay attention to while making their selection. The experiment lasted approximately 5 minutes.

4.2   Results (Dutch)

The Dutch results are given in Table 7.2. The overall distribution is significantly different from chance ($\chi^2(2) = 34.8$, $p < 0.001$). Looking at the top row in this table, it can be seen that there is a mild preference for the eyebrow movement to be aligned with the first word in the all-focus (double contrast) case, which is realized in our Dutch speech data with a double accent. However, the next two lines with results on utterances with a single accent, clearly indicate that Dutch subjects disprefer cases where the eyebrow movement and the pitch accent do not coincide. Arguably, such stimuli are 'inconsistent' in that the speech cues indicate that one word is in focus, while the eyebrows suggest that the other word is in focus. Apparently, Dutch subjects prefer cases where pitch and eyebrows are synchronized. This preference is clearest in the case where the pitch accent falls on the first word (CG); in 75% of these cases, the Dutch listeners prefer the eyebrow movement on the first word as well. This is in accordance with our earlier speech-only results (Krahmer and Swerts (2001)). In Dutch the default position for the nuclear accent (basically, the most prominent accent in a phrase) is the final word. When the pre-final word is in focus (and the final word is given), the nuclear accent shifts to a non-nuclear position and as a consequence it is somewhat more 'conspicuous' than when the nuclear accent appears in default position.

4.3   Results (Italian)

The Italian results can be found in Table 7.3. Again, the overall distribution is significantly different from chance ($\chi^2(2) = 106.92$, $p < 0.001$).

Table 7.3. Preference judgements (Italian) for eyebrow movement on first or second word as a function of context ($N = 300$; 12 stimuli × 25 subjects).

	Eyebrow preferred on	
Context	First word	Second word
CC	.84	.16
GC	.76	.24
CG	.79	.21

Inspection of the table reveals that Italian subjects have a clear preference for the eyebrow movement to coincide with the first word, irrespective of the context. This is in line with the earlier observation that even though both words always receive an accent, the accent on "triangolo" is more prominent than the one on "nero".

4.4 Discussion

The Dutch and Italian results are significantly different (Pearson $\chi^2(5)$ = 49, $p < 0.001$). Interestingly, these differences can be reduced entirely to prosodic differences between the two languages. The Italian subjects prefer the animations with the eyebrow movement on the first word, irrespective of the context. This can be explained through the fact that the first accent is the most prominent one. In the cases where our two Dutch speakers produced a single accent (CG and GC) the Dutch subjects prefer the animation in which eyebrow movement and pitch accent fall on the same word. So, in general, if an animation contains an eyebrow movement, *both* Dutch and Italian subjects prefer the eyebrow movement on the most prominent word, the difference being that in Italian the most prominent word is always the first one while in Dutch this depends on the context (see Swerts et al. 2002 for more details).[5] The fact that in Dutch pitch accents and eyebrow movements are preferred to be aligned, suggests that they may serve the same purpose, namely to render a word more prominent. This issue is investigated further in study 2.

5. Experiment 2: Perceived Prominence

5.1 Method

Subjects were again confronted with pairs of animations that have identical speech properties (including pitch accent distribution), but differ in the presence and placement of eyebrow movements. Unlike in the previous study, however, for experiment 2 each pair of stimuli consisted of one animation without any eyebrow movements and one animation with an eyebrow movement on either the first or the second word of the utterance. Given the finding of the previous experiment that listeners disprefer cases where pitch accents and eyebrows do not coincide (a situation that can only arise in Dutch), the eyebrow movements in the second study always accompanied a pitch accent. This implies that Dutch subjects had to make less pairwise comparisons than Italian ones, since the two 'inconsistent' kinds of Dutch stimuli (i.e., $\overline{G}C$ and $C\overline{G}$) are left out of consideration. For both the Dutch and the Italian study, the same 25 subjects from study 1 participated. Moreover, the same two male voices for each language were used.

The second experiment consisted of four different sessions. In two sessions subjects had to focus on the first word (the adjective "blauw" for Dutch and the noun "triangolo" for Italian), once for each male voice. In the two other sessions, subjects had to focus on the second word (the noun "vierkant" for Dutch and the adjective "nero" for Italian). In all four sessions, subjects had to determine by forced choice which of the two animations contained the most prominent realization of the word of interest. The stimuli were presented in two different random orders to compensate for any learning effects. For both Dutch and Italian, half of the stimulus pairs in each session were distractors. These consisted of utterance pairs that were not only different in terms of eyebrow movements, but also used different speech realizations (taken from different contexts), in an attempt to deliberately confuse subjects about the purpose of the experiment. Before a session started, subjects again entered a brief training session (one stimulus pair per session) to make them acquainted with the material and the task. Again, no feedback was given on the 'correctness' of their answers and there was no further communication with the experimenter. Apart from the distractors, each Dutch session consisted of 4 pairs of stimuli and each Italian session of 6 pairs. Subjects were not informed about the kinds of cues they could pay attention to while making their selection. The second experiment lasted approximately 15 minutes.

5.2   Results (Dutch)

Table 7.4 gives a summary of the results obtained for Dutch. To keep the table readable, we do not present separate results for each individual pairwise comparison. In fact, the different speech conditions gave rise to very little variation anyway; all pairwise comparisons yielded significant differences, with χ^2 scores in the range of 28.8 and 42.3, $df = 1$,

Table 7.4. Prominence judgements (Dutch) for the first word ("blauw") and the second word ("vierkant") in animations with an eyebrow movement either on the first or second word (indicated by a line on top of the relevant word). ($N = 400$; 2 words × 4 comparisons × 2 voices × 25 subjects).

Word	Pairwise comparisons	
Blauw	$\overline{\text{blauw}}$ vierkant .95	blauw $\overline{\text{vierkant}}$ .05
	blauw $\overline{\text{vierkant}}$ .10	$\overline{\text{blauw}}$ vierkant .90
Vierkant	$\overline{\text{blauw}}$ vierkant .14	blauw $\overline{\text{vierkant}}$ .86
	blauw $\overline{\text{vierkant}}$ .90	$\overline{\text{blauw}}$ vierkant .10

$p < 0.001$) (the interested reader may consult Krahmer et al. (2002b) for the detailed tables).

Looking at the results for the first word, "blauw", it is clear that the presence of an eyebrow movement on this word (marked by an over-line) has an effect on the perceived prominence; in 95% of the cases, subjects consider "blauw" more prominent in the animation where this word is associated with an eyebrow movement. Whether the phrase contains only one accent (CG) or two accents (CC) does not influence the result. This suggests that pitch and eyebrows have an additive effect for prominence ratings. Interestingly, eyebrow movements also appear to downscale the perceived prominence of words that appear in the immediate context of a word which is accompanied by an eyebrow movement. This can be seen from the second row of Table 7.4; when the word "vierkant" is associated with an eyebrow movement, subjects consider the utterance of "blauw" in the animation *without* eyebrow movements the most prominent one (and recall that the speech in the two animations is identical).

The results for "vierkant" in the lower half of Table 7.4 mirror those for "blauw" in the upper half: when an eyebrow movement accompanies "vierkant", this boosts the perceived prominence of this word (fourth row), but when the eyebrow movement is associated with "blauw", the word "vierkant" is perceived as less prominent (third row).

Table 7.5. Prominence judgements (Italian) for the first word ("triangolo") and the second word ("nero") in animations with an eyebrow movement either on the first or second word (indicated by a line on top of the relevant word). ($N = 600$; 2 words × 6 comparisons × 2 voices × 25 subjects).

Word	Pairwise comparisons	
Triangolo	t̅r̅i̅a̅n̅g̅o̅l̅o̅ nero .85	triangolo nero .15
	triangolo n̅e̅r̅o̅ .35	triangolo nero .65
Nero	t̅r̅i̅a̅n̅g̅o̅l̅o̅ nero .29	triangolo nero .71
	triangolo n̅e̅r̅o̅ .71	triangolo nero .29

5.3   Results (Italian)

The overall Italian results are summarized in Table 7.5. All but one of the pairwise comparisons are statistically significant, with χ^2 values in the range of 3.92 ($df = 1$, $p < 0.05$) and 35.28 ($df = 1$, $p < 0.001$). The only non-significant comparison is one in which subjects had to focus on "triangolo" in a GC context.

The general picture that emerges from Table 7.5 is the following. If "triangolo" is accompanied by an eyebrow movement, subjects rate its prominence higher than when it is not accompanied by such a movement. Alternatively, if the eyebrow movement occurs on the word "nero", in 65% of the cases, subjects consider "triangolo" more prominent in the animation without eyebrows. The basic picture for the second word ("nero") is essentially the same; the presence of an eyebrow movement on "nero" increases its perceived prominence, but when the eyebrow movement is associated with "triangolo" this reduces the perceived prominence of "nero".

5.4   Discussion

The results for Dutch and Italian are very similar: the presence of an eyebrow movement boosts the perceived prominence of the associated word and downscales the prominence of the preceding or following word. This effect holds for both the first and the second word, and is independent of the context in which the speech was uttered. This is in line with earlier observations from Krahmer and Swerts (2001) that prominence judgements are very much dependent on the prosodic context, in that an isolated pitch peak is perceived as more prominent than the same peak presented in the context of an intonationally comparable pitch peak. The results for Italian are somewhat less pronounced than the Dutch ones, in particular when the eyebrow movement occurs on "nero" or when "nero" is the word of interest. This is might be due to the inherent prominence of "triangolo" in these utterances.

So far, the results for both languages are consistent with claims that eyebrow movements are relevant for prominence perception. In the next experiment it is examined to what extent subjects *use* information from eyebrow movements when processing utterances.

6. Experiment 3: Functional Analysis

6.1 Method

In the third study it is investigated to what extent Dutch and Italian subjects use audio-visual cues when interpreting utterances. For this purpose a "dialogue reconstruction" experiment is used (Swerts et al. (2002)). Subjects watch and listen to the Talking Head uttering (the Dutch and Italian) counterparts of "blue square" (i.e., "blauw vierkant" or "triangolo nero"), with a certain intonation contour (taken from its original context) and an eyebrow movement on either the first or the second word. This gives rise to six different kinds of stimuli ($\overline{C}C$, $C\overline{C}$, $\overline{G}C$, $G\overline{C}$, $\overline{C}G$, and $C\overline{G}$). For Italian, four male voices were used. For Dutch, six male voices were used; four human speakers recorded in the earlier dialogue game experiment and in addition, two synthetic speakers (copying intonation contours of two human speakers).[6]

The task for the subjects is to decide by forced choice what the *preceding* utterance would have described: (1) a red square, (2) a blue triangle or (3) a red triangle. To perform this task subjects have to determine what the focus of the *current* utterance is: (1) the first word ("blue"), (2) the second word ("square") or (3) both. See Table 7.1 for the actual Dutch and Italian phrases used in the third experiment.

Subjects were 25 native speakers of Dutch (different from those used for studies 1 and 2) and 25 native speakers of Italian (the same as those for studies 1 and 2).[7] Before the actual experiment started, subjects entered a brief training session (3 stimuli), to make them acquainted with the experimental setting and the kind of stimuli. No feedback was given about the 'correctness' of their answers, and there was no further communication with the conductor of the experiment. The experiment

Table 7.6. The perception of focus in Dutch as a function of context ($N = 900$; 6 conditions × 6 voices × 25 subjects).

| | | Focus perceived on | |
Context	Blauw	Vierkant	Both
$\overline{C}C$	.30	.27	.43
$C\overline{C}$	.14	.47	.39
$\overline{G}C$	.17	.61	.22
$G\overline{C}$	.18	.60	.22
$\overline{C}G$	.75	.15	.10
$C\overline{G}$	.70	.20	.10

consisted of 36 stimuli for Dutch (6 voices × 6 conditions) and 24 for Italian (4 voices × 6 conditions). The experiment lasted approximately 10 minutes.

6.2 Results (Dutch)

In Table 7.6 the results of the dialogue reconstruction experiment for Dutch are given. The overall distribution is significantly different from chance ($\chi^2(10) = 292.2$, $p < 0.001$). First consider the cases where the speech has a single pitch accent, either on the adjective (CG) or the noun (GC). In the first case, the majority of the subjects perceives the focus on the word "blauw", while in the second case, the majority of subjects perceives the focus on the word "vierkant". Hence, in both cases subjects perceive the focus on the accented word, irrespective of the position of the eyebrow movement. Nevertheless, if we compare the distribution obtained with an eyebrow movement on the first word with the distribution obtained with such a movement on the second word, a significant difference is found (Pearson $\chi^2(8) = 19$, $p < 0.025$). This difference is primarily due to the cases where both words receive a pitch accent (CC). In those cases, a word which is associated with an eyebrow movement is perceived to be in focus roughly twice more often than when the word is *not* accompanied by a brow movement. Thus, if the eyebrow movement coincides with "blauw", subjects perceive the focus on this word in 30% of the cases (as opposed to 14% of the cases when no eyebrow movement accompanies "blauw"). And, if the eyebrow movement is aligned with "vierkant", this word is perceived to be the focussed one in 47% of the cases (as opposed to 27% of the cases when no eyebrow movement accompanies "vierkant"). So, for Dutch both pitch

Table 7.7. The perception of focus in Italian as a function of context ($N = 600$; 6 conditions × 4 voices × 25 subjects).

| | | Focus perceived on | |
Context	Triangolo	Nero	Both
$\bar{C}C$	.36	.31	.33
$C\bar{C}$	.35	.28	.37
$\bar{G}C$	.37	.29	.34
$G\bar{C}$	.26	.49	.25
$\bar{C}G$	.25	.36	.39
$C\bar{G}$	.32	.38	.30

accents and eyebrow movements can influence the perception of focus, albeit that the effect is much larger for pitch.

6.3 Results (Italian)

The Italian results are rather different, as the reader can observe in Table 7.7. The overall distribution is not significantly different from chance ($\chi^2(10) = 16.8$, n.s.). Moreover, the distribution obtained with the eyebrow movement on the first word is not significantly different from that with the movement on the second word (Pearson $\chi^2(8) = 10.84$, n.s.) This indicates that Italian subjects can not reconstruct the dialogue history on the basis of the audio-visual properties of the stimuli. Put differently, the placement of pitch accents and eyebrow movements does not provide any clues for our Italian subjects about the context.

6.4 Discussion

The results show that Dutch subjects are capable of "reconstructing the dialogue history" in the current experiment, while Italian subjects are not. The results for both languages confirm the earlier speech-only results of Swerts et al. (2002). In the Dutch speech-only results, subjects could reconstruct the dialogue history best in the CG case (because the nuclear accent falls on a non-default position) and least in the CC case. In the current experiment we can basically observe the same picture. Interestingly, the eyebrow movements contribute only in the all contrast (CC) case, which is the one where the speech cues are least informative. Overall we see somewhat more confusion in the current experiment than was found in the speech-only experiment. This might indicate that the presence of the face is somewhat distracting for subjects. Similar observations have been made for 'real' face-to-face communication (Doherty-Sneddon et al. (2001)).

In our earlier speech-only experiment for Italian we found that subjects are incapable to reconstruct the dialogue history on the basis of prosodic cues. This was not surprising, since our Italian speakers always pronounced "triangolo nero" with the same contour irrespective of the context. On the basis of this, and in analogy with the Dutch CC case, one might hypothesize that eyebrow movements would contribute more for Italian than they did for Dutch. This would also be in line with observations from Rimé and Schiarature (1991) that gestures occur more when speech cues are underspecified. But in fact, the opposite of our expectation turned out to be true: eyebrows contributed *less* for Italian than they did for Dutch.

Thus, again we find differences between Dutch and Italian (eyebrows do something for focus perception in Dutch and nothing in Italian) and again these differences seem related to prosodic differences between the two languages (prosodic cues contribute to focus perception for our Dutch but not for our Italian speech materials).

7.   General Discussion

7.1   Eyebrows in Dutch and Italian

This chapter has reported on three experiments with an embodied agent, in an attempt to gain more insight into the cue value of eyebrow movements for the perception of focus in Dutch and Italian.

The first experiment tested how Dutch and Italian listeners react to two-word stimuli with an eyebrow movement either on the first or on the second word. Results showed that our Dutch subjects prefer those animations in which the eyebrow movement is synchronized with a word that carries a pitch accent (due to contrastiveness) rather than with an unaccented word. Our Italian subjects preferred the eyebrow movement to occur on the first word, irrespective of its information status. So Dutch and Italian subjects appear to have different preferences, but these differences can be explained entirely by the prosodic differences between the two languages. Essentially, both Dutch and Italian subjects prefer the eyebrow movement to coincide with the most prominent word in the utterance, which is determined by context in Dutch and always is the first word in our Italian speech data.

The second experiment investigated whether listeners are sensitive to eyebrow movements when they have to rate the prominence of particular words. This experiment showed that for both the Dutch and the Italian stimuli, eyebrow movements boost the perceived prominence of the word they are associated with and simultaneously downscale the prominence of words in the immediate preceding or following context. The situation was somewhat more clear for Dutch than for Italian, which again can be ascribed to prosodic differences between the languages (in particular to the inherent prominence of the first pitch accent with respect to the second, downstepped one in the Italian stimuli).

The third experiment tried to found out the relative contributions of pitch accents and eyebrow movements for the perception of focus in Dutch and Italian. Our Dutch listeners use both cues to determine the focus of an utterance, albeit that the effect of pitch accents is much larger than that of eyebrow movements. The latter only contribute when speech cues are relatively unclear (i.e., the double contrast, CC case). Our Italian subjects, however, were unable to determine the focus of the utterances. The differences between the Dutch and Italian results once again mirror prosodic differences between the two languages. In earlier work (Swerts et al. (2002)) we have found that Dutch listeners can and Italian listeners cannot determine the focus of utterances on the basis of auditory cues alone.

This suggests that the two questions from the introduction may be answered as follows. About question one: eyebrow movements seem to play only a secondary role for the perception of focus; they follow pitch accents and mainly enhance the perceived prominence of words. And concerning question two: the proper placement of eyebrow movements is language dependent and their functional contribution may differ per language. Interestingly, however, to the extent that eyebrow movements have different functions in the languages under consideration here, these differences can be fully explained from the prosodic differences between the languages.

The first two experiments confirm the earlier claims that eyebrow movements and pitch accents are related for communicative purposes; both the Dutch and Italian subjects prefer the eyebrow movement to coincide with the most prominent word, and the brow movement indeed seems to perform some accentuation function. Still, it remains puzzling that eyebrow movements play only a small (Dutch) or no (Italian) role for the perception of focus. It might be that eyebrow movements are exploited more consistently as a cue to different kinds of conversational phenomena.[8] Another explanation might be that listeners are simply more biased to auditory cues than to visual cues for focus perception. This would be in line with the earlier observation that speakers do more with pitch than with eyebrows. Many accented words are not accompanied by a baton or an underliner, so it is not unlikely that we are most sensitive to verbal prosody.

7.2   About Analysis-by-Synthesis

Analysis-by-synthesis is a powerful evaluation method, which may provide useful empirical data about the relation between verbal and visual prosody. The two main advantages of the method are that (a) one has direct control over all the relevant parameters, and (b) once a theory has been implemented (and evaluated positively) it can be applied directly in an embodied conversational agent. One can think of many variations on the three experiments discussed above that could be pursued using the analysis-by-synthesis method. For instance, we have only looked at one eyebrow movement (AU 1+2). Ekman and Friesen (1978) also describe another brow movement that may serve as a baton or an underliner, namely AU 4 (in which the brows are lowered and drawn). According to Ekman (1979) this movement can have a similar function as AU 1+2, but seems to contain an element of doubt as well. It would be interesting to test this.[9] Other variations involve manipulating the duration and the strength of the brow movement. What happens if we would use shorter/longer movements, where the eyebrows move upwards to a lesser extent? Would they still increase the perceived prominence of words? For such research questions, the analysis-by-synthesis method seems very useful.[10]

There is also a potential disadvantage of the analysis-by-synthesis method, however, in that the results may be incomplete. In the three experiments described above, we only manipulated one parameter (brows) and measured the results. Still, it might be that some other visual factor or combination of factors is more relevant for focus perception. Since no other parameters were manipulated in the experiments, such an alternative explanation cannot be ruled out. Of course, we can redo the experiments with, say, head nods, in combination with or instead of eyebrow movements. It might, for instance, be the case that head nods are more convincing visual cues than eyebrow movements for reconstructing the dialogue history (experiment 3). But even if that were the case, it would not solve the general problem. After all, it might be that there still is another cue or combination of cues which more accurately corresponds with focus signalling. The number of potential cue combination grows explosively and it does not seem feasible to try out all of them via analysis-by-synthesis experiment. In our opinion, the best way to address this potential problem is by combining analysis-by-synthesis with *analysis-by-observation*. Below we describe such an analysis.

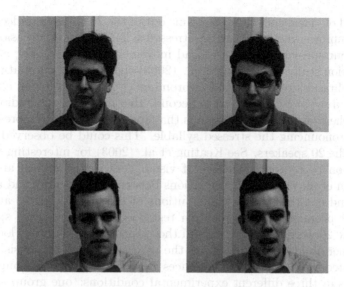

Figure 7.2. Representative stills of two subjects uttering unstressed (left) and stressed (right) syllables.

7.3   Analysis-by-observation

To gain insight into which audio-visual prominence cues human speaker actually use, an analysis-by-Observation test was conducted. Twenty (Dutch) subjects were asked to pronounce nonsense words consisting of three CV (consonant vowel) syllables: /ma ma ma/ and /ga ga ga/.[11] In each utterance, subjects had to emphasize one syllable. To achieve this, they were given cards with the three syllables, one of which was printed in upper case. The text on a card could be, for instance, "ma MA ma," which indicated that the second syllable should be pronounced with more emphasis than the other two. Subjects were not instructed about the kinds of cues they could use for emphasizing a syllable. They were given six cards in total (2 words × 3 stressed syllables). After looking at the top card, they were asked to pronounce the word printed on this card while looking into the camera. They did so in two different conditions: *neutral* and *exaggerated*. This process was repeated for each of the six cards, which resulted in 12 utterances per speaker (240 utterances in total).

As expected, almost all speakers used verbal cues to stress the designated syllable, but many speakers used visual cues as well. See Figure 7.2 for some illustrative screen shots. Two findings are particularly noteworthy for the purposes of this chapter. First, speakers clearly *differ* in the kind of visual cues they use. Nine out of the 20 speakers indeed raise their eyebrows when uttering the stressed syllable (at least occasionally), while four speakers would use head movements. Interestingly, a recent production study by Keating et al. (2003) showed clear correlations between phrasal stress (the kind of prominence related to focus) and *both* head and eyebrow movements. Second, the most obvious audio-visual cue in the exaggerated condition is that speakers articulate more clearly when pronouncing the stressed syllable. This could be observed for 18 out of the 20 speakers. See Keating et al. (2003) for interesting related results on perceptual relevance of visual cues in the mouth area and Erickson et al. (1998) for correlations between jaw opening and accent.

To find out the relative contributions of the visual and the auditory cues for prominence, a perception test was conducted. Five speakers from the 20 were selected (we used those speakers who always looked in the camera and always produced the utterances with emphasis on the designated syllable). Their utterances were offered to three groups of 15 subjects in three different experimental conditions: one group saw the utterances as they were recorded (audio+vision), one group only heard the speech (audio) and the last group only saw the speakers (vision). All subjects were asked to determine which of the three syllables was the emphasized one. As expected, in both the audio+vision and in the audio condition, subjects were very good at determining the stressed syllable (97.1% and 97.3% correct, respectively). In the vision condition subjects scored significantly less good, confirming our earlier observation that auditory cues are more important for the perception of prominence than visual ones. Nevertheless, subjects in this condition performed still surprisingly good, with overall 92.89% correct guesses. What this indicates is that there are clear visual cues for prominence besides the well-known auditory ones.[12]

The analysis-by-observation approach does not suffer from the potential problems that may plague analysis-by-synthesis. Still, the approach cannot give us all the information that we would like to have. In particular, while the perception test clearly shows that there are audio-visual cues that Dutch people may use when interpreting an utterance (e.g., to detect prominence), we do not know *which* cues people actually use. In fact, one way to find out would be using an analysis-by-synthesis experiment. This illustrates that the combination of analysis-by-observation with analysis-by-synthesis is a good way to gain insight in functions of audio-visual prosody, because it enables us to get insight in which cues human speakers employ, but also in how human listeners interpret stimuli which include these cues.

Acknowledgments

This research was partly conducted within the VIDI-project "Functions of audio-visual prosody (FOAP)", sponsored by the Netherlands Organization for Scientific Research (NWO). Parts of the Dutch results have been presented at the Workshop on Coordination and Fusion in Multimodal Interaction (Dagstuhl, November (2001)), Speech Prosody (Aix-en-Provence, April 2002), and ICSLP (Denver, September (2002)). The Italian results appear here for the first time. We would like to thank Han Noot, Zsófi Ruttkay and Wieger Wesselink for their help in making the animations, and Cinzia Avesani and Jeannine de Raad for their help in carrying out the Italian experiments. Iris Boshouwers has been a great help in the analysis-by-observation study. We have benefitted from comments by Matthew Stone, Mariët Theune, Loredana Cerrato and an anonymous reviewer.

Notes

1. Embodied Conversational Agents (e.g., Cassell et al. (2000)) are also referred to as Virtual Humans (e.g., Gratch et al. (2002)) or Talking Heads (e.g., Rubin and Vatikiotis-Bateson (1998)). In this chapter we mainly concentrate on Talking Heads although the methodological part of the story is applicable to any kind of embodied agent.

2. There is even some evidence that the presence of Perlin noise results in animations which are slightly *less* functional than animations without Perlin noise, since subjects are somewhat more likely to miss potentially informative facial cues when random movements are present (van de Laar (2003)).

3. Their usage of the term *flash* for an eyebrow movement does not coincide with Ekman's usage of the term. The flashes of Cassell et al. (2001) are really batons or underliners, while Ekman's flashes refer to repeated brow raises which do not coincide with speech (i.e., emblems).

4. The Dutch and Italian subjects came from different parts of The Netherlands and Italy, respectively. For methodological reasons, it would have been better to have Italian subjects from Tuscany only (the dialect of the speakers), as Italian dialects are known to vary regarding their intonation structures. Unfortunately, we were unable to find enough Tuscanian subjects. However, since the Italian results are so unequivocal, we suspect that the results would not have been dramatically different from the ones reported here.

5. Of course, it might be that our Dutch and Italian subjects would have preferred an animation *without* eyebrow movements, but the experiment was not designed to test this. It would be interesting, however, to redo the first experiment including animations without eyebrow movements, and ask subjects for their preference.

6. The synthetic voices were added to see to what extent naturalness of the voice influences the perception of focus. Arguably, a human voice has more natural and better sounding prosody, but a synthetic voice might be more suitable as the auditory counterpart of a synthetic character. It turned out that this was not the case: the results for the 4 human voices did not differ significantly from the results for the 2 synthetic voices.

7. The order of presentation in this chapter is a historical falsification. The Dutch experiments were carried out first. This was done in two steps: first, we performed the functional analysis, and in a later stage we did the subjective preferences and perceived prominence tests to get a better understanding of the results of the functional analysis. The Italian experiments were done at a later date, but in the same order as the Dutch experiments (i.e., 3, 1, 2).

8. Ekman (1979) also mentions other conversational functions of brows besides accenting, in particular they may cue punctuation, question marks, word search, and agreement between dialogue participants. None of these functions seems intuitively right for the stimuli used in the three experiments. It is interesting to observe that all of the functions Ekman mentions are also typical functions of verbal prosody.

9. It seems that a study along these lines has been carried out by O'Sullivan and Eyman (1978). We have not been able to consult this paper, but O'Sullivan (p.c.) informed us that they compared AU 4, AU 1+4 and AU 1+2+4, combined with neutral statements, and found that different brows affected the interpretation.

10. Along the same lines, it might be worth investigating subtle interactions of visual cues with other auditory cues to prominence, such as different pitch accent types and voice intensity.

11. The motivation to select /m/ and /g/ was that the former phoneme is pronounced in the front of the articulatory channel, while the latter is pronounced in the back. It was hypothesized that the /m/ is visually easier to perceive than the /g/. This turned out not to play a role for prominence perception.

12. More details about this and some related experiments will be given in a sequel to this paper.

References

Bolinger, D. (1985). *Intonation and its parts*. Edward Arnold, London.

Birdwhistell, R. (1970). *Kinesics and context*. University of Pennsylvania Press.

Cassell, J., Sullivan, J., Prevost, S., and Churchill, E., editors (2000). *Embodied Conversational Agents*. The MIT Press, Cambridge, MA.

Cassell, J., Vihjálmsson, H., and Bickmore, T. (2001). BEAT: The Behavior Expression Animation Toolkit. In *Proceedings of SIG-GRAPH'01*, pp. 477–486, Los Angeles.

Cavé, C., Guaïtella, I., Bertrand, R., Santi, S., Harlay, F., and Espesser, R. (1996). About the relationship between eyebrow movements and F_0 variations. In *Proceedings of the International Conference on Spoken Language Processing (ICSLP)*, pp. 2175–2179, Philadelphia.

Chafe, W. (1974). Language and consciousness. *Language* 50: 111–133.

Condon, W. (1976). An analysis of behavioral organization. *Sign Language Studies*, 13: 285–318.

Cutler, A. (1984). Stress and accent in language production and understanding. In Gibbon, D. and Richter, H., editors, *Intonation, accent and rhythm. Studies in Discourse Phonology*. pp. 77–90, de Gruyter, Berlin.

Cruttenden, A. (1997). *Intonation*, 2nd edition. Cambridge University Press, Cambridge.

Darwin, Ch. (1872). *The Expression of the emotions in man and animals*. Philosophical Library, New York.

Doherty-Sneddon, G., Bonner, L., and Bruce, V. (2001). Cognitive demands of face monitoring: Evidence for visuospatial overload. *Memory and Cognition*, 29(7): 909–919.

Efron, D. (1941). *Gesture and environment*. King's Crown Press, New York.

Eibl-Eibesfelt, I. (1972). Similarities and differences between cultures in expressive movements. In Hinde, R., editor, *Non-verbal communication*. Cambridge University Press, Cambridge.

Ekman, P. (1979). About brows: Emotional and conversational signals. In von Cranach, M., Foppa, K., Lepenies, W. and Ploog, D., editors, *Human ethology: Claims and limits of a new discipline*. pp. 169–202, Cambridge University Press, Cambridge.

Ekman, P. and Friesen, W. (1978). *Facial Action Coding System*. Consulting Psychologists Press, Inc, Palo Alto.

Erickson, D., Fujimura, O., and Pardo, B. (1998). Articulatory correlates of prosodic control: Emotion and emphasis. *Language and Speech*, 41(3-4): 399–417.

Granström, B., House, D., and Lundeberg, M. (1999). Prosodic cues to multimodal speech perception. In *Proceedings 14th International Conference of the Phonetic Sciences (ICPhS)*, pp. 655658, San Francisco.

Granström, B., House, D., and Swerts, M. (2002). Multimodal feedback cues in human-machine interactions. In *Proceedings of Speech Prosody 2002*. pp. 347–350, Aix en Provence, France.

Gratch, J., Rickel, J., André, E., Badler, N., Cassell, J., and Petajan, E. (2002). Creating interactive virtual humans: Some assembly required. *IEEE Intelligent Systems*, 17(4): 54–63.

Hirschberg, J. (1993). Pitch accents in context: predicting intonational prominence from text. *Artificial Intelligence*, 63: 305–340.

Keating, P., Baroni, M., Mattys, S., Scarborough, R., Alwan, A., Auer, E., and Berstein, L. (2003). Optical phonetics and visual perception of lexical and phrasal stress in English. In *Proceedings 16th International Conference of the Phonetic Sciences (ICPhS)*, pp. 2071–2074, Barcelona, Spain.

Krahmer, E. and Swerts, M. (2001). On the alleged existence of contrastive accents, *Speech Communication*, 34: 391–405.

Krahmer, E., Ruttkay, Zs., Swerts, M., and Wesselink, W. (2002a). Pitch, eyebrows and the perception of focus. In *Proceedings of Speech Prosody 2002*, pp. 443–446, Aix en Provence, France.

Krahmer, E., Ruttkay, Zs., Swerts, M., and Wesselink, W. (2002b). Perceptual evaluation of audio-visual cues to prominence. In *Proceedings of International Conference on Spoken Language Processing (ICSLP'02)*, pp. 1933–1936, Denver, CO.

Ladd, D. (1996). *Intonational phonology*. Cambridge University Press, Cambridge.

van de Laar, L. (2003). *Influence of eyes on the interpretation of utterances of embodied conversational agents: An experimental inquiry.* MA thesis, Tilburg University.

Morgan, B. (1953). Question melodies in American English. *American Speech*, 2: 181–191.

Nass, C., Isbister, K., and Lee, E. (2000). Truth is beauty: Researching embodied conversational agents. In Cassell, J., Sullivan, J., Prevost, S., and Churchill, E., editors, *Embodied Conversational Agents*. The MIT Press, Cambridge, MA.

O'Sullivan, M. and Eyman, J. (1978). The signal value of eyebrow movements in conversation. *J. Western Psychological Association Convention*. San Francisco.

Pelachaud, C., Badler, N., and Steedman, M. (1996). Generating facial expressions for speech. *Cognitive Science*, 20: 1–46.

Perlin, K. (1995). Real time responsive animation with personality. *IEEE Transactions on Visualization and Computer Graphics*, 1(1): 5–15.

Rimé, B. and Schiaratura, L. (1991). Gesture and speech. In Feldman, R. and Rimé, B., editors, *Fundamentals of nonverbal behavior*. pp. 239–281, Cambridge University Press, Cambridge.

Rubin, P. and Vatikiotis-Bateson, E. (1998). Talking heads. In Burnham, D., Robert-Ribes, J. and Vatikiotis-Bateson, E., editors, *International Conference on Auditory-Visual Speech Processing (AVSP'98)*, pp. 233238, Sydney, Australia

Ruttkay, Zs. (2001). Constraint-based facial animation. *Journal of Constraints*, 6: 85–113

Ruttkay, Zs. and Noot, H. (2000). Animated CharToon Faces. In *Proceedings of NPAR 2000 - First International Symposium on Non Photorealistic Animation and Rendering*, pp. 91–100, Annecy, France.

Sanderman, A. and Collier, R. (1997). Prosodic phrasing and comprehension. *Language and Speech*, 40(4): 391–409.

Swerts, M., Krahmer, E., and Avesani, C. (2002). Prosodic marking of information status in Dutch and Italian: A comparative analysis. *Journal of Phonetics*, 30(4): 629–654.

Terken, J. (1984). The distribution of pitch accents in instructions as a function of discourse structure. *Language and Speech*, 27: 269–289.

Terken, J. and Nooteboom, S. (1987). Opposite effects of accentuation and deaccentuation on verification latencies for Given and New information. *Language and Cognitive Processes*, 2(3-4): 145–163.

Zappa, F. (1989). *The Real Frank Zappa Book*, Poseidon Press, New York.

Chapter 8

EVALUATION OF MULTIMODAL BEHAVIOUR OF EMBODIED AGENTS

Cooperation between Speech and Gestures

Stéphanie Buisine, Sarkis Abrilian, and Jean-Claude Martin

> *They define being and body as one, and if any one else says that what is not a body exists they altogether despise him, and will hear of nothing but body.*
>
> —Plato, Sophist

Abstract   Individuality of Embodied Conversational Agents (ECAs) may depend on both the look of the agent and the way it combines different modalities such as speech and gesture. In this chapter, we describe a study in which male and female users had to listen to three short technical presentations made by ECAs. Three multimodal strategies of ECAs for using arm gestures with speech were compared: redundancy, complementarity, and speech-specialization. These strategies were randomly attributed to different-looking 2D ECAs, in order to test independently the effects of multimodal strategy and ECA's appearance. The variables we examined were subjective impressions and recall performance. Multimodal strategies proved to influence subjective ratings of quality of explanation, in particular for male users. On the other hand, appearance affected likeability, but also recall performance. These results stress the importance of both multimodal strategy and appearance to ensure pleasantness and effectiveness of presentation ECAs.

Keywords: Embodied conversational agent, evaluation, multimodal behaviour, redundancy, complementarity.

Z. Ruttkay and C. Pelachaud (eds.), From Brows to Trust, 217–238.
© *2004 Kluwer Academic Publishers. Printed in the Netherlands.*

1.   Introduction

In order to make Embodied Conversational Agents (ECAs) more believable (Nijholt (2001)) and more comfortable (Ball and Breese (2000)), attempts are made to give them some aspects of emotions and personality during the interaction with human users (see Ball and Breese (2000) for a review; Workshops AAMAS (2002) and (2003)). Personality contributes to a large extent to defining ECAs as individuals: extraversion, agreeableness or friendliness are some personality traits that have been most studied. They affect all verbal and nonverbal modalities of communication: content of speech, intonation, facial expression, body posture, arm movements, etc.

Personality can be given to ECAs whatever their function. In assistance tasks, some ECAs (André et al. (2000)) combine specific behaviours depending on their personality (on the dimensions of extraversion and agreeableness) and presentation acts, which are not based on individual characteristics. To increase again ECAs' believability, we could also imagine to associate presentation acts themselves to individual strategies. In human behaviour, speech-accompanying arm movements can be considered as an integral part of individual communicative style (Kendon (1980)) and their occurrences could depend on the tactic of expression temporarily preferred by the speaking person (McNeill (1987), quoted by Rimé and Schiaratura (1991)).

During presentation tasks, ECAs have to relate speech and pictorial information. In such a context, cooperation between modalities observed in humans could be used to specify ECAs' behaviour. In social sciences, spontaneous gestures produced by a speaker were mostly studied for themselves (see Goldin-Meadow (1999a) for a review). Authors classically tried to observe and classify these gestures independently of the context and the speech content. The categorizations that emerged from these works show different levels of granularity but there seems to be a consensus on the following categories (see for example McNeill (1992)):

- *Emblems* are gestures that have a signification per se, for example waving the hand to say hello.

- *Iconic gestures* capture aspects of the semantic content, for example when the speaker mimes an action or symbolizes an object with his hands.

- *Metaphoric gestures* are pictorial gestures like iconics but displaying rather an abstract content, for example shrugging the shoulders to say "I don't know".

- *Deictic gestures* designate something in the conversational space, for example pointing at an object.

- *Beat gestures* are movements along with the rhythm of speech.

However, these categories do not detail to which extent the meanings conveyed by speech and gestures cooperate in the discourse. Simultaneous speech and gestures were related in some studies (e.g., Goldin-Meadow et al. (1999b)), but only in terms of match/mismatch of information. The framework provided by this field of research appears to be inadequate to the study of cooperation between modalities for ECAs.

On the other hand, the development of multimodal interfaces raised new needs in terms of analysis of human multimodal behaviour. Thus, on the basis of a survey of video corpora, we have proposed a taxonomy for the cooperation between modalities. The following types of cooperation are extracted from this taxonomy (see Martin et al. (2001) for more details):

- *Redundancy*: modalities cooperating by redundancy produce the same information.

- *Complementarity*: different chunks of information are produced by each modality and have to be merged.

- *Specialization*: a specific kind of information is always produced by the same modality.

In a presentation context, redundancy consists in giving verbal information and repeating it either with an iconic gesture or a deictic gesture towards an object. Although not explicitly named, this kind of strategy seems to be most frequently adopted for animated presenters or pedagogical agents (André et al. (2000); Rickel and Johnson (1999)). Conversely, cooperation by complementarity enables a decrease in the amount of information given by each modality. For example, the ECA talks about an object and gives information (e.g., shape or size) by hand gesture without mentioning this information by speech (Cassell et al. (2001)).

Some other presentation agents could be designed to give verbally the whole content of the presentation. This happens when the agent is embodied as an animated face without any body (e.g., Pelachaud et al. (2002)). A fully-embodied agent could also display no semantic content through gestures. In this case, modalities cooperate by speech-specialization. This type of cooperation corresponds to the 'elaborate speech-style', which is likely to occur in humans when the discourse content is distant from personal experience, conventional, abstract, and objective (Rimé and Schiaratura (1991)). This strategy also constitutes a kind of control condition in comparison to redundancy and complementarity.

The primary goal of this study was to determine whether individual multimodal strategies, when exhibited by ECAs, would be perceived by a human listener and/or would have an impact on the effectiveness of the presentation. In these cases, what strategy would be the best one? We decided to test the effect of three multimodal strategies — cooperation by *redundancy, complementarity* and *speech-specialization* — in ECAs short presentations. We have selected these three strategies as they are rather different from one another and thus one could expect significant results when comparing them (although we did not make any preliminary hypothesis about which one would be perceived best). Another important issue in such a context is the influence of ECA's look on the effectiveness of presentation. As a secondary goal, we decided to test the effects of ECA's appearance independently from its multimodal strategy. Thus, the three selected strategies were randomly attributed to three different-looking ECAs. We investigated the impact of these two factors on two kinds of variables: subjective impressions of users (in a post-experimental questionnaire) and recall performance of the information provided in the presentations. Finally, we included in the questionnaire items about ECAs' personality, in order to test whether multimodal strategy and/or appearance influenced users' perception of ECAs' personality. In order to fully control the parameters of the ECAs' behaviour, the users could not interact with them. Thus, the users' task consisted in listening to three short technical explanations (60 to 75 seconds), trying to recall the maximum of information, and then filling out a questionnaire.

Next section presents the experimental setting. The results are described in section 3 and discussed in section 4. A few concluding remarks are presented in section 5.

2.   Experimental Setting

In this section, we present our methodology in details.

2.1   Participants

Two groups of users from our laboratory participated in the experiment: 9 male adults (age range 23 to 51, *mean* = 30.7) and 9 female adults (age range 22 to 50, *mean* = 29.2). These two groups did not differ in age ($F(1/16) = 0.129$; N.S.).

2.2   Apparatus

Animations were presented on a 19″ computer screen (1024 × 768 resolution) and loudspeakers were used for speech synthesis with IBM ViaVoice[1]. In addition to speech synthesis, the text of the ECA's presentation was displayed sentence by sentence on the top of the screen (see Figure 8.1; the initial text was in French).

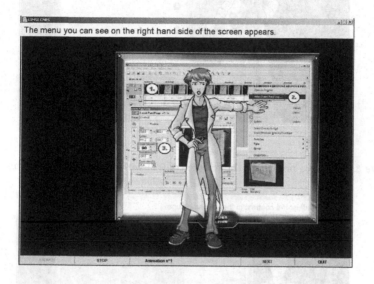

Figure 8.1.   Lea presenting a software with a redundant strategy. Other examples of Lea's behaviour can be seen on Figure 8.4.

2.3   Scenarios

The presentations were three short technical explanations, dealing with the functioning of a video-editing software, a remote control for video-projector and a copy machine. The main difficulty lay in ambiguities of position, colour and shape of keys or menu items which are on the three objects. These objects were thus particularly relevant to study multimodal spatial references. They also involved similar functional behaviours, and were of the same complexity.

The explanations addressed on the position of buttons or menu items, on their function, etc. The ECAs appeared in front of a black background and a whiteboard. Each explanation was associated with a single picture displayed on this whiteboard (see Figures 8.1 to 8.3).

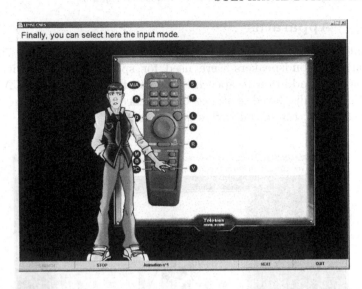

Figure 8.2. Marco presenting the remote control with a complementary strategy.

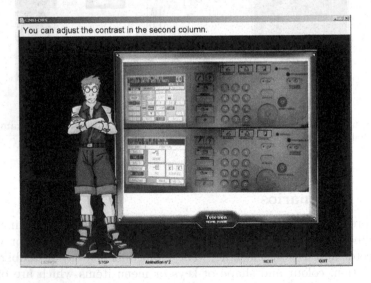

Figure 8.3. Julien presenting the copy machine with a speech-specialized strategy.

2.4   Independent Variables

The primary variable tested was the *multimodal strategy* of the ECAs. It had the following three values:

- *Cooperation by redundancy*: relevant information (e.g., position, shape, size of items) was given both by speech and arm gesture (deictic gesture towards the picture or iconic gesture when possible, see Figure 8.1).

- *Cooperation by complementarity*: half of relevant information was given by speech, and the other half was given by gesture (deictic gesture towards the picture or iconic gesture, see Figure 8.2).

- *Cooperation by speech-specialization*: all information was given by speech. Gestures did not convey any semantic content (see Figure 8.3).

The *appearance* of the ECAs was the second variable investigated in this experiment. We used three 2D cartoon-like Limsi Embodied Agents that we have developed. The 2D ECAs technology we used was described by Abrilian et al. (2002). Multimodal behaviour of all ECAs was specified using a low-level XML language. In this experiment, we used one female ECA and two male ECAs, namely Lea, Marco and Julien (see Figures 8.1 to 8.3). A demonstration is available on the Web[2].

Combinations between ECAs' appearance, multimodal strategy and content of presentation were determined by means of a Latin square design (Myers (1979)). Each ECA used each strategy and presented each object the same number of times across each group of users. For example, Figure 8.4 shows Lea presenting the remote control with the three different strategies. Such a design enables investigating the three variables with less expenditure of time (each user saw 3 presentations) than complete factorial designs would involve (27 presentations). It also removes some sources of error variance such as repetition effects. However, with this design, tests of interactions between these three variables are impossible to extract. We could only test the effect of ECA's appearance and multimodal strategy independently.

Finally, the influence of users' *gender* on dependent variables was tested. The two groups were paired regarding the Latin-squared combinations. Additional variables such as the content of the presentations or the order of presentations were considered as subsidiary variables. The presentations were equivalent in duration for the three contents (75 seconds for redundant and speech-specialized scenarios, 60 seconds for complementary scenarios). The presentation order of the three explanations, of the three strategies and of the three ECAs were neutralized across each group of users.

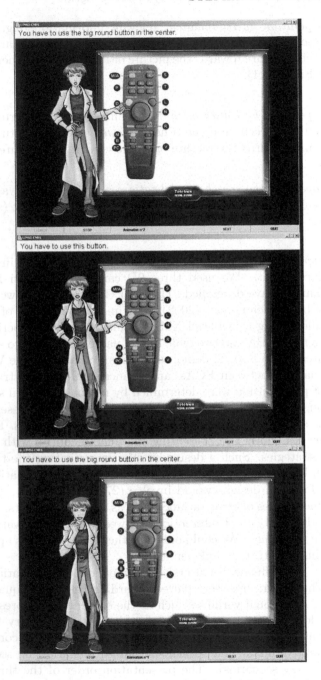

Figure 8.4. Each ECA (Lea in this screenshot) was tested with the three strategies: redundant (upper window), complementary (middle window) and speech-specialized (lower window).

2.5 Generation of Multimodal Behaviour

In this section, we present the way we specified the ECAs' behaviour whatever their appearance. All the animations were made manually. We first present the simple specifications we used for the animations that were common to the three strategies. Then, we describe the rules underlying each strategy, which were the focus of this study.

2.5.1 Common Animations Each feature of the ECA was manually animated in accordance with the content of the discourse. Lip movements, periodic eye blinks, and eyebrow movements were appropriately inserted in order to have a natural-looking animation. The ECAs also periodically turned the head towards the whiteboard, and emphasis was displayed via eyebrows on certain words (e.g., "on the **right**", or "the **blue** button"). Voice intonation was set to neutral.

The gestural modality was of prior importance in this study. We made sure that the number of gestures was exactly the same for all strategies so that we could compare them — any difference in users' reactions to the three strategies could not be attributable to variations in the *amount* of gesticulation. The rate of semantic gestures (deictic or iconic) among arm/hand movements was maximal in redundant scenarios, intermediate in complementary scenarios, and null in speech-specialized scenarios.

Hand shapes and movements for non-semantic gestures (e.g., laying the hand on the hip, moving the arm downwards, touching one's chin, folding the arms, etc.) were selected in our database according to the naturalness of their combination with each specific utterance. Since no intonation specifications were included, strokes of all gestures were placed manually in the speech course.

2.5.2 Rules for Generating Redundant Multimodal Behaviour Redundant presentations were created by including the following rules in ECAs' animations:

- Speech: for items of interest, absolute localization (e.g., "on the top left side") was used whenever it was possible; otherwise the ECA used relative localization (e.g., "just below, you will find..."). Shape, colour and size of items were given whenever it was a discriminative feature.

- Hand and arm gestures: shape and size were displayed via an iconic gesture when possible (with both hands). A deictic gesture was used for every object. Finger or palm hand shape was selected as a function of the precision required (size of the item to be designated). Non-semantic gestures (as described above) were used when no other gesture was possible.

- Gaze: the ECA glanced at target items for 0.4 second at the beginning of every deictic gesture.

- Eyebrows: shape of big objects was not only displayed with speech and gestures, but also via raised eyebrows.

- Locomotion: if needed, the ECA moved closer to the target item before deictic gesture.

2.5.3   Rules for Generating Complementary Multimodal Behaviour   The following rules define complementary presentations:

- Speech: in comparison with redundant scenarios, information concerning localization, shape, colour or size was given for half of the items.

- Hand and arm gestures: deictic or iconic gestures were used every time the information was not given by speech. Non-semantic gestures were used the rest of the time.

- Gaze: the ECA glanced at target items for 0.4 second at the beginning of every deictic gesture.

- Locomotion: if needed, the ECA moved closer to the target item before deictic gesture.

2.5.4   Rules for Generating Speech-specialized Multimodal Behaviour   In speech-specialized presentations, ECAs were animated as follows:

- Speech: the same information as in redundant scenarios was given by speech (localization, shape, colour, size of items).

- Hand and arm gestures: only non-semantic gestures (as described in section 2.5.1) were displayed.

2.6   Dependent Variables

In this section we describe the variables we investigated and how they were collected.

2.6.1   Subjective Variables   The users filled out a questionnaire in which they had to grade the three ECAs for the following questions:

- Which ECA gave the best explanation?

- Which ECA do you trust the most?

- Which ECA is the most likeable?

- Did the ECAs have the same personality? Which one had the strongest personality? (in French, the expression "strong personality" corresponds more or less to extraversion).

- Which ECA was the most expressive?

The users could also add free comments, and were particularly prompted to explicit their observations about the way each ECA gave explanations.

2.6.2   Recall Performance   After viewing the presentations, the users were given the three pictures used in the experiment. On this basis, they had to recall the maximum of information they remembered. The experimenter marked out the performance (between 0 and 10) according to the number of information recalled (e.g., "this is the start button" counts for one information).

2.7   Data Analysis

Subjective variables as well as performance data were submitted to analysis of variance with user's gender as the between-user factor. For each dependent variable, the analysis was successively performed using ECA's strategy and ECA's appearance as the within-user factor. By way of control, the effects of the content of explanation were also tested. All the analyses were performed with SPSS[3].

3.   Results

The results described in this section will be discussed globally in the next section.

3.1   Subjective Variables

3.1.1   Quality of Explanation   The main effect of ECA's strategy on ratings of quality of explanation proved to be significant ($F(2/32) = 5.469$; $p = 0.009$; see Figure 8.5). Indeed, ECAs with

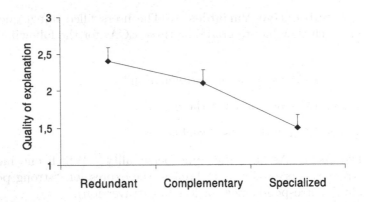

Figure 8.5. Ratings of the quality of explanation as a function of ECA's multimodal strategy.

a redundant or a complementary strategy obtained equivalent ratings ($F(1/16) = 1.000$; N.S.) but were both rated better than ECAs with a speech-specialized strategy (respectively $F(1/16) = 13.474$; $p = 0.002$, and $F(1/16) = 4.102$; $p = 0.060$).

The interaction between strategy and user's gender was also significant ($F(2/32) = 4.980$; $p = 0.013$; see Figure 8.6): the strategy effect was significant for male users ($F(2/16) = 19.000$; $p < 0.001$) but not for female users ($F(2/16) = 0.757$; N.S.). Ratings of male users could thus be considered as responsible for the previous main effect. Male users rated the ECAs with a redundant strategy better than the others ($F(1/8) = 12.000$; $p = 0.009$ for complementary strategy and $F(1/8) = 100.000$; $p < 0.001$ for speech-specialized strategy). They also tended to rate complementary strategy better than speech-specialized strategy ($F(1/8) = 4.000$; $p = 0.081$).

No effect of ECA's appearance or content of presentation was observed.

3.1.2   Trust   No main effect of ECA's strategy arose in subjective ratings of trust, but an interaction between strategy and user's gender appeared ($F(2/32) = 3.735$; $p = 0.035$). In a similar way as for quality of explanation, the effect of ECA's strategy tended to be significant for male users ($F(2/16) = 2.868$; $p = 0.086$), whereas it was not for female users ($F(2/16) = 2.500$; N.S.).

A positive linear correlation was found between this variable and ratings of quality of explanation (Pearson's correlation between 0.630 and 0.757, $p < 0.005$ for the three strategies). This result not only confirms

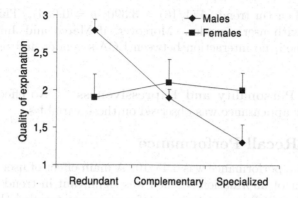

Figure 8.6. Ratings of the quality of explanation as a function of ECA's multimodal strategy and user's gender.

that the interaction effect was of the same kind for the two variables, but also shows that ratings of trust were linked to ratings of quality of explanation.

No effect of ECA's appearance or content of explanation was observed on ratings of trust.

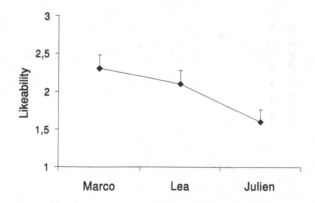

Figure 8.7. Ratings of likeability as a function of ECA's appearance.

3.1.3   Likeability   Analyses on this variable yielded no effect of ECA's strategy, but a main effect of appearance proved to be significant ($F(2/32) = 3.328$; $p = 0.049$; see Figure 8.7). It showed that no preference arose between Marco and Lea ($F(1/16) = 0.471$; N.S.), but Julien appeared less likeable than Marco ($F(1/16) = 6.479$; $p = 0.022$)

and than Lea (in trend: $F(1/16) = 3.390$; $p = 0.084$). This effect did not vary with user's gender. Moreover, if Marco and Julien's scores are combined, no interaction between ECA's gender and user's gender appears.

3.1.4   Personality and Expressiveness   No effect of ECA's strategy or appearance was observed on these variables.

3.2   Recall Performance

The average performance was 6.45/10. A main effect of user's gender on the amount of information recalled was significant in trend ($F(1/16) = 4.174$; $p = 0.058$), suggesting that female users recalled slightly more information (7.1/10) than male users (5.8/10).

ECA's strategy did not influence recall performance, but a main effect of ECA's appearance neared significance ($F(2/32) = 3.215$; $p = 0.053$; see Figure 8.8), suggesting that recall was slightly better when Marco had given the explanation, and slightly worse with Julien — recall with Lea being intermediate. This decrease of performance seems to follow the ratings of likeability, but no significant correlation between these two variables was found.

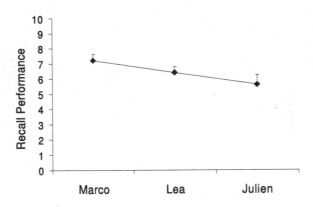

Figure 8.8.   Recall performance as a function of ECA's appearance.

Concerning the influence of the content of explanation, no main effect arose, but an interaction between content and user's gender proved to be significant ($F(2/32) = 5.150$; $p = 0.012$). The effect of the content of explanation on recall performance was significant for female users ($F(2/16) = 9.838$; $p = 0.002$) but not for male users ($F(2/16) = 0.683$; N.S.). Actually, female users recalled more information about the copy machine than the two other objects. This effect, which constitutes a bias in our experiment, could come from a better previous familiarity of females with this object, although our two groups of users were homogeneous regarding socio-professional category.

4. Discussion

Table 8.1 summarizes the main results of this experiment.

Table 8.1. Summary of our results: our two main independent variables are presented in column and dependent variables are listed in raw.

	Multimodal Strategy	ECA's Appearance
Quality of Explanation	Main effect: *redundant = complementary* *redundant > specialized* *complementary > specialized*	no effect
	Interaction with gender: *Effect of strategies for males,* *no effect for females.*	
Trust	Interaction with gender: *Effect of strategies for males,* *no effect for females.* Correlation between trust and quality of explanation.	no effect
Likeability	no effect	Main effect: *Marco = Lea* *Marco > Julien* *Lea > Julien* No gender effect (ECA or user).
Personality, Expressiveness	no effect	no effect
Recall Performance	no effect	Main effect (trend): *Marco > Lea > Julien* No correlation between performance and likeability.

4.1   Effects of Multimodal Strategies

The main goal of this experiment was to study the effect of multi-modal strategies of ECAs. Before discussing the results, we would like to emphasize that these strategies were hardly consciously noticed by the users. The analysis of free comments given after the experiment shows that only 10 users (5 males, 5 females) from the 18 reported that they had observed differences in how the three ECAs gave explanations. Moreover, they noticed that some ECAs made deictic gestures, but nobody mentioned differences between redundant and complementary strategies. This is consistent with Rimé's figure-ground model (Rimé and Schiaratura (1991)) in which the speaker's nonverbal behaviour is usually at the periphery of the listener's attention.

The effect of multimodal strategies on ratings of quality of explanation was globally significant. However, considering the interaction with user's gender, this main effect proved to be produced by ratings of male users only. For this group of users, the preference for redundant ECAs was clear, though unconscious as underlined above. In contrast, ratings of female users yielded no preferences among strategies. This gender difference was unexpected. Before interpreting this result, we may point out that the number of users we tested may cast doubt on interaction effects. Indeed, we may consider that we had a fair number of users to test main effects, but the interactions arisen from our data will surely have to be confirmed in further experiments.

Nevertheless, the interaction we obtained raises interesting hypotheses on gender differences. We cannot assume that females were less focused on the ECAs than males. Indeed, our female users made a lot of comments about ECAs' appearance and did not notice fewer differences in ECAs' strategies than males did.

The literature on recognition of nonverbal behaviours cannot explain either our result, because it usually reports that women have greater decoding skills than males (Feldman et al. (1991)). Besides, no gender differences have been described in biological motion recognition (see Giese and Poggio (2003)).

Finally, we could tentatively explain this result by the well-known cognitive differences between men and women (e.g., visual-spatial vs. auditory-verbal preferences, see Kimura (1999)). However, our protocol was too different from classical cognitive studies to claim that the same processes were involved. Thus we will conduct further experiments not only to verify our result with a greater number of users, but also to relate it to a cognitive model.

This gender difference is not clarified either by performance data, since ECA's strategy had no effect on user's recall in our experiment. Similar pattern of results (effect on subjective but not on objective variables) was previously found for example with the persona effect (van Mulken et al. (1998)). The fact that ECA's strategy influenced subjective variables without affecting performance does not in any way detract from the importance of these multimodal strategies. Indeed, we think that subjective variables remain a crucial factor of engagement and determine, to a certain extent, the success of such multimedia tools.

Ratings of trust yielded the same kind of interaction between ECA's strategy and user's gender. Actually, trust proved to be linked to the perceived quality of explanation. This result could be confirmed by more indirect questions, such as: "Would you buy a mobile phone from this ECA?" If it is confirmed, the influence of multimodal strategy on trust could be of interest in applications where trust is required (e.g., e-commerce).

4.2 Effects of ECAs' Appearance

The ECA's appearance had no effect either on ratings of quality of explanation or ratings of trust. However, it had a significant effect on likeability, which was independent of user's gender. This result showed that Marco and Lea were preferred to Julien. Marco's smile happened to be designed broader than the smile of the other ECAs, and this was appreciated by the users, as they indicated after the experiment. Comments about Lea were more contradictory, because of her white coat: some users found her nicer and more serious; some others found her too strict. The influence of ECAs' clothes on their evaluation was previously mentioned in some empirical research (McBreen et al. (2001)). Finally, the fact that Julien's eyes were not so visible through his quite opaque glasses was negatively perceived by most of the users. Besides, his position at rest consisted in having his arms folded, and several users found it unpleasant.

ECA's appearance also tended to influence recall performance of the users. Although this result lacks statistical significance, it warns us about the consequences of ECA's design not only on user's satisfaction, but also on the effectiveness of the application. Performance was not shown to be correlated to ratings of likeability. In a similar way, Moreno et al. (2002) found that pedagogical efficacy of ECAs varied with their appearance, but they failed to find a link with any subjective variable (likeability, comprehensibility, credibility, quality of presentation, and synchronization of speech and animation). Further experiments are thus needed to confirm and interpret the influence of ECA's appearance on recall performance.

4.3   Additional Results

No effect of multimodal strategy or appearance of ECAs arose in perceived personality or expressiveness. Comments given by users at the end of the experiment indicated that three dimensions influenced their judgments for these variables: ECA's appearance, amount of movements, and voice. The importance of this last parameter was emphasized in recent research (Chapter 10 by Darves and Oviatt), but it was not controlled in our experiment: we used only one male voice and one female voice from IBM ViaVoice speech synthesis. It should also be noticed that 4 users (1 male and 3 females) did not find any personality differences between the three ECAs.

Finally, the bias produced by the content of presentation (better recall for females about one of the objects) could possibly explain the overall better performance of female users (obtained in trend).

5.   Conclusions and Future Directions

Our results stress the importance of both multimodal strategy and appearance to ensure the design of pleasant and effective presentation ECAs. As highlighted by Table 8.1, multimodal strategies and ECAs' look did not influence the same variables. We then could suspect these two factors to be independent. However, a factorial design would be necessary to validate this assumption.

Taken as a whole, males and females subjective ratings showed no preference between redundant and complementary scenarios. The advantage of complementary strategy lies in the possible reduction of the amount of information transmitted by each modality: it enables avoiding both an overload of verbal information and an exaggerated gesticulation, which can be perceived as unnatural (Cassell et al. (1994)). As a consequence, complementary scenarios could also save presentation time (to provide the same information, complementary scenarios were 20 % shorter than redundant and specialized scenarios in our experiment). However, if it is confirmed that male users find redundant strategies better, it could be interesting to use redundancy when target users are males or when the duration of presentation matters little. Benefits of redundancy in pedagogical applications were previously observed (e.g., Craig et al. (2002); Moreno and Mayer (2002)), but they concerned multimedia presentations (addition of text to auditory material) rather than multimodal behaviour of ECAs. In humans, teachers' hand gestures were shown to be useful in a math classroom (Goldin-Meadow et al. (1999b)), but the redundant or complementary nature of these gestures was not investigated.

Our findings about multimodal behaviour of ECAs might not be generalized to other contexts. This experiment investigated only a presentation task with some spatial aspects — positions of items were crucial. The importance of multimodal strategies might be lowered in a more narrative or conversational context. But it could also be increased in other situations, for example when the data to process are more complex. We might even hypothesize that multimodal strategies could yield differences in performance in more complex tasks.

Users' comments about ECAs' appearance suggested avoiding teacher-like features (such as a white coat), avoiding behaviours such as folding arms, and keeping eyes and gaze clearly visible. Conversely, a cartoonish broad smile seemed to be a predominant factor of likeability. Dramatized characters, because of the emotions they display, have previously been claimed to make better interface ECAs than do more realistic and human-like characters (Kohar and Ginn (1997)).

In the near future, we will carry out further experiments within the same methodological framework, in order to complement this study with data on more users. We also intend to improve our 2D ECAs technology by going up from manual specification of behaviour to higher-level specification language. Such a language should include rules for synchronizing not only gestures to speech, but all the modalities (e.g., for the role of eyebrow movements, see Chapter 7 by Krahmer and Swerts). It could also be interesting to include different speech intonations, different energies and temporal patterns in movements, and some idiosyncratic gestures. 2D ECAs with individual behaviour can be of interest for mobile applications, but the design of 3D ECAs should also be considered.

We also suggest building ECA's individuality from corpora of individual human behaviours. We believe that ECAs look as if they came from the same mould because they are usually specified by the same set of general psycholinguistic rules. So far, both the literature on individual multimodal behaviour and the automatic extraction of context-dependent and individual rules from corpora annotation were neglected in the field of ECAs.

More experimental results could lead to recommendations for ECA design in various application areas such as games or educational tools, which could also include teams of ECAs having each their own multimodal behaviour. One issue will be the granularity of such design guidelines which should not be too specific in order to be useful to ECA designers.

Acknowledgments

The work described in this chapter was developed at LIMSI-CNRS and supported by the EU/HLT funded project NICE[4] (IST-2001-35293). Our ECAs were designed by Christophe Rendu. The authors wish to thank their partners in the NICE project as well as William Turner and Frédéric Vernier for their useful comments and Guillaume Pitel for his kind help.

Notes

1. http://www-3.ibm.com/software/speech/ (last accessed 2003-11)
2. http://www.limsi.fr/Individu/martin/research/projects/lea/ (last accessed 2003-11)
3. http://www.spss.com/ (last accessed 2003-11)
4. http://www.niceproject.com/ (last accessed 2003-11)

References

AAMAS (2002). Marriott, A., Pelachaud, C., Rist, T., Ruttkay, Zs., and Vilhjálmsson, H., editors. *Proceedings of Workshop on Embodied Conversational Agents — Let's Specify and Evaluate them!*. AAMAS02, Bologna, Italy.

AAMAS (2003). Pelachaud, C., Marriott, A., and Ruttkay, Zs., editors. *Proceedings of Workshop on Embodied Conversational Characters as Individuals*. AAMAS03, Melbourne, Australia.

Abrilian, S., Buisine, S., Rendu, C., and Martin, J.-C. (2002). Specifying Cooperation between Modalities in Lifelike Animated Agents. In *Proc. PRICAI02 Workshop on Lifelike Animated Agents: Tools, Functions, and Applications*, pp. 3–8, Tokyo, Japan.

André, E., Rist, T., Van Mulken, S., Klesen, M., and Baldes, S. (2000). The automated design of believable dialogues for animated presentation teams. In Cassell, J., Prevost, S., and Churchill, E., editors, *Embodied Conversational Agents*. pp. 220–255, MIT Press, Cambridge.

Ball, G. and Breese, J. (2000). Emotion and personality in a conversational character. In Cassell, J., Prevost, S., and Churchill, E., editors, *Embodied Conversational Agents*. pp. 189–219, MIT Press, Cambridge.

Cassell, J., Bickmore, T., Vilhjálmsson, H., and Yan, H. (2001). More than just a pretty face: Conversational protocols and the affordances of embodiment. *Knowledge-Based Systems*, 14: 55–64.

Cassell, J. and Stone, M. (1999). Living hand to mouth: Psychological theories about speech and gesture in interactive dialogue systems. In *Proc. of AAAI99*, pp. 34–42, North Falmouth, MA.

Craig, S. D., Gholson, B., and Driscoll, D. (2002). Animated pedagogical agents in multimedia educational environments: Effects of agent properties, picture features, and redundancy. *Journal of Educational Psychology*, 94: 428–434.

Feldman, R. S., Philippot, P., and Custrini, R. J. (1991). Social competence and nonverbal behavior. In Feldman, R.S. and Rimé, B., editors, *Fundamentals of Nonverbal Behavior*. pp. 329–350, Cambridge University Press, Cambridge, England.

Giese, M.A. and Poggio, T. (2003). Neural mechanisms for recognition of biological movements. *Nature Reviews*, 4: 179–192.

Goldin-Meadow, S. (1999a). The role of gesture in communication and thinking. *Trends in Cognitive Sciences*, 3(11): 419–429.

Goldin-Meadow, S., Kim, S., and Singer, M. (1999b). What the teacher's hands tell the student's mind about math. *Journal of Educational Psychology*, 91: 720–730.

Kendon, A. (1980). Gesticulation and speech: two aspects of the process of utterance. In Key, M. R., editor, *The relationship of Verbal and Nonverbal Communication*. pp. 207–228, Mouton Publishers, The Hague, The Netherlands.

Kimura, D. (1999). *Sex and Cognition*. MIT Press, Cambridge.

Kohar, H. and Ginn, I. (1997). Mediators: Guides through online TV services. In *Electronic Proc. CHI97*.
URL: http://www.acm.org/sigchi/chi97/proceedings/demo/hk.htm/

Martin, J. C., Grimard, S., and Alexandri, K. (2001). On the annotation of the multimodal behavior and computation of cooperation between modalities. In *Proc. AAMAS01 Workshop on Representing, Annotating, and Evaluating Non-Verbal and Verbal Communicative Acts to Achieve Contextual Embodied Agents*, pp. 1–7, Montreal, Canada.

McBreen, H., Anderson, J., and Jack, M. (2001). Evaluating 3D embodied conversational agents in contrasting VRML retail applications. In *Proc. Int. Conf. on Autonomous Agents Workshop on Multimodal Communication and Context in Embodied Agents*, pp. 83–87, Montreal, Canada.

McNeill, D. (1987). *Psycholinguistics: A new approach*. Harper and Row, New York.

McNeill, D. (1992). *Hand and Mind*, University of Chicago Press, Chicago, IL.

Moreno, K. N., Klettke, B., Nibbaragandla, K., and Graesser, A. C. (2002). Perceived characteristics and pedagogical efficacy of animated conversational agents. In *Proc. of ITS02*, pp. 963–971, Biarritz, France and San Sebastian, Spain.

Moreno, R. and Mayer, R. E. (2002). Verbal redundancy in multimedia learning: when reading helps listening. *Journal of Educational Psychology*, 94: 156–163.

van Mulken, S. André, E., and Müller, J. (1998). The Persona effect: How substantial is it? In *Proc. of HCI98*, pp. 53–66, Berlin, Germany.

Myers, J.L. (1979). *Fundamentals of Experimental Design*. Third Edition, Allyn and Bacon Inc, Boston.

Nijholt, A. (2001). Towards multi-modal emotion display in embodied agents. In *Proc. of Artificial Neural Networks and Expert Systems 2001*, pp. 229–231, Dunedin, New Zealand.

Pelachaud, C., Carofiglio, V., De Carolis, B., De Rosis, F., and Poggi, I. (2002). Embodied contextual agent in information delivering application. In *Proc. of AAMAS02*, pp. 758–765, Bologna, Italy.

Rickel, J. and Johnson, W. L. (1999). Animated agents for procedural training in virtual reality: Perception, cognition, and motor control. *Applied Artificial Intelligence*, 13: 343–382.

Rimé, B. and Schiaratura, L. (1991). Gesture and speech. In: Feldman, R.S. and Rimé, B., editors. *Fundamentals of Nonverbal Behavior*. pp. 239–284, Cambridge University Press, Cambridge, England.

Chapter 9

ECA AS USER INTERFACE PARADIGM

Experimental Findings within a Framework for Research

Richard Catrambone, John Stasko, and Jun Xiao

> *Beware of pretty faces that you find*
> *A pretty face can hide an evil mind*
> *Ah, be careful what you say*
> *Or you'll give yourself away*
> *Odds are you won't live to see tomorrow*
> *Secret agent man, secret agent man*
> *They've given you a number and taken away your name*
> —Performed by Johnny Rivers, written by P.F. Sloan and S. Barri 'Secret Agent Man'

Abstract   A strong debate has ensued in the computing community about whether Embodied Conversational Agents (ECAs) are beneficial and whether we should pursue this direction in interface design. Proponents cite the naturalness and power of ECAs as strengths, and detractors feel that ECAs disempower, mislead, and confuse users. As this debate rages on, relatively little systematic empirical evaluation on ECAs is actually being performed, and the results from this research have been contradictory or equivocal. We propose a framework for evaluating ECAs that can systematize the research. The framework emphasizes features of the agent, the user, and the task the user is performing. Our goal is to be able to make informed, scientific judgments about the utility of ECAs in user interfaces. If intelligent agents can be built, are there tasks or applications for which an ECA is appropriate? Are there characteristics (in appearance, in personality, etc.) the ECA should have? What types of users will be more productive and happy by interacting with an ECA? Our initial experiment within this framework manipulated the ECA's appearance (realistic human versus iconic object) and the objectivity of the user's task (editing a document versus deciding what to pack on a trip). We found that the perception of the ECA was strongly influenced by the task while features of the ECA that we manipulated had little effect.

Keywords: Embodied conversational agent, evaluation, research framework, task, Wizard of Oz.

Z. Ruttkay and C. Pelachaud (eds.), From Brows to Trust, 239–267.
© *2004 Kluwer Academic Publishers. Printed in the Netherlands.*

1.   Introduction

If you could ask for assistance from a smart, embodied conversational agent (ECA) that provides help via spoken natural language, would that be an improvement over an on-line reference manual? Presumably the answer, in most cases, is yes for two reasons. First, the spoken natural language aspect would allow you to speak your questions rather than having to type them. Generally this is a faster approach for most people. Second, the smart aspect would improve the chance of the help system finding the information you want even if you do not state the query using the correct or most appropriate terms. The state of the art in this style of interface is a human consultant.

Would it matter that the ECA has a face and that the face can have expressions and convey a personality? Would a face affect you in terms of your comfort and satisfaction with the interaction? Would the presence of a face make the help or advice you receive more persuasive? The answers to such questions have implications for the design of systems for training, customer service, kiosks, etc.

ECA-based interfaces, particularly those with a human appearance, are still relatively uncommon. Human-like assistants who answer questions and perform tasks through conversational, natural language-style dialogs with users contrast the traditional view of computers as enabling tools for functional purposes.

Many researchers believe that ECA interfaces have great potential to be beneficial in HCI for a number of reasons. ECAs could act as smart assistants, much like travel agents or investment advisors, aiding people in managing the ever-growing amount of information encountered today (Lyman and Varian (2002)). Further, a conversational interface appears to be a more natural dialog style in which the user does not have to learn complex command structure and functionality (Laurel (1990)). People are adept at communicating with others and a conversational interface would be easy to learn and adopt.

Advocates also note how the human face seems to occupy a privileged position for conveying a great deal of information, including relatively subtle information, efficiently (Collier (1985)). An ECA with a face that grows more confused by the second might be better at letting a user know that the path he or she is following is wrong than simply displaying "I am getting confused" on the screen. This is because the text requires screen real estate and requires the user to read that text, which each may be disruptive to the main task being worked on.

These potential advantages are balanced by strong negatives. ECA interfaces are viewed by some researchers as being impractical and inappropriate. Current speech recognition, natural language understanding, and learning capabilities of computers still fall far short of any human assistant. Further, technologies for interaction production and synthesis also are in their infancy and just being developed.

More specifically, Lanier (1995) believes that ECA systems disempower users by clouding issues such as who is responsible for a system's actions. Shneiderman (1997) feels that user interfaces are more beneficial when they clearly reflect the commands available to a user and present the objects that a user can act upon. Furthermore, critics argue that ECAs may mislead both users and designers, increase user anxiety, reduce user control, undermine user responsibility, and destroy a user's sense of accomplishment (Shneiderman and Maes (1997)). For example, the powerful human ability to interpret faces, cited as a positive above, might lead a user to overinterpret the feedback from an ECA's face, particularly if that face is human-looking, and conclude the ECA knows or understands more than it does.

Although strong opinions have been voiced both positively and negatively for ECAs, relatively little empirical research has been conducted on the topic as noted by (Dehn and Van Mulken (2000); Ruttkay et al. (2002); Sanders and Scholtz (2000)). Erickson (1997) states: "First it must be acknowledged that in spite of the popularity of the agent metaphor, there is remarkably little research on how people react to agents." Cassell (2000) notes: "To date, few researchers have empirically investigated embodied interfaces, and their results have been equivocal". Isbister and Doyle (2002) comment: "Rigorous evaluations of benefits to the user are rare, and even when performed are subject to considerable criticism owing to the difficulty of finding objective measures of success." Shneiderman and Maes (1997) echo the need for more study: "Please, please, please do your studies – whether they are controlled scientific experiments, usability studies, or simply observations, and get past the wishful thinking and be a scientist and report on real users doing real tasks with these systems".

Other researchers have laid out a research agenda for the area. Laurel (1990) discusses one component of such an agenda:

> In the theoretical arena, work must proceed on the analysis of user needs and preferences vis-à-vis applications and environments. What are the qualities of a task that make it a good candidate for an ECA-style interface? What kinds of users will want them, and what are the differences among potential user populations? How might interface agents affect the working styles, expectations, productivity, knowledge, and personal power of those who use them?
>
> In terms of design, the meatiest problem is developing criteria that will allow us to elect the appropriate set of traits for a given ECA – traits

that can form coherent characters, provide useful cues to users, and give rise to all of the necessary and appropriate actions in a given context.

1.1   Our Research Objectives

The objective of our research is to gain an understanding of the utility and usability of ECAs in user interfaces. Our particular focus is on conversational, anthropomorphic and personified agents.

Before proceeding further, we need to define some important terms or at least clarify how we use them throughout this chapter. The term *anthropomorphic* user interface refers to an interface that has a realistic, human guise as its chief contact. Typically, such systems utilize a conversational interaction style with a natural language dialog between the human user and the interface character. The term *personified* user interface typically refers to an interface in which human characteristics, abilities, and foibles are attributed to something that is not human, such as a pet or a toaster. Often, these terms are confused.

Another cause of confusion and disagreement is the use of the term *agent* itself (Bradshaw (1997)). The term 'agent' takes on many different meanings, although most software agent researchers feel that a software system should exhibit some non-trivial level of autonomy or proactive behaviour in order to be termed an agent. For instance, agents might answer particular email messages or schedule appointments for a human user.

In this chapter, we will use the term '*ECA* simply to mean an interface character that users interact with. For instance, an anthropomorphic or personified character who simply answers user questions would be considered an ECA to us, while other stronger definitions of 'agent' may not consider it so. Our focus is primarily on human-like characters who play an important role in the interface to an underlying software application. We will use the term ECA frequently throughout this chapter as a textual shorthand for these types of interfaces.

Our primary motivation is to learn about how people view and interact with ECA interfaces in order to determine when ECAs can be used to benefit the user. A second motivation of our work is to inform ECA-application builders. Systems with ECAs *are* being developed and ideally research, in addition to intuition, should guide their designs. It is important for the developers of ECA applications to know how the attributes, features, and characteristics of the ECAs will affect their users in order to build appropriate systems.

Four key queries guide our research program:

- How do people react to ECA-based user interfaces? That is, how do people subjectively assess them? This question should be investigated with potential users of many different characteristics.

- How do different attributes of the interface (appearance, personality, gender, speech qualities, etc.) affect people's perceptions and subjective and objective performance?

- For what types of tasks, if any, are these interfaces best suited?

- Broadly, is this a user interface metaphor worth pursuing? That is, is this a user interface metaphor that is appropriate and useful?

We propose that three main factors influence people's perceptions of this style of interface and therefore these factors frame our planned experimentation. The first factor is the *user* of the system. It is likely that different types of people will have different reactions to ECA interfaces. Such differences of users may be computer-experience, age, or gender-based, for example. The second factor is the *ECA* itself including its appearance, personality, and degree of reactivity/proactivity. Numerous aspects of how the ECA looks, sounds, and behaves can be manipulated. The third factor is the *task* and *task domain* involved. For instance, is the ECA assisting the user in making investment decisions or is the ECA playing a game against the user? Is the task relatively objective (e.g., making pre-determined editing changes in a document) or is it more subjective (e.g., deciding what items to pack on a trip)? Is the ECA assisting students learn math or helping shoppers at an information kiosk in a store? People may perceive the value of an ECA differently in different task contexts.

In general, we focus on two main evaluation dimensions in our research. First, does the ECA enhance task performance by people? Are users able to learn new software faster, find information more easily, come to decisions quicker, complete design or implementation tasks more efficiently, and show greater persistence on tasks? Second, how do people subjectively assess the appeal of such interfaces? Do they like ECA interfaces and feel comfortable working with them, or are these interfaces awkward and annoying? Clearly, people's subjective impressions of ECAs will have a strong influence on future adoption and continued use.

In the rest of this chapter, we describe a framework that we have developed for conducting systematic research on evaluating ECAs in user interfaces. The framework is based on the three chief factors identified above: user, ECA, and task. The framework is not meant to be exhaustively comprehensive. Rather, it provides a structural background that is useful to discuss evaluation research in this area. In the next section, we situate existing research within the framework, and we describe how the framework relates to those developed by others.

Later in the chapter, we present an initial experiment we conducted to examine the effects of user personality, ECA appearance, and task being performed – three important variables identified in the framework – on how well people perform tasks and on their perception of ECAs. Our long-term goal is to use the framework to guide a set of studies that will hopefully provide coherent results that will be of use to developers designing ECA-based systems.

2.   Research Framework

An important event in the history of ECA research was Apple Computer's late 1980's production of the video titled *Knowledge Navigator* (Sculley (1989)). The video showed a university faculty member in his office interacting with his computer. The computer's chief interface metaphor was an anthropomorphic, 3-D talking head, a computerized assistant named Phil with whom the professor interacted *via* natural language. Phil answered questions directed to him and took the initiative in carrying out important actions that would benefit the professor. *Knowledge Navigator* was a thought-provoking film, and it has been the source of much discussion in the HCI and agent communities since its production, gaining its share of both praise and criticism.

In the past 10-15 years, quite a bit of effort has been made toward building autonomous ECAs like 'Phil' in the *Knowledge Navigator* video. For examples of recent work in system development, see (Cassell et al. (2000)). Of course, these efforts have been initial steps toward that advanced vision, and much work remains.

It is probably safe to say that the most widely used system in this space, at least in spirit, is the Paper Clip assistant from Microsoft. The Paper Clip's pervasive presence in Microsoft Office tools such as Word and PowerPoint has influenced many people's opinions of user interface agents like this, often negatively (Xiao et al. (2003)).

Another recent boom in ECAs has occurred on the World Wide Web. Sites seek to provide human-like hosts or guides that will assist a person browsing web pages or that will read news much like an evening TV newsperson. Noteworthy sites utilizing or providing such capabilities are Virtual Personalities[1], Artificial Life[2], FaceWorks[3], Haptek[4] and Ananova[5] – ECA no longer present.

So, systems are being built, but what about studies of the use of ECAs? When we began our research inquiries, we could not find an encompassing summary of potential directions of inquiry and a guide to evaluations that had already been performed. Thus, we performed an analysis by reviewing related work and carefully considering the factors that could influence ECA adoption and use. The result of that analysis was a framework for thinking about evaluations of the effectiveness of ECAs. The framework is not meant to be an exhaustive taxonomy of all potential ECA-related issues. Rather, it provides an organizational structure to help us review studies and to guide our own work. Other evaluation frameworks do now exist, see for instance the Chapter 2 by Ruttkay et al. in this book, and they too will help other researchers better understand the issues present in this area.

Each of the three factors – user, ECA, task – in our framework involves many variables and provides many opportunities for interactions. The number of variables within each factor is definitely quite extensive and is certainly larger than the number we identify here.

In the first two factors, User and ECA, for brevity we provide more thorough discussions only of the variables manipulated in the experimental study reported in this chapter or of variables that we believe have not been adequately discussed in prior work. In the Task factor, we provide a more extensive discussion of all the listed variables because this appears to be an area that has not been as thoroughly considered in existing research.

2.1   Features of the User

Potential users of ECA technology vary, of course, in many ways. However, there are certain features that may be more likely to affect how useful a user perceives an ECA. Below we list some of those features:

- prior (domain) knowledge;

- personality;

- social context;

- gender;

- age;

- ethnicity;

- familiarity with ECA technology;

- cultural context;

- ability;

- computer experience;

- physical capability.

Below we elaborate on some of the variables listed above. For a more extensive discussion of user characteristics and how they may affect interaction with and perceptions of ECAs, please see the Chapter 2 by Ruttkay et al. in this book.

Personality features: Researchers have identified what are referred to as the 'Big Five' traits that seem to be quite useful in describing human personalities (see McCrae and Costa (1987)). These traits are: extraversion, openness, agreeableness, neuroticism, and conscientiousness. An important quality about these traits is that they appear to be orthogonal, that is, a high or low score on any one of these traits does not predict the score on any of the other traits. While researchers in the field continue to debate the Big Five notion, it seems reasonable to examine whether users' positions on these trait dimensions is predictive of how they will respond to ECAs. For instance, one might hypothesize that an introverted person might find a proactive ECA to be intimidating while a more extroverted person would enjoy interacting heavily with the ECA.

A relevant body of related work is that of Nass, Reeves and their students at Stanford. Their efforts focus on the study of "Computers as Social Actors." They have conducted a number of experiments that examined how people react to computer systems and applications that have certain personified characteristics (Moon and Nass (1996); Nass et al. (1994); Nass et al. (1995); Nass and Lee (2000); Rickenberg and Reeves (2000)). Their chief finding is that people interact with and characterize the computer systems in a social manner, much as they do with other people. This can occur in spite of the fact that participants know that it is only a computer with which they are interacting. More specifically, Nass and Reeves found that existing, accepted sociological principles (e.g., similar personality individuals tend to get along better than do differing personality individuals) apply even when one of the two participants is a machine. A potential implication of their findings is that a 'one size fits all' approach in designing ECAs simply may not provide enough flexibility for conversational style interactions in which manner, personality, and appearance seem to be so important. One person may be engaged by a sarcastic, talkative ECA while another might find such an ECA to be annoying.

Ability: Barker (2003) found that participants who either performed very well or very poorly on a task perceived that an ECA had a more negative effect on their performance, while those who performed near the average had a more positive perception.

2.2 Features of the ECA

Like users, ECAs can vary on a wide number of features. For a thorough discussion of the dimensions in which ECAs can vary, and thus could be studied, please see the Chapter 2 by Ruttkay et al. Also, discussions of the multitude of dimensions in which the design of an ECA can vary are presented in the article by Griffin et al. (2003).

In this subsection, we focus more on 'high-level' variables or design characteristics, such as expressiveness, rather than lower level agent characteristics such as hair colour or accent, for example. The list of potential high-level variables within this factor includes:

- fidelity/realism;

- expressiveness;

- personality;

- presence;

- initiative;

- coordination of multiple modalities.

Below we elaborate on the variables listed above.

2.2.1   Fidelity/realism How lifelike or real an ECA appears may influence users' perceptions of the ECA and its capabilities. In this variable we include the notions of representational appearance, such as an anthropomorphic representation versus one that is not, and proximity to reality, such as a lifelike 3D rendering versus a cartoon. A study by King and Ohya (1996) suggested that ECAs with more realistic-appearing, 3D human representations are perceived by users as being more intelligent. This might be viewed as either as a positive or a negative. From another perspective, realistic-appearing ECAs are more difficult to implement, so if user performance is improved by the presence of an ECA, but does not vary according to appearance, simpler caricature style characters would be advantageous.

McBreen et al. (2000) studied people observing an interaction between an ECA acting as a sales assistant and a customer. They found that study participants significantly preferred ECAs presented through videos and as disembodied voices because participants' expectation of a high level of realistic and human-like verbal and nonverbal communicative behaviour in synthetic ECAs was not met.

Haddah and Klobas (2003) further explore the issues of fidelity and realism. The authors note that designer and user impressions of realism differ. ECA designers tend to focus on the graphical, photo-realistic aspects, while users tend to characterize realism according to the integrity of the ECAs action within the application domain.

2.2.2   Expressiveness   Within realistic-appearing ECAs we might vary both the diversity of expressions, such as facial expressions, gesture, emotions, and the intensity of expressions as well. Animated, expressive ECAs again may be viewed as more realistic and intelligent, but they might also unduly draw the viewer's attention and thus be distracting and annoying.

Walker et al. (1994) created a study involving a questionnaire that was administered both textually on a computer screen and by a synthesized talking face. They found that people who interacted with the talking face spent more time on the questionnaire, made fewer mistakes, and wrote more comments. Furthermore, people who viewed a stern face spent more time, made fewer mistakes, and wrote more comments than those who viewed a more neutral-appearing face, although the people with the stern face liked the experience and the face less.

2.2.3   Personality   A further important component of an ECA's profile is its personality. Should it be dominant or humble? Should we adapt the personality of the ECA according to the preferences of different users? Design decisions on the ECA's personality should be made consistently with other characteristics of the ECA, such as appearance.

As we have mentioned before, Nass and his colleagues (Moon and Nass (1996); Nass and Lee (2000)) have shown that when the personalities of the ECA and the user match along the introvert/extravert dimension, users tend to be more positive about the interaction, regardless of whether the personality is manifested through text or speech.

2.2.4   Presence   Is the ECA's face always present on the screen or does the ECA appear only when it is engaged in a conversation by the user or does the face never appear but rather the agent exists as only a disembodied voice? One might hypothesize that an ever-present ECA would make users uneasy by producing an effect of being watched or evaluated all the time. Related to this notion is the location of the ECA. When it appears, should it be off to the side or directly in the work area? One might hypothesize that how an ECA integrates with its application depends heavily on the application domain and the nature of task.

Takeuchi and Naito (1995) studied people playing a card matching game with ECAs. The researchers found that facial displays on the ECAs attracted the participants' attention and prevented them from concentrating on the game as effectively as participants who did not see human faces. Specific facial mannerisms in the agents were not explicitly noted by the participants, but apparently were attended to at some level.

2.2.5   Initiative   Related to the 'presence' dimension is the degree to which an ECA initiates interactions. Should it proactively make suggestions and offer guidance or should it only respond when directly addressed? A proactive ECA might be viewed as being obnoxious and might bother users, or it could be viewed as being extremely helpful and intelligent if it acts in situations in which the user is unsure of how to proceed or is so confused that he or she is unable to form a coherent help request.

Xiao et al. (2003) studied the proactive behaviour of an ECA to help people learn and use an unfamiliar text-editing tool. The researchers found that performance with both reactive and proactive ECAs was equivalent to that with printed help. Proactive suggestions made by the ECA did not improve performance, but were viewed as being helpful by study participants.

2.2.6   Coordination of Multiple Modalities   One might expect multimodal ECAs to be more effective and enjoyable than just ECAs with only one input/output modality. For example, an ECA could respond auditorally and/or through text and image 'thought bubbles' on the screen. Mayer et al. (1999) and Sweller et al. (1998) have shown that the types of input and output have implications for cognitive load.

On the input side, if a user has to type her question to the ECA, this would presumably be more cognitively demanding than just speaking it because it requires more of an attention shift. Alternatively, the simple act of speaking may engage particular brain functions that compete with cognition. On the output side, if the ECA provides its responses through on-screen thought bubbles and/or diagrams, this could cause cognitive load problems when the task itself is inherently spatial due to working memory limits within a particular modality. An auditory response would not compete with a visual task for visual working memory. Conversely, encoding responses as on-screen text gives them persistence, something notably lacking in auditory responses.

A few empirical studies have been carried out to investigate the effect of different communication modalities and their combinations on people's perception about ECAs. Lai et al. (2000), Nass and Lee (2000), and Chapter 10 by Darves and Oviatt in this book explore user perceptions of speech quality. Finally, Buisine and her colleagues in Chapter 8 applied a framework for observing and analyzing human cooperative multimodal behaviour proposed by Martin et al. (2001) and investigated the cross-modality effect. They found that coordinating the speech and gestures of an ECA making an explanatory presentation about technology devices to people influenced the people's subjective ratings of the quality of the presentation, but not their recall performance about the topic.

2.3   Features of the Task

While several researchers, including us, have proposed factors concerning users and ECAs that will affect ECA success, it appears that relatively little attention has been paid to features of tasks. Tasks can vary in many different ways. Some tasks can be opinion-like (e.g., choosing what to bring on a trip) while others are more objective (e.g., solving a puzzle). Some involve a good deal of high-level planning (e.g., writing a talk) while others are more rote (e.g., changing boldface words into italics).

As with features of ECAs and users, we list below a set of variables on which tasks might be classified. After that we elaborate on some of those features because they are not discussed much in the literature. A list of potential variables within this factor includes, but is not limited to:

- domain;

- objectiveness;

- intent;

- difficulty;

- importance of task;

- longitudinal features;

- nature of interaction;

- primacy of task;

- duration of task;

- degree of time pressure;

- consequences of task performance quality.

Below we elaborate on some of the features listed above.

2.3.1 Domain The domain in which the user is working (e.g., music vs. construction) might affect ECA acceptance and effectiveness. Van Mulken et al. (1998) studied people's reactions to presentations made by an ECA on both technical and non-technical topics. They found that participants perceived the ECA to be more of an aid in the technical presentations.

Koda (1996) created a Web-based poker game in which a human user could compete with other personified computer characters. The study used realistic (image) and caricature (cartoon) male and female characters, as well as a smiley face, no face, and a dog. Data were gathered on people's subjective impressions of the characters; no actual 'performance' data were gathered because of the style of task. Koda concluded that: 1) Personified interfaces are engaging and appropriate for entertainment tasks and domains; 2) People's impressions of a character are different in a task context than in isolation, and their impressions are strongly influenced by perceived ECA competence; and 3) A dichotomy (favourable versus unfavourable) exists with respect to people's impressions of the ECAs.

2.3.2 Objectiveness The situation in which an ECA is being used might be an opinion-based one in which the user is seeking advice and recommendations on some topic (e.g., which items to pack for a trip to a foreign country). Alternatively, the user might be carrying out an objective task such as simply acquiring facts (e.g., finding the keystroke combination for a particular command in a software application).

2.3.3 Intent The user could be doing a task for a variety of reasons. The user might wish to learn something (e.g., algebra). The user might be carrying out a procedure (e.g., editing a document). The user might be playing a game. The intent of the user will play a role in the type of help and interventions from an ECA that are considered acceptable. For instance, in carrying out a familiar procedure, a user might prefer to have an ECA provide help with low-level details when asked whereas when playing a game the user might welcome high-level strategy advice, at least during the user's early experiences with the game.

2.3.4   Difficulty   Some tasks might be more difficult for a particular user than other tasks. Perhaps an ECA would be more welcomed for more difficult tasks.

Importance of Task: Tasks that are more important to the user might lead him or her to be less willing to accept advice from the agent or to be willing to assign only the most mundane subtasks to the agent.

2.3.5   Longitudinal Features   If a user interacts with an ECA over several (or many) sessions versus a one-time interaction, will that play a role in how the other factors will influence performance and perceptions? For instance, an ECA that helps with a short task such as using an Automatic Telling Machine (ATM) or getting information from a kiosk might be better if it was fairly proactive, verbose, and amusing; the user would have to silence those features if desired. Conversely, a task that is done on a regular basis by the user, and therefore one can assume a high level of competence or at least familiarity by the user, might be better served by a terse ECA that gets involved only when explicitly invited.

2.3.6   Nature of Interaction   Some tasks might require a user to essentially hold a dialog with an ECA while other tasks might lead to more minimal interactions. For instance, an ECA that is helping a person do her taxes might engage the user in a conversation about various aspects of her finances; in this case there would be more 'face-to-face' communication. On the other hand, an ECA that is merely responding to a user's queries about particular keystroke commands for an editor would primarily be attended to auditorally by the user and in addition the user would less likely feel engaged by the ECA.

2.3.7   Primacy of Task   An ECA's assistance may be directly involved with the primary task upon which a user is engaged. On the other hand, ECAs might be helpful with 'side' tasks such as looking up a phone number quickly while a user attends to some other primary task. Would people perceive an ECA as being more useful in one of the scenarios compared to the other?

2.3.8   Duration of Task   Tasks that require a larger amount of time, particularly in one session, might lead the user to be more willing to accept help from an agent.

2.3.9   Degree of Time Pressure   If a task needs to be completed quickly, a user might be more willing to use an agent if the user is confident the agent can complete certain subtasks correctly.

2.3.10   Consequences of Task Performance Quality   Consequences of how well a task is performed, which presumably are related to the importance of the task, vary greatly. Some tasks, such as games, have relatively minor consequences associated with quality of performance while others, such as banking, have much larger consequences. ECAs might be less accepted in areas such as banking. However, would such results be due to the specific ECAs tested or are they truly due to importance issues?

2.3.11   Other Variables   Other task-related variables to consider are duration of task and degree of time pressure. Further, the Chapter 1 by Isbister and Doyle stresses that understanding the use of an ECA in specific application domains is one of the four key research areas in the general research agenda for ECAs.

2.4   Interaction of Variables

While each of the above identified variables alone may have implications, interactions among the variables will be crucial to evaluating ECAs as well. For instance, a novice attempting to carry out a task in a particular domain might welcome proactive comments/advice from an ECA while someone with more experience could get annoyed; these reactions might be reversed in another domain or task. Thus, a person packing for her first trip abroad could be pleased to get advice from an ECA (such as a critique of her packing choices) while a seasoned traveller would be offended by suggestions.

While such predictions seem reasonable for an 'opinion' task like packing, the predictions might be reversed for a more objective task such as text editing. Here, a novice, at least one who is interested in learning, might not want help from an ECA unless explicitly asked because the novice wants to be an active learner and thereby increase his or her chances of remembering the information. Conversely, an expert would be happy to have the ECA take over a set of lower level editing tasks while the expert can concentrate on the overall flow of the argument in the text.

Our main point here is that the variables listed under each factor cannot be adequately examined in isolation. Each will likely interact with other factors, an important consideration for researchers evaluating the use of ECAs.

2.5   Approaches to Assessing ECAs

With respect to approaches for evaluating ECAs, we have to consider which dependent measures are most appropriate. Towards the more objective end, a user's performance on a task in terms of accuracy, time, and persistence – when such measures are meaningful – can be one measure when evaluating an ECA. For instance, time, errors, and number of sub-tasks successfully completed would be appropriate measures for a text-editing task. Towards the more subjective end, a user is likely to have a number of affective reactions to an ECA that are extremely important as well (see Chapter 5 by Höök). These reactions might manifest themselves in terms of how much users like the ECA, how intrusive they found the ECA, how they perceived the ECA's personality, and how willing they are to use the ECA in the future. We can certainly assess a user's liking of and satisfaction towards an ECA, but if the user can carry out the tasks more effectively with the ECA, then how important are liking and satisfaction? On the other hand, long-term use of an ECA might be predicted by liking, satisfaction, and stated desire to have the ECA.

The likelihood of a user following an ECA's advice might be another interesting measure to evaluate an ECA. While advice-following would certainly be at least partly a function of the quality of the advice, it will also be impacted by how the user feels about the ECA. How many children ignore the advice of their parents merely because it is the parents giving the advice?.

Dehn and Van Mulken (2000) provide a careful examination of the many different ways to evaluate animated interface agents. In particular, they identify three main effects on users to be observed in empirical studies: the user's subjective experience of the system, the user's behaviour while interacting with the system, and the outcome indicated by performance data. For more discussion of the dimensions of evaluation in studies of ECAs, see Chapter 2 by Ruttkay et al. where evaluation methods are divided into two main categories, usability and user perceptions, and lists a number of more specific subtopics under each.

In the next section, we describe an initial experimental study that we conducted to begin examining variables within the factors of our evaluation framework.

3.   An Experimental Study

The goal of our research is to begin to systematically examine the factors that influence the usefulness of agents. Our initial experiment manipulated the ECA's *appearance* and the *task* being performed by participants. More specifically, we varied the ECA's appearance with respect to the *fidelity* and *expressiveness* dimensions. Here, we use the general notion of 'fidelity' to include the actual representation of the ECA (human appearance versus light bulb) and the lifelike quality of that representation (realistic appearance versus cartoon). For the task, we varied the *objectiveness* dimension: all participants interacted with an ECA in order to do a document editing task (acquiring and using facts) as well as a travel task (deciding which items to take on a trip). These variables were chosen because prior work and our framework suggested they would be likely candidates to have an effect on the perception and effectiveness of ECAs. Also, as this was an initial experiment, we decided to vary the ECA's appearance significantly to observe if that would have any effect on performance and user perceptions.

3.1   Goal and Hypotheses

We had four primary hypotheses in our study. We based these hypotheses on a variety of reasons including our personal beliefs and prior research performed by others, where appropriate. After listing the hypotheses below, we explain the rationale for them.

> **H1:** The fidelity of the ECA does not affect user performance on either task.

> **H2:** There is a positive association between fidelity of the ECA and personality and intelligence ratings of the ECA by the users.

The more human and life-like the ECA appears, the more likely the user might be to ascribe qualities such as personality and intelligence to the ECA, but objective performance would likely not be affected by appearance because the particular tasks are not very personally important to users. Therefore users are unlikely to use appearance to judge whether to trust the agent's responses.

> **H3:** Users rate the ECA as being more useful in the editing task than in the travel task.

Users will find the ECA to be more useful in its role as a reference source rather than as an entity that provides opinions, particularly when the opinions are uninvited (as is the case in the present experiment for the travel task).

> **H4:** There is an association between task objectiveness and personality ratings of the ECA by the users.

A task that requires the user to debate the merits of his or her opinion (about items to pack on a trip, for example) might lead the user to feel the ECA has more of a personality (for good or for bad) compared to a task in which the user makes use of the ECA more as a reference tool (e.g., reminding the user of keystroke commands for a text editor).

3.2   Participants, Materials, and Procedure

3.2.1   Participants   Thirty-nine undergraduates participated for course credit and were randomly assigned to conditions. Participants had a variety of majors and computer-experience backgrounds. There were not enough participants with any particular background to allow us to look for effects of background on performance.

3.2.2   Materials and Procedure   Participants performed two tasks: a travel task and an editing task. The travel task was chosen to be a type of creative, opinion-based task in which interacting with an agent might be viewed as an opportunity to think more deeply about the task by discussing points of view about the importance of travel items. The editing task was chosen to represent an opportunity to use an agent primarily as a reference source rather than as a guide or teacher.

The *travel task* involved a hypothetical situation in which the participant had an American friend who was flying overseas on his first vacation to Europe. The task was to recommend six items for the person to take with him from a pool of 12 items and to rank the six items in order of importance. This task was similar to the desert island survival problem used in studies by Nass, but was more realistic for our participants. After the participant did the initial ranking using a simple software interface, a computer agent who supposedly had knowledge about international trips appeared. The agent made a predefined set of suggestions in which it recommended changing the rankings of four of the six choices and it agreed with the ranking of two other items.

For example, the agent first suggested promoting the person's fourth item (e.g., backpack) to the first position, demoting the first item (e.g., walking shoes) but keeping it in the top six by saying:

> I think that the backpack should be the most important item not the fourth. Backpacks are very handy for carrying many different items, and your friend will be out and about quite a bit on the trip. I still think that your friend should take the walking shoes that you ranked first. I just don't think they should be the most important item. While they likely will be helpful, an extra pair of shoes will take up quite a bit of space.

As the above example illustrates, the ECA explained the reasoning for its suggestion at every stage. The ECA also asked the participant what he or she thought about the suggestion (e.g., "How does that sound?"). After the participant responded to the agent's comment on a particular item, the agent would say one of several conversational conventions (e.g., "OK, let's continue") so that it could move on to the next suggestion.

After the agent finished providing feedback on the rankings, the original rankings were displayed on the screen and the participant was given the opportunity to change the rankings.

The *editing task* required participants to use an unfamiliar emacs-like text editor to modify an existing document by making a set of prescribed changes to the document. Participants first viewed a short video that described the various functions (e.g., copy, paste) and the specific key combinations needed to issue the commands. Participants were then shown a marked-up document that required a set of changes such as deletions, insertions, and moves, and they were instructed that if at any time they could not remember the keystrokes for a particular function, they could ask the agent for help. Pilot testing was conducted to ensure that the number of commands was sufficiently large so that participants would be likely to need to ask the agent for help.

The ECA always answered editing questions in the following predefined manner: To X press Y (e.g., "To delete a character press control-d"). The experimenter controlling the agent determined which answer best fit the participant's question. A variety of responses covering other situations were also prepared. This included responses such as asking the participant to repeat the question or to state that the ECA was not able to provide an answer (in cases in which a participant asked for a function that the editor did not possess).

After completing each task (i.e., the set of editing tasks and the travel task), participants filled out a questionnaire about the agent and were asked a few questions about the agent and related issues by the experimenter. The items in the questionnaire and the questions asked by the experimenter were developed based on our review of the agent literature as well as our beliefs about which aspects of the agent were likely to be salient to the user.

The ECAs Three different ECA designs were used in the experiment. We will use the terms animated, stiff, and iconic to identify the three different ECAs. The animated ECA (developed using software donated by Haptek) had a realistic, animated 3D female appearance (though somewhat androgynous) that blinked and moved its head occasionally in addition to moving its mouth in synchronization with the synthesized voice. The female appearance was chosen because of neutral responses from several participants during pilot tests. Certain gaze patterns (e.g., glancing aside), facial expressions (e.g., smile), and other facial movements (e.g., nod) were applied, in a pre-defined manner, where they were appropriate. The stiff agent had the same realistic face as the animated agent but moved only its mouth, thus it was less expressive. The left side of Figure 1 shows the face of the agent in the animated and stiff conditions. The iconic agent, shown in the right side of Figure 1, was a light-bulb icon that "turned on" (arrows appeared and background changed) whenever it spoke.

Figure 9.1. Appearance of Agent in Animated and Stiff Conditions (left) and Iconic Condition (right).

We used the DECtalk speech synthesizer to generate the voice for all the ECAs. Because we had limited control over the speech synthesizer, no intonation was used to convey additional information. Each ECA stayed in a small window at the upper-right corner of a participant's computer screen.

Design   Two between-subjects variables were manipulated: ECA appearance (animated, stiff, iconic) and task order (travel task then editing task or vice versa). The within-subjects variable was task objectiveness (more subjective: travel task; more objective: editing task).

Participants were run individually using a computer equipped with a microphone and speaker. The ECAs were controlled through a Wizard of Oz technique (Dahlback et al. (1993)). One experimenter was in the room with the participant to introduce the experimental materials, and a second experimenter was in an adjacent room, monitoring the questions and responses made by the participant. The second experimenter insured that the ECA responded in a consistent manner using a prepared set of replies.

One design issue about this experiment should be flagged. Although our key task manipulation was the 'objectiveness' of the task (i.e., the travel task being less objective and the editing task being more objective), the nature of the agent also was varied as a function of the task. The agent was completely reactive in the editing task; it provided information only when requested. However, in the travel task the agent provided feedback regardless of the participants' desire. A cleaner version of the experiment would have been to hold the 'nature' of the agent constant across the tasks. For example, we could have made the agent merely respond to users' questions about travel items rather than offering unrequested advice. We allowed this confounding to occur here because we felt participants were unlikely to ask for 'help' with the travel task.

Measures   Both objective and subjective measures were used.

The objective measure for the travel task was whether participants changed their rankings as a function of the ECA's feedback. For four items the ECA suggested a change in position and for two items the ECA did not suggest a change. For the four items that the ECA suggested be changed, we calculated the proportion of them that did get changed when participants re-ranked them. Similarly, for the two items that the ECA suggested not be changed, we calculated the proportion of them that did get changed when participants re-ranked them. This is a gross measure because it ignores how much the rankings changed as well as whether participants moved items to the exact positions recommended by the ECA. Nevertheless, it does provide some assessment of how much participants were influenced by the ECA's comments.

The objective measure for the editing task was how long (in seconds) it took participants to complete the edits.

The primary subjective measures for both tasks were the responses to the individual items in the questionnaires and the answers to the questions posed by the experimenter. The questionnaire items used a five-point Likert scale (1 = strongly agree, 5 = strongly disagree) that addressed a number of qualities of the agent (see Table 9.2). The questions posed by the experimenter during the interview were open-ended and provided participants an opportunity to give their impressions about the agent's personality, helpfulness, and intelligence. Each interview lasted about 5-10 minutes.

3.3   Results

Task order had no effect on the results and therefore we collapse over this factor in the analyses below.

Performance Measures   With respect to more objective measures, Table 9.1 shows that participants were more likely to change the rankings of items that the agent disagreed with in the travel task compared to items that the agent agreed with, $F(1, 36) = 38.48$, *Mean Square Error (MSE)* $= .07$, $p < .0001$). There was no effect of type of agent, $F(2, 36) = 0.9$, $MSE = .11$, $p = .42$. There was no interaction, $F(2, 36) = 1.25$, $p = .30$.

The time (in seconds) to do the editing task did not differ significantly as a function of agent (animated: 714.8, stiff: 568.7, iconic: 671.1); $F(2, 31) = 1.78$, $MSE = 37637.22$, $p = .19$ (5 participants did not do the editing task). As expected in Hypothesis 1, fidelity of the ECA that we manipulated had little effect over the performance of the user.

Table 9.1. Proportion of Travel Items with Changed Rankings as a Function of Type of Agent and Agent Advice.

	Animated (n=14)	Stiff (n=12)	Iconic (n=13)	AVG
Agent suggested change	.82	.90	.77	.83
Agent agreed with ranking	.57	.42	.38	.46

Questionnaire Responses   Table 9.2 shows the mean responses to the questionnaire items for the different agent conditions in the travel and editing tasks. There were 5 participants who did not do both tasks because either they aborted the second task voluntarily or sudden equipment failures caused us to end the session early. Their data are excluded from Table 9.2.

Contrary to Hypothesis 2, there was no effect of agent type for any of the questions. For two of the items, worthwhile and intrusive, there was an effect of task (worthwhile: $F(1, 31) = 15.68$, $MSE = .45$, $p = .0004$; intrusive: $F(1, 31) = 20.28$, $MSE = .23$, $p = .0001$), which was consistent with Hypothesis 3 and Hypothesis 4 (effects of task on perception of agents). The agent was rated more worthwhile and less intrusive after the editing task compared to the travel task. These results make sense. First, the editing task required most participants to rely heavily on the agent to remind them of commands, thus making the agent seem worthwhile. Second, the uninvited critique of participants' rankings of travel items could certainly have seemed intrusive.

While group differences did not exist on most of the questionnaire items, it is interesting that for most items, the average response tended

Table 9.2. Responses to Questionnaire Items as a Function of Type of Agent and Task.

Agent was...	Animated (n=12) Travel	Edit	Stiff (n=12) Travel	Edit	Iconic (n=10) Travel	Edit	AVG. Travel/Edit
Worthwhile	2.50	1.58	2.25	1.42	2.30	2.10	2.35/1.57
Intrusive	2.83	3.50	3.50	4.00	3.40	3.80	3.24/3.76
Friendly	2.67	2.67	2.42	2.50	2.40	2.80	2.50/2.65
Annoying	3.25	3.33	2.83	3.25	3.20	3.80	3.09/3.44
Intelligent	2.58	2.92	2.58	2.50	2.40	2.70	2.53/2.71
Cold	3.25	3.08	3.00	2.67	3.70	3.30	3.29/3.00
Agent has clear voice	2.33	2.58	2.58	2.33	2.50	2.40	2.47/2.44
Enjoyed interacting with agent	3.08	3.17	2.75	2.83	2.70	2.90	2.85/2.97
Agent helped with task	2.25	1.50	1.67	1.50	2.00	2.30	1.97/1.74
Like to have agent	2.83	2.67	2.58	2.33	2.20	2.40	2.56/2.47

Note: Responses were on a scale from 1 (strongly agree) to 5 (strongly disagree).

to be in the positive direction. Participants felt positively, on average, about the agent.

Interview Responses While participants made a number of interesting and insightful comments about the agent in response to questions from the experimenter, a simple tally of responses shows reactions to the agent that again varied as a function of task. Virtually all participants found the agent helpful for both tasks. Participants were much less likely to consider the agent to have a personality after doing the editing task compared to the travel task. This makes sense because the agent was merely providing subjects with information on commands in the editing task. In the travel task the agent expressed its 'opinions.'

Finally, it is worth noting that the agent was perceived as more intelligent after the travel task than after the editing task. At one level this seems odd because the agent had all the answers for the editing task. However, as demonstrated by some participants' comments, the agent was perceived as very limited in the editing task; it knew about editing commands and probably little else (despite the fact that it also appeared to understand spoken language!). In the travel task though it presumably gave the impression of having sufficiently deep knowledge about travel such that it could give feedback on the importance of various items one might take on a trip. While some of the participants' responses to the agent indicated that they disagreed with its suggestions, they appeared to believe that the suggestions were at least thoughtful.

Finally, one striking difference in behaviour in the interviews was whether a person referred to the agent using words such as 'agent' or 'it,' versus the gender pronouns 'she,' 'her,' 'he,' or 'him.' Eleven of the 39 participants used the gender pronouns. Of those 11, five saw the animated agent, four saw the stiff agent, and two saw the iconic agent. Thus, it appears that the 3D human-like appearance did promote this reaction to some degree. The study participants included 15 women and 24 men. Curiously, eight of the 11 participants who used the gender pronouns were women and only three were men. Thus, over half the women in the study referred to the agent this way and only 13% of the men did so.

3.4 Additional Observations from the Experiment

In addition to the results reported above, we recorded all the sessions and we learned a great deal by observing participants' behaviours and responses in the sessions. One key question we had was how would the participants interact with the agents in the two different tasks. In the editing task, participants seemed very comfortable asking the agents for assistance. Participants requested help an average of 6.5 times. However, in the travel task participants seemed reluctant to engage the agents in a dialog. Only a few replied with more than a few words when the agents attempted to engage them.

The agents' social abilities and personality (or lack thereof) were noted by a number of the participants. In the travel task, we intentionally had the agents begin the session saying: "Hello, [person's name]." Three participants explicitly mentioned this feature, one stating, when asked if the agents had a personality: "Yes, respectful. It said: '[my name]', and 'I agree with this.'... I thought that was very funny. That was really cool." The small talk capability of the ECA, as pointed by Cassell and Bickmore (2001), can increase the likelihood that people will be comfortable and respond to it in a social manner.

Other comments implying a personality included: "Seemed a lot like a travel agent that was in a hurry," and "helpful, but kind of annoying," and "he seemed almost irritated when I didn't agree with him." One participant who did the editing task first, stated after the task that the agent did not have a personality: "It was just directed at answering questions. It had no inflections." But when asked again after the travel task, the participant responded: "It was still mechanical, but you could feel the attempt at being more personable. It acknowledged my responses, asking me to elaborate. The responses were at a more personal level." Participants' willingness to ascribe a personality to the agents based on a few comments by the agent in one task suggests that people might be predisposed to 'finding' a personality in an agent. If the effects of seeing a personality in an agent can be better understood, such a predisposition might be exploited for good purpose by designers.

4. Conclusions

Embodied conversational agents might be one of the best interface approaches ever devised. Or they might not. Equivocal results from prior research make it virtually impossible to decide this matter. The difficulty with prior work has been its lack of systematicity in examining key factors and the use of dependent measures that often did not appropriately assess subjective experience and objective performance.

The goal of our research is to begin to systematically examine the factors that influence the usefulness of such agents. Prior work and our own analyses helped us develop a three-factor approach for systematically examining the effects of ECAs on user performance and subjective responses. We performed an initial experiment within this framework that suggested that type of task may play an outsized role in the perception of agents. While we were surprised to find no effect of agent appearance, this might have been due to the limited range in which we manipulated this factor as well as the fact that participants did not need to look at the agent very much in order to do their tasks. These issues can be addressed in future studies which manipulate the likelihood of users looking at the ECA. For instance, a task that involves the user being 'interviewed' by the ECA, such as a tax preparation task, would presumably require more face-to-face interaction and therefore provide an opportunity for ECA appearance to make a difference in subjective and objective measures. It would be interesting to contrast various ECA appearances with a condition that involved only a voice in order to explore whether the visual aspect of the ECA matters at all.

We will explore the effects of key variables within each factor on agent usefulness. Through our unified framework – and related frameworks suggested by others – we believe we will obtain results that will provide more definitive answers about the features of agents, users, and tasks that predict success. Such results can guide developers as they pursue ECA interfaces. Alternatively, the results might show convincingly that such an interface is not the interface of the future. We plan to use our framework to guide additional studies and hope other researchers find it useful and that it will allow future experiments to build on each other more effectively than in the past.

Notes

1. http://www.vperson.com.
2. http://www.artificial-life.com.
3. http://interface.digital.com/overview/default.htm.
4. http://www.haptek.com.
5. http://www.ananova.com.

References

Barker, T. (2003). The Illusion of Life Revisited. In *Proceedings of AA-MAS 2003 Workshop on Embodied Conversational Characters as Individuals*, Melbourne, Australia.

Bradshaw, J.M. (1997). An introduction to software agents. In Bradshaw J.M., editor, *Software Agents*, pp. 3–46, AAAI Press/MIT Press.

Cassell, J. (2000). Embodied conversational interface agents. *Communications of the ACM*, 43(4): 70–78.

Cassell, J., Sullivan, J., Prevost, S., and Churchill, E., editors (2000). *Embodied Conversational Agents*, MIT Press, Cambridge.

Cassell, J. and Bickmore, T. (2001). A Relational Agent: A Model and Implementation of Building User Trust. In *Proceedings of the ACM CHI 2001 Conference*, pp. 396–403, Seattle, Washington.

Collier, G. (1985). *Emotional Expression*, Lawrence Erlbaum Assoc., Hillsdale, NJ.

Dahlback, N., Jonsson, A., and Ahrenberg, L. (1993). Wizard of Oz studies - why and how. In *Proceedings of the 1993 International Workshop on Intelligent User Interfaces*, pp. 193–200, Orlando, FL.

Dehn, D.M. and Van Mulken, S. (2000). The impact of animated interface agents: A review of empirical research. *International Journal of Human-Computer Studies*, 52(1): 1–22.

Erickson, T. (1997). Designing agents as if people mattered. In Bradshaw J.M., editor, *Software Agents*, pp. 79–96, AAAI Press/MIT Press.

Griffin, P., Hodgson, P., and Prevost, S. (2003). Character User Interfaces for Commercial Applications. In *Proceedings of AAMAS 2003 Workshop on Embodied Conversational Characters as Individuals*, Melbourne, Australia.

Haddah, H. and Klobas, J. (2003). The Relationship between Visual Abstraction and the Effectiveness of a Pedagogical Character-Agent. In *Proceedings of AAMAS 2002 Workshop on Embodied Conversational Agents - Let's Specify and Evaluate Them!*, Bologna, Italy.

Isbister, K. and Doyle, P. (2002). Design and Evaluation of Embodied Conversational Agents: A Proposed Taxonomy. In *Proceedings of AAMAS 2002 Workshop on Embodied Conversational Agents — Let's Specify and Evaluate Them!*, Bologna, Italy.

King, W. J. and Ohya, J. (1996). The representation of agents: Anthropomorphism, agency and intelligence. In *Proceedings of CHI 1996 Conference Companion*, pp. 289–290, Vancouver, B.C..

Koda, T. (1996). *Agents with faces: A study on the effect of personification of software agents*. MIT Media Lab, MS thesis.

Lai, J., Wood, D., and Considine, M. (2000). The effect of task conditions on the comprehensibility of synthetic speech. In *Proceedings of the ACM CHI 2000 Conference*, pp. 321–328, The Hague, Netherlands.

Lanier, J. (1995). Agents of alienation. *Interactions* 2(3): 66–72.

Laurel, B. (1990). Interface agents: Metaphors with character. In Laurel B., editor, *The art of human-computer interface design*, pp. 355–365, Addison-Wesley, New York.

Lyman, P. and Varian, H. (2002). How Much Information?, available at http://www.sims.berkeley.edu/how-much-info/.

Martin, J.C., Grimard, S., and Alexandri, K. (2001). On the annotation of multimodal behavior and the computation of cooperation between modalities. In *Proceedings of AAMAS 2001 Workshop on Representing, Annotating, and Evaluating Nonverbal and Verbal Communicative Acts to Achieve Contextual Embodied Agents*, pp. 1–7, Montreal, Canada, 2001.

Mayer, R. E., Moreno, R., Boire, M., and Vagge, S. (1999). Maximizing constructivist learning from multimedia communications by minimizing cognitive load. *Journal of Educational Psychology*, 91(4): 638–643.

McBreen, H.M., Shade, P. Jack, M.A., and Wyard, P.J. (2000). Experimental Assessment of the Effectiveness of Synthetic Personae for Multi-Modal E-Retail Applications. *Proceedings of Fourth International Conference on Autonomous Agents*, pp. 39–45, Barcelona, Spain.

McCrae, R. and Costa P. (1987). Validation of the five-factor model of personality across instruments and observers. *Journal of Personality and Social Psychology*, 52(1): 81–90.

Moon, Y. and Nass, C. (1996). How 'real' are computer personalities? Psychological responses to personality types in human-computer interaction. *Communication Research*, 23(6): 651–674.

Nass, C., Steuer, J., and Tauber, E. (1994). Computers are social actors. In *Proceedings of the ACM CHI 1994 Conference*, pp. 72–78, Boston, MA.

Nass, C., Lombard, M., Henriksen, L., and Steuer J. (1995). Anthropocentrism and computers. *Behaviour and Information Technology*, 14(4): 229–238.

Nass, C. and Lee, K.M. (2000). Does computer-generated speech manifest personality? An experimental test of similarity-attraction. In *Proceedings of the ACM CHI 2000 Conference*, pp. 329–336, The Hague, Netherlands.

Shneiderman, B. and Maes, P. (1997). Direct manipulation vs. interface agents. *Interactions*, 4(6): 42–61.

Shneiderman, B. (1997). Direct manipulation versus agents: Paths to predictable, controllable, and comprehensible interfaces. In Bradshaw J.M., editor, *Software Agents*, pp. 97–106, AAAI Press/ The MIT Press, Menlo Park, CA.

Rickenberg, R. and Reeves, B. (2000). The effects of animated characters on anxiety, task performance, and evaluations of user interfaces. In *Proceedings of the ACM CHI 2000 Conference*, pp. 329–336, The Hague, Netherlands.

Ruttkay, Z., Dormann, C., and Noot, H. (2002). Evaluating ECAs - What and How?. In *Proceedings of AAMAS 2002 Workshop on Embodied Conversational Agents — Let's Specify and Evaluate Them!*, Bologna, Italy.

Sanders, G. and Scholtz, J. (2000). Measurement and Evaluation of Conversational Agents. In Cassell J., Sullivan J., Prevost S., Churchill E., editors, *Embodied Conversational Agents*, pp. 346–373, MIT Press, Cambridge, MA.

Sculley, J. (1989). The Relationship Between Business and Higher Education: a Perspective on the 21st Century. *Communications of the ACM*, 32(9): 1056–1061.

Sweller, J., van Merrienboer, J. J. G., and Paas, F. G. (1998). Cognitive architecture and instructional design. *Educational Psychology Review*, 10(3): 251–296.

Takeuchi A. and Naito, T. (1995). Situated facial displays: Towards social interaction. In *Proceedings of the ACM CHI 1995 Conference*, pp. 450–455, Denver, CO.

Van Mulken, S., Andre, E., and Muller, J. (1998). The Persona Effect: How substantial is it?. In *Proceedings of the ACM CHI 1998 Conference*, pp. 53–66, Los Angeles, CA.

Walker, J. H., Sproull, L., and Subramani, R. (1994). Using a human face in an interface. In *Proceedings of the ACM CHI 1994 Conference*, pp. 85–91, Boston, MA.

Xiao, J., Catrambone, R., and Stasko, J., (2003). Be Quiet? Evaluating Proactive and Reactive User Interface Assistants. In *Proceedings of INTERACT '03*, pp. 383–390, Zurich, Switzerland.

IV

EVALUATION OF APPLICATIONS

Chapter 10

TALKING TO DIGITAL FISH

Designing Effective Conversational Interfaces for Educational Software

Courtney Darves and Sharon Oviatt

> *A Locanian, having plucked all the feathers off from a nightingale and seeing what a little body it had, "Surely," quoth he, "thou art all voice and nothing else."*
>
> —Plutarch, Laconic Apothegms

Abstract   Conversational interfaces that incorporate animated characters potentially are well suited for educational software, since they can engage children as active learners and support question asking skills. In the present research, a simulation study was conducted in which twenty-four 7-to-10-year-old children used speech and pen input to converse directly with animated fish as they learned about marine biology. The animated fish responded with TTS voices crafted to sound either extroverted or introverted in accordance with the speech signal literature. During these interactions, children became highly engaged, asking an average of 152 questions during a 45-minute session. Self-report measures further confirmed that children liked "talking to the animals and that the TTS and interface were easy to understand and use. The auditory embodiment of animated characters as TTS output also had a significant selective impact on children's engagement in asking science questions. Specifically, children asked +16% more science questions when conversing with animated characters embodying an extrovert TTS voice that resembled the speech of a master teacher (e.g., higher volume and pitch, wider pitch range), rather than an introvert TTS voice, although no differential impact was found on social questions. These findings reveal that conversational interfaces can be designed that effectively stimulate children during learning activities, thereby supporting the goals of next-generation educational software.

Keywords: Children's speech, animated software characters, conversational interfaces, text-to-speech, audio interface design, science education, educational software.

Z. Ruttkay and C. Pelachaud (eds.), From Brows to Trust, 271–292.
© *2004 Kluwer Academic Publishers. Printed in the Netherlands.*

1.   Introduction

Researchers, educators, and industry alike all have explored the effective integration of computers in education (Cassell and Ryokai (2000); Haughland (2000); Kulik et al. (1983)). Computer-based instruction can lead to higher test scores and better attitudes toward computers, and can reduce the amount of time needed to learn a subject matter (Haughland (2000); Kulik et al. (1983)). It clearly also can play a major role in making education more accessible and better tailored for all children. For example, audio-visual multimedia systems have the potential to provide better support for children with different learning styles, in comparison with previous text-based information delivery (Druin (1996); Moreno et al. (2001)).

Although computer-based instruction historically has relied on rote-learning strategies, newer interfaces now are being designed that give children a more active role in the learning experience (Haughland (2000)). Recently, researchers have emphasized the importance of children having more active control and creative input during computer-based learning. One trend has been to make students designers of the technology they use (Cassell and Ryokai (2000); Druin (1996); Druin (1999)). For example, in one application children added the graphics, animation, and sound to their own original story (Cassell and Ryokai (2000)). In another application, students learned about plant physiology by designing roots, stems, and leaves appropriate for different environments (Moreno et al. (2001)).

Another emerging trend in educational software is the incorporation of animated characters, which can provide an interface design vehicle for engaging children and managing the overall tutorial exchange (Lester et al. (1997); Oviatt and Adams (2000)). When animated characters are embedded within a conversational interface, they quite naturally can become the central focus of the content exchange as an interlocutor, rather than playing a subsidiary and sometimes distracting "help-agent role. As an example, in the course of learning about science, a child could converse directly with an animated parasite or sea creature to extract information about it. The immediacy of such an interaction could be designed to facilitate children's engagement as "active learners such that they seek answers to questions that they care about as they construct an understanding of science[1] (Richmond et al. (1987)). Consistent with a constructivist view of educational theory, one goal of the present research was to investigate how animated character technology can be designed to bring out the best in student's question asking skills.

1.1 Evaluating Animated Characters in Educational Software

While past research has confirmed animated characters' ability to engage and motivate users (Cassell et al. (2000); Dehn and Van Mulken (2000); Lester et al. (1997); Moreno et al. (2001)), it rarely has shown any task-relevant performance enhancement as a function of a character's presence or specific design (Dehn and Van Mulken (2000)). Likewise, most research on animated character design has focused on rendering them with high-fidelity graphics and animation, and on the impact of visual embodiment, but has ignored the question of whether auditory embodiment also can provide powerful cues that influence user behaviour. However, in one study involving web-based book reviews, the TTS voice used for animated characters influenced users' self-reported book preferences and purchasing behaviour (Nass and Lee (2001)). In another web-based study, children rated TTS sentences with focal F0 doubling as more fun than control sentences, whereas they rated sentences with focal duration lengthening as more boring than control sentences (Gustavson and House (2001)). In another web-based study, the presence of animated agents that actively monitored users' behaviour as they worked was found to decrease users' performance and increase their anxiety level (Rickenberg and Reeves (2000)). Unfortunately, there are few compelling demonstrations that animated characters significantly improve users' learning-oriented behaviour in any way during a tutorial exchange. One exception to this is a recent study which demonstrated that when students interacted with animated characters that provided spoken versus text-based feedback, they showed increased interest, learning, and performance on transfer tests (Moreno et al. (2001)). However, the specifics of spoken interface design and different TTS voice types in particular were not assessed.

Since conversational interfaces are social in nature (Nass et al. (2000); Nass and Lee (2001); Nass et al. (1994)), in the present research the voice characteristics of a "master teacher were used as a design metaphor for integrating animated characters into an educational software application. The education literature indicates that students respond with increased attention and on-task behaviour to dynamic and energetic speech (Bettencourt et al. (1983); Sallinen-Kuparinen (1992)), or to an extroverted speech style that is higher in volume and pitch and more expanded in pitch range (Nass and Lee (2001); Nass and Lee (2000); Scherer (1979)). As a result, we might expect that animated characters that respond in an extroverted voice would be more effective in stimulating children's learning-oriented behaviour, including their level of spontaneous question asking about educational content.

1.2   Goals of the Study

In the present study, children conversed directly with animated fish using the Immersive Science Education for Elementary kids (*I SEE!*) interface as they learned about marine biology. This research was designed to:

- explore whether conversational interaction with animated characters can be engaging for children, as measured by time spent interacting with the software, quantity of spontaneous question asking, and children's self reports;

- determine whether the TTS voice characteristics used for animated characters influence children's learning-oriented behaviour (e.g., question asking), and what the implications are for designing educational software;

- assess the overall usability of the *I SEE!* conversational interface prototype.

With respect to the second goal, children's queries were compared when they interacted with animated characters embodying different TTS voice profiles. In a comparison of introvert versus extrovert voices, it was predicted that an extrovert voice that shares features in common with master teachers' speech would be more effective in stimulating children to ask task-appropriate questions during learning activities. In particular, it was predicted that children would ask more biology questions when conversing with an extrovert TTS voice (compared with an introvert voice), although no differential impact would occur for general social-interaction questions. The long-term goal of this research is to design effective conversational interfaces, in particular ones that have a desirable behavioural impact on users for the application being designed.

2.   Methods

2.1   Participants, Task, and Procedure

Twenty-four elementary-school children participated in this study as paid volunteers. A median split divided the participants into two age groups, younger children (mean age 8.2, range 7.7. to 8.8.), and older ones (mean age 9.7, range 9.4 to 10.1), with each age group gender balanced. All participants were native English speakers without known behavioural or linguistic impairments. Participants also represented different personality types as assessed by parent and teacher ratings, with

13 rated by parents and/or teachers as extroverts versus 11 rated as moderately introverted. Participation was conducted at an elementary school field site.

Children interacted with an educational software program called Immersive Science Education for Elementary kids (*I SEE!*), which is an application designed to teach children about marine biology, simple data tabulation, and graphing. The interface permitted children to use speech, pen, or multimodal (speech and pen) input while conversing with animated software characters as they learned about marine biology. Figure 10.1 illustrates the *I SEE!* Interface. An animated "Spin the Dolphin character, shown in the lower right corner of Figure 10.1, also was co-present on the screen and available as a conversational partner. The child could control the marine animals by asking Spin the Dolphin to start, stop, or replay the videos. When the movie stopped, the marine animal was embellished with animated eyes that gazed at the child and blinked naturally. At this point, the animal became available as a "conversational partner" for answering questions about itself using text-to-speech (TTS) output. For example, an animated manatee could identify its species, diet, habitat, unique behaviour, endangered species status, and so forth. Essentially, the animated eyes that gazed at the child and blinked provided attentional cues that marked the transition from a passive movie-viewing experience to active availability of the animal as the child's conversational partner.

During data collection, children queried the marine animals to collect information and build a graph representing information about them (e.g., "Can this animal change colours rapidly?"). Children also were encouraged to ask any questions they wished and to have fun learning new things about the animals. The marine animals were responsive but did not direct the conversation. Therefore, children's spontaneous conversations with the animals primarily were self-initiated, reflecting their own curiosity and interests about the marine creatures. When each child had finished asking a marine animal questions, he or she could request that Spin the Dolphin start the next movie with a new animal.

Before starting a session, each child received instructions and practice with a science teacher on how to use the *I SEE!* interface on a small hand-held computer, shown in Figure 10.2. During the ten- to fifteen-minute hands-on orientation, children interacted with and graphed information about three practice animals. Following the practice session, the experimenter left the room, and the child used the *I SEE!* application to view and interact with 24 different marine animals (e.g., octopus, shown in Figure 10.1) that were sequenced in three task sets of eight animals apiece. Each task set had a different target question (e.g., "Is this

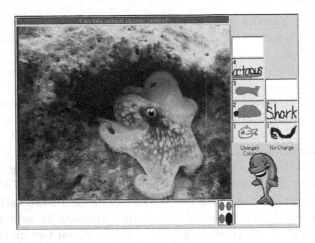

Figure 10.1.   I SEE! Interface.

animal common or endangered?") and presented a new set of animals. Children could spend as much time as they liked interacting with each individual animal, and whenever they were ready could ask to see the next one.

During data collection, no teacher or adult was present to influence what children asked, or how long they interacted with the animals in *I SEE!*. After the child finished interacting with all 24 animals, the experimenter returned and conducted a post-experimental interview related to the *I SEE!* system and its animated characters. A video record was made of all human-computer interaction with the interface during each session and interview, including all of children's spoken and pen-based input and a close-up view of their face and hands.

2.2   Simulation Environment

The *I SEE!* interface is a simulated conversational system that was designed to support proactive research on conversational interaction and interface design. As such, children's input was received by an informed assistant who interpreted their queries and provided system responses. System responses to high-frequency child queries were pre-loaded into a database, which is a feature that supported rapid simulated responding for the majority of children's questions. An automatic error generator produced general failure-to-understand messages in response to 4-5% of child queries in order to enhance the simulation's credibility. During testing, children believed that they were interacting with a fully func-

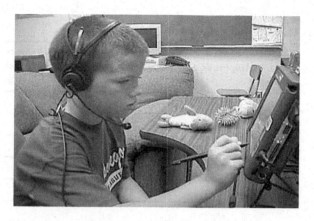

Figure 10.2. Eight-year old boy at school as he asks an animated marine character questions about itself.

tional system. The simulation environment ran on a PC, and it received input from a Fujitsu Stylistic^{TM} 2300 that was used by the children. Details of the simulation infrastructure, its performance, and its use in research with children have been described elsewhere (Oviatt and Adams (2000)).

2.3 Text to Speech Manipulation

Text-to-speech voices from Lernout and Hauspie's TTS 3000 were used to convey the animated characters' spoken output. TTS voices were tailored for intelligibility of pronunciation. They included both male and female American English prototype voices, which were further tailored to represent opposite ends of the introvert-extrovert personality spectrum as indicated by the speech signal literature (Scherer (1979); Smith et al. (1995); Tusing and Dillard (2000)). Introvert and extrovert voices were selected because they are relatively well understood, highly marked paralinguistically, and have been used in previous research on the design of animated characters (Nass and Lee (2001)). In addition, the extrovert TTS voice was selected to model the speech of an engaging teacher (e.g., higher volume and pitch, wider pitch range), as described in the education literature and in the introduction of this chapter (Bettencourt et al. (1983); Sallinen-Kuparinen (1992)). As such, comparison of children's behaviour in the two TTS conditions permitted an assessment of whether an interface with a TTS voice modelled after that of an expert teacher (Extrovert), as opposed to its acoustic opposite (Introvert), could be used to facilitate children's question-asking behaviour. In

Table 10.1. Characteristics of the four TTS voice conditions.

TTS Voice	Mean Amplitude	Mean Pitch Range	Utterance Rate	Dialogue Response Latency
Type	(dB)	(Hz)	(syl/sec)	(sec)
FE	60	186	5.2	1.65
ME	58	106	5.2	1.65
FI	45	71	3.3	3.36
MI	44	58	3.3	3.36

total, four TTS voices were used in this study: (1) Male Extrovert (ME), (2) Male Introvert (MI), (3) Female Extrovert (FE), and (4) Female Introvert (FI).

The introvert and extrovert TTS voices were designed to represent the upper and lower bounds of speech signal features (e.g., amplitude, duration) in order to determine whether users' behaviour could be influenced by a TTS target voice when an optimal degree of contrast is present. The TTS voices also were designed to maintain an identifiable social presence. To achieve this, features of the extrovert and introvert TTS voices were manipulated together as they tend to co-vary in real speakers' voices. That is, individual parameters were not manipulated in isolation in order to avoid producing artificial voices with no recognizable social personality or realism. Table 10.1 summarizes these differences in global speech signal features between the introvert and extrovert TTS voices.

It is important to note that due to pre-loading of system responses, lexical content was controlled in the different TTS voice conditions. In addition, the TTS voice conditions were counterbalanced across task sets, which controlled for the visual appearance of different animated characters presented during the study. Therefore, the only experimentally manipulated variable was the acoustic-prosodic characteristics of the TTS output.

2.4   Research Design and Analyses

The research design for the larger data collection effort, within which this study was situated, was a completely crossed factorial. The main within-subject factor was (1) Type of TTS Voice (Introvert, Extrovert).

This factor remained constant for the first 16 animals, but switched for the remaining 8 (from I to E, or E to I). To test the generality of any TTS effects, I and E voices were tested using both male and female voice prototypes, which resulted in four voices total (ME, FE, MI, FI). Other between-subject comparisons included (2) Child Gender (Male, Female) and (3) Child Age (Young, Old), which was categorized using a median split to divide children into a younger (average 8 yrs., 2 mos.) and older (average 9 yrs, 7 mos.) group.

With respect to the main comparison involving TTS voice type, the marine animals were assigned one of the four TTS voices during practice and task sets 1 and 2. However, the introvert-extrovert dimension of the TTS voice then was switched for task set 3 (e.g., MI switched to ME; FE switched to FI). The TTS voices were distributed equally across subjects, with 6 children assigned each of the 4 voices for the initial task set. Participants were assigned semi-randomly to ensure equal numbers of male and female and older and younger children in each of the 4 TTS voice conditions. Figure 10.3 illustrates the main manipulation involving the TTS voice types and their switch for the marine characters before task 3 during each session.

In the present evaluation, time to complete activity, number of questions asked, and self-report comments were used to assess children's engagement with the interface. In addition, the total number of different types of questions that children asked (e.g., biology, social, interface help) was evaluated to compare the impact of E versus I TTS voices on children's active initiation of learning-oriented behaviour. Further details of the dependent measures used in this study are outlined in section 2.5. In accord with the hypotheses and directional predictions outlined in section 1.2, a priori paired t-tests were used to compare children's specific question asking behaviour during the E versus I TTS voice conditions. Independent t tests were used to confirm that children's differential question asking behaviour in the E versus I TTS voice conditions did not vary as a function of TTS voice gender, children's gender, or children's age.

2.5   Data Coding and Dependent Measures

Human-computer interaction was videotaped and conversational interaction transcribed. Children's conversations with the animated characters were coded for the following dependent measures: (1) time to complete activity, (2) number and type of child questions, and (3) children's self-report comments about the interface and its ease of use.

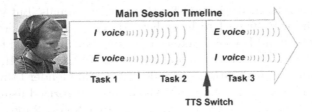

Figure 10.3. TTS voice for animated characters before and after switch task.

Time to Complete Activity   For all subjects, total time spent engaged with the *I SEE!* interface after practice was measured to the nearest second.

Number and Type of Self-Initiated Queries   The number and type of children's spontaneous queries to the animated characters and Spin the Dolphin were counted and coded into separate genre types. Table 10.2 provides descriptions and sample questions representing the main genres. The four genres were used to classify the questions into the following categories: (1) Biology, (2) Social, (3) Interface Help, and (4) Other questions. Questions coded in the Biology genre focused on factual educational information about the marine animal, including its diet, habitat, predators, and so forth. In contrast, the Social genre encompassed questions that were social-interactive in nature, including questions about family life, friends, personal preferences, as well as ritualized social greetings. The Interface Help genre included questions on how to use the *I SEE!* Interface. The Help genre served as an indicator of ease and naturalness of the interface. The Other genre included miscellaneous questions not classifiable into the other main genres, for example "What's behind you?" In addition, the number of child requests for an animated character to repeat an utterance was counted separately to assess TTS intelligibility. Children's commands (e.g., to start the movies introducing new animals), responses to system initiations, and simple acknowledgments were relatively infrequent, and were separated from the other main categories of interest.

Interview Self-Reports   At the end of each child's session, the experimenter returned to interview the child. Children were told that their responses would be used to help improve future versions of the computer. The following questions were used to summarize the children's appraisal of the interface and its ease of use:

Table 10.2. Description of query genres.

	Description and Examples
Biology	Questions about biology. - *What kind of marine animal are you?* - *How do you defend yourself?*
Social	Questions about social and personal issues. - *What's your name?* - *What's your favorite color?*
Help	Questions about how to use the *I SEE!* interface. - *How do I stop the movie?* - *How do I change the ink color?*

- What did you think of this computer?

- Would you like to have a computer like this? (If so, what would you do with it?)

- Was the computer easy or hard to use? (If hard, what was hard?)

- What did you think of the ocean animals?

- What were the animals likea stranger, friend, teacher, parent, or what?

- What about this computer did you like?

Children's responses to these questions were easily separated into categories for qualitative description. The percentage of children who gave positive appraisals of the system was summarized based on responses to the first question, and the percentage of children who appraised the marine animals positively was assessed using the fourth question. Assessments of children's desire to own such a computer, its ease of use, and beliefs about what the animals were like were evaluated from the second, third, and fifth questions, respectively. Finally, children's qualitative comments about the animated characters and system were summarized based on responses to the fourth and sixth questions.

Inter-coder Reliability   In total, 17% of child queries were second-scored by an independent coder for genre classifications, and these judgments between coders matched over 99% of the time.

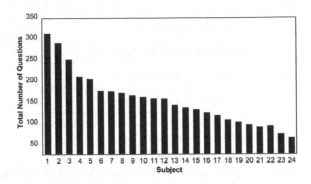

Figure 10.4. Individual differences in total number of questions asked.

3.   Results

Our study of twenty-four children's interactions with the *I SEE!* interface yielded approximately 36 hours of videotape data. A total of 3,643 child queries were coded for genre classification, of which 3,340 were directed to the animated marine animals, and another 303 to Spin the Dolphin. Figure 10.3 shows an example of a transcribed question-answer exchange between a child and a marine animal, which illustrates very typical content for these dialogues.

3.1   Engagement in Interface and Ease of Use

Even though children were alone in the classroom with no teacher present, they spontaneously asked an average of 152 queries of the animated marine animals while engaged with the interface. The total questions asked per child ranged from 62 to 309. Figure 10.4 displays the total number of questions asked by each subject. During these interactions, children spent an average of 45.9 minutes engaged in conversation with the animated characters.

In spite of the fact that children were introduced to Spin the Dolphin as a character who could provide them with help using the computer, less than 0.25% of all children's queries to either the animated marine characters or to Spin involved requests for help with the interface, including help constructing graphs. In addition, children rarely (less than 1% of the time) requested repetition of TTS feedback from the animated characters or Spin, which confirmed that the TTS was adequately intelligible for the present application.

Based on self-reports collected during post-experimental interviews, 100% of the 24 children gave a positive assessment of the interface, with

Table 10.3. Description of query genres.

Child: Are you an octopus?
Octopus: I'm an octopus.
Child: What is your name?
Octopus: My name is Ollie the Octopus. What is your name?
Child: Jake.
Octopus: Hello, Jake.
Child: Do you have any brothers and sisters?
Octopus: I have many brothers and sisters.
Child: Do you know any of them?
Octopus: They have gone away.
Child: Do you have teeth?
Octopus: I don't have teeth. I have a beak instead.
Child: What do you eat?
Octopus: I eat crustaceans and sometimes smaller mollusks. I hunt them at night.
Child: How warm is it in the ocean?
Octopus: About 73 degrees.
Child: Do you move a lot?
Octopus: I can crawl with my arms. I can also swim using my arms or by shooting out water from my siphon.
Child: What kind of octopus are you?
Octopus: I'm an Atlantic octopus.
Child: Can I see another movie now?

79% reporting that it was "easy to use," and 96% reporting that they wanted one to own. Typical qualitative comments included that the computer was "cool," "fun," and something they would "like to play with all day." Children's most common spontaneous comments were that they liked "talking to the animals" (50%), "being able to write and speak to the computer" (29%), and "being able to get answers to questions and learn things" (21%). In terms of the animated characters, 96% of children assessed them positively, with 83% describing them as

Table 10.4. Distribution of total queries to marine animals by topic.

Genre	Occurrences	Percent of Corpus
Biology	2493	74.6
Social	794	23.8
Other	53	1.6
Interface Help	0	0

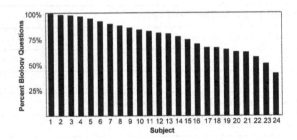

Figure 10.5. Percentage biology questions asked by each subject of their total social and biology queries.

being like "friends" or "teachers" (i.e., rather than parents, strangers, or other).

3.2 Distribution of Question Types

As shown in Table 10.4, the majority of children's queries to the animated marine characters (75%) focused on marine biology factual information. The remaining questions (24%) were social in nature, with only a small percentage on miscellaneous topics. As shown in Figure 10.5, all but one child asked more factual questions than social questions.

3.3 Impact of TTS Voice Type on Child Queries

Children asked more questions overall when interacting with animated marine characters embodying the extrovert TTS voice, compared with the introvert voice (mean 141 vs. 126 questions, respectively). Figure 10.6 illustrates children's differential level of question asking when interacting with the introvert and extrovert voices, broken down into the two main genre types of biology versus social questions. A priori paired t-tests confirmed that children asked a greater number of biology questions when conversing with the extrovert voice, rather than the introvert one (mean 108 and 93 biology queries, respectively), paired t=2.08 (df=23), p < .025, one-tailed. This represented a 16% overall increase in children's educationally-relevant question asking when interacting with the extrovert TTS voice. Further, the majority of children, or 17 of 24, responded in this manner. Table 10.5 shows individual differences in the relative increase in total biology questions asked when children interacted with characters speaking in extrovert versus introvert TTS voices. In contrast, no significant difference was found in the level of children's social queries when interacting with these two voice types, t < 1, N.S.

Comparison of the difference in biology questions asked as a function of the TTS voice condition revealed no significant difference between the younger and older children, t = 0.165 (df = 22), p = 0.871 (separate variances), N.S. There also was no difference between male and female children, t = 0.465 (df = 22), p = 0.647, N.S. Finally, these results also generalized across testing with the male and female TTS voice prototypes, for which no significant differences were observed, t = 1.377 (df = 22), p = 0.18, two-tailed, N.S.. That is, all of these analyses confirmed that the extrovert TTS voice stimulated significantly and selectively more biology queries. A summary of these results on the impact of TTS voice type on children's question asking is shown in Tables 4.5 and 4.6.

4. Discussion

The primary aim of this chapter has been to explore aspects of conversational interfaces and animated character design within the context of an empirical evaluation of an educational interface prototype. We explored both the auditory embodiment of animated characters, which will be especially important for future mobile interfaces, as well as how to design animated characters for educational software in a way that engages children and facilitates their learning-oriented behaviour. Within the framework of proposed evaluation taxonomies for animated character design (see Chapter 1 by Isbister and Doyle in this book), the present work represents an Application Domain research focus.

4.1 Acoustic Characteristics of Animated Character Design

Auditory embodiment alone, independent of an animated character's visual appearance or lexical output, can be highly influential in stimulating users' behaviour in task-appropriate ways. In the present conversational

Table 10.5. Individual differences in percentage increase in biology questions asked when interacting with extrovert versus introvert TTS voices.

Subject	Percent Change
S1	100%
S2	68%
S3	64%
S4	58%
S5	52%
S6	37%
S7	34%
S8	33%
S9	31%
S10	25%
S11	24%
S12	17%
S13	13%
S14	10%
S15	9%
S16	6%
S17	3%
S18	-1%
S19	-13%
S20	-14%
S21	-17%
S22	-24%
S23	-39%
S24	-53%

interface, children's question asking was substantially affected by the acoustic-prosodic features of the TTS output they heard. When interacting with the extrovert voiced characters, which in many ways repre-

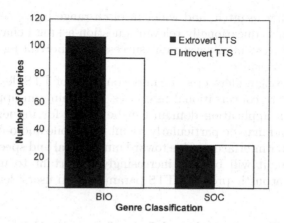

Figure 10.6. Number of biology (BIO) and social (SOC) queries asked by children when interacting with characters using extrovert versus introvert TTS voices.

Table 10.6. Impact of extrovert (E) versus introvert (I) TTS voice type on number of educationally-relevant child queries.

Dependent Measure	P value	Magnitude and Direction of Effect
Total queries	<.09	+12% more questions in E condition
Biology queries	<.025*	+16% more questions in E condition
Social queries	0.968	N.S.

Table 10.7. Generality of effect (increased biology-content questions) across child gender, age, and TTS voice gender.

Comparison Groups	P value	Magnitude and Direction of Effect
Male TTS vs. Female TTS	0.183	N.S.
Male children vs. Female children	0.647	N.S.
Younger children vs. Older children	0.871	N.S.

sented the rhetorical style of a master teacher (Bettencourt et al. (1983); Sallinen-Kuparinen (1992)), children were stimulated to ask 16% more marine biology questions. In contrast, children's general social questions were not differentially affected by the same introvert and extrovert voices. In other words, using an extrovert TTS voice that was louder,

faster, higher in pitch, and wider in pitch range had a selective impact
on children's educationally relevant question-asking behaviour. The extrovert voice essentially was more successful in motivating and managing
a tutorial exchange.

This finding underscores the important role of TTS design in the success of future conversational interfaces. Matching an appropriate TTS
voice to an application domain can be a tool for influencing user behaviour, and may be particularly useful for mobile audio-only interfaces.
As computer interfaces evolve toward multimodal and speech-based communication, it will become increasingly important to understand the
impact of acoustic-prosodic TTS parameters on users' learning and behaviour.

4.2   Conversational Interfaces as Educational Interfaces

One goal of this research was to investigate the quantity and quality of
children's question asking when using a relatively unstructured conversational interface. We found that when left alone, children spontaneously
asked an average of 152 questions of the digital fish, and in some cases
over 300 questions. The majority of children's questions, or 75%, focused
on marine biology, and this pattern was consistent for the majority of
the children. The large volume of questions focusing on marine biology suggests that conversational interfaces can be successfully designed
to promote children's mastery of science through active question-asking
(Richmond et al. (1987)). Beyond this, even children's questions that
focused on social interaction and bonding with the marine animals may
have indirectly stimulated learning by engaging them in marine science
content.

Children's most common positive comment about the computer was
that they liked "talking to the animals," which may in part reflect the
"immediacy characteristics" of this interface (Richmond et al. (1987)),
as well as the self-reinforcing nature of conversation itself. The majority of children also reported that the animated characters were like
"friends" or "teachers", with 96% of the children assessing the characters
positively. Children's engagement with the characters was corroborated
by the social quality of their conversations. For example, they gave
the fish compliments ("You're pretty"), showed empathy toward them
("I'm sorry you're endangered"), and displayed emotional attachment
("I'll miss you, Spin!"). Finally, past work with the *I SEE!* interface
has revealed that children predominantly use personal pronouns when
addressing these animated characters (Oviatt and Adams (2000)).

The ease and naturalness of conversational interfaces make them good candidates for educational software, especially among young children who may be unable to read or spell consistently. After only brief exposure, young children using *I SEE!* were able to converse with the fish, extract large amounts of information about marine biology, and construct graphs tabulating this new information. In post-experimental interviews, 79% of children reported that the system was "easy to use," and children rarely requested help using the interface. Future uses of conversational interfaces may include handheld computers that serve as "interactive tour guides" at aquariums, zoos, or museums. Rather than passively reading exhibit signs or listening to an audio-taped tour, visitors could use the conversational interface to obtain answers to specific questions quickly and easily.

4.3 Conclusion

In the present research, the interpersonal and educational literature provided a point of departure for designing effective TTS voices for a tutorial exchange. TTS voices modeled after expert teachers' voices were the most effective at stimulating learning-oriented interactions. Specifically, these voices increased the number of science questions asked by children, although they had no differential impact on the number of general social questions asked. Furthermore, both behavioural and self-report measures indicated that the young children in this study enjoyed the conversational interface, and especially "talking to the animals." When working alone in a classroom, children asked the digital fish over 150 questions during a 45-minute session. They also found the interface easy to use and rarely requested help or repetition of the TTS output.

These results indicate that conversational interfaces can facilitate learning through direct question and answer exchanges that are easy, natural, and highly engaging for users. Furthermore, the specific characteristics of animated character voices can influence users' behaviour in task-relevant ways. In different application contexts with other user groups, undoubtedly different social metaphors and associated TTS profiles will be needed to achieve the most desirable impact. Future research should continue to pursue understudied aspects of the design of animated characters, including their auditory embodiment. The long-term goal of this research is the design of effective conversational interfaces, in particular ones that have a task-appropriate behavioural impact on users for the application being designed.

Acknowledgments

This research was supported in part by Grants IRI-9530666 and IIS-0117868 from the National Science Foundation, Special Extension for Creativity (SEC) Grant IIS-9530666 from NSF, and a gift from the Intel Research Council to the second author. Thanks to Matt Wesson for implementing simulation, transcription, and data analysis tools and for assisting during testing. Thanks also to Rachel Coulston for reliability scoring of the genre coding. Finally, we are grateful to the students who participated in this research.

Notes

1. Everyday Classroom Tools Project, Harvard Graduate School of Education
    http://hea-www.harvard.edu/ECT/Inquiry/inquiry1.html

References

Bettencourt, E., Gillett, M., Gall, M., and Hull, R. (1983). Effects of teacher enthusiasm training on student on-task behaviour and achievement. *American Educational Research Journal*, 20(4): 435–450.

Cassell, J. and Ryokai, K. (2000). Story Spaces: Interfaces for Children's voices. In *Proc. of ACM SIGCHI Conference of Human Factors in Computing Systems: CHI 2000*, pp. 243–244.

Cassell, J., Sullivan, J., Prevost, S., and Churchill, E., editors (2000). *Embodied conversational agents*. MIT Press, Cambridge, MA.

Dehn, D.M. and Van Mulken, S. (2000). The impact of animated interface agents: A review of empirical research. *International Journal of Human-Computer Studies*, 52: 1–22.

Druin, A.e., editor (1996). *Designing Multimedia Environments for Children*. John Wiley & Sons, USA.

Druin, A.e., editor (1999). *The Design of Children's Technology*. Morgan Kaufmann, San Francisco, CA.

Gustavson, K. and House, D. (2001). Fun or Boring? A web-based evaluation of expressive synthesis for children. In *Proc. of Eurospeech 2001*, pp. 565–568, Aalborg, Denmark.

Haughland, S.W. (2000). *Computers and young children*. Report available from the Educational Resources Information Center, ERIC Document Reproduction Service No. ED 438 926.

Kulik, J.A., Bangert, R.L., and Williams, G.W. (1983). Effects of computer-based education on secondary school students. *Journal of Educational Psychology*, 75(1): 19–26.

Lester, J.C., Converse, S.A., Stone, B.A., Kahler, S., and Barlow, T. (1997). Animated pedagogical agents and problem-solving effectiveness: A large-scale empirical evaluation. In *Proc. of Eighth World Conference on Artificial Intelligence in Education*, pp. 23–30, Kobe, Japan.

Moreno, R., Mayer, R., Spires, H., and Lester, J. (2001). The case for social agency in computer-based teaching: Do students learn more deeply when they interact with animated pedagogical agents?. *Cognition and Instruction*, 19(2): 177–213.

Nass, C., Isbister, K., and Lee, E. (2000). Truth is beauty: Researching embodied conversational agents. In Cassell, J., Sullivan, J., Prevost, S., and Churchill, E., editors, *Embodied Conversational Agents*, pp. 374–402, MIT Press, Cambridge, MA.

Nass, C. and Lee, K.L. (2001). Does computer-synthesized speech manifest personality? Experimental tests of recognition, similarity-attraction, and consistency-attraction. *Journal of Experimental Psychology: Applied*, 7(3): 171–181.

Nass, C. and Lee, K.L. (2000). Does computer-generated speech manifest personality? An experimental test of similarity-attraction. In *Proc. of Conference on Human Factors in Computing Systems: CHI 2000*, pp. 329–336, ACM Press, New York, NY.

Nass, C., Steuer, J., and Tauber, E. (1994). Computers are social actors. In *Proc. of Conference on Human Factors in Computing Systems: CHI 1994*, pp. 72–78, ACM Press, Boston, MA.

Oviatt, S.L. and Adams, B. (2000). Designing and evaluating conversational interfaces with animated characters. In Cassell, J., Sullivan, J., Prevost, S., and Churchill, E., editors, *Embodied Conversational Agents*, pp. 319–343, MIT Press, Cambridge, MA.

Richmond, V., Gorham, J., and McCroskey, J. (1987). The relationship between selected immediacy behaviours and cognitive learning. *Communication Yearbook*, 10: 574–590.

Rickenberg,R. and Reeves, B. (2000). The effects of animated characters on anxiety, task performance, and evaluations of user interfaces. In *Proc. of Conference on Human Factors in Computer Systems: CHI 2000*, pp. 49–56, ACM Press, The Hague, Amsterdam.

Sallinen-Kuparinen, A. (1992). Teacher communicator style. *Communication Education*, 41(2): 153–166.

Scherer, K.R. (1979). Personality markers in speech. In Scherer K.R. and Giles H., editors, *Social Markers in Speech*, pp. 147–209, Cambridge Univ. Press, Cambridge, UK.

Smith, B.L., Brown, B.L., Strong, W.J., and Rencher, A.C. (1995). Effects of speech rate on personality perception. *Language and Speech*, 18: 145–152.

Tusing, K.J. and Dillard, J.P. (2000). The sounds of dominance: Vocal precursors of perceived dominance during interpersonal influence. *Human Communication Research*, 26: 148–171.

Chapter 11

EXPERIMENTAL EVALUATION OF THE USE OF ECAS IN ECOMMERCE APPLICATIONS

Three Studies

Hazel Morton, Helen McBreen, and Mervyn Jack

> *We live in a fantasy world, a world of illusion. The great task in life is to find reality.*
>
> —Iris Murdoch

Abstract   This chapter describes an experimental approach to the evaluation of embodied conversational agents (ECAs) within eCommerce contexts and exemplifies the approach with three case studies. Results are presented from three experiments into the usability of eCommerce applications employing 3D ECAs within the domain of eRetail and eBanking.

The findings described here confirm user preferences for applications in which the agent acts as a conversational partner compared with a non-visual telephone application using speech recognition. Further, data in this chapter confirm the positive role of ECAs in interfaces and the benefits to that role of adding other modalities such as text output.

Keywords: Conversational agents, evaluation, eCommerce.

Z. Ruttkay and C. Pelachaud (eds.), From Brows to Trust, 293–321.
© *2004 Kluwer Academic Publishers. Printed in the Netherlands.*

1.   Introduction

A complex activity such as interacting with an embodied conversational agent (ECA) requires a sophisticated, multivariate approach to its investigation. This chapter describes an experimental approach to the evaluation of ECAs that combines rigorous control of variables in the context of eCommerce application user interfaces and task scenarios. Results are presented from three experiments into the usability of eCommerce applications employing 3D ECAs, all of which use applications within the domain of eRetail and eBanking.

Rigorous control of recruitment of participants and experiment procedures is important when investigating user responses to applications in order to ensure valid, statistically reliable results. The experimental approach is particularly relevant when the study focuses on perceptual and other relatively low-level psychomotor characteristics of the user interface or ECA, for example as in the study of eyebrow movements for ECAs described in the Chapter 7 by Krahmer and Swerts in this book; in such cases careful control of the participants' experiences and environment is required. Experiment procedures of this kind are usually carried out under laboratory conditions on relatively short time scales, ensuring that the results are rapidly available to the service designers. The drawback with the experimental approach in the context of usability studies is that it tends to tell designers and service providers relatively little about the user's holistic response to the complex activity of engaging with an interface to complete real-world tasks. It can be argued that what is ultimately most important is to understand users' responses to ECAs when engaged in realistic tasks performed in well defined and clearly understood eCommerce contexts (Bersen et al. (1998)).

Field trials, using fully implemented services with actual customers carrying out real-world tasks, may be used to gather realistic data on customers' behaviour and usage of a service. However, from a usability perspective such trials suffer from a number of serious drawbacks. Often, the data gathered by such studies is limited in its depth and sophistication when compared with the data obtained from a laboratory-based experiment. Real-world field trials are very costly and time consuming to run and the data gathered may be too informal and qualitative to contribute to a detailed assessment of the usability of the interfaces and specifically the causes of the expressed attitudes to the interfaces. What is more, because of the investment required for the implementation of large-scale field trials, the results usually come too late in the design cycle to prompt improvements in the interface design, thus reducing considerably their usefulness to the interface design team. What is required is a usability evaluation approach that combines the rigour, speed and depth of insight offered by experimental procedures with the realism and holistic experience offered by field trials. A general discussion of evaluation research is given in the Chapter 3 by Christoph in this book.

The experimental approach described in this chapter deploys expert resources and interface programming in order to provide a realistic interface and context for the research. Importantly for this approach, a contrastive study is carried out using two or more versions of an interface, differing in some crucial design characteristic. Participants are given detailed personal data for their fictitious personae and realistic, professionally produced supporting documentation such as, in the assessment of banking applications, bank statements, priming and information leaflets. The results obtained from this procedure are considered to approximate the responses the service would generate in a real world context of use.

This chapter details three experimental studies in the use ECAs in eCommerce applications. The background to each of the studies is described, followed by the main experimental findings and general conclusions based on the results.

2.   Experimental Approach

In this approach, a repeated-measures design is used to ensure maximum control over between-subject variability and a rich set of data is collected based on objective, performance measurements (such as time taken to complete tasks and success rates) and subjective attitudes to the experiences of using the different versions of the interface.

Participants' attitudes are measured using questionnaires usually completed after experiencing each version of the service. The approach uses attitude questions having a Likert (Likert (1932)) format where each usability attribute to be measured is presented to the participant in the form of a stimulus statement followed by an agree-disagree scale. The advantages of this format are described in Coolican (1994):

- Participants prefer the Likert scaling technique because it is "more natural" to complete and because it maintains their direct involvement in the process.

- The Likert technique has been shown to have a high degree of validity and reliability.

- The Likert scale has been shown to be effective in measuring changes over time.

In the approach used for the three experiments described in this chapter, 7-point Likert response scales were used with a balance of positively and negatively worded stimulus statements in the questionnaire. The phrasing of the stimulus statements was made as succinct as possible, compatible with a clear identification of the usability attribute being measured. In all cases, the statements were evaluated before use by a team of human factors specialists experienced in the specific issues of evaluating user interfaces and ECAs in particular. A score over 4.0 represents a positive attitude; scores below 4.0 represent negative attitudes to the identified attributes. Overall usability scores were obtained by taking the mean of all the items in the questionnaire. Analysis of the attitude data also involved breaking down the results by between-subject factors such as gender and age group.

In addition to performance data and user attitudes, the approach also provides for the gathering of qualitative data through the use of structured interviews with participants after they have completed all their tasks and through more detailed focus group sessions with a subset of participants who had already completed the experiment session. Data gathered in these ways tend to be more difficult to analyse but can be very useful in providing insights into why participants responded in the ways they did and suggesting causes for their responses, thereby allowing researchers to "probe the user more deeply on interesting issues as they arise." (Dix et al. (1993)).

A sample experimental procedure used in this approach is as follows:

1 Brief explanation of research session: that the participant is, for example, a banking customer who will try two versions of a banking service.

2 Participant given realistic 'customer' details to use in the research session.

3 Participant given task sheet containing tasks relevant to the application, which offers enough time and experience with the application that the participant is able to form judgements about it.

4 Participant uses first application to accomplish the tasks.

5 Participant completes subjective questionnaires on their attitudes to the usability of the application.

6 Participant given second task sheet which contains similar tasks for completion with the second application version.

7 Participant uses the second application to accomplish the tasks.

8 Participant completes second subjective usability questionnaire.

9 Participant completes structured verbal interview questionnaire, designed to give participants the opportunity to discuss their opinions and preferences of the two applications they had used.

10 Participant completes demographic and technographic questionnaire, which establishes participants' characteristics such as age, gender, previous experience of automated telephone services and frequency of Internet use.

3. The Phoebe Experiment

This experiment was designed to evaluate the addition of an ECA, Phoebe (Figure 11.1), to an established telephone banking service. The service is used on a standard PC with a spoken language interface capability. The telephone version of the banking service and the Phoebe version are directly comparable as they have exactly the same functionality and use the same dialogue flow and voice recordings. The aim of the experiment reported here was to assess users' responses to both versions of the service using the repeated-measures design described above. It was also of interest in this experiment to investigate potential crossmodal perceptual effects (see the *McGurk effect*, McGurk and MacDonald (1976)) which might cause users to view the voices differently given the contrasting implementations.

Phoebe was created using Poser 4, a character animation tool, which was then exported to a VRML (Virtual reality Modelling Language) format model for use on a Web page. The world in which Phoebe resided was then created using a 3D package supporting VRML. The environment was kept relatively simple in order to ensure that there were few distractions, making comparison with the telephone version straightforward. A female ECA was used because the (previously developed) telephone service used a female voice. The agent was dressed formally because previous research had shown that users preferred formally dressed agents in banking applications (McBreen et al. (2001)). Within the scenario, Phoebe was provided with a computer monitor to which she could refer at relevant times in the interaction and a keyboard with which she could simulate the input of data provided by the user. These served to boost the realism of the scene. In addition, there was a dynamic message board to the agent's left side that displayed the service options at relevant points in the dialogue. The user therefore received both spoken and visual cues during the ECA version of the service.

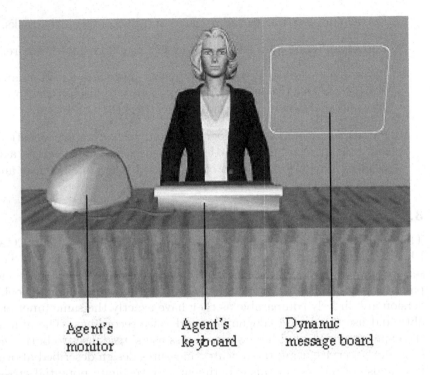

Agent's monitor   Agent's keyboard   Dynamic message board

Figure 11.1. Phoebe banking agent.

The ECA's verbal behaviour dialogue was adapted from an established automated telephone banking service in use at the time of the experiment by a well-known UK bank. A set of movements was created to represent the agent's non verbal behaviour, from which the various gestures used by the ECA could be drawn. Table 11.1 details the ways in which body parts of the agent could move; a series of these movements synchronized together would constitute a gesture.

The gestures were made relevant to the environment in which the agent was situated. For example, deictic gestures were implemented in order that the dynamic message board and agent's computer monitor could be referenced. Facial expressions, lip synchronisation and gestures for keyboard use were also created. Each of the service prompts in the dialogue was categorised according to discourse type. Because the dialogue represents an information exchange, where the user attempts to find out certain information or accomplish some task and the system has the capability to impart the information or execute a transaction, most of the dialogue constitutes discourse types such as requests, questions,

Table 11.1. Agent non-verbal behaviour

Body part	Movement
Torso	move towards her monitor, message board or towards user
Head	move to the left or right, tilt to the left or right, nod
Eyes	blink, gaze, narrow
Eyebrows	raised, normal, frown
Mouth	lip synching, smile
Hands	rest on keyboard, type on keyboard, left hand point to message board, and open closed gesture, clasped at front, left hand move to ear

clarifications, confirmations and the giving of information. For each of these discourse types, gestures were derived from the gesture library.

Table 11.2 gives an example dialogue between agent and user and describes the gestures employed by the agent for each of the prompts. The first prompt is classified as a Request Beat, where the system requests that the user chooses from a number of options. For this prompt type, the agent employs hand beat gestures, (described by Cassell et al. (1994) as "small formless waves of the hand that occur with heavily emphasized words") when pointing at the message board synchronized with each option offered. For the direct question, the agent focuses on the user,

with a slight tilt of the head. The last prompt in Table 1.2 is classified as a Rheme (Halliday (1970)) because the system is giving new information to the user. The first part of the prompt is the thematic part which recalls the user's previous request; the second part of the prompt, the rhematic part, expresses the new information, and the agent highlights this by giving a slight nod of the head when she reads it out.

In the case of communication difficulties between the user and the application, Phoebe demonstrated non-verbal communicative strategies such as moving closer to the user and cupping her left ear with her hand in the case where the user does not respond and head tilting and frowning in the case of a rejection of the user's utterance. In addition, Phoebe exhibited a set of life-signs, such as breathing and blinking motions.

3.1   Experimental Procedure

A total of 48 participants took part in this study, balanced for gender and age group, (ages 18–35, 36–49 and 50+). Half of the participant cohort had used an automated telephone banking service before. As all interactions with both applications were by speech, participants in this study were not required to have had prior computer experience.

Table 11.2.   Example agent speech and gesture.

Interlocutor	Speech	Gesture
Phoebe	*"Please select Balance, Recent Transactions or another service."*	**Request Beat:** Torso and head is turned to message board, hand points to each option as spoken. (options displayed on dynamic message board)
User	"Balance please"	
Phoebe	*"Is that for your current account?"*	**Direct Q:** Head tilts to the side, raised eyebrows, right hand open
User	"Yes"	
Phoebe	*"The balance of your current account...*	**Theme:** Head turned towards computer monitor, hands on keyboard, typing
	...is 200 pounds"	**Rheme:** Turns and looks back to user, gives a slight nod of her head

A repeated measures design was used with all participants using both versions of the service, (telephone vs. Phoebe), balanced for order of presentation. Between-subject variables of order of experience, age group and gender were balanced across the sample.

In order to create a realistic experience, participants were given realistic 'customer' details to use in the research session. These included a 'customer' name, a membership number and a corresponding security number, which were used to pass the identification and verification stage of the dialogue. In addition, participants were given a task sheet containing relevant banking tasks: to find out their current account balance, and to transfer £200 into their account. The participants were asked to complete two tasks with the application so that they have enough time and experience with the application to form judgements about it.

Following the use of each application, participants were asked to complete a usability questionnaire, followed by a voice semantic differential questionnaire on their attitudes to the voice of the application agent. Once participants had tried both applications, participants then completed a structured verbal interview questionnaire, followed by a demographic and technographic questionnaire.

3.2   The Usability Questionnaire

Based on a definition of usability, (ISO (1998)), previous work by the authors (e.g. Love et al. (1992); Love et al. (1994); Love (1997); Foster at al. (1993)) has identified salient attributes of the perceived usability of interactive systems, and a usability questionnaire in Likert format has been constructed to measure these attributes.

The questionnaire covers the following attributes of conversational agent applications: *cognitive issues*, (level of concentration required by users, and how stressful the application was to use), the *fluency and transparency* of the application, (ease of use and degree of complication), *application performance*, (the efficiency of the application and users' preferences for a human agent), and issues relating to the *agent voice*, (politeness and clarity).

3.3   Results

The pooled mean attitude to the telephone service for all 20 items in the usability questionnaire was 4.99; the pooled mean attitude to the application with the ECA was 5.10, on a 7-point scale with a mid-point of 4. Although the difference was not significant, it suggests a slight preference for the banking service with the animated agent. Repeated measures ANOVAs were carried out over each of the 20 questionnaire items, taking into consideration the between subjects factors of order of experience, age, and gender.

Four items in the questionnaire showed main effects for attitudes towards the two services, pooled across all participants. A significant difference ($p<.02$) was found between the two services with regards to degree of complication: the telephone service had an overall mean score of 5.19 while the service with the ECA had an overall mean score of 5.65. The service with the ECA was therefore perceived to be less complicated to use than the telephone service. In addition, the service with the ECA was also found to be more enjoyable to use than the telephone service, with a mean score of 5.10 against 4.54. Although in this case the effect was not significant, this result does show a strong tendency in that direction. In contrast, in terms of the efficiency of the service, the telephone service scored significantly higher than the service with the ECA ($p<.03$).

The telephone service was rated slightly better in terms of knowing what to do than the service with the ECA. Although not a significant difference, results do indicate that with the telephone service, users felt they knew better what to do when compared with the service with the ECA. Note that the majority of participants in the study (69%) had used an automated telephone service prior to their participation in the experiment, whereas few participants (15%) had ever seen an embodied conversational agent before. Also, there was a tendency for the service with the ECA to be seen as more friendly. This suggests that social aspects of the interaction were enhanced when using the ECA.

When considering just the first use of each application, both degree of complication and enjoyment of use of service showed significant differences depending on the application. Participants in a between-subjects comparison rated the service with the ECA significantly less complicated to use than the telephone service, (with mean scores of 5.83 compared to 4.87), and found the service with the ECA to be significantly more enjoyable to use than the telephone service (mean scores of 5.46, compared to 4.58). These results follow the patterns shown for degree of complication and enjoyment of use across all participants in the pooled data analysis.

In addition to assessing the usability of each application, the voice was also assessed. A semantic differential questionnaire was used to gather the data on user perceptions of the voice of the agent in each application. In the semantic differential questionnaire, a 7-point scale was provided between two polar opposite adjectives (e.g., clear/unclear) or descriptive phrases.

A core set of twenty-two pairs of antonymous descriptions were used to cover the following attributes of the voice personality of the conversational agent: *voice quality* (friendliness and approachability), *excitement* attributes (reserve and assertion), *sincerity* issues (reliability and seriousness), *sophistication* traits (confidence and glamour), and *professional* traits, (efficiency and responsibility). In a similar way to the usability data, within and between subjects comparisons were made with respect to the voice personality of each agent.

The pooled mean attitude to the voice of the telephone service across all 22 items in the voice personality questionnaire was 5.00; the pooled mean attitude to the voice of the service with the ECA was 5.16. Although the difference was not significant, it does suggest a preference for the voice of the service with the ECA. The spoken dialogue for both services was exactly the same, and the same voice prompts were used for both the telephone and ECA versions of the service. The difference found here in attitudes to the voice may therefore be attributable to the different media.

Two of the individual questionnaire items showed significant differences between the perceived voices of the two services. Attitudes with regards to excitement showed a significant difference (p<.02), with the voice of the service using the ECA being rated as less boring than the voice of the telephone service. In addition, a difference was found for the degree of relaxation in the voices of the two services. The voice of the service with the ECA was perceived to be significantly more relaxed (p<.03) than the voice of the telephone service. Although only two of the items showed significant differences, many of the items in the questionnaire did indicate a preference for the voice of the service using the ECA over that of the telephone, as can be seen from figure 11.2 which takes the mean values for each of the categories within the voice personality questionnaire for both the telephone and the service with the ECA.

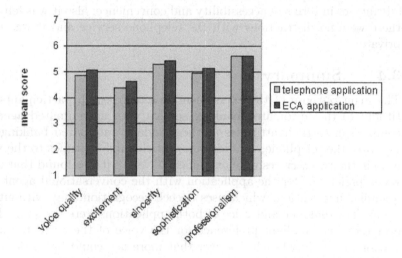

Figure 11.2. Overall voice attribute category means by application.

Despite this tendency, however, there were few if any clear cross-modal effects on the perception of the voice. Adding an ECA to the dialogue did not in itself change attitudes to the service voice.

3.3.1   Qualitative Results   Qualitative data were collected from the exit interview questionnaire, after participants had used both applications. When asked to say which service they preferred to use, 28 participants (58.3%) expressed a preference for the application with the ECA. Some participants found it easier to use. One participant stated that *"even though* [it was] *an animated agent, I felt as if I was really speaking to someone"*. A total of 17 participants (35.4%) preferred the telephone application. Some participants thought the telephone version was quicker to use, and found it more familiar. One participant expressed anxiety in the interaction with the ECA: *"Felt on the spot with the agent- felt I was being watched"*.

Some 40 of the 48 participants (83.3%) felt that the appearance of the agent was a good match for the voice. One participant stated that the agent looked *"pleasant and competent"*; however, another participant stated that they *"would have preferred her to look more real, rather than cartoon-like"*. Participants commented that the service with the ECA had the advantage of displaying visual information for the user, with the menu options; however, it was felt that more use could have been made of this to incorporate balance and transaction information visually. Participants commented that the telephone service had some advantages in terms of accessibility and convenience; also it was felt that there were no distractions with the telephone service and it was more private.

3.4   Summary

The main purpose of the experiment was to research participants' attitudes to the automated banking service with an animated agent in comparison to their attitudes to the standard automated banking service over the telephone. In addition, participants' attitudes to the voice used in the two services were examined. Overall, it was found that there was a preference for the application with the conversational agent over a similar application, which uses speech recognition, but without the agent. The dialogue and voice of both applications were the same, however there was a slight preference for the voice of the animated agent version. Participants felt however that more use could be made of the application in which the agent was used, particularly in exploiting the screen to display dialogue options and account information. This is clearly an issue meriting further research. Similarly, the application described above would be a convenient interface with which to investigate a more sophisticated use of non-verbal modalities.

4.   The Voice Personae Experiment

The second study was an extension of the work on evaluating voices in an eBanking application. The research aimed to assess the perceived personality of an agent from their way of speaking: exploring how the agent's verbal style has an effect on the perceived personality of the conversational agent. The work focused on three traits of helpfulness, carefulness and competence which are central to the effectiveness of eCommerce services employing ECAs. The work also extended to exploring the role of involving the user in the choice of ECA characteristics.

Sociolinguistic studies show that an individual's verbal style is affected by many different factors: gender, age, geographical place of childhood, social class, and relationship with interlocutor (Trudgill (2000)). Any utterance may be expressed in a number of different ways. Aspects of our background, characteristics and personality are evident in our speech, from lexical choice, grammatical structures and pronunciation, and can have an effect on how we are perceived by others. The aim in this study was to investigate how the personality of the agent was perceived depending on their verbal style.

Four different voice personae were created for an automated banking service with which the user could interact in order to perform simple banking tasks. The voice personae differed in terms of gender and formality. With two male and two female voice personae, one version of each gender was designed to be more casual (and younger); the other to be more formal (older). The dialogues were designed in order to suggest a casual male, a casual female, a formal male and a formal female agent, which were named as in Table 11.3.

Table 11.3. Four Voice Personalities.

	Male	Female
Casual Style	John	Kate
Formal Style	Mark	Emma

The linguistic repertoire detailed here assumes the existence of negative politeness and positive politeness as introduced by Brown and Levinson (1987) who state that negative politeness "is the heart of respect behaviour, just as positive politeness is the kernel of 'familiar' and 'joking' behaviour" (1987: 129). As such, the two casual personae were created to exhibit the *chummy* characteristics which assume that speaker and hearer are alike: "to imply common ground...to a limited extent even between strangers who perceive themselves, for the purposes of the interaction, as somehow similar." (p.103). Whereas, the two formal personae exhibit more elaborate and conventionalised linguistic strategies, such as the use of modifying clauses, which imply 'distance' between speaker and hearer.

Because this study focussed on the language and style of speaking of the agents, (not on their regional variety), a Southern British English accent was chosen for all four voices. Assessing the effect of regional varieties on the perception of agents could be an area of further research. Table 11.4 gives a brief overview of the distribution of linguistic features (Crystal (1997)) between the older and younger personae; examples of the personae dialogues follow.

Table 11.4. Linguistic features for formal and casual personae.

Feature	Formal personae	Casual personae
(i) Voice	Passive	Active
(ii) Modals	Conditional modals *(would, could)*	Non-conditional *(will, can)*
(iii) Speech style	Standard	Colloquial
(iv) Discourse markers	Standard *(actually, now, so)*	Standard + non standard *(like, you know)*
(v) Error level	Apologies	Alerts
(vi) Modifying clauses	If-clauses	None
(vii) Phonological	Careful enunciation	Assimilation, elision, glottal stops

Using the same eCommerce banking dialogue as in the previous study, dialogue prompts were tailored for each of the four voice personae, varying in style and language to suggest the different personality traits of the four voice presentations. The functionality of the banking service remained the same, however the four personae had their own distinct style of offering the service. Recordings of the prompts were made by one male and one female professional recording artists each with a Southern British English accent.

It was judged essential for the visual interface that some sort of iconic image was offered, implying embodiment of the agent. However, in order to avoid assessment of the voice personae being confounded by other visual aspects of the agent, the graphical representation of the agents was limited to a silhouetted head and shoulders image. In this way, the research was focussed on the assessment of the voice of the agent.

4.1 Voice Personae

The following describes some features of the language of each of the four voice personae.

4.1.1 John (casual male)

John's speech was characterised by direct questions using unconditional modal verbs as in the following example.

> *"So, what dyu want to do? Dyu want balance, recent transactions or another service?"*

As John displayed a more casual style of speaking, his speech included elision, as with many younger speakers in British English, his 't's were glottalised (so that the 't' in 'want' was realised by a stop at the glottis rather than a stop in the mouth ridge) which allowed for a quicker pace of speaking:

> *"Dyu wan-h another service?"*

4.1.2 Kate (casual female)

Kate's language was similar to that of John's with shorter, snappier prompts recorded in a breezy, upbeat style. Some verb phrases in Kate's dialogue were reduced by the removal of the auxiliary to produce a more informal, chatty style:

> *"The statement'll cost £3. You want one?"*

A warning strategy was adopted in Kate's dialogue to indicate a problem in recognition of the spoken input with a short hesitation before her prompt:

> *"Uh listen, I'm having a problem with this."*

In the recording of Kate's prompts, some glottalisation of her t's was also incorporated into her speech style, although in a more subtle form to that of John's.

4.1.3 Mark (formal male)

Mark's style of speaking was characterised by slower, more verbose prompts. His language was more formal, using conditional modals in dialogue prompt messages:

> *"Would you like to select another service?"*

In cases of a speech recognition problem, Mark used an explicitly overt style of language, with an apology strategy to introduce the difficulty:

> *"I'm afraid there is a problem confirming which service you would like."*

Mark's prompts were recorded with a well enunciated, more deliberate style which highlighted his more formal speech style.

4.1.4   Emma (formal female)   As with Mark, Emma's language followed a traditionally formal style. Emma also used conditional modal verbs, expressing explicit politeness to her customer:

> *"Please choose which service you would like."*

Emma, like Mark, adopted an apologetic strategy for indicating a problem to the customer, but with a more self-effacing attitude than Mark.

> *"I'm afraid I'm having a problem understanding which service you would like."*

In the recordings, the Emma prompts were read with a soft, calming voice, in comparison to the upbeat, chirpy and 'younger' Kate.

4.2   Experimental Procedure

The same approach was employed as was highlighted in the approach section, using the usability evaluation questionnaire as described in the last study. To explore the process of voice selection and change, participants were first asked to experience the standard voice banking service, which exhibited a neutral professional verbal style. Following this, they had the opportunity of changing the voice personality of the service. Participants were informed that they could opt for a new personality if they wished, but did not have to do so. They were given the chance to listen to excerpts of each of the personae dialogues, and then were able to choose one of the personae that they would interact with to accomplish some banking tasks. In other words, each participant experienced the standard service and either the same version again or their preferred new voice personae. Upon completion of the banking tasks, participants were asked to complete the usability questionnaire to assess their attitudes to the usability of the banking service with their chosen voice persona.

Further, in order to gather reasons for each participant's choice, a short questionnaire was designed to elicit reasons for the personality choice as well as participants' impressions of the personae they heard. The questionnaire included both open and closed questions regarding participants' perceptions and impressions of their chosen personality. In addition, adapted from the Five-factor model of personality, (neuroticism, extraversion, openness to experience, agreeableness, and conscientiousness), a series of cards was devised with descriptions to represent these traits, from which the user could choose in order to describe the voice personality with which they had interacted (Table 11.5).

The descriptive examples used in Table 11.5 are not an exhaustive list of traits which have been associated with this model of personality (Costa and McCrae (1995)). However, they were chosen as rele-

Table 11.5. Descriptive examples of personality categories.

Personality category	Descriptive examples
Openness	open-minded - narrow-minded unconventional - conventional
Conscientiousness	competent - incompetent careful - careless
Extraversion	cheerful - moody outgoing - reserved
Agreeableness	helpful - unhelpful easy-going - irritable modest - arrogant
Neuroticism	calm - agitated

vant for evaluation within the context of the eBanking application. Had the study been assessing voice personae across a number of application domains, for example in the assessment of social agents, it may have included some other traits which fall into these personality categories. Within the banking application, it was not possible to assess, for example, the trait 'talkative-quiet', since by design in the experiment, all the agents exhibited the same degree of talkativeness. This highlights the importance of designing any assessment within the context of the application under evaluation.

4.3 Results

A total of 100 participants took part in this study, balanced for gender and two age groups (ages 18–34 and 35+), though with a slight bias (60%) towards the younger age group.

A within-subject comparison was made between the standard banking service and the personalised banking service with respect to the voice persona chosen. Using paired-sample t-tests, certain items in the usability questionnaire were found to be significantly different between the standard service and the service with a different voice persona. Three of the voice personae (John, Kate and Mark) were found to be friendlier than the standard service. Further, participants felt that the banking service with John (casual male) was *too fast*, compared to the standard service. Participants who experienced the personalised banking service with Kate (casual female) were *less likely to prefer a human agent*, and thought the service was *more reliable* than the standard banking service. The increased attitude score for (non) preference for a human is particularly encouraging here. With respect to Emma (formal female), no individual items came out as being significantly different to those of the standard service; in terms of formality and speech style, the version using Emma was the most similar to the standard service.

Overall attitude scores increased for the personalised versions of the banking service in comparison to the standard banking service, and certain individual attributes were significant for the different. However, no single voice persona emerged as a dominant winner. Participants were given a free choice of which persona to choose, and with that choice they could make a comparison with the standard service which they had tried. Table 11.6 gives a breakdown of persona chosen against participant age and gender.

Table 11.6.   Distribution of personae chosen by participant demographic.

	John (casual male)	Kate (casual female)	Mark (formal male)	Emma (formal female)	No choice made
Male 18–34	25%	17.5%	10.5%	12.5%	35.5%
Female 18–34	25%	23.5%	9.5%	15.5%	26.5%
Male 35+	9.5%	16.5%	7%	28.5%	38%
Female 35+	8%	2.5%	16%	26.5%	47.5%
Total	18.5%	16.5%	10.5%	19.5%	35%

As can be seen from the above table, younger participants in the study had a stronger preference for choosing the younger voice personae of both genders; whereas, the older participants had a preference for choosing the formal female persona.

Participants expressed their opinions on the voice personae. Each of the personae scored highly in terms of helpfulness. The casual male voice persona, John was perceived as being easy going, cheerful and outgoing, but also unconventional and a little arrogant; the casual female voice persona, Kate, was perceived as being cheerful, outgoing and competent; both the formal personae, Mark and Emma, were perceived as being calm, careful and competent. In addition, Emma was thought to be modest and conventional. Figure 11.3 highlights the differences found between the four personae over three pooled attributes which were considered to be applicable to the banking context.

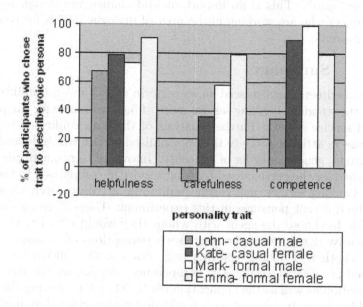

Figure 11.3. Comparison of personality traits for four personae

4.3.1 Qualitative Results In the verbal interview, qualitative data was collected on the personae and the appropriateness of their language and style in a banking application. Asked what type of person they thought John (casual male) was, one participant commented *"young, confident, knows what he's talking about"*, while another stated that he *"didn't sound professional"*. Of the participants who chose John to interact with, 71% thought his language and style of speaking was too casual for a banking application. With Kate (casual female), one participant stated that they thought she was *"smart, young, out going, friendly"*, while another stated that she *"sounds as if she is in a hurry"*; 57% of participants who experienced the service with Kate found her style of speaking to be about right for a banking application; although 43% found it too casual for the banking application. Both the Mark and Emma applications, with their more formal speech styles, were found to be appropriate for a banking application in terms of language and style of speaking.

Interestingly, many participants commented that the conversations they had with the personae felt natural and almost humanlike, although one participant stated that *"the closer the voice comes to the human norm then the more distressing it is when the voice says it doesn't un-*

derstand you". This is an important and challenging design issue for developers who are working in the area of dialogue design for conversational agents.

4.4   Summary

The experiment data showed an increase in overall mean usability score from the standard banking service score of 5.45 to a score for the personalised service of 5.61. Further analysis of the data confirmed that this increase in attitude score to the personalised service was independent of age group, gender or order of exposure. In overall terms, attitude scores increased for the personalised banking service in comparison to the standard banking service, and certain individual attributes were significant for the different personae in this experiment. Users were also keen to be able to choose the agent with whom they would interact; moreover, qualitative data showed that one user's perceptions of an agent differed from another. Previous research (e.g. Nass et al. (2000)) found that desired personality traits (e.g. competence) depend on the user of the application as well as the application itself. Therefore, having the choice of which agent to interact with could be an important design issue for developers.

The difference in linguistic style is only one factor which could affect the perceptions of the agent. Therefore it is important to be able to define a particular agent in terms of their voice, lexical choice, linguistic variation, and possibly regional variety, to coincide with choices made to the agent's gender, perceived age, style of dressing, movement, and emotional displays.

Further research in the mapping of voice personae to the appearance, movement and gestures of embodied agents is required in order to generalise which agent type would be best for the application. In addition, it would be necessary to detail which of the above traits would be optimal for an eCommerce banking agent to have.

5.   The Trust Experiment

The third study discussed here evaluated added features in the interface for the improvement of agent trustworthiness. This study assessed the introduction of text input and text output in eCommerce interfaces in combination with speech input and speech output as mechanisms to increase user confidence and infer a greater degree of trustworthiness when users must disclose financial information. Bickmore and Cassell (2000) demonstrated that users are initially reluctant to disclose personal and financial information to an agent but that by establishing a social relationship with a conversational agent users can become more engaged in a trusting relationship which then leads to a more successful interaction. On the other hand, Van Mulken et al. (1999) found that anthropomorphising an interface with lifelike agents was not sufficient in itself to maintain trust and confidence in the interface. This important finding suggests that it is this maintenance of a consistent level of trust that may encourage further interactions and provide users with an environment in which they can confidently disclose information. This section introduces mechanisms that may thus maintain, arouse, and improve user's confidence, improving perceived trustworthiness of ECA and the applications in which they appear.

The experiment aimed to investigate the effects of text output to examine if the user is assisted during the conversation with an ECA when the agent uses text output. In addition, the user was given the option of entering details with the keyboard instead of through speech. It was considered that this could improve user confidence in the system from two perspectives. Firstly, from a security and privacy perspective by not vocalising the information users may have more confidence in the system. Secondly, in the event of users not being confident with the system's speech recognition capabilities, text entry may be preferred. To provide a medium in which trust can be examined, two applications were selected: a virtual cinema box-office and a virtual banking application as seen in the Phoebe experiment. Participants interacted with ECA's who were dressed casually in the cinema application and formally in the banking application (McBreen et al. (2001)) and were asked to complete questionnaires after they experienced the various interface conditions in both applications.

Text input and text output facilities were added to the interfaces of both applications. In total four experiment conditions were created:

1 Speech Input; Speech Output

2 Speech and Text Input; Speech Output

3 Speech Input; Speech and Text Output

4 Speech and Text Input; Speech and Text Output

The experiment platform was set up so that users could speak to the ECA's and their speech output was captured and processed using a speech recogniser. Participants were informed that when completing application tasks with the agent, they would sometimes have the option to type the required task information, instead of entering the details via speech. When this condition was available, the user had the choice of when to use speech input and when to use text input. To capture the text input a command line appeared in the interface. A text recognition function, activated by the dialogue manager, recognised keywords relevant to each task. This text function permitted the participants to type entire sentences or just the keywords. It also was capable of recognising numbers in the form of digits. Participants also had the opportunity to enter security number details using their mouse via a virtual number pad, which appeared on the desk in the retail environment. In the virtual world, a computer monitor appeared on the assistant's desk and this was normally facing the agent. For the text output condition, this monitor was rotated so that the user could see the screen and the details of the information they had entered. As the conversation progressed more of the data input appeared on the screen, (see Figure 11.4).

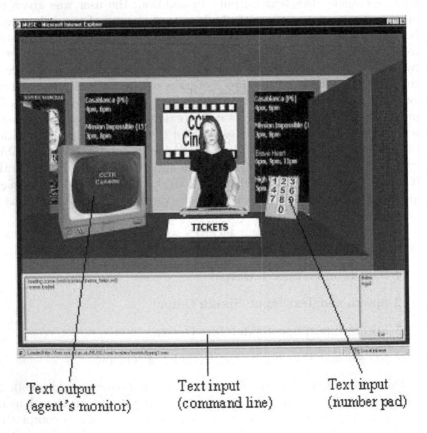

Text output
(agent's monitor)

Text input
(command line)

Text input
(number pad)

Figure 11.4.   Agent in cinema application: text input and output options

5.1   Experimental Procedure

A total of 48 participants balanced for age and gender took part in the experiment. For this experiment, it was essential that, as a recruitment requirement, research participants had prior experience of using computers, as they would have the opportunity to use the mouse or keyboard at points during the interactions. Participants received priming regarding the application they were to use, including tasks which they were asked to accomplish. Directly before experiencing each experiment condition, participants were reminded about the features of the interface, e.g. that they had the option to use the keyboard and number pad or that they would see the assistant's computer screen.

In this repeated measures design the presentation of the experiment conditions to the participants was randomised across applications and the presentation of the two applications was balanced amongst the participants. After the participants experienced each experiment condition they were asked to complete a questionnaire (7-point Likert attitude questionnaire statements) relating to the agent and the application. Based on research by McKnight and Chervany (1996), questionnaire items were chosen to provide indications of user trust in the role of the ECA within the interface: reliability, confidence, dependability, competence, goodness and shared understanding. When participants had experienced all four conditions in both applications they took part in an interview designed to elicit further information about the agents, which also gave participants the opportunity to make suggestions for improvements to the system.

5.2   Results

Participants felt that both the cinema and banking applications were equally efficient and useful, and that they were equally confident using either application. Significant differences emerged due to users' attitudes toward the reliability of the applications, and the cinema application was thought to be more reliable than the banking application (mean cinema = 5.05, mean bank = 4.68). A marginally significant interaction between participant age and application also emerged and a post hoc t-test showed participants in the younger age group (18–35) felt that the cinema application was significantly more reliable than the banking application.

It was found that for most of the usability attributes, the mean scores for experiment conditions favoured interfaces that included text output. In addition, t-tests showed that interfaces with both text input and text output were thought to be a significantly better idea than those with text input alone, p<0.01. There was also a preference for the cinema application with respect to the participant's perceived level of control (mean cinema = 4.92, mean bank = 4.60). The qualitative results will show that the cinema application was preferred because many participants were uncomfortable with the notion of divulging financial information to an animated agent, regardless of the fact that in many cases they had the opportunity to enter more crucial information using the keyboard as opposed to speech entry.

5.2.1   Attitude to Agents   The second set of quantitative data addressed participants' attitudes toward various aspects of trustworthiness with respect to the embodied agents who appeared as assistants in the application environments. Figures 11.5 and 11.6 below illustrate the pattern of results for the agents with respect to application and experiment condition.

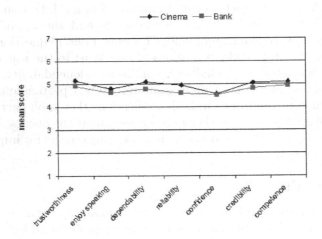

Figure 11.5. Usability Attributes for Agents by Application.

A difference in trust might be anticipated, which would typically apply to a real world agent providing a frivolous service like selling cinema tickets and one providing a serious service like a bank transfer. Interestingly, this has not been bourn out in these data for ECAs in the role as a component in a user interface.

As can be seen from Figure 11.6, participants rated the agent in the cinema application higher across all attributes than the banking agent. With respect to experiment condition (Figure 11.6), a significant effect emerged for the usability attribute 'confidence', and post-hoc t-

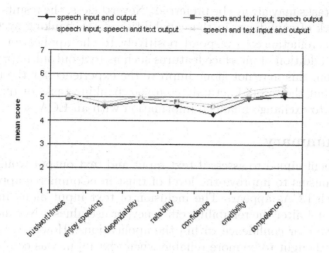

Figure 11.6. Usability Attributes for Agents by Experiment Condition.

tests showed that participants significantly felt more *confident* that the agents understood them when text output also appeared in the interface. Similarly, there was a significant effect with 'credibility' for experiment condition and post hoc t-tests showed that the agents in the interfaces that displayed text output were thought to be significantly more *credible* than the agents in the interfaces where text output was not visible. In addition, an effect emerged indicating that agents in the interfaces which displayed text output scored significantly higher in terms of *competence* than those without text output and these agents were perceived as being more competent.

5.2.2   Qualitative Results   Participants had the opportunity to express their application preference and were encouraged to give reasons for their choice. The results show that the role of the ECA in the cinema application was preferred to the role of the ECA in the banking application. These qualitative results augment the quantitative results already reported and the results can be neatly summed up by quoting one of the participants, who stated that *"Although the experiences were similar, I preferred the cinema because it was a more entertaining service and was more enjoyable than the bank, but this is the difference between the nature of the services and I prefer to do more entertaining things"*. The results suggest that no matter what additional features are added to the interface, as long as they improve the interaction for the user, more entertaining tasks may always be preferred. Nevertheless, the results also indicate a lack of confidence in the capabilities of the banking system, resulting in a reluctance to respond positively to the application and although the addition of interface features such as text output improved the interaction, this may not alone improve the experience for the user, so much so that they would actually complete banking tasks or display a willingness to exchange financial information with an ECA.

5.3   Summary

This experiment aimed to assess if text input and text output would be useful mechanisms to improve the level of trust in eCommerce applications in which ECAs appear. The inclusion of text input alone in the interface did not alter the reliability, efficiency, or usefulness. Nor indeed did it improve user confidence within the applications. However, applications were thought to be more reliable when text input was combined with text output. Combining text input and text output was judged to be an improvement for the applications. Moreover, although text input alone did not improve user confidence, when text input was offered with text output the improvement in user confidence in the application was significant. The participant cohort also felt that the ECAs themselves were more credible and competent when the interface combined text input and text output together with speech input and speech output.

The results favoured the ECA in the cinema application, who was thought to be significantly more trustworthy, dependable, reliable, and credible than the ECA in the banking application. Independent of application however, the addition of text output did improve other aspects of the perception of the agent. Users felt significantly more confident that the ECA understood them better when the interface had text output and the presence of the information in the interface reassured the user that the information was correct. In addition, the ECA was also thought to be more credible and competent when the interface had text output, with or without text input. Although there was no significant difference with respect to trustworthiness itself, the associated attributes of confidence, credibility and competence were significantly improved by the presence of text output.

The evaluation has shown that including text output in the interface can generate greater agent credibility, competence and confidence of understanding although these alone are not sufficient to create a more trusting environment for users to disclose financial information. Trust remains difficult to establish and maintain especially in ECA banking applications. However, it is known that trust can be established through displays of competence, and the results of this evaluation show that text output in the interface produces greater competence, making it possible to infer that text output in ECA interfaces may be at least a factor in improving user trust in banking applications.

6. Conclusion

It is important for the developer of embodied conversational agents to have available a means of assessing agents within the environment or application for which they are intended, using an approach that combines experimental control with realistic use. The research reported in this chapter illustrates three different eCommerce applications in which ECAs were employed. Much of the evaluation of the conversational agents concentrated on the usability of the application, when the user is interacting through speech technology with the agent. In addition, this chapter described research conducted to assess the perceived trustworthiness of an agent in two eCommerce environments when varying text input and output functionalities are employed. Further, methods of assessing the voice of agents, which can be seen to be a tangible realisation of the agent's personality, were addressed.

In this work, a usability assessment approach, which merges experimental rigour with task realism, has been shown to be a valid approach to assessing the roles of ECAs in eCommerce applications. The data presented in this paper confirm:

- Users prefer applications in which the agent acts as a conversational partner compared with a non-visual telephone application using speech recognition.

- Users clearly appreciate the opportunity to personalise the ECAs involved in eCommerce services in the dimension of selection of voice.

- Extending the role of the ECA to allow text modalities boosts user confidence in the eCommerce applications. These were judged to be more reliable when text input was coupled with text output.

- Users feel significantly more confident that the ECA has understood them when the interface used text output.

- Data in this paper confirm the positive role of ECAs in interfaces and the benefits to that role of adding other modalities such as text output.

References

Bersen, N., Dybkjær, H., and Dybkjær, L. (1998). *Designing Interactive Speech Systems: From First Ideas to User Testing*. Berlin, Springer-Verlag.

Bickmore, T. and Cassell, J. (2000). How about this weather? Social Dialogue with Embodied Conversational Agents. In *Proceedings of Socially Intelligent Agents: the Human in the Loop*, AAAI Fall Symposium, pp. 4–9. North Falmouth, MA, USA

Brown, P. and Levinson, S.C. (1987). *Politeness: Some Universals in Language Usage*. Cambridge, Cambridge University Press.

Cassell, J., Stone, M., Douville, B., Prevost, S., Achorn, B., Steedman, M., Badler, N., and Pelachaud, C. (1994). Modeling the Interaction between Speech and Gesture. In Ram, A. and Eiselt, K., editors, *Proceedings of the Sixteenth Annual Conference of the Cognitive Science Society*, pp. 153–158, Georgia, Atlanta, Lawrence Erlbaum Associates.

Coolican, H. (1994). *Research Methods and Statistics in Psychology*, Hodder and Stoughton, London.

Costa, P.T. and McCrae, R.R. (1995). *NEO Personality Inventory-Revised: Professional Manual*, Psychological Assessment Resources, Florida.

Crystal, D. (1997). *A Dictionary of Linguistics and Phonetics*, Blackwell, Oxford.

Dix, A.J., Finlay, J.E., Abowd, G.D., and Beale, R. (1993). *Human-Computer Interaction*, Pearson Education Limited, Essex.

Foster, J.C., Dutton, R.T., Jack, M.A., Love, S., Nairn, I.A., Vergeynst, N.A., and Stentiford, F.W.M. (1993). Intelligent dialogues in automated telephone services. In Baber, C. and Noyes, J.M., editors, *Interactive Speech Technology: Human Factors Issues in the Application of Speech Input/Output to Computer*, pp. 167–175, Taylor and Francis, London.

Halliday, M.A.K. (1970). Language Structure and Language Function. In Lyons, J., editor, *New horizons in Linguistics*, pp. 140-165, Penguin, Aylesbury.

ISO International Standardisation Organisation (1998). ISO-9241: Ergonomic requirements for office work with visual display terminals (VDTs). Part 11: Guidance on usability.

Likert, R. (1932). Technique for the Measurement of Attitudes. *Archives of Psychology*, 140: 5–53.

Love, S. (1997). *The Role of Individual Differences in Dialogue Engineering for Automated Telephone Services*, University of Edinburgh, PhD thesis.

Love, S., Dutton, R.T., Foster, J.C., Jack, M.A., Nairn, I.A., Vergeynst, N.A., and Stentiford, F.W.M. (1992). Towards a usability measure for automated telephone services. In *Proceedings of Institute of Acoustics Speech and Hearing Workshop*, vol.14(6): 553–559. Bowness-on-Windermere, UK.

Love, S., Dutton, R.T., Foster, J.C., Jack, M.A., and Stentiford, F.W.M. (1994). Identifying salient usability attributes for automated telephone services. In *Proceedings of International Conference on Spoken Language Processing*, pp. 1307–1310. Yokohama, Japan.

McBreen, H.M., Anderson, J.N., and Jack, M.A. (2001). Evaluating 3D Embodied Conversational Agents in Contrasting VRML Retail Applications. In *Proceedings of Autonomous Agents 2001 Workshop: Multimodal Communication and Context in Embodied Agents*, pp. 83–87. Montreal, Canada.

McGurk, H., and MacDonald, J. (1976) Hearing lips and seeing voices. *Nature*, 264: 746–748.

McKnight, H. and Chervany, N. (1996). *The Meaning in Trust*, Working paper 96-04, Carlson School of Management, University of Minnesota, MN.

Nass, C., Isbister, K., and Lee, E.J. (2000). Truth Is Beauty: Researching Embodied Conversational Agents. In Cassell, J., Sullivan, J., Prevost, S., and Churchill, E., editors, *Embodied Conversational Agents*, pp. 374–401, MIT Press, Cambridge, Ma.

Trudgill, P. (2000). *Sociolinguistics*, Penguin, Harmondsworth.

Van Mulken, S., André, E., and Müller, J. (1999). An empirical Study on the Trustworthiness of Lifelike interface Agents. In Bullinger, H.J. and Ziegler, J., editors, *Proceedings of HCI International 1999: Human Computer Interaction: Communication, Cooperation and Application Design*, pp. 152–156, Munich, Germany.

Chapter 12

WHAT WE CAN LEARN FROM AVATAR-DRIVEN INTERNET COMMUNITIES

Case Studies on Two Commercial Applications

Brigitte Krenn, Barbara Neumayr, Christoph Schmotzer,
and Martine Grice

> *Hiro's not actually here at all. He's in a computer-generated universe that his computer is drawing onto his goggles and pumping into his earphones. In the lingo, this imaginary place is known as the Metaverse. Hiro spends a lot of time in the Metaverse.*
>
> —Stephenson, Snow Crash

Abstract   In this chapter we describe a commercial platform for the development of net environments, virtual spaces inhabited by avatars which have been created and are subsequently visited and instructed by users via the Internet. The platform allows extensive data collection. Which data are collected and the scope of analysis will be explained on a theoretical level and by examples from data sets gathered from different applications.

Keywords: Evaluation methodology, case studies, avatar, Internet community, human-like agent, user modelling, virtual characters.

Z. Ruttkay and C. Pelachaud (eds.), From Brows to Trust, 323–352.
© *2004 Kluwer Academic Publishers. Printed in the Netherlands.*

1.   Introduction

In this chapter we focus on case studies using data collected from commercial (multi-user) community applications on the Internet where the users are represented by avatars. These applications are, on the one hand, fun and constitute entertainment for the users. On the other hand, they help sponsors to better get to know the interests and preferences of the users attracted by a certain community. The avatars are instrumental for both goals. As a side-effect, the analysis of usage of these applications provide information about the users who like this type of application.

In particular, we describe a platform, called sysis NetLife, and two of its applications, Flirtboat and derSpittelberg, which provided data for our case studies. The case studies cover a development and operation time-frame of about 2.5 years. During this period the analysis of the collected data was used to develop a classification scheme for data collection. The final classification scheme, as described in section 3.3, is backed up by 16 launches of 7 different applications in various countries. Flirtboat, for instance, has been customized for the Austrian, the UK and the Croatian market. Sample applications can be found under the sysis web site[1]. A discussion of language and culture-specific customization of Flirtboat is presented in Krenn et al. (to appear).

With sysis NetLife, we present an approach to applications featuring virtual characters where the character is an integral part of the system and not an added extra to the interface, which has typically been the case in the (commercial) use of virtual characters on the web. See, for instance, the broadcasters Ananova[2] and Chase Walker[3],

characters interfaced with a text-to-speech system so that they can read out news to the user. Another example are classical chatterbots such as Cybelle[4] which pretend to communicate with the user.

In sysis NetLife, the avatar is a vehicle for gathering data over a period of time. The applications typically have a runtime of three months. From the different launches of Flirtboat we have learned that the individual user on average logs onto the system on 33 days, and visits her avatar 34 times. In the present study, we employ the data to assess the patterns of usage, as well as the characteristics, preferences and attitudes attributed by the users to their avatar representatives. Such data only become available when the user is closely interconnected with the system via the avatar and returns to the application over a longer period of time. The assumption that long-term users do consider their avatar as their alter-ego is also of considerable benefit to the operator or sponsors of the system, as the system can be used as a tool for online market studies. However, a word of caution is in order. It must be understood that the personal data accessible through NetLife applications cannot be sufficiently checked for their substance. People may or may not be sincere as regards their personal data such as age, gender, and so forth. What can be done, however, is to increase the incentive for users to be sincere, or to find a metaphor which fosters the identification of the user with the application and thus reinforces the tendency of the user to be sincere. In sysis NetLife applications, the avatar metaphor is used as a means of increasing identification of the user with the system. How far this assumption is valid cannot fully be answered, but there is evidence from informal feedback, and from a survey on user satisfaction based on the first launch of Flirtboat in Austria that users tend to perceive the avatar to be their virtual representative. To fully answer this question, however, a series of qualitative experiments would be required; this is clearly outside the scope of the work presented in this chapter.

A further advantage of data collection via NetLife is that it provides access to a large group of users and at the same time makes it possible to focus on a specific target group via the theme and scenario of the particular application. Thus, major questions addressed in this chapter are: Which system functionalities are useful, how avatar/user profiles can be established and what types of data can be collected. In this respect, our work considerably differs from other work on the evaluation of applications with animated characters, such as the one described in Chapter 11 by Morton et al. The reader must also keep in mind that data collection in NetLife originated from a clearly commercial perspective of market analysis. And even though one of the intentions of NetLife is to evoke an affective relationship between user and application via the avatar, the kind of data collected do not allow for an assessment of the human-avatar relationship. In our approach, the user and the avatar merge. Nevertheless, NetLife applications are a useful means for quantitative studies on user behaviour in avatar-driven, targeted web communities.

In sysis NetLife, virtual characters are referred to both as *avatars* and *agents*. The characters are avatars, because they represent the users who initially define and subsequently refine them. Apart from that, the virtual characters act autonomously like agents, driven by application-specific needs and desires. The platform has been developed by sysis from scratch, and the different applications have been built on the basis of this platform.

NetLife applications offer different types and qualities of data. Summing up, we have large amounts of data of various types, data from long term usage of NetLife applications (the runtime of a commercial

application is typically 3 months), data from Internet users under real
world conditions (as opposed to laboratory experiments), data from different applications (Flirtboat and derSpittelberg), data from launches
of an application in different countries (launches of Flirtboat in Austria,
Croatia and the UK), data on usage and activity (see section 4.1.1),
data on user generated content (see section 4.1.2), data on avatar characteristics as they have been attributed to avatars by their users (see
sections 4.1.3 and 4.1.4), and, last but not least, avatar mediated data
on user preferences and attitudes (see section 4.1.6). Note that all data
analysis is made on a quantitative basis. Nevertheless, especially the
user generated content calls for qualitative analysis, which is a topic of
future research.

Section 2 describes the NetLife platform and its applications, Flirtboat and derSpittelberg. Section 3 discusses data collection methods
and strategies. Section 4 explains our evaluation strategies and presents
evaluation results. It should be noted that in a commercial context it
is not possible to disclose all data. We can therefore only show samples of the data analyses and where necessary they have been further
generalised.

2.   The sysis NetLife

In this section, we first describe the platform on which the applications,
Flirtboat and derSpittelberg, are based. We then present the specific
characteristics of the respective applications.

2.1   The NetLife Platform

Sysis has developed the NetLife platform which serves as the basis for a
special kind of web community, which is avatar driven and focussed on
bringing users together under different metaphors of community. The
users are represented by avatars which are situated in a virtual world,
engage in social relations (in Flirtboat and derSpittelberg making friends
with others) and fulfil specific tasks depending on what is required of
them in a given application. The user is able to design her avatar with
respect to its graphical representation by choosing from a number of
predefined characters. In Flirtboat, for instance, the user may select
from 16 female and 16 male characters which differ in hair style, hair
and skin colour, and the way they dress. The user also defines her avatar
with respect to its socio-demographic coordinates age and gender, and
its personality traits and interests.

Once the avatars have been created by the user, they act autonomously. Driven by the needs built into the system, the agents search

their habitat for friends, food and drink, or sleep. The most urgent need will always be fulfilled first. The model output, i.e., the activities of an agent, the friends it has met and what has happened during such a meeting is represented in the form of template generated stories. In other words, the stories are written representations of the simulation parameters relevant in a certain application at a certain time. The presentation is supported by graphical representations in the form of still pictures showing the avatar in an application-typical environment. The user gives constant input to the system by choosing to look at particular stories, booking events, answering questions to refine the avatar's (or indirectly the user's own) profile, writing e-mail to the avatars of other users, or chatting. All input is by mouse and keyboard. The application runs 24 hours a day, 7 days a week. The application works asynchronously. This means that the avatar does not react immediately or directly to the user input, but the input of the user influences how the avatar proceeds in the community. The user can always access the stories representing the past life of the avatar in the community. All past model output is accessible for 35 days.

Apart from the user's own agent, there are also so-called *system avatars*, which are — as might be guessed — system driven and have been developed for two reasons: First, they are an important means for the designers to give more atmosphere to the application and transport the respective community metaphor. In Flirtboat, for instance, a typical system avatar is the playboy on board who approaches the user avatars and gives them flirt tips. Second, system avatars have been designed to pose questions about user preferences and attitudes. Thus they are one of the vehicles that allow longterm collection of user responses. In the commercial applications, they are used for market studies.

Other important features of the platform are the means offered for direct communication between users, like internal mail system, chat, nickpage and guestbook. The usage of e-mail and chat will be addressed in section 4.1.2.

2.2   The Flirtboat Application

Flirtboat is an application where avatars meet on behalf of the users on board a cruise liner with the aim of finding partners to flirt with, perhaps even of finding the optimal partner. With this aim in mind the avatars move around the virtual Flirtboat, meeting and assessing other avatars, making friends and reporting their experiences back to the user whose objective is to help the avatar to become popular. Based on Flirtboat, we give a short overview of the most important characteristics of a NetLife application from a user's perspective. In particular, we describe the steps a user typically takes through the application.

As a first step, the user creates her own avatar — which is conceived as a virtual representation of the user's self — by answering a number of questions about sociographic aspects and personality traits. Based on the user answers, the model generates an individual profile for each avatar which also contains the user's choice of appearance for the avatar.

The avatar profile can be refined throughout the runtime of the application as the user answers additional questions about the avatar's preferences and way of thinking.

A personality related question might for example be:

> Got up late, missed the bus, left my shoes at home. Do I go berserk or do I keep calm?

This particular question is aimed at the thinking versus feeling dimension of a Jungian type personality classification. (See Section 3.3.4.0 "Personality" for more details.) Selection of the answer "I go berserk" is considered to belong to the feeling type whereas the answer "I stay calm" indicates the thinking type.

After creation of the avatar, when the user enters the community for the first time, she is shown an animated sequence where a helicopter takes the avatar to the Flirtboat. The user can now access all functionalities of the simulation, or in other words all areas of the avatar's life on the boat. The user might first look into her diary, where she will find a report on the arrival and first impressions the avatar has gained. In the course of the game the diary will be the central area of communication with the avatar, because it is the means of access to the stories where the avatar reports back to the user what has happened to her/him while the user was off-line. As part of these stories the user is asked to decide on the next steps such as arrange a meeting with another avatar, send e-mail to another avatar, select a certain action the avatar should take during the next meeting/date with another avatar. It is also possible to cancel previously arranged dates. When the user logs in the system the next time, she is informed by her avatar what has happened during the previous meetings/dates. All information is presented in a setting as shown in Figure 12.1. In the middle of the screen, the avatar representing the user is shown at the location of a previous date. The current picture refers to a meeting at the 'Largo Amore pool'. The text underneath is a monologue of the avatar summarizing what has happened during the date. To be able to customize the wording and style of text to the particular application and the envisaged target user group, we employ a template-based approach to generation. The text in our Figure 12.1 reads:

Hi!
Imagine what happened! popeye_3rd and I had our second date at the
Largo Amore pool. That's someone I wouldn't push off the edge of my
bed! I invited popeye_3rd to another date on 28.06. at 19hrs with all
my charm. We're going to have a game of pool. Bye bye lonely hearts
club!
What shall I do?

When the user clicks on the "What shall I do?" link, she is asked to
select an action from a list of actions the avatar may instigate at the
upcoming date. The user's choice influences the avatar behaviour at the
date, which in turn influences the state of the avatar named popeye_3rd.

The middle frame at the left of the screen shot represents the avatar
diary (see "My Travel Diary"). Via the links in the lower left frame the
user can access pictures and stories representing past dates of the avatar.

The right upper frame provides access to "Pick-up Pete's Flirting
Tips". Pick-up Pete is the playboy system avatar in the UK version of
Flirtboat. For a country-specific customization of the playboy/playgirl
type in Flirtboat see Krenn et al. (to appear).

Figure 12.1. The user interface of Flirtboat.

In NetLife applications there are usually more system avatars which
try to talk to the user and tell her the latest gossip or ask questions

about her attitudes or preferences. An example is the Reverend on the
Flirtboat. One of his question is:

> God bless you, my child! I've just spoken to Father Gregory. He's at
> home looking after the poor and deprived people on the streets. It's not
> an easy job. Have you ever helped out those in need or do you think
> the authorities are dealing with the problem well enough?

Potential answers are: "I pay my rates" or "I like to help". The question
is targeted at assessing the social orientation of the user.

As an incentive for answering questions posed by the system, the users
are awarded points for each question they answer. The top ten avatars
which have acquired the highest number of points during one week are
presented to the community as 'champion flirts'.

Another important area of activity is the avatar profile which is derived from the information given during registration and can be updated
throughout the duration of participation. As this profile is presented to
the other users in the form of an individual profile page (called *nickpage*).
Apart from the data given during registration, except for personal data
(such as real name, postal address and e-mail of the user, etc.) which
of course are not made available, the profile contains user generated
content such as, in the case of Flirtboat, a description of the partner
of one's dreams, and any photograph the user might choose to upload.
The nickpage is accessible via the right bottom frame ('Flirting Style').

Flirtboat was first launched in Austria in November 2000 via
jet2web.at which is the Internet affiliate of the Telekom Austria. After two re-launches Flirtboat is still running in Austria at the time of
writing and currently has 17 150 registered users.[5] Localised versions of
Flirtboat were running in the UK (06/2001 – 03/2003) and in Croatia
(12/2001 – 03/2002). In the UK, Flirtboat was hosted on iCircle which is
the woman's portal of Freeserve, by that time the largest Internet portal
in the UK. Freeserve is a subsidiary of Wanadoo. In Croatia, Flirtboat
was launched via VIPnet which is a subsidiary of the Mobilkom Austria.

2.3   The derSpittelberg Application

derSpittelberg has been developed in cooperation with an Austrian newspaper and was targeted at a young urban audience, for whom the context
of flat sharing and student life is appealing. The newspaper is positioned
in the high income, high education consumer segment, and wanted to
offer an online community to its younger readers.

Thus this particular application is set within the context of student
life with locations like the flat shared with other students, the library
or the cafeteria of the university and locations for going out such as the
cinema or the dance club.

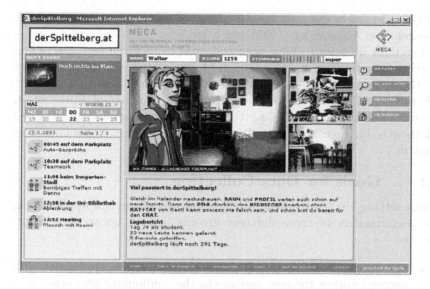

Figure 12.2. The user interface of derSpittelberg.

A particular sociocultural context is set through reference to the Spittelberg area of Vienna. As is the case with all sysis NetLife applications, the whole front end, especially the verbal and graphical representation of the setting was carefully designed for the target group. See Figure 12.2 for an example of the user interface of derSpittelberg.

In our study, derSpittelberg serves as an example for a market analysis based on lifestyle clusters which have been developed especially for sysis NetLife. The application was launched in May 2002 via the online version of the newspaper. It was conceived to run as a sponsor financed campaign with a previously fixed end, and had 4 500 users within three months. 12 sponsors took part in this project. The application also serves as the basis for one of the demonstrators developed in the European research project Neca[6]. Here we have exchanged the presentation of avatars using still pictures, with movies of animated agents interacting with each other. At the time of writing, user studies are underway to evaluate the appropriateness of the communicative behaviour expressed by the animated agents.

3. User Data Analysis

In the following we will describe the general patterns of data types and data collection we have extracted from sysis NetLife applications. According to the basically commercial setting, initial data collection and analysis did follow the principles of empirical social research and market research (see Atteslander (1995) and Friedrichs (1990)).

The data we refer to have been collected from three launches of the Flirtboat application and one launch of derSpittelberg. In the case of Flirtboat, we refer to three subsequent Austrian launches (if not stated otherwise AUT Flirtboat refers to the second launch of Flirtboat in Austria), one UK launch (UK Flirtboat), and one Croatian launch (CRO Flirtboat). In the case of derSpittelberg, we refer to a single launch in Austria.

3.1   Goals for Data Collection

When setting the goals for data collection in commercial applications, the requirements of three different groups had to be accounted for, namely:

- the *user*, who wants to find entertainment in the application and access to other Internet surfers via the community platform.

- the *operator*, who needs to improve customer retention on her site and/or wants to know her customers better.

- the *system developer*, who needs to prove that the platform is accepted well by the users and supports the operator in achieving her goals.

Thus the motivation to collect certain data partially differs and partially overlaps for the three user groups.

Functionality of the operational core is relevant for all three user groups. Its assessment includes data such as which avatars have met in the application, what has happened in the meetings, what are the personality traits and interests of the individual users/avatars.

Commercial evaluation, for obvious reasons, is desirable for both the operator and the designer, in order to be able to evaluate the performance of an application. In NetLife applications this refers to questions on how many users registered, how often users visit the application, etc.

Commercial benefit is of clear interest to the operator. In the early stages of NetLife, the commercial benefit consisted mainly of good performance, but as the market developed it became a necessity to find more benefits for the operator. The possibility of conducting market research in NetLife applications has turned out to be such a benefit.

To successfully connect users via an application the following goals must be met.

Individualisation: The user must be able to personalise her avatar, and thus present herself to the community as an individual. It was therefore necessary to offer a number of opportunities in the NetLife applications to distinguish oneself from the others. In particular these are the user defined avatar profile including age, gender, personality, attitudes, preferences, and looks (especially in Flirtboat), as well as the individual profile page which is created and maintained by the user on behalf of the avatar.

Communication: Users must be able to communicate with each other. In sysis NetLife this is achieved via e-mail and chat, as well as via actions. On behalf of their avatars users send e-mails to other avatars in the environment. Alternatively, users communicate directly with each other via chat. Moreover, actions can be selected by the users as advice/directive for the avatar on what to do in a specific meeting with a particular avatar.

Appraisal: Users should be motivated to give feedback to other members of the community and also should want to learn what others think. In derSpittelberg, for instance, a means of appraisal is the election of the best nickpage by the collective of users via rating. This form of appraisal can be easily gathered automatically.

All data used for evaluation are automatically collected by the system and stored in a database. In the following, we will concentrate on those aspects of data collection that are motivated by user related goals.

3.2   Methodology

Before we go on with the discussion of the data, a few words are in order about the general methodological aspects of data collection as well as NetLife specific features.

3.2.1   General Considerations

Sampling   In the context of NetLife applications, sampling only has influence insofar as the operator defines the target group correctly and the final customisation of the application is compatible with that target group. Apart from that, a NetLife application is accessible for anyone with an Internet connection. This aspect alone accounts for the sample not being representative of the total population, but — based on the assumption that the application has been appropriately customized for a certain target group — theoretical requirements regarding sampling are fulfilled.[7]

Profiling   As explained, the user is represented by an avatar in
NetLife applications. This raises the question as to how far avatar profiles actually correspond to user profiles. Do users tend to give information on themselves or rather invent some fantasy characters. Before we
go into this issue in detail, it should be noted, that important parts of
the user profile, especially the tracking of user activity and any conclusions drawn from that are completely independent from this question.
Apart from that, we work with the assumption that users identify with
their avatar and therefore give information on their actual personality,
preferences and attitudes. The following observations support this assumption:

- In a survey performed after the first run of Flirtboat in Austria,
  users were asked directly if they felt well represented by the avatar.
  69 % said that their own personality had been embodied very well
  or well by their avatar. However, the response rate was rather low,
  with only 83 respondents.

- User questions to the operators like "Where can I change my flat?"
  or "Why am I sometimes matched with people who are not in my
  age group?" indicate that users are indeed interested in presenting
  themselves to the community.

- User input in the discussion forum and in the guest books indicate
  that people upload photos showing themselves and things that
  are important to them into their nickpages, they discuss current
  developments in politics and society, but also personal issues. Some
  users update their nickpage daily.

Our hypothesis is that people who construct a different identity from
their own do not build a relationship to the community, and therefore do
not return sufficiently often to be included in our data analysis. Based
on experience from 16 launches of 7 different NetLife applications this
hypothesis holds strongly enough to enable further development, especially from a commercial point of view. To back this up scientifically,
however, a systematic analysis of user created content and a user survey still needs to be conducted. We assume that it is not possible for
users to answer questions on attitudes and preferences consistently if
the answers do not actually reflect their true opinions and feelings. A
consistency test could easily be integrated into NetLife applications via
the questions posed by system avatars, although we have not yet done
so.

3.2.2   Collection Methods   Technically, NetLife offers an ideal platform for extensive collection of data, since it:

- takes data any time, i.e., the system is online all the time, thus the user can visit her avatar any time of day;

- works with a database and therefore collects data automatically;

- produces high quality data, i.e., maximum reliability in data acquisition is achieved as user input equals system output. Error rate is reduced as no human observer is involved in registration and interpretation of the data.

As regards the user, data are collected in three ways:

1 tracking of user actions: tracking investigates all explicit user actions and aims at deriving valid conclusions about implicit or underlying dimensions such as user preferences or interests.

2 collection of direct user answers to questions by the system: a major advantage of the anytime approach in NetLife is that the user gives answers over time, and whenever she wants. As a result the user tends to answer many questions. Another advantage is that the user answers questions on different days when she may be in different moods and situations. As input from the user is distributed over many days and times of the day, biases due to varying daily performance are statistically levelled out.

3 input from other users/voting by all users: user content can be rated by other users (in the case of NetLife the personal nickpage), in other words users may give their opinions on other users. Voting is used to find the collective opinion of the community on a certain topic.

The above three way distinction has formed the basis for what we call the generalized avatar/user profile, a classification of data collected via NetLife applications. All data apart from tracking and user generated content are acquired by means of multiple choice questions. The results are aggregated automatically by the system over all answers per person.

3.3   Generalized Avatar Profile

The avatar profile (which, as described earlier, is assumed to reflect the characteristics of the user) constitutes a very important component of the application as a whole.Most of the dynamic content of the database can be related to individual users, and the user avatars are the central driving force of the simulation. Figure 12.3 gives an overview of the generalised avatar/user profile as it occurs in sysis NetLife applications. The individual aspects will be explained in the following sections. The picture shows the connection between data collection methods (like tracking, direct user input) and the data types acquired (like usage and activity, user generated content). In addition, example classes are presented. Shaded fields with text in italics indicate areas that are part of the user profile concept but have not been fully analysed up to date.

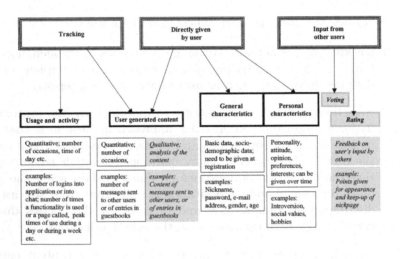

Figure 12.3.   Generalized avatar/user profile.

3.3.1   Usage and Activity

Analyses of usage data, usually performed in combination with interpreting data from the 'general characteristics' class, help to assess user attraction and persistence. Parameters representing the 'usage and activity' type of data are the number of registered agents over time, and number of user visits (logins) to their avatars. Parameters representing 'general characteristics' are avatar age and gender. These are used for cross classification with the usage data, see section 4.1.5.

A very specialised item is 'visits to locations', i.e., the number of times a specific location has been visited. As locations can be branded by sponsors, this is a particularly vital piece of information for the commercial evaluation part. Additionally, the mere counting of user generated content items allows conclusions as to which functionalities of the platform work particularly well for the user. In section 4.1.1 we will give figures on the number of registrations, the visiting rate of users to their avatars and the number of daily logins to different launches of Flirtboat.

3.3.2   User Generated Content   The user has four ways of adding personal content.

1 **Creating and maintaining a nickpage:** The nickpage contains free descriptions of, for example, the partner one is looking for or the things the user hates most etc. Each item can be counted and assessed for its degree of user acceptance.

2 **Taking an action at a date:** When instructing her avatar to seek a date with another avatar, the user can specify an action that the avatar should take at this meeting. Basically, actions are predefined and parameterised, which enables the other avatar to interpret the action as something to be considered positive or negative. As parameterization takes place during the production phase with the main purpose of adding more of a game feel to the simulation, it must be acknowledged that actions might not be considered equally positive or negative in all cultural circumstances and by all users, but indicators used in this area are highly aggregated and can safely be assumed to even out statistically. Moreover, they are chiefly used in customisation projects to assess number and types of items needed so as to create an entertaining application. In addition, at each date the user can enter a message that her avatar will give its counterpart at the meeting (and which will then turn up in the accounts of both avatars). Number and content of such messages can also be used to guide further development especially as regards the game aspect of the community. In the context of the work presented, we only use number of actions and action type as indicators.

3 **Asynchronous communication:** The user may write e-mails on behalf of her avatar to the avatar's friends or partners. As an indicator we use the number of mails sent.

4 **Synchronous communication:** The user may directly engage in communication with other users via the chat facility. Indicators are how many users use chat during a day, at what times and on which days.

In section 4.1.2, we will give a quantitative analysis of Flirtboat data concerning the usage of actions, e-mail and chat. Assessment of the content of such messages, however, is outside the scope of the work presented in this chapter.

3.3.3   General Characteristics   These aspects of the user are static and are given during registration. They mainly cover socio-demographic data. Thus they are different from personal characteristics which develop over time. In our studies the general characteristics, avatar age and gender, are used as the determinants of primary cluster analyses.

It must be noted that the distinction between general characteristics and personal characteristics has been made primarily to facilitate working on and with the NetLife platform and less for theoretical reasons.

3.3.4   Personal Characteristics: Most of the questions a user will answer during participation in the platform will be targeted at her personal profile, or more specifically the avatar's personal profile. In particular these questions relate to personality, opinions and attitudes, preferences and interests.

Personality   The personality model – together with a need model which controls the agents – forms the core of the virtual life in Flirtboat. The model is based on the Jungian theory of personality, Jung (1937). In particular it is an adaptation of the Myers-Briggs Type Indicator (see Keirsey and Bates (1984)), a paper-and-pencil personality test, according to which personality is modelled along the dimensions extroversion – introversion, intuiting – sensing, thinking – feeling, and judgment – perception. Combinations of these dimensions lead to 16 personality types.[8]

This particular approach has been chosen, because it can be easily adapted for the matching and dating mechanism underlying the applications, and also for the assignment of personality to the avatars by means of an online questionnaire which is presented to the user as part of the registration process.

The model provides precise indications as to the personal relationships each personality type may have with any of the other types and how they are expected to develop over time, see Socionics Relations[9]. Question-answer lists in the style of Flirtboat texts have been designed for each personality type by a psychologist addressing several areas of (the users') lives such as social behaviour, partnership, career etc. The answers to these questions are used to attribute individual Jungian dimensions resulting in personality profiles. See Boeree web site[10] for an online description of the Myers-Briggs types. Examples for question-answer pairs as presented in the UK Flirtboat are given in Table 12.1.

3.3.5 Opinions and Attitudes

Questions on opinions and attitudes aim to identify the respondent's value system. Attitudes are defined as "an organismic state of readiness to respond in a characteristic way to a stimulus (as an object, concept, or situation)" whereas opinions are described as "a view, judgment, or appraisal formed in the mind about a particular matter".[11]

In short, attitudes are more generalised and consistent over time, while opinions refer to a specific issue that may only be relevant at one point in time. In NetLife applications, these questions are asked over time. In part they are needed to refine avatar profiles for matching with other avatars, in part they are used to profile the data for lifestyle analysis.

3.3.6 Preferences and Interests

Preferences and interests are the main indicators used in life style analysis. Two types of questions relating to preferences and interests are used: 1) general questions that follow the lifestyle analysis concept described in section 3.4 and are employed for assigning a lifestyle type to the profile, and 2) specific questions which are asked by a concrete sponsor and relate either to the sponsor's products or to sponsor-specific segmentation criteria.

Data on gender, age, and personality traits of the avatars in Flirtboat are presented in sections 4.1.3 and 4.1.4, respectively. The assessment of opinions/attitudes and preferences/interests is of relevance for the analysis of lifestyle, see section 4.1.6.

3.3.7 Rating

We talk about rating if users give an evaluation of user generated content, such as for example the nickpage. It is a means for the community to manage its standards itself. In Netlife, ratings are used for the nickpages and are simply given on a scale from 1 to 5, according to whether users like or dislike them.

Voting: Technically, voting follows the same mechanisms as rating, but has a slightly different focus and outcome. As opposed to rating which refers to personal topics such as the individual nickpages, voting refers to general topics in the particular community. Voting is neither implemented in Flirtboat nor in derSpittelberg.

Table 12.1.   Examples for question-answer pairs for the assignment of avatar personality.

Imagine your date is keeping you waiting. How long does it take before you start to feel annoyed?	5 minutes 10 minutes 15 minutes 30 minutes
What would you say sounds more like you: "Hello, here I come!" or "Lets wait and see."	Hello, here I come! Lets wait and see
Are you a dreamer or more of a practical type?	Dreamer Practical type
Are you a rational or an emotional person?	Rational Emotional
Do you like to keep everything in good order or are you inspired by chaos?	Order Chaos
How do you feel when you are in a crowd?	Relaxed Tense
What do you think about visionaries?	They're tedious They're fascinating
Be honest: Are you likely to be impressed by an emotional speech or will only hard facts convince you?	Emotional speech Hard facts
Do you like to check things out first or do you act on the spur of the moment?	Investigate first I'm impulsive

3.4   Lifestyle Analysis

During the conceptual work on derSpittelberg, an additional user profiling-module has been developed and integrated into the NetLife platform to carry out market segmentation based on lifestyle questions.

As sysis provides avatars equipped with personality traits, it is a consequential extension to undertake lifestyle classifications. Information about lifestyle group-affiliations is very useful for commercial applications as well as it serves for matching purposes, especially user-to-user or content-to-user matching within applications.

On the basis of theories on lifestyle (Hartmann (1999)), lifestyle and identity and the relevance of lifestyle classifications for marketing purposes (Mitchell (1983)), and socio-scientific research on different dimensions of behaviour that make up the frame for each lifestyle-concept (Bortz and Dring (2002)), the following three main dimensions (a priori typology) were formulated to classify avatars/users in derSpittelberg leading to 8 lifestyle types.

- *Spare time behaviour* (active versus passive) investigates the principal preference for spending one's spare time, i.e., relaxing or looking for action, organising or participating in events.

- *Buying motivation* (usefulness versus prestige) investigates the principal preference in buying goods, in terms of what the main motivation is when a customer decides among similar products.

- *General mindset* (conventional versus unconventional) investigates the principal attitude and perspective of a person when judging or decision making.

To determine lifestyle segment affiliations of users, a set of related questions is used to assess the position of a user on each dimension. All questions are formulated dichotomously reflecting the two opposite perspectives. The predominant perspective is used for the assessment of each dimension, undecided cases are omitted from further statistical analysis. Due to practical needs or application constraints the number of questions used for lifestyle type assessment must be variable. For der-Spittelberg, for instance, each dimension was covered by a maximum of eight questions. In addition, sponsors were given the possibility to pose questions concerning their products. As a tribute to the entertaining character of the application, most questions were randomly presented and users could skip answers if they wished. This led to a relatively large number of missing values in the data-set.

In the following we present two examples for questions that survey the lifestyle type of a user in derSpittelberg. A question to test egotism versus social attitude was:

> You and your friend suddenly feel ravenous for something sweet but there's only one of your favourite chocolate bars left. What will you do?
> — eat it in private versus share with my friend.

A question to test status orientation was:

> Which would be your holiday hire car? — stretch limousine versus compact car.

4.   Data Evaluation

Generally, one must differentiate between quantitative analysis of the data like counting the times a user has logged onto the system, or the number of items in all nickpages and the like, and qualitative analysis of the data like an analysis of users, their motives and use of the community. User generated content, for instance, would be an appropriate resource for qualitative analysis. A qualitative approach, however, is out of the scope of this study. All evaluation results presented in section 4.1 are based on quantitative analysis.

The following main aspects were addressed when analysing the data collected:

Performance should be watched closely as it is the main determinant deciding about the further fate of a community. Typical questions are:

- How many logins occur per day?

- How often do users return?

- Which functionalities are most widely used?

Typical conclusions are:

- measures to retain users,

- development of the functionalities most used, or of functionalities undersized etc., depending on qualitative conclusions.

Cross classification is relevant to answer questions such as, what are the characteristics of the avatars being visited often or rarely, or more indirectly who are the users logging in often/seldom? (males? young? etc.). This serves as a mechanism to check if the target group defined prior to the application development has been reached or to adapt promotion measures to sharpen the definition of the target group if it was only defined very broadly beforehand.

Lifestyle modelling is a further means to support matching of users in the community, as lifestyle stands for an expression of one's personal image on the basis of given living conditions, and for a means of sustaining one's identity. It has shown that people tend to participate in groups with similar lifestyle characteristics. Items and actions with a distinct symbolic meaning are used to communicate lifestyle-group affiliation to others, see Mitchell (1983). In derSpittelberg lifestyle clusters are used for market analysis, see section 4.1.6.

4.1   Evaluation Results

As already stated, we can only give some samples of the evaluation performed within the methodology described in the previous section. We believe, however, that these samples show well what can be achieved by collecting and analysing data in the way described above, both in terms of commercial sustainability and further development. All data presented in sections 4.1.1 to 4.1.5 stem from Flirtboat applications. The data in section 4.1.6 originate from derSpittelberg.

4.1.1 Usage and Activity

Number of Registrations   AUT Flirtboat had a total of 11,053 agents registered, 4,233 (38.3%) of which were inactive, i.e., the user visited her avatar (i.e., log into the application) only on one day. For comparison, UK Flirtboat had a total of 22,681 agents registered, 12,421 (54.8%) of which were inactive and for CRO Flirtboat 6,718 avatars were registered, with 2,126 (31.65%) inactive.

Average Number of Visits   The average number of visits to the application per registered user was just under 35 in AUT Flirtboat, with average time on board amounting to 36 days. In UK Flirtboat on average an avatar was only visited 21 times over a duration of 27 days. In CRO Flirtboat avatars were visited on average nearly 47 times during a period of 37 days. In AUT Flirtboat, 25% of the users had a time on board of more than 60 days, visiting their avatar more than 34 times. The duration is the same for the top quartile in CRO Flirtboat, whereas the number of visits (more than 52 for the top user group) is the highest of all three countries. In the UK, the quartile with the most visits had over 20 visits and an average duration on board of more than 42 days. The fact that the median (50% quartile) of visits is much lower than the mean, and only the 75% quartile is about as high as the mean, leads to the conclusion that among the top 25% of the users the number of visits is actually well above the mean. In fact, the maximum number of visits by an individual user in AUT Flirtboat was over 1,000. In CRO Flirtboat it was 1,174 and in UK Flirtboat over 800.

Daily Logins   After approximately one and a half months of runtime, daily logins were established at a fairly constant level for all three applications, see Figure 12.4. The average number of logins per day amounted to 2,734 in the UK, 1,941 in Croatia and 2,265 in Austria. As we learn from AUT Flirtboat 3, the application with the longest runtime of all NetLife applications up to date, the number of daily logins eventually stagnates at a considerably lower level.

4.1.2 User Generated Content

Actions   In AUT Flirtboat 1, one out of ten meetings were accompanied by an action. 80% of these actions had a positive character, and 4% were negative actions. The picture changed in AUT Flirtboat 2, where the number of actions decreased (only 8 out of 100 meetings were accompanied by a user-defined action), and the percentage of negative actions

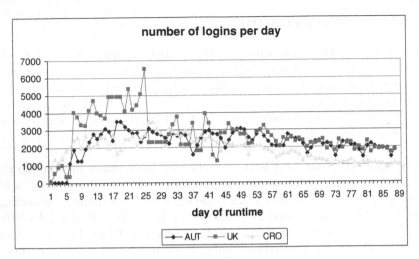

Figure 12.4. Flirtboat: daily logins

increased to 28%, mainly replacing neutral actions, which decreased to 2%. In UK Flirtboat, 50% fewer actions are taken by the users than in AUT Flirtboat 2. However 60% of these actions are accompanied by text input, and 80% of all actions have a positive character. In all applications, utterances accompanying an action are typically quite short 38 characters on average.

E-mail   In AUT Flirtboat 1, on average 19 mails were sent per avatar. The average number of mails per avatar was almost halved in AUT Flirtboat 2, i.e., there was an average of 10 mails per user. For UK Flirtboat there was only an average of 8 mails per user. This may be due to the chat facility available in UK Flirtboat and AUT Flirtboat 2. The average length of a mail in AUT Flirtboat 2, however, considerably increased from 191 characters in AUT Flirtboat 1 to 295 characters in AUT Flirtboat 2. Mails are even longer in UK Flirtboat, 374 characters on average.

Chat   The data from UK Flirtboat and AUT Flirtboat 2 have shown that the frequency of chat usage was different on different week days with the most intensive use on Sunday in the UK and on Monday in Austria. The chart of logins per time of day also shows clear differences with peak- and off-peak times, largely corresponding in both countries. The only time with hardly any chat traffic at all was between 3AM and 8AM, the busiest time was between 9PM and 10PM. Surprisingly the youngest age group (13–19) in both countries had the lowest mean for chat login frequency. At the other extreme, in the Austrian sample the highest mean for chat logins was observed in the oldest age group (above 50). Generally, the chat facility was used more by English users, not only in total numbers, but also in relative numbers (logins per user), and UK males use the chat slightly more frequently than females. Chat content was not logged.

4.1.3   General Characteristics

Age Groups of Avatars   Age is grouped into five broad classes (≤19, 20–29, 30–39, 40–49, ≥50), and the users assign one of these age groups to their avatars. Comparing the Austrian and UK Flirtboat, we find that the age distribution of avatars is fairly similar in the three countries. Differences are particularly small in the Austrian and the UK application. See figure 12.5 for illustration. The majority of avatars belong to the group of under 30s, whereas the over 40s are strongly underrepresented, and there are even fewer avatars in the age group over 50.

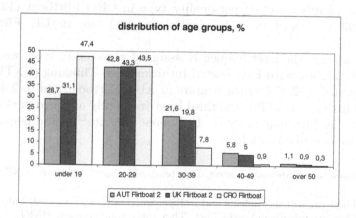

Figure 12.5.   Flirtboat: distribution of age groups among avatars.

Avatar Gender   Female avatars outnumber male ones in UK Flirtboat and CRO Flirtboat, with 51.5% versus 48.5% and 53.2% versus 46.8%, respectively. In AUT Flirtboat, however, the distribution is inverse, with 58% male avatars versus 42% female ones. These data refer to avatars contacted more than once.

4.1.4   Personal Characteristics

Personality   Even though avatar personality is modelled along the four dimensions of the Mayers-Briggs Indicator only data related to the dimensions extroversion – introversion and thinking – feeling showed significant results. In Austria and the UK, more than half of the avatars were created with introverted personality, and more than half of the avatars were created with a feeling type personality. In other words, Flirtboat attracts the introverts and the emotional ones.

Comparing the personality types assigned to the avatars in the Flirtboat applications in Austria, the UK and Croatia, we find that there is little variation in the most frequently assigned personality types in all three counties. Note that the names used for labelling the personality types are standard terminology, cf. for instance Keirsey and Bates (1984). In particular we found that:

Extroverted Feeling with Intuiting (ENFJ) is the most frequently assigned personality type in UK Flirtboat (10.64% of the avatars) and in CRO Flirtboat (17.51%), and it is the second most frequently assigned personality type in AUT Flirtboat (11.22%);

Introverted Intuiting with Feeling (INFJ) is the most frequently assigned personality type in AUT Flirtboat (11.41%), the second most frequently assigned personality type in CRO Flirtboat (12.18%) and still the third most frequently assigned one in UK Flirtboat (9.48%).

Considering the least frequently assigned personality type, we again find similarities, with Extroverted Intuiting with Thinking (ENTP) being assigned to 2.37% of the avatars in AUT Flirtboat and to 2.42% in CRO Flirtboat. ENTP is the third least frequently assigned personality type in UK Flirtboat (4.08%). In Boeree web site[12], these personality types are described as follows:

> These people are easy speakers. They tend to idealize their friends. (ENFJ)

> These are serious students and workers who really want to contribute. They are private and easily hurt. They make good spouses. (INFJ)

> These are lively people, not humdrum or orderly. As mates, they are a little dangerous, especially economically. (ENTP)

4.1.5   Cross Classifications

Apart from the analysis of single avatar characteristics, cross classifications are analysed, in order to see if there are differences in usage between the basic sociodemographic user clusters gender and age.

Logins and Avatar Gender   The question investigated is: Do females use this application more than males? As regards gender, there are hardly any differences between the UK and the Austrian application. In general the average number of visits is slightly lower for males than for females, but the difference is less than 1 average visit. The difference in the average duration of visits in days to female and male avatars is four in the Austrian sample and three in the UK sample. Again, male avatars are visited less often than female ones. CRO Flirtboat shows a different picture. Here male avatars on average have 9 more visits than female ones, although the average time on board is slightly higher for female avatars (39 and 37 respectively).

Logins (visits) and Avatar Age   Does this application appeal more to the young or to the older audience? The average number of visits is highest in all three samples among the 30 to 39 year olds. In the Austrian data the difference is more pronounced than in the UK data.

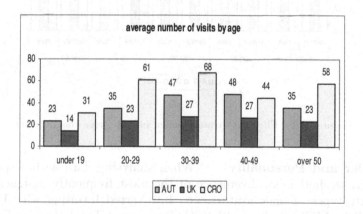

Figure 12.6. Flirtboat: average number of visits by age.

Avatar Gender and Avatar Age   How well balanced is the community in terms of the basic characteristics? This question is particularly important for a dating platform like Flirtboat where the vast majority of users prefer to be matched with people of their age group. In connection with derSpittelberg it was important for the operator to know if the pre-specified target group (students between 18 and 25) had been reached, and ideally males and females in a 50:50 split. The predominance of male avatars is particularly interesting in the UK version of Flirtboat, as it is hosted on a women's channel. The Austrian data reflect the gender distribution of Austrian Internet users as reported in the Austrian Internet Monitor URL[13].

The distribution of (avatar) gender over (avatar) age groups is comparable for the Flirtboat applications in the UK, Austria and Croatia. In all three launches female avatars clearly outnumbered the male ones in the group of subject younger than 19. For all other age groups in all launches male avatars outnumber female ones.

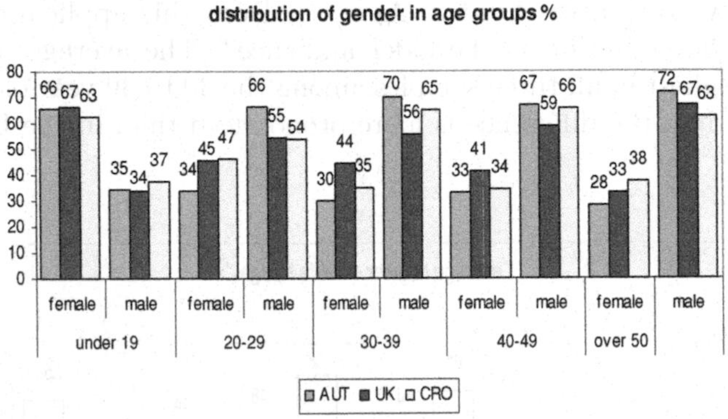

distribution of gender in age groups %

Figure 12.7. Flirtboat: avatar gender and age cross classification.

Gender and Personality   When analysing data with respect to gender, we find more divergence of the most frequently assigned personality types of male avatars, i.e., Introverted Intuiting with Feeling (INFJ) in AUT Flirtboat (10.48%), Introverted Thinking with Sensing (ISTP) in UK Flirtboat (10.35%) and the generally high scoring type Extroverted Feeling with Intuiting (ENFJ) in CRO Flirtboat (14.68%).

Looking at female avatars, we find ENFJ as most frequent type in AUT Flirtboat (14.37%) and CRO Flirtboat (20.18%). It is again the UK sample which clearly differs, with INFP (introverted feeling with intuiting) as most frequently assigned personality type (13.49%).

Interestingly much more convergence can be found for the least frequently assigned personality type, ENTP (extroverted intuition with thinking) which was assigned least in five of six clusters in total, namely in AUT Flirtboat (1.99% of the male avatars, 3.00% of the female avatars), CRO Flirtboat (2.43% male, 2.41% female), and UK Flirtboat (3.34% female). In Boeree (url) we find:

> These people are action-oriented and fearless, and crave excitement.

(ISTP)

> These people are idealistic, self-sacrificing, and somewhat cool or re-served. They are very family and home oriented, but don't relax well.

(INFP)

Age and Personality   In AUT Flirtboat the proportion of avatars designed as introverts is particularly high among those specified as aged above 40. While in the Austrian sample the proportion of introverts in the different age groups varies between 52% and 67%, in the UK the variation is small (ranging from 53% to 57%).

4.1.6   Lifestyle Analysis   In Table 12.2, we present the distri-bution of derSpittelberg users across the eight lifestyle types defined at sysis. Absolute and relative frequencies of valid cases are listed.

Table 12.2. User lifestyle classification within derSpittelberg

	Life-style Type	Buying Motivation	Spare Time Behaviour	General Mindset	Freq.	Valid %
Valid	A:	prestige	active	conventional	13	3.7
	B:	prestige	active	unconventional	38	10.7
	C:	prestige	passive	conventional	6	1.7
	D:	prestige	passive	unconventional	7	2.0
	E:	usefulness	active	conventional	70	19.7
	F:	usefulness	active	unconventional	149	41.9
	G:	usefulness	passive	conventional	36	10.1
	H:	usefulness	passive	unconventional	37	10.4
	Total				356	100.0
Missing	System				3964	
Total					4320	

We see that type F (usefulness active unconventional) is overrepre-sented (41.9%) whereas Types A, C, and D are underrepresented (3.7%, 1.7%, 2%). A result which meets our assumptions about the target group of this application.

From evaluation of the lifestyle typology, we see that types A,C and D can be neglected for the analysis of product related questions of sponsors due to their insignificant representation within the community. Thus for investigations into specific consumer behaviour only user types B, E, F, G and H are taken into consideration.

5. Conclusion

In this chapter, we have presented sysis NetLife — an application platform for the development of avatar-driven multi-user Internet communities — and two of its applications: Flirtboat and derSpittelberg. The most distinctive feature of NetLife applications is that users are represented and integrated in the community via their avatars. Thus the avatar is the principal means or metaphor for data collection.

We have presented a way of classifying the data collected by NetLife applications, and have discussed in more detail data which stem from the users' activities in creating, visiting and supporting their avatars. In particular, these are data on usage and activity, user generated content, and general and personal avatar characteristics.

As regards usage and activity, the data from Flirtboat show high user retention: almost two thirds of the users return to AUT Flirtboat, and more than two thirds do so in CRO Flirtboat. User retention is less strong for UK Flirtboat, here just under half of the users return to the application. Moreover, data on the average number of visits strengthen the evidence that user retention is best in CRO Flirtboat, closely followed by AUT Flirtboat, and less strong in UK Flirtboat, users of CRO Flirtboat visit their avatar 47 times over 37 days, users of AUT Flirtboat do so 35 times over 36 days, whereas users of UK Flirtboat on average visit their avatar 21 times over 27 days. Another valuable insight from usage data is that the interest in the application levels off after a certain period of time, for example, approximately after one and a half months for the Flirtboat applications. In other words, after a certain period of time a core user group is established. This core further reduces with increasing runtime. We consider such cores of particular value for qualitative studies on the impact of community applications with virtual user characters (avatars).

Our evaluation of user generated content can also be subsumed under usage and activity, because the results presented stem from quantitative analysis, such as how frequently are e-mail and chat facilities used, compared to a such indirect means for communication as the actions that can be selected to accompany a date.

Regarding avatar characteristics, for example, the distribution of age groups among the avatars in Flirtboat shows that in all three countries most avatars belong to the group of under 30s, whereas the distribution of female and male avatars differs between UK and Croatia on the one hand, and Austria on the other hand, with more female avatars in the application for the former, and more male ones for the latter. This knowledge may be used for further design decisions to improve the work on male or female avatars, to set new incentives to balance or, on the contrary, to sharpen the gender distribution, depending on the goals pursued with the application. As regards personality, we find that there is little variation in the most frequently assigned personality types over the applications in Austria, Croatia and the UK. We conclude that certain types of users can be reached particularly well by the application.

From a cross classification of items we get insights at a more fine grained level, e.g. we learn that even if the most prominent group of avatars belongs to the under 30s, older ones are more frequently taken care of than younger ones (less than 19 year olds). Given we accept the assumption that avatar age reflects user age, the data reveal that older user groups are more engaged in the application. We also learn that in all cases (all age groups and all Flirtboat applications) except for the under 19's, male avatars outnumber female ones. Also lifestyle analysis (presented and analysed from a commercial point of view in the context of derSpittelberg) is of more general interest for avatar-based applications, especially its potential for user-to-user and content-to-user matching.

In this contribution we have shown which possibilities such avatar-driven communities open up for data collection across large populations. As the users interact with the system over a longer period of time by creating, modelling and influencing their avatar representatives, these communities are suitable testbeds for the evaluation of different types of animated characters.

Acknowledgments

The Austrian Research Institute for Artificial Intelligence (OFAI) is supported by the Austrian Federal Ministry for Education, Science and Culture and the Austrian Federal Ministry for Transport, Innovation and Technology. This research is partly supported by the EC Project NECA IST-2000-28580. We would also like to thank the people at sysis who have been strongly involved in the design and implementation of the NetLife platform and the applications Flirtboat and derSpittelberg.

Notes

1. http://sysis.at/website/web/pages/portfolio/community/.
2. http://www.cnn.com/2000/TECH/computing/04/18/ananova.launch/
3. http://www.cnn.com/2000/TECH/computing/04/18/ananova.launch/

4. http://www.agentland.com/
5. The figure dates from June 2003.
6. http://www.oefai.at/NECA/
7. Sampling methods are described in Atteslander (1995) and Friedrichs (1990).
8. See also Socionics Types (http://www.socionics.com/main/types.htm) and Socionics Profiles (http://www.socionics.com/advan/prof/), respectively.
9. http://www.socionics.com/rel/rel.htm
10. http://www.ship.edu/~cgboeree/jung.html
11. See Merriam Webster (www.m-w.com/home.htm).
12. foot-Boeree
13. http://www.integral.co.at

References

Atteslander, P. (1995). *Methoden der empirischen Sozialforschung*, Walter de Gruyter, 8.Auflage.

Boeree, C.G., URL: http://www.ship.edu/~cgboeree/jung.html

Bortz, J. and Dring, N. (2002). *Forschungsmethoden und Evaluation*, Springer, Berlin.

Friedrichs, J. (1990) *Methoden empirischer Sozialforschung*, Westdeutscher Verlag, 14. Auflage.

Hartmann P.H. (1999). *Lebensstilforschung. Darstellung, Kritik und Weiterentwicklung*, Opladen.

Jung, C.G. (1937). *Psychologische Typen*, Rascher, Ges. Werke, Bd. 6.

Keirsey, D. and Bates, M. (1984). *Please Understand Me: Character and Temperament Types*, 5th Edition, Prometheus Nemesis Book Co, Del Mar, CA.

Krenn, B., Neumayr, B., Gstrein, E., and Grice, M. (to appear) Life-Like Agents for the Internet: A Cross-Cultural Case Study. In Payr, S. and Trappl, R., editors, *Agent Culture: Designing Human-Agent Interaction in a Multicultural World*, Lawrence Erlbaum Associates, New York.

Mitchell, A. (1983). *The Nine American Lifestyles*, Warner Books, New York.